AUSTRALIA'S GREAT BARRIER REEF

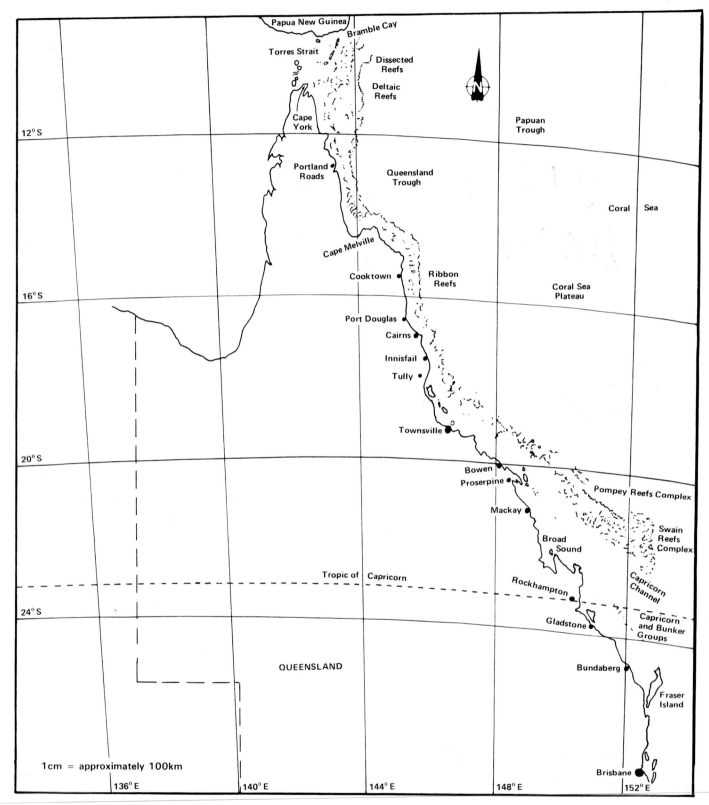

Map 1. Map of Queensland showing the Great Barrier Reef region. Details of the reefs can be seen in maps 2, 3 and 4 on pages 12 and 13.

AUSTRALIA'S GREAT BARRIER REEF

Robert Endean

University of Queensland Press
St Lucia • London • New York

Typeset by Savage & Co. Pty Ltd
Printed and bound by Silex Enterprise & Printing Co., Hong Kong

Distributed in the United Kingdom, Europe, the Middle East, Africa, and the Caribbean by Prentice-Hall International, International Book Distributors Ltd, 66 Wood Lane End, Hemel Hempstead, Herts., England.

National Library of Australia
Cataloguing-in-Publication data
Endean, R. (Robert).
   Australia's Great Barrier Reef.

   Includes index.
   ISBN 0 7022 1678 X.

   1. Coral reef biology — Queensland — Great Barrier
   Reef. 2. Natural history — Queensland — Great
   Barrier Reef. 3. Great Barrier Reef (Qld.) —
   Description and travel — Guide-books. I. Title.

574.9943

Library of Congress Cataloguing in Publication Data
Endean, R.
   Australia's Great Barrier Reef.

   Includes index.
   1. Coral reef biology — Australia — Great Barrier
   Reef (Qld.) 2. Great Barrier Reef (Qld.) I. Title.
   QH197.E53   508.943   82-2063
   ISBN 0-7022-1678-X   AACR2

Designed by Horsley Dawson

Contents

Illustrations

Figures

Maps

Preface

The Great Barrier Reef is many things to many people. To some, the term conjures up visions of a tropical sea studded with coral reefs and islands and represents a place of adventure, romance and recreation. Some see the Great Barrier Reef as a place of beauty, a kaleidoscope of colour and a refuge for a host of strange but interesting animals and plants. Still others see it as the most complex ecosystem on this planet, posing a major challenge to scientists wishing to unlock the store-house of new knowledge it contains.

To me it is all of these things and I am grateful that I had the opportunity over the last thirty years to travel along its length, to visit hundreds of its reefs and to study the fauna and flora of those reefs. Everywhere, from the atoll-like platform reefs of the Bunker and Capricorn Group and the magnificent underwater citadels of the Swain Reefs complex at its southern end to the precipitous ribbon reefs north of Cairns, and to the tide races of Torres Strait and the huge Warrior Reefs near its northern limit there is variety, colour and spectacle that are more than sufficient to make the Great Barrier Reef qualify as the Eighth Wonder of the World.

The Royal Commissions into Oil Drilling on the Great Barrier Reef and the enquiry into the crown-of-thorns starfish on the Great Barrier Reef sponsored by the Commonwealth and Queensland governments during the early 1970s revealed the apparent depth of our ignorance of many aspects of the biology of corals, starfish, and other organisms associated with coral reefs, and of the general ecology of coral reef communities. Yet, a great mass of new data on coral reefs generally and on the reefs of the Great Barrier Reef and their fauna and flora in particular had been obtained since the Second World War and had accumulated in various scientific journals. Some of it was brought together during the 1970s in the four volume work entitled *Biology and Geology of Coral Reefs* which was edited by O. A. Jones and myself and published by Academic Press. By the early 1980s the time was opportune for the production of a book incorporating new advances in our knowledge of this vast area.

Initially it was intended that the book be written for biologists and biology students. However, Mr Frank Thompson, Manager of the University of Queensland Press, persuaded me to write what was hopefully termed a definitive book on the Great Barrier Reef for a general audience. The task of writing a book suitable for both university students and a general audience was a daunting one, but it occurred to me that anybody interested in the natural sciences is a student in a sense. Moreover, there was an urgent need to provide members of the general public with sufficient information to enable them to assess logically the major threats now faced by the fauna and flora of the Great Barrier Reef as a result of past, present and projected human activities in the region. Accordingly, this book has a core of classical biology. Most of the groups of animals and plants occurring on the Great Barrier Reef, as well as many of the recent advances in our understanding of major ecological problems relating to them are dealt with in this book. In addition topics such as the importance and the future of the Great Barrier Reef, its geography and topography, its geology and mode of formation, its recent history, tourist resorts in the region, fishing, reef-walking and diving on the reefs, strange and dangerous animals that might be encountered there, and the pressing need for conservation of its fauna and flora are included. As well as providing a reliable source of information for both students of and visitors to the Great Barrier Reef it was intended that the book would be a practical memento of a visit to the Great Barrier Reef. For these reasons it was decided to illustrate this book with colour photographs showing not only the diversity of the fauna and flora of the Great Barrier Reef but also its grandeur and beauty.

Because of limitations on book size it was decided that animal groups found on the Great Barrier Reef would be dealt with principally at the family level.

A discussion of the manner in which zoologists arrange animals in taxonomic groupings will be found in chapter four and descriptions of the various family groups will be found under appropriate headings. These descriptions should be used in conjunction with relevant diagrams and colour illustrations in order to obtain an idea of the basic characteristics of each family group. Genera found on the Great Barrier Reef and belonging to each family mentioned are listed. (Plans are in hand to produce a series of books in which species belonging to each family of animals found on the Great Barrier Reef are discussed so that detailed information on the various species occurring there will ultimately become available.) The general reader of this book who is not particularly interested in descriptions of animal groups could skip through these descriptions leaving them for later reference and concentrate on the remainder of the book so as to obtain an overview of the nature of the Great Barrier Reef, of the general biology of the major groups found there, of the general ecology of coral reef communities and of the conservation problems bearing on these communities.

Most of the colour photographs appearing in this book were taken by Mr John Paterson of the Zoology Department of the University of Queensland. These photographs were augmented by inclusion of a number of pictures taken by Mr Doug Henderson of Brisbane (Illustrations no. 54, 65, 102, 103, 106, 107, 109, 111, 118, 121, 122, 157, 168, 175, 203, 204, 210, 239, 247, 268, 279, 283, 284, and 287).

Also, colour pictures were made available by Mr Russel Reichelt of A.I.M.S. Townsville (Illustrations no. 1, 5 and 6), Mr Theo Brown of Newport Beach, NSW (Illustration no. 294) and Mr John Harding of Sydney (Illustration no. 296). Colour pictures of algae (Illustrations no. 38, 39, 41, 43, 44, 45, 46, and 47) were provided by Dr A. B. Cribb of the Botany Department of the University of Queensland.

The author wishes to thank all these people for generously making photographs available for inclusion in this book. A number of pictures (Illustrations no. 12, 19, 49, 50, 56, 59, 61, 67, 68, 128, 139, 141, 142, 149, 151, 155, 178, 197, 198, 200, 201, 209, 222, 223, 240, 242, 245, 250, 251, 271, 274, 289, 290, 295, 297, 298, and 299) are from the author's collection.

It is a pleasure to acknowledge the assistance given by Dr A. B. Cribb who read the chapter dealing with algae and made several helpful suggestions for its improvement. Dr Richard Willan of the Zoology Department, University of Queensland, contributed valuable information to the chapter on molluscs and his assistance is gratefully acknowledged. Thanks are also due to Dr B. Jamieson of the Zoology Department, University of Queensland, who provided information on marine oligochaete worms; and to Miss Annabelle Monaghan and Mr W. Stablum who assisted with the preparation of diagrams and maps. Dr Ann M. Cameron, who read the book in its entirety, detected several errors, and made a number of useful suggestions for improving the presentation of subject matter.

This book is dedicated to the memory of my friends Dr Owen A. Jones, a former Chairman of the Great Barrier Reef Committee; and Mr Robert Poulson, a former Manager of Heron Island Pty Ltd. Owen Jones made a major contribution to the successful establishment of the Heron Island research station. A great deal of the new information in this book has stemmed from studies made by workers operating from this station. Bob Poulson often placed his boats at the disposal of myself and colleagues enabling us to visit numbers of reefs of the Great Barrier Reef. Some of the new information in this book was obtained during these visits. Proceeds from the sale of this book will be used to fund further research into the coral reef communities of the Great Barrier Reef.

R. Endean
1982

1

Definition, Attraction, and Importance of the Great Barrier Reef

Off the tropical north-eastern coastline of Australia is a shallow-water platform that for millennia has provided ideal conditions for coral growth. As a result, a remarkable system of coral reefs is found in this region — the Great Barrier Reef. It is the largest single collection of coral reefs known at the present time or throughout geological history.

Coral reefs may be defined as rigid shallow-water structures formed from the skeletal remains of corals, coralline algae, and other lime-secreting organisms. Usually, the remains are associated with fine detritus and compacted to form limestone. A veneer of living animals and plants that constitute the coral reef community hides the limestone core of each reef.

Although the reefs of the Great Barrier Reef collectively form a barrier to waves moving towards the eastern Queensland coast from the Coral Sea, and although they are a barrier to the unrestricted movement of shipping, they do not constitute a barrier reef as envisaged last century by the famed naturalist Charles Darwin. His now classical theory about the genesis of coral reefs was an attempt to explain the origins of coral reefs found in oceanic waters and may be summarized as follows: In the shallow water surrounding tropical oceanic islands, where conditions were favourable for coral growth, reefs grew encircling the shorelines; these Darwin termed *fringing reefs*. Owing to subsidence of the sea-floor in certain areas over the ages, some islands began to sink. As an island sank (and its area above sea-level consequently diminished), the outer edge of its fringing reef continued to grow upwards towards the sea surface, while the growth of corals near the island slowed because of the creation of unfavourable conditions. Eventually this erstwhile fringing reef was separated from the shrinking island by a body of water too deep for the growth of corals (see fig. 1). So a reef located at some distance from the island, which Darwin termed a *barrier reef*, was formed. Continued subsidence could lead ultimately to the disappearance of the island, and the former barrier reef would then appear as a ring-like structure — an atoll. In recent years Darwin's theory of the origin of oceanic atolls has been confirmed by drilling at places such as Bikini Atoll.

The geological history of the Great Barrier Reef, however, has followed a course different from that of reefs around oceanic islands. The Great Barrier Reef is a shallow-water structure which consists of numerous individual and discrete reefs, and it is only in its northern sector that chains of offshore reefs form a more or less continuous rampart extending parallel to the Queensland mainland coast. Elsewhere, the reefs occur mainly as isolated offshore structures separated one from another by bodies of water of considerable extent. Indeed, such reefs have been aptly described as "oases in the oceanic desert". The communities of animals and plants found on the coral reefs of the Great Barrier Reef are discrete assemblages, vastly different in species composition from the communities of animals and plants found in, on, and above the sea-floor separating the reefs.

A reasonably well-defined channel utilized by shipping separates the offshore reefs from the Queensland mainland and associated rocky islands. Many of these rocky islands possess narrow fringing reefs around their shorelines, and fringing reefs are also found on the mainland shore in a few places. There has been much debate whether the term *Great Barrier Reef* should include these fringing reefs as well as the larger offshore reefs. As applied to the offshore reefs, the term *barrier reef* is a misnomer, as we have seen. The term *Great Barrier Reef* can, with advantage, be applied to the whole collection of the coral reefs found on the shallow-water platform off the eastern Queensland coast between the mainland shore and the hundred-fathom (180-metre) line, and this course will be followed in this book. However, it should be appreciated that there are basic differences between the offshore reefs and the near-shore fringing reefs. These differences involve not only their structure and geological history but also the composition of their fauna and flora.

The Great Barrier Reef is important for many reasons. First it is a wilderness area — a place for natural adventure, contemplation, and recreation. Such areas become fewer each year on our crowded planet as human populations increase and urban industrialization spreads. Few terrestrial areas can rival the beauty of the reefs themselves. Seen from an aircraft, the offshore reefs appear as white-encircled emeralds set in a sapphire blue sea. The variety of form and colour exhibited by the animals and plants of the reef is more than enough to arouse the interest of even the most jaded jet-setter. Then there are the coral islands, with their dazzling white beaches fringing in many cases

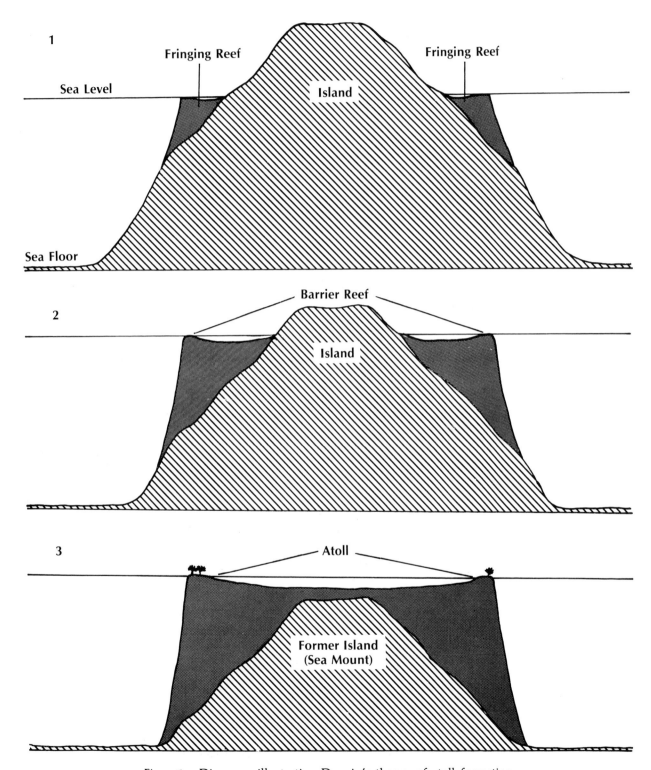

Figure 1. Diagrams illustrating Darwin's theory of atoll formation.

luxuriant vegetation. Skin and scuba diving, swimming, angling and big-game fishing, fossicking at low tide on reefs, examining and photographing the diverse fauna and flora of reefs, sailing and boating among reefs, and exploring islands associated with reefs are among the recreational activities that the Great Barrier Reef has to offer. It can be predicted that in the future there will be a marked increase in the use of underwater aquaria, illuminated underwater entertainment and conference areas, and tethered and free submersibles to enable visitors to obtain glimpses of the fauna and flora of the reefs by day and by night.

As yet, the full potential of the Great Barrier Reef as a tourist attraction and recreational centre has not been appreciated. Only a relatively small percentage of Australians, let alone overseas visitors, have seen the reefs of the Great Barrier Reef. To a large extent the relative inaccessibility of the reefs and tourist resorts of the Great Barrier Reef has been responsible for this state of affairs. The eastern Queensland coast off which the reefs are found is thousands of kilometres long; the coastal towns that provide gateways to the reefs are hundreds of kilometres apart; and the reefs and tourist resorts themselves are a long way from the coastal towns and widely scattered. Until recent years access was principally by boat, frequently involving trips of several hours duration, often in rough seas. Furthermore, as the tourist resorts located on islands are necessarily small, it was uneconomic in most cases to run daily boat services, which meant visitors were expected to stay several days at least. In some seasons, accommodation was often in short supply and booked up weeks ahead. The relative isolation of the tourist resorts has also meant that their operations have had to be self-contained, and consequently the provision of facilities such as electric power and fresh water has been expensive. Those visitors who did not wish to stay at tourist resorts have had to charter boats to see the reefs.

All this has meant that, in the past, visitors to the Great Barrier Reef have found access difficult, time-consuming, often uncomfortable, and usually expensive. Indeed, many Australians have found it cheaper and easier to visit coral reefs in such South Pacific countries as Fiji and New Caledonia. The lot of the international visitor has been worse. Prior to the 1980s the lack of an international airport to cater for visitors who wished to see the Great Barrier Reef forced them to travel to Sydney or Melbourne before changing planes and flying north again to Queensland coastal towns, there to embark on boats for the final leg of their pilgrimage to the Great Barrier Reef.

In recent years, airstrips suitable for light planes have been constructed at tourist resorts situated on the larger islands, and helicopter services have been instituted at other islands. If the tourist trade is to prosper, however, it will be necessary to operate regular and reasonably cheap aerial services, in addition to boat services, to all of the present Barrier Reef tourist resorts and to other strategically situated tourist resorts yet to be constructed. An increase in the use of helicopters (involving helicopter landing platforms on reefs) and amphibious planes is called for, as is the upgrading of airports on the eastern Queensland coast to cater for international tourist traffic to the Great Barrier Reef. Also, there is a need for radically new types of accommodation to be provided. Attention should be given to floating and submerged hotels, marinas, and specially constructed submersibles in the immediate vicinity of offshore reefs. It can be confidently predicted that when access and accommodation are improved in the ways mentioned, Barrier Reef tourism will become Australia's greatest earner of foreign exchange.

The coral reef communities of the Great Barrier Reef are among the most biologically productive of all natural communities. Their potential to provide food for humans has not been systematically investigated. Even the exploitation of obvious food sources such as fish and

Chains of offshore reefs near Lizard Island form a barrier to waves moving towards the Queensland coast from the Coral Sea.

crustaceans has been haphazard, and the harvesting of the less familiar foods (at least to Australians) provided by algae, molluscs, holothurians (*bêche-de-mer*), and the like, has been negligible. Because of the phenomenal increase in the world's population that is now occurring, it is vital that optimal use should be made of all renewable food resources. As matters stand, commercial fishing on the Great Barrier Reef is a small but important industry; many coral reef fishes, such as coral trout and the various emperors, are highly prized as food and command high prices. However, most commercial fishing for coral reef fishes is carried out by hand-lining. Better methods have not been investigated. Nor have the effects of over-fishing on some accessible reefs been investigated until recently. It is already apparent that in some areas commercial fishing on the reefs themselves will have to be carefully regulated. On the other hand, there appears to be plenty of scope for increased exploitation in the waters among the reefs of pelagic fishes such as mackerel, tuna, and bonito as well as demersal fishes such as various snappers.

The delectable crayfish found on reefs will not enter baited craypots and must be hand-collected by divers. Not a great deal is known about reef crayfish on the Great Barrier Reef, and their commercial exploitation should be put on a scientifically managed basis. Prawns and other crustaceans, and scallops, squid, and other molluscs have been exploited regularly only in a few areas in the deeper waters among the reefs and between the reefs and the Queensland mainland; again, a systematic investigation of these resources should be carried out so that the various fishing industries can be put on a secure economic basis and their full potential realized. Additional information is also needed to ensure that the exploitation of the renewable marine food resources of the Great Barrier Reef area can be so regulated that it is compatible with their conservation.

Toxic products from terrestrial plants — for example, atropine, morphine, curare, and digitalis — have long been used in medicine, and studies of the pharmacological activities and chemical structures of these products have enabled hundreds of new drugs to be synthesized. The clinical use of penicillin and other anti-microbial compounds derived from fungi has revolutionized the treatment of certain diseases. In recent years it has become apparent that a wide variety of toxic compounds, including anti-microbial agents, are elaborated by marine organisms and especially by those found on coral reefs. New therapeutic drugs are already being developed by some pharmaceutical firms from several of these toxic products, including those elaborated by Great Barrier Reef organisms. Biological activities exhibited by compounds already isolated from Great Barrier Reef organisms include activity on the central nervous system, the autonomic system, the sensory system, the neuro-muscular system, the cardio-vascular system, the respiratory system, the renal system, and the hormonal system as well as anti-inflammatory, antiviral, antibacterial, antiyeast, antifungal, antiprotozoan, antihelminthic, molluscididal, and insecticidal activity. There are cogent reasons for believing that novel compounds isolated from toxins and other bioactive compounds elaborated by Barrier Reef marine organisms will provide a major source for the new therapeutic drugs, antibiotics, and possibly the anticancer agents of tomorrow.

Portions of two platform reefs in the Capricorn Group. In the foreground is part of the tourist complex on Heron Island and a man-made boat passage and swing basin which bisects the adjacent Heron Island reef. This reef is separated by a deep channel from Wistari reef in the background.

High-grade lime for cement manufacture, constructional activities, manufacturing, treatment of ores, and agriculture is present in enormous quantities on the Great Barrier Reef. It is believed by many people that substantial amounts of this lime, particularly in the form of coral sand, could be removed in some cases without appreciable damage to coral reef communities if appropriate techniques were used. However, others doubt this and believe that the fabric of the reefs should not be interfered with in any way under any circumstances.

Oil has been found associated with fossil coral reefs in some countries, and this association has sparked interest in searching for oil in the Great Barrier Reef area. This interest was heightened by the realization that thick layers of sedimentary rocks of the type that could contain oil lay off the Queensland coast. The possibility of massive oil spills with disastrous consequences for the flora and fauna of the area has generated a wave of popular opposition to drilling for oil on the Great Barrier Reef that to date has prevented any drilling from occurring in the region. In the absence of suitable alternative fuels, however, it would seem inevitable that as the world's oil supplies run low and fuel costs increase there will be increasing agitation and political pressure for the tapping of the reservoirs of oil believed by some to be under some sections of the Great Barrier Reef and beyond in the Coral Sea. Some hard decisions will have to be made in the near future regarding the oil-prospecting leases that now cover most of the Barrier Reef area.

Many people make a hobby of collecting the beautifully coloured and often exquisitely patterned and spectacularly shaped shells of Great Barrier Reef molluscs. Also, a number of cottage industries — shell buttons, buckles, lamps, ornaments, and bric-à-brac — are based on these shells. So-called black corals (antipatharians) found in the Great Barrier Reef area provide the raw material for a form of jewellery that is rapidly increasing in popularity. Coral ornaments and utensils inlaid with turtle shell are also much in demand by tourists as mementoes of their visit to the Great Barrier Reef.

It is not generally appreciated that coral reefs possess a vast bacterial flora which together with most attached bottom-dwelling animals remove organic materials from sea water. Accordingly, coral reefs appear to act as gigantic filters helping to purify sea water and to remove pollutants. This role of coral reefs will assume ever-increasing importance in the future, as the tropical shallow-water areas off the eastern Queensland coast are particularly prone to pollution by man-made chemicals carried there by mainland streams. Moreover, the Great Barrier Reef acts as a self-repairing breakwater, giving protection to hundreds of kilometres of continental coastline and permitting the continued existence of hundreds of islands.

Because the coral reef community is the most complex of all ocean ecological systems, and because it is also the oldest ecological system in geological history, it has a powerful attraction for scientists, particularly biologists. Accordingly, biologists from diverse disciplines find much to interest them in the fauna and flora of the greatest collection of coral reefs that ever existed. Indeed, the reef communities of the Great Barrier Reef pose numerous questions. Why, for example, are there so many species of animal and plant represented

Some of the platform reefs of the Capricorn Group. The lagoon on Wistari reef with its maze of coral pinnacles is prominent in the foreground.

in these communities? How do they share out among themselves the limited living space available? Why are so many highly specialized but apparently rare species present? Why do so many coral reef animals produce toxic materials? Why are so many coral reef animals so brilliantly coloured? Do the populations of animals and plants present fluctuate wildly, or do they remain relatively stable? How are so many animals able to obtain sufficient food? Questions such as these tax the minds of many scientists and, of course, are also of interest to many non-scientists. Other scientists pursue goals that to some members of the public might appear more practical, such as obtaining data on animals that are to be exploited as food, or data on animal and plant products that could have a use in medicine or in industry. Indeed, the Great Barrier Reef can be regarded as a huge natural laboratory for the scientific study of marine organisms and their interactions. The few research stations that have been established on the Great Barrier Reef warrant the full support of the Australian government and people, and at least one of these stations should have international status as a centre for coral reef studies in the Indo–West Pacific region. There are few species of coral reef animal about which it could be said that adequate information on their life histories, let alone other aspects of their general biology, is available. However, the Great Barrier Reef is not the preserve of the scientist. Anybody with an enquiring mind can derive hours of pleasure from observing the animals and plants found there and can contribute to knowledge of these organisms. The educational value of the Great Barrier Reef and its fauna and flora should be far more widely appreciated than it is at present.

Much of the scientific research undertaken at the research stations on the Great Barrier Reef should be directed towards the conservation of the flora and fauna of reefs and associated islands. It should be noted that the Great Barrier Reef is unquestioningly accepted by international authorities as part of the World Heritage and is regarded by many people as the eighth wonder of the world. However, the fauna and flora of the reefs and islands of the Great Barrier Reef are under threat from human activities. The nature of the activities that affect coral reefs are outlined in chapter 24 of this book. These activities should be widely publicized so that an informed Australian public can compel their legislators to ensure that the fauna and flora of the Great Barrier Reef are conserved for future generations to wonder at, learn from, and derive pleasure from. Now is the time for action to conserve this fauna and flora.

2

Geography, Topography, and Hydrographic Conditions

The Great Barrier Reef region embraces that section of the continental shelf of eastern Queensland which lies between the mainland coast and the hundred-fathom line to the north of Fraser Island (see map p. 00). The northern limit is usually placed at Bramble Cay, situated at approximately 9°13′ south latitude, just south of Papua New Guinea. The western boundary in Torres Strait between Papua New Guinea and Queensland may be placed conveniently at 142°30′ east longitude. Thus defined, the region occupies an area of about 250,000 square kilometres. To the north the shelf is bounded by Papua New Guinea and by the deep Papuan Trough. To the east in the northern part of this region the continental shelf drops steeply to the Queensland Trough, which is over two thousand metres in depth. In the central part the extensive (approximately 177,400 square kilometres) Coral Sea Platform, much of which is less than a thousand metres in depth, lies almost immediately to the east of the shelf. This platform also carries reefs but has a different geological history from the Great Barrier Reef region. To the south, near latitude 22°30′S, a tongue of deep water, the Capricorn Channel, intrudes into the region. The shelf is narrowest (about 36 kilometres wide) off Cape Melville (lat. 14°10′S). Both to the north and to the south of this point its eastern boundary diverges seaward from the Queensland coastline, attaining a maximum width in the north of about 350 kilometres in the Torres Strait region, and a maximum width in the south of about 412 kilometres near Broad Sound (lat. 22°S). The mean depth of the shelf increases progressively from north to south. North of latitude 16°S the shelf is generally less than 40 metres deep. Between latitudes 16°S and 20°S, depths usually range from about 40 to 70 metres. South of latitude 20°S, depths on the shelf usually range from about 60 to 130 metres.

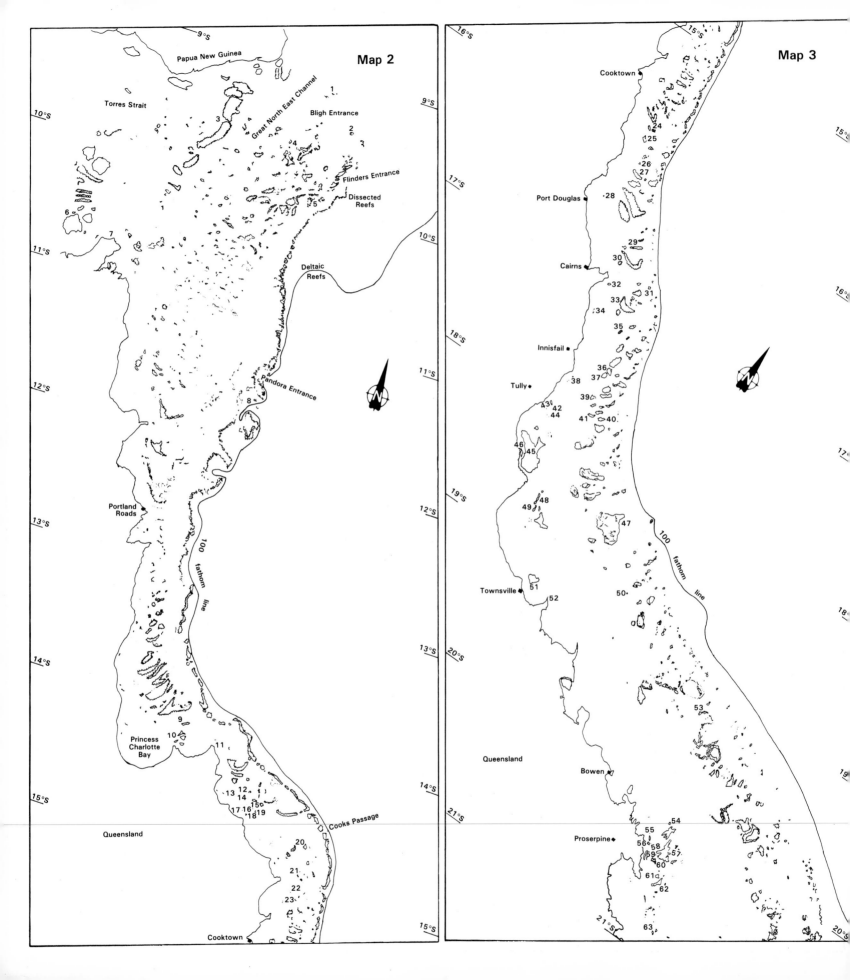

Map 2

Papua New Guinea

Torres Strait

Great North East Channel

Bligh Entrance

1

3

2

Flinders Entrance

4

Dissected Reefs

5

6

Deltaic Reefs

7

10°S

11°S

Pandora Entrance

8

12°S

Portland Roads

100 fathom line

9

13°S

Princess Charlotte Bay

10

11

14°S

12
13
14
17 16 15
18 19

Cooks Passage

Queensland

20

21

22

23

Cooktown

Map 3

16°S

15°S

Cooktown

24

25

26
27

Port Douglas

28

29

30

Cairns

32

31

33

34

35

Innisfail

36
37

Tully

38

39

43
42
44

41

40

46
45

48

49

47

100 fathom line

Townsville

51

52

50

53

Queensland

Bowen

54

Proserpine

55

56
58
59
57
60

61

62

63

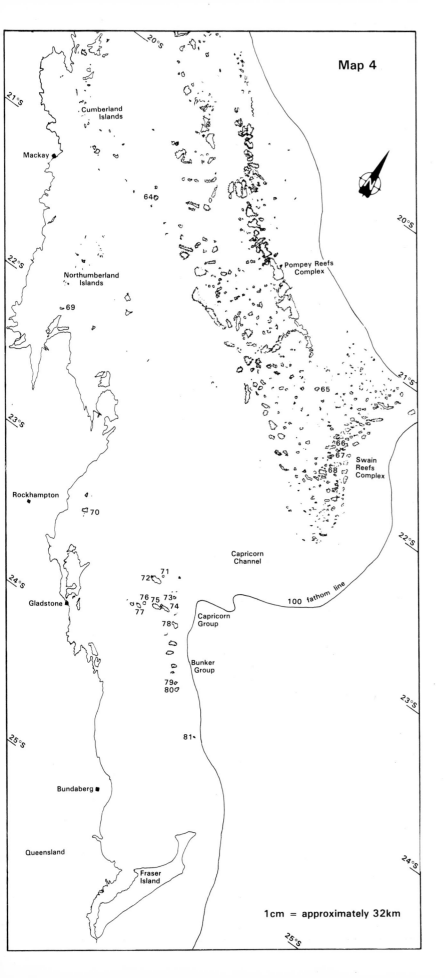

Map 4

1cm = approximately 32km

Key to Maps

MAP 2

1. Bramble Cay
2. Anchor Cay
3. Warrior Reefs
4. Darnley Island
5. Murray Islands
6. Thursday Island
7. Cape York
8. Raine Island
9. Clack Reef
10. Flinders Group
11. Cape Melville
12. Ingram Island
13. Bewick Island
14. Watson Island
15. Howick Group
16. Newton Island
17. Sand Reef
18. Houghton Island
19. Coquet Island
20. Lizard Island
21. Eye Reef
22. Two Isles
23. Three Isles

MAP 3

24. Endeavour Reef
25. Pickersgill Reef
26. Mackay Reef
27. Undine Reef
28. Low Isles
29. Michaelmas Reef
30. Green Island
31. North-West Reef
32. Fitzroy Island
33. Sudbury Reef
34. Frankland Group
35. Flora Reef
36. Peart Reef
37. Feather Reef
38. Barnard Isles
39. Ellison Reef
40. Taylor Reef

41. Beaver Reef
42. Dunk Island
43. Bedarra Island
44. Family Group
45. Hinchinbrook Island
46. Hinchinbrook Passage
47. Slasher Reefs Complex
48. Orpheus Island
49. Palm Islands
50. Wheeler Reef
51. Magnetic Island
52. Cape Cleveland
53. Kangaroo Reef
54. Hayman Island
55. South Molle Island
56. Daydream Island
57. Whitsunday Island
58. Whitsunday Passage
59. Long Island
60. Hamilton Island
61. Linderman Island
62. Cumberland Group
63. Brampton Island

MAP 4

64. Bushy Island
65. Mystery Cay
66. Gillett Cay
67. Bylund Cay
68. Poulson Cay
69. Wild Duck Island
70. Great Keppel Island
71. Tryon Island
72. North West Island
73. Wreck Island
74. Heron Island
75. Wistari Island
76. Erkine Island
77. Masthead Island
78. One Tree Island
79. Fairfax Island
80. Lady Musgrave Island
81. Lady Elliot Island

Note Maps 2, 3 and 4. Base maps were supplied by the Surveyor-General of Queensland and reproduced by arrangement with the Queensland government. Crown copyright reserved.

Map 2. The northern section of Great Barrier Reef, see key.

Map 3. Central section of the Great Barrier Reef, see key.

Map 4. The southern section of Great Barrier Reef, see key.

Continental Islands

Islands and coral reefs stud the continental shelf in the Great Barrier Reef region. Near the mainland coastline numerous rocky islands occur, the largest being Hinchinbrook Island, near Tully. Many of the rocky islands are clustered at intervals to form island groups. Among the major groups are the Keppel Islands near Rockhampton, the Northumberland Islands near Mackay, the Cumberland Islands near Proserpine, the Palm Islands near Townsville, the Family group near Tully, the Barnard Islands near Innisfail, the Frankland group near Cairns, the Howick group near Cooktown, the Flinders group in Princess Charlotte Bay, and the Murray Isles near the northern tip of the Great Barrier Reef. All these rocky islands, except the Murray Isles and adjacent islands, are detached pieces of the adjacent mainland, and hence are known as continental islands. They represent the tops of partially submerged hills and mountains, and their geological structure is similar to that of the adjacent mainland.

Continental islands are at times little more than rocky outcrops protruding above the waves. Some, however, are impressive, with high mountains or steeply sloping hills. Sometimes they are bare of shrubs and trees, but often they are clothed in dense scrub and occasional patches of jungle. Some rise sheer from the water, surrounded by steep cliffs. Others are encircled by sandy beaches. Hoop pines (*Araucaria cunninghami*) are conspicuous among the trees of some of the rocky islands. The lee sides of many of the larger ones provide a haven for small craft. Passages between the large islands and the mainland, such as Whitsunday Passage and Hinchinbrook Passage, are justly famed for their scenic beauty.

Volcanic Islands

The Murray Isles formed part of a volcanic crater that was active in recent times. Likewise both Bramble Cay and Darnley Island, which lie north-east of Cape York and which are composed of andesitic lavas and ash beds, have had a volcanic origin.

Coral Reefs

The narrow coral reefs known as fringing reefs grow on the shores of many of the rocky islands and occur in places on the mainland shore itself. Elsewhere on the shelf there are reefs belonging to four different categories. Between latitudes 10°40'S and 17°S (approximately) the outermost of these reefs are situated close to the edge of the continental shelf, but north of 10°40'S and south of 17°S they are set back several kilometres from the shelf edge. From about 11°14'S to about 16°S these outer reefs form an almost continuous belt of linear reefs with recurved ends known as *ribbon reefs*. Their long axes parallel the edge of the continental shelf and they are separated one from another by narrow channels. They range from five to twenty-five kilometres in length and from three hundred to five hundred metres in width. North of this area the appearance of the outer reefs changes. Between latitudes 11°14'S and 10°S (approximately) the outer reefs occur as elongate patches which are separated by shallow meandering channels giving the appearance of

Fitzroy Island, a rocky continental island lying near Cairns.

a river delta. Hence the reefs are known as *deltaic reefs*. Their form has no doubt been influenced by the strong tidal currents found in the Torres Strait region. From about 10°S to about 9°45′S, where the outer reefs terminate, the channels between the reefs become straighter and the reefs in this region have been termed *dissected reefs*.

Between the outer reefs and the Queensland mainland, *platform reefs* occur. These are basically knoll-like formations, but the reefs present a variable surface geometry. Generally their maximum horizontal dimensions range from five to ten kilometres. Some of those lying near the Queensland mainland are only one to two kilometres in greatest dimension but bear complex assemblages of shingle ridges, exposed limestone platforms, mangrove areas, and small islands.

South of latitude 16°S, ribbon reefs are absent from the shelf, the outer edge of which gradually diverges seaward from the mainland coast. The offshore reefs in this section are all platform reefs. The innermost platform reefs of the shelf are separated by a channel from the mainland. Some of these inner platform reefs are large, up to twenty kilometres in maximum horizontal dimension, and some contain lagoons. Platform reefs become increasingly sparsely distributed as one proceeds southwards from 16°S to 19°S. However, between 19°S and 20°S they become more numerous, and from 20°S to 21°10′S, in the Pompey Reefs complex, the outer reefs are densely packed and of variable size and shape. All, however, are set well back from the hundred-fathom line. The channel separating the mainland and associated rocky islands (which usually have fringing reefs) from the innermost platform reefs of the shelf increases in width towards the south. Between latitudes 21°10′S and 22°30′S the platform reefs of the shelf are widely dispersed and form a veritable maze in the Swain Reefs complex. To the south-west this complex is separated by the Capricorn Channel from the Capricorn and Bunker Groups, which represent the southernmost reefs of the Great Barrier Reef. These lie only eighty kilometres approximately from the mainland coast.

Thus the reefs of the Great Barrier Reef span fifteen degrees of latitude and ten degrees of longitude. They are scattered over a distance of approximately two thousand kilometres. A study of recent charts indicates that there are approximately 30 dissected reefs, 30 deltaic reefs, 1,290 platform reefs, and 130 ribbon reefs on the continental shelf in the Great Barrier Reef region. Because many of the fringing reefs around continental islands and on the mainland coast are very small, their number cannot be determined with any certainty, but it is estimated there are about a thousand. While the reefs vary in size and shape, the mean area occupied by each in flat projection is estimated to be approximately ten square kilometres. Thus only about 10 per cent of the Great Barrier Reef region is occupied by reefs. The principal areas of a reef are depicted in figure 2.

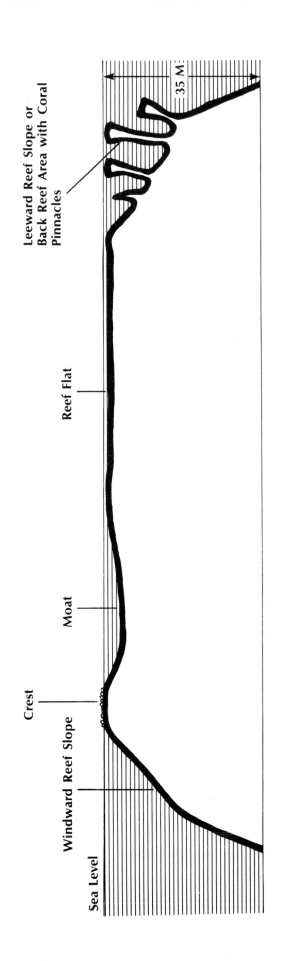

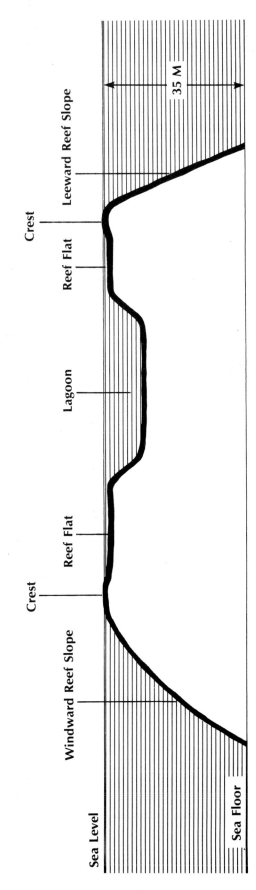

Figure 2. Vertical sections through two generalized platform reefs showing principal topographic features. Not to scale. *Top:* Platform reef with moat on outer reef flat behind crest. *Bottom:* Platform reef with lagoon.

Coral Islands

On many platform reefs there are small sandbanks, formed predominantly of pulverised foraminiferal, coral, and molluscan fragments. These materials accumulate on the lee side of the reef flats, usually in the region where waves driven around either side of the reef by the prevailing south-easterly trade winds converge. However, most of the sandbanks are unstable and alter their position, shape, and size considerably with time. They occur on platform reefs which are usually relatively large, contain a shallow lagoon, and are situated towards the outer edge of the continental shelf. If such an accumulation of sand becomes emergent above the level of the sea at high tide it forms an island known as a sand cay. It is not known precisely how this emergence comes about. Possibly cyclones associated with abnormally high tides cause a piling up of sand and debris at a level higher than usual. The island may then act as a barrier to water currents crossing the reef flat, causing the deposition of additional material around its periphery. Usually, sand cays occupy only a small proportion of the reef surface and emerge only a few metres above the level of mean low water. Many of the sand cays, such as Mystery Cay and others in the Swain Reefs area, Taylor, Beaver, Flora, and Wheeler in the central region, and Pickersgill, Undine, and Mackay in the northern region, are completely unvegetated. Others, such as Sudbury and Michaelmas in the central region, carry a few wisps of grass and sometimes a few succulents. Still others, such as Erskine Island in the Capricorn Group, carry stunted shrubs in addition to grasses and succulents. A sand cay in its climax state may carry a stand of trees or a veritable forest of trees as well as shrubs, succulents, and grasses. Most of the islands in the Bunker and Capricorn Group, Bushy Island off Mackay, and Green Island and several other sand cays in the region north of Cairns are of this kind.

Another type of coral island is the shingle cay. Some islands on platform reefs are formed basically of medium-sized fragments of corals. Pieces of branching corals, particularly *Acropora* species, are major constituents. Such shingle cays are often located on the windward side (the south-east side) of high reefs (e.g., Watson, West Hope, and Sand reefs), particularly when they are near the mainland in the northern part of the Barrier Reef where fringing reefs also occur. Typically, they occupy 5 to 10 per cent of the reef top area. Shingle islands may carry vegetation similar to that carried by sand cays. For example, cays in the southern region of the Swain Reefs complex, such as Poulson Cay, Bylund Cay, and Gillett Cay, carry coarse grasses. However, mangroves often colonize the lee side of the shingle island if it is situated near the mainland. A few cays are composed of an intimate mixture of sand and shingle, while others have regions where shingle predominates in some parts and sand in other parts.

Sometimes a reef supports more than one island. The islands may be sand cays (e.g., Low Isles, Two Isles, Three Isles, Bewick, Newton, and Ingram) or composite shingle and sand cays in addition to a shingle cay (e.g., Coquet, Houghton). The sand cay at Two Isles, with an area of some 195,000 square metres, is the largest sand cay on the Great Barrier Reef.

Water Movements

Currents

Surface currents within the Great Barrier Reef region are complex, being affected by tidal movements and varying with the seasons. Two

Lizard Island, a rocky continental island with an extensive fringing reef.

Portion of a ribbon reef near Lizard Island. The bare pavement-like reef crest on which waves from the Coral Sea are breaking can be clearly seen. A reef flat shelving into the channel lying between the offshore reefs and the mainland is visible on the landward side of the reef.

major westward-flowing currents in the Coral Sea impinge on the region. These currents are the South Equatorial Current in the far north and, further to the south, the Trade Wind Drift. During the monsoon season, from January to March, these currents combine and veer south, forming the East Australian Current. At such times water from the Arafura Sea flows through Torres Strait and also contributes to the general southerly set of the currents along the outer edge of the Great Barrier Reef region. During the remainder of the year the southerly set persists in the region south of approximately latitude 18°S, but in the region north of about that latitude the currents flow north-west along the outer edge of the Great Barrier Reef region towards Torres Strait. On the continental shelf within the region, surface currents have been little studied. When south-easterly trade winds blow, surface currents in the Townsville-Cooktown region flow north-west parallel with the coastline. During November-December, when winds blow frequently from the north, surface currents flow to the south-east in the region between Townsville and the Whitsunday Isles.

Tides

Tidal waves move westward towards the Queensland coast where they impinge on the Great Barrier Reef region. The tides are mixed semi-diurnal; that is, a high and a low tide occur within every twelve-hour period approximately. During the flood tide a build-up of water occurs in the region on the shallow continental shelf, particularly at its southern and northern ends. In the vicinity of Broad Sound (lat. 22°S), where the shelf is widest, there is a tidal rise and fall of approximately 11 metres during periods of spring tides. Further south in the Capricorn and Bunker groups the tidal range at springs is about 3 metres, and in the vicinity of the Northumberland and Cumberland Islands off the central Queensland coast it is about 4 to 6 metres. In the narrow waterways between the coast and the Cumberland Islands, maelstrom effects caused by tidal currents have been identified in satellite pictures of the area. Further north, in the Cairns region, the tidal range at springs is only 1.7 metres. This range increases again to the north, attaining a maximum of about 4 metres in the Torres Strait region. The biggest spring tides occur in December–February at night and in May–August during the day. At extreme low water there may be considerable exposure of reef flats.

Tidal currents in channels around and between reefs can attain considerable velocities, particularly in regions where the tidal range is great and gaps between reefs are narrow, as in the Pompey Complex east of Mackay or in the deltaic reef area near the extreme northern end of the Great Barrier Reef.

Winds

South-east trade winds blow almost constantly from March to November in the Great Barrier Reef region. Mean wind velocities range from 18 to 29 kilometres per hour (10 to 15 knots). During the summer months (December–February) the dominant winds are north-westerlies in northern parts of the region. These are linked to the arrival in December of the north-west monsoon off Cape York. Usually the monsoon front extends southwards during January and early February, often as far as the Cairns-Innisfail districts, before retreating northwards. Over the remainder of the Great Barrier Reef region, winds may be variable during the summer months. In some years periods of calm weather, each period extending over several days, have been recorded during summer months.

Erskine Island, a coral cay surmounting a platform reef in the Capricorn Group.

Cyclones

Tropical storms known as cyclones, with centres of low pressure ranging down to 950 millibars, are spawned most years in the Coral Sea or further east in a belt lying between latitudes 8°S and 18°S. They can occur from December to April, but usually occur in January, February, or March. Two or three appear each year, on average, but only about half those generated move into the Great Barrier Reef region. The remainder move southwards parallel with the Queensland coast or in a general south-easterly direction. Initially, their course is frequently erratic. Violent winds, gusting to velocities in excess of 200 kilometres per hour, occur near the centre of the cyclone.

Often the cyclones move in a westerly or south-westerly direction and eventually cross the Queensland coast. Huge seas are often generated by the cyclonic winds, and these also cause a piling up of water in shallow-water areas, giving the impression of abnormally high tides. Naturally, cyclones wreak havoc with small ships, and prudent sailors run for shelter when the "glass begins to fall" during the cyclone season. Extensive damage is caused to corals on coral reefs in the path of a cyclone, particularly if the cyclone strikes what is normally the lee side of a reef.

Water Temperature

Except between latitudes 14°S and 15°S, water temperatures in the Great Barrier Reef region vary rather uniformly with latitude. Mean temperatures range from about 27.5° at the northern end to about 24°C at the southern end. Highest sea temperatures occur in January in the northern region (approximately 30°C) and in February in the southern region (approximately 28°C). Lowest sea temperatures occur in June–July in the northern region (approximately 24°C) and in July–August in the southern region (approximately 20°C).

Between latitudes 14°S and 15°S, periods occur, particularly in February and May, when sea temperatures are lower than those to the north and south. This section of the Great Barrier Reef region is the narrowest section, and water temperatures there are probably affected more by mixing with Coral Sea water than are water temperatures in other sections.

Rainfall, Freshwater Run-off, and Salinity

The south-east trades are dry, and rainfall in the Great Barrier Reef region is concentrated over the summer months. It is heaviest in the Cairns region, where annual totals are around 2,000 millimetres, and decreases both to the north and south of this region. Outflow from coastal rivers during the summer monsoon season can be considerable. For example, the outflow from the Johnstone River at Innisfail during the three-month period December 1978 to February 1979 was approximately 3.43 million megalitres. At such times sediment is carried considerable distances out to sea, and waters bathing the reefs of the Great Barrier Reef in the region can be quite turbid.

3

History of the Great Barrier Reef

Coral reefs have had a long evolutionary history. Calcareous structures formed by living organisms and which could be termed reefs began to appear in the earth's tropical seas at least two billion (2,000 million) years ago. However, the calcareous deposits formed, called stromatolites, were the work of plants known as blue-green algae. It was not until the Cambrian period, some 600 million years ago, that animals became associated with the algae. These primitive animals resembled sponges and were called archaeocyathids. After 60 million years they became extinct. Then, some 480 million years ago, two other groups of animals, the bryozoans and the first corals (the *tabulate corals*) became associated with algae on reefs in a major way. Stromatolites persisted on these reefs, but other calcareous algae, called *coralline algae*, began to flourish there about the same time as the tabulate corals. The latter were later joined by another group of primitive corals called *rugose corals*. These coral reef communities persisted for about 100 million years, then they suffered a catastrophic collapse. During the next 100 million years, tabulate and rugose corals played a minor role as reef builders and, indeed, they became extinct about 215 million years ago.

About 200 million years ago the first representatives of the modern group of corals, the *scleractinian corals*, appeared and became associated with coralline algae on reefs. They flourished for the next 130 million years, and at one stage the group contained more genera than it does today. Other animals became associated with them on reefs; sometimes, as was the case with a group of molluscs called *rudists*, they played a greater part in reef formation than the corals. Then about 70 million years ago coral reefs disappeared abruptly from the fossil record for a period of about 20 million years. Subsequently coral reefs gradually reappeared and coral reef communities similar to those existing today were formed. The dominant feature of these communities was the association between scleractinian corals and coralline algae, a feature that has persisted to the present day.

Of course, the history of coral reefs just outlined did not run its course in the Great Barrier Reef area. That area did not exist as a geographical entity until a few million years ago. Indeed, Australia itself has not always had its present geographical position relative to other continents and to the poles. Near the beginning of the Triassic period about 225 million years ago, the present continents were fused into a single super-continent named Pangaea, which had a peripheral shallow-water margin on which reefs grew. Marine climates were mild and water temperatures were much warmer, even at higher latitudes, then they are today. Subsequently Pangaea broke up, splitting initially into a northern super-continent called Laurasia and a southern super-continent called Gondwana. In turn, these super-continents gradually fragmented, and the fragments became the continents of today. Slowly their positions relative to one another changed, the land masses being propelled by forces generated deep within the earth's crust. This is the phenomenon of continental drift.

By late Cretaceous times, some 65 million years ago, Gondwana had fragmented into South America, Africa, India, and Australia-Antarctica. Australia-Antarctica was then situated near the South Pole. Subsequently Australia-Antarctica split apart and Australia drifted north towards the Equator. By Miocene times, some 28 million years ago, the north-eastern coast of Australia had moved into the tropics and was favourably placed for the development of coral reefs. Apparently, as a result of faulting or down-warping of the continental margin, a shallow marine basin had been formed off the north-eastern coast. Corals flourished in this basin, which underwent slow subsidence during most of the Miocene period, which lasted for about 16 million years. As a result, the north-eastern coast became a drowned coast with coastal mountains plunging into the sea and isolated peaks protruding from the sea as rocky islands. Also, the coral reef communities grew upwards towards the sea surface from the sinking ocean floor. Sediment was trapped in the framework formed by corals and coralline algae, and the calcareous material became consolidated, then lithified as reef limestone. This material provided the foundation for attachment of later organisms, and so reefs were gradually built up, their sizes and positions being governed by the topography of the marine basin and by hydrographic conditions operating there. Probably the subsidence and reef building continued through the Miocene and the succeeding Pliocene period, up to the beginning of the Pleistocene period about a million years ago. By that time the major zones of the Great Barrier Reef and the positions of the reefs there must have been much as they are today. However, at the extreme northern end of the Great Barrier Reef region, volcanic activity occurred during the Pleistocene period and affected the development of reefs in that area.

There then occurred the remarkable Pleistocene lowerings of sea level stemming from the locking up of water in massive ice-caps, particularly in polar regions. It has been estimated that, overall, mean sea level was lowered by fifty to sixty-five metres. This would have resulted in the draining of much of the shallow water areas lying off the Queensland coast and their exposure to sub-aerial erosion for extended periods. At such times the former platform reefs of the Great Barrier Reef must have stood up from a gently sloping plain as flat-topped limestone mesas and the erstwhile ribbon reefs in the northern part of the Great Barrier Reef region must have resembled enormous dykes running along the edge of a shrinking sea. It seems likely that early Australian Aborigines lived on the coastal shelf and gazed on these massive limestone ramparts before the sea finally returned to the shelf some ten thousand years ago, when the ice-caps melted. As the water rose, it gradually covered the eroded cores of the earlier reefs. Corals and other members of the coral reef community once again settled on these limestone cores. Again the reefs grew vertically towards the surface, although their rate of growth failed to keep pace with the rate of increase in water depth. Finally the sea stopped rising and even fell slightly about three thousand years ago, and this established an upper limit to vertical growth of the reefs. The reefs reached this upper limit at various times during the last three thousand years. Only some peripheral growth was then possible, depending on local conditions. Coral islands formed on some reefs as a result of the accumulation of debris. Also, exposed rubble accumulating on some reefs near the coast acted as a trap for silt carried from the mainland and this in turn led to the establishment of mangrove forests. So the stage was set for the arrival of Europeans, the beginning of the recorded history of the Great Barrier Reef and the unravelling of its prehistory.

Australian Aborigines probably lived for several thousand years on parts of the coastal shelf where the reefs of the Great Barrier Reef now stand before the region was gradually flooded by the rising sea between about ten thousand and six thousand years ago. As the waters rose, the Aborigines would have gradually withdrawn to higher coastal land. Subsequently, after sea-level stabilized near its present height, they probably made frequent visits to many of the newly formed fringing reefs and some of the more accessible platform reefs in search of fish, turtles, molluscs, and crustaceans. Recent archaeological evidence indicates that some of the Queensland continental islands have long been used by Aboriginal groups who foraged on near-by reefs. Much of the food gathered on the reefs was eaten around the camp fires, but some of the shells collected, such as baler shells (species of *Melo*) were traded with inland tribes. Art created by the Aborigines centuries ago still adorns the walls of caves and rock overhangs on some of the islands.

A few hundred years ago, navigators from other lands began visiting the Great Barrier Reef region. Although the Englishman James Cook is usually credited with the discovery of the Great Barrier Reef in 1770 during his epic voyage along the eastern Australian coast, it is likely that other navigators preceded him. The Frenchman Bougainville saw reefs of the Great Barrier Reef from the Coral Sea side in 1768. Indonesians, Malays, Chinese, Moors, and even ancient Egyptians have been thought by some to have ventured into the region centuries before Cook. However, supporting evidence is virtually non-existent. On the other hand, there is supporting evidence for the view that the Portuguese discovered the Great Barrier Reef and charted much of Queensland's eastern coastline in the early sixteenth century. This evidence takes the form of maps produced at Dieppe, France, in about 1540. The maps were based on earlier maps smuggled out of Portugal. (The Portuguese of the early sixteenth century pursued a policy of keeping secret discoveries made by their mariners.) When adjustments are made for magnetic deviation and type of projection originally used to maps produced at Dieppe of a large land mass shown lying to the south of Java, Australia's northern and eastern coastlines become apparent, the Queensland coast, in particular, being depicted with remarkable accuracy.

As a result of his researches, K. G. McIntyre has suggested that the Portuguese navigator Cristovao de Mendonca sailed through Torres Strait from west to east in 1521 before turning to the south and charting the eastern Australian coast as far to the south as eastern Victoria. Be that as it may, one of the Dieppe maps (that prepared by the cartographer Desliens) shows what appears to be reefs beginning near a point where Cooktown now stands. The near-by coast was appropriately named "coste dangereuse" on the map, and it is in this region that the platform reefs of the Great Barrier Reef come closest to the mainland. Ironically, one of the reefs prominently marked on the map could well be Endeavour Reef, which Cook's vessel struck and on which it was almost wrecked in 1770, more than two centuries after Desliens produced his map of the region.

After the *Endeavour* was lightened by jettisoning ballast and equipment, such as six of the guns (recovered in 1969), the ship was hauled from the platform reef that almost claimed her and taken for repair to the mainland river that now bears her name. When their ship was repaired and revictualled, Cook and his crew continued their voyage northwards. They immediately found their passage impeded by the numerous islands, fringing reefs, and platform reefs that lie near the mainland between latitudes 15°30'S and 14°30'S. From the highest point on one of the islands, which he named Lizard Island, Cook obtained his first glimpse of the ribbon reefs of the Great Barrier Reef. He wrote: "When I looked around I discovered a reef of rocks, lying between two and three leagues without the islands and extending in a line N.W. and S.E. farther than I could see, upon which the sea broke in a fearful surf; this however made me think that there were no shoals beyond them and I conceived hopes of getting without these, as I perceived several breaks or openings in the reef." Cook took the *Endeavour* through one of these openings to the deep water of the Coral Sea. However, further to the north, near latitude 12°30'S, he was forced by a combination of events to re-enter the reef and island-strewn channel between the ribbon reefs and the mainland coast and to sail within this channel until Cape York was reached. There he turned west through Torres Strait.

Another remarkable mariner, William Bligh, was soon to follow Cook through Torres Strait. After the mutiny on the *Bounty*, Bligh and loyal members of the crew were cast adrift in an open boat near Tahiti. By an astonishing piece of seamanship, Bligh took his puny craft across the Coral Sea to a point near the northern tip of the Great Barrier Reef where he found a passage that permitted him to enter Torres Strait.

Yet another famous navigator was soon to pit his skills against the hazards posed by the Great Barrier Reef. During a voyage in 1802, Matthew Flinders charted the more southerly of the Cumberland Isles and then sailed northwards to a point near latitude 20°S before turning to the east and passing through a passage in the Great Barrier Reef that now bears his name.

Initially, trading ships plying between the new colony of New South Wales and Europe sailed in the Coral Sea to the east of the Great Barrier Reef on their northerly run before turning west and passing through one of the many passages in the Great Barrier Reef in the vicinity of Torres Strait. By the 1840s, however, some ships had begun to use the channel that lay between the offshore reefs of the Great Barrier Reef and the mainland. Although shorter, it was more hazardous than the Coral Sea route. Pilots with detailed knowledge of the channel were soon employed. This embryonic pilot service was ultimately to become the famous band of master mariners known as the Torres Strait Pilots. The hazard that the Great Barrier Reef posed to navigation in the days of sail is attested to by the hundreds of wrecks that lie in the region. One of the most famous is that of the *Pandora*, which was returning to England with some of the hapless mutineers from the *Bounty* in 1797. The *Pandora* was wrecked at the entrance to a passage at latitude 11°22'S which now bears her name. The wreck was located in November 1977.

Low Isles, a coral cay near Port Douglas. Buildings associated with the lighthouse establishment were used by scientific expeditions in 1928–29 and in 1954.

In order to make navigation safer in the channel between the reefs and the mainland, comprehensive surveys of the channel were undertaken. Initially these involved ships of the British navy. The first systematic survey of the Great Barrier Reef region extending from its southern to its northern tip was made by HMS *Fly* and HMS *Bramble*, under the command of Captain Blackwood, in the period 1842–46. Subsequent surveys attempted to fill in some of the many gaps in knowledge of the region. This century, survey and hydrographic vessels of the Royal Australian Navy have taken up the task. Despite all this survey activity, the sea-floor contours in the immediate vicinity of platform reefs that do not abut on the channel used by shipping are still usually poorly charted, as are the reefs themselves in some areas such as the Swain Reefs complex. Indeed, even some of the cays in this complex were still being "discovered" and placed on official charts in the 1960s.

Some of the reefs and many of the continental islands of the Great

Barrier Reef were named by Cook in 1770. Others were named by officers on various survey vessels. Not surprisingly, many of the reefs were often named after ships and naval officers. Some, however, were named after animals and two after gin distillers! Many reefs are still without official names.

During the nineteenth century, settlement gradually moved north along the Queensland coast, and the resources of the Great Barrier Reef began to be utilized. By the 1870s *bêche-de-mer* was being collected for export at places such as Green Island, near Cairns. Pearl-shell was at that stage being fished intensively in the Torres Strait region. Trochus-shell and green snail were subsequently taken in quantity from the reefs. In 1893 the commissioner of fisheries to the government of Queensland, William Saville-Kent, in a fascinating book dealing with the Great Barrier Reef, wrote: "Large quantities of bleached coral are utilized, in conjunction with Barrier Reef shells, as the orthodox adornment of innumerable oyster saloons throughout the Australian colonies, while many of the more ornamental varieties find a ready sale among retail purchasers for household decoration." Apparently the Great Barrier Reef fishing industries were slower to establish themselves. Saville-Kent noted in 1893, "The fishing industries of Queensland, as far as they relate to the fresh fish supplies of the larger centres of population, are particularly in their infancy." Towards the close of the nineteenth century some of the rich guano deposits on islands of the Great Barrier Reef were worked by phosphate companies. However, the deposits were soon worked out. Turtle meat and turtle soup canning activities began at the southern end of the Great Barrier Reef in the early years of this century. Decimation of turtle stocks in the area put an end to the turtle canning industry but gave birth to another industry in the area — tourism. The turtle cannery at Heron Island was converted into a tourist resort in 1932. It is tourism that appears likely to be the major industry on the Great Barrier Reef in the forseeable future.

As far as scientific exploration of the Great Barrier Reef is concerned, naturalists on board the *Endeavour* were the first to collect and record some of the plants and animals of the region. Joseph Beete Jukes, naturalist on board HMS *Fly*, visited many of the reefs in 1842–43 and produced an account of his visit in 1847. He was followed by three famous scientists: T. H. Huxley, on HMS *Rattlesnake* in 1848–49; Charles Darwin, on board the *Beagle* in 1859; and the American Alexander Agassiz, who visited the region in 1896. Unfortunately, circumstances prevented them from carrying out major studies in the region. In his celebrated work dealing with the Great Barrier Reef, Saville-Kent provided in 1893 superb photographs of corals and other reef organisms. He also initiated some experiments relating to the growth of massive corals that were completed early this century by the American worker A. G. Mayer. H. L. Clark, another American worker, visited the Murray Islands at the northern end of the Great Barrier Reef in 1921 and laid the foundation of much of our knowledge of the echinoderm fauna of the Great Barrier Reef. During the first half of this century many Australian workers, particularly workers from the Australian Museum such as Charles Hedley, Tom Iredale, Frank McNeill, and Gilbert Whitley, contributed significantly to our knowledge of the marine fauna of the region and Australian scientists have subsequently figured prominently in Great Barrier Reef research.

In 1922 a scientific society, the Great Barrier Reef Committee, was founded to expedite the scientific investigation of the Great Barrier Reef. In attempts to determine whether subsidence was involved in the formation of this extensive structure, the committee organized the sinking of two bores. One was sunk to a depth of approximately 183 metres at Michaelmas Cay, near Cairns, in 1926, the other to a depth of approximately 223 metres at Heron Island, near the southern end of the Great Barrier Reef, in 1937. Neither bore reached the basement rocks underlying the reefal sediments, but information derived from the cores obtained has been supplemented by more recent data derived from deeper exploratory bores sunk by oil companies at the northern and southern ends of the Great Barrier Reef. All this information has enabled geologists to provide an account of the geological history of the Great Barrier Reef.

The Great Barrier Reef Committee was also deeply involved with the planning and organization of two expeditions to Low Isles. There was a major expedition in 1928-29, involving mostly British scientists, which laid the foundations of much of our knowledge of the general biology and taxonomy of Great Barrier Reef organisms, and a short expedition in 1954 which examined changes that had occurred at Low Isles in the intervening twenty-five years. In 1951 the committee began the construction of the Heron Island Research Station. Construction of this station was a pioneering venture by a scientific society which is without parallel in the relatively brief history of Australian science. It has enabled hundreds of scientists both from Australia and from other countries to live and work right on a reef of the Great Barrier Reef. As a result, there has been a marked increase in our knowledge of the biology of organisms found at the southern end of the Great Barrier Reef. The Heron Island Research Station was recently given to the University of Queensland by the Great Barrier Reef Committee.

In recent years other research stations have been opened on the Great Barrier Reef. These include the small One Tree Island Research Station (adjacent to Heron Island), operated by the University of Sydney; the Lizard Island Research Station, operated by the Australian Museum; and the Orpheus Island Research Station, operated by James Cook University. In addition, many scientists at the Australian Institute of Marine Science at Cape Cleveland, near Townsville, are involved with studies of problems relating to the adjacent area of the Great Barrier Reef. An increase in scientific knowledge of this central region and its fauna and flora can now be expected. In order to facilitate the obtaining of scientific information from the northern region of the Great Barrier Reef, a field station is now required somewhere near the northern tip of this region, possibly in the Murray Isles area.

4

Classification and Naming of Animals and Plants

Before discussing the living animals and plants that constitute the coral reef communities found on the Great Barrier Reef, it will be necessary to consider briefly the system of naming and classifying animals and plants used by zoologists and botanists.

The animal kingdom includes such diverse members as corals, birds, crabs, and starfish. Moreover, there is a bewildering array of different kinds of coral, bird, crab, and starfish. Zoologists seek order amidst this apparent chaos. By comparing the structural features of animals it is possible to split the animal kingdom into groups, the members of each group having many features in common. Thus corals, birds, crabs, and starfish are obviously different structurally and can be placed in separate groups. Each group can be subdivided further, still on the basis of differences in structural features (the process is known as classification) until a group of animals is obtained whose members resemble each other so closely that no structural basis can be found for subdividing them further. This final grouping is the species. The species is a fundamental unit in biology, just as atoms and sub-atomic particles are fundamental units in physics and chemistry. It is a criterion of a species that the members of such a grouping can interbreed and that they do not normally interbreed with other species, or if they do, the resultant offspring are incapable of breeding.

In the eighteenth century the famed Swedish naturalist Linnaeus proposed a system of classification which, in its essentials, is accepted today. His first major division or splitting of the animal kingdom gave rise to groups called phyla (sing. phylum). There are over twenty phyla recognized today, but many of them contain relatively few species. A phylum may be subdivided progressively into subphyla, classes, subclasses, orders, suborders, families, subfamilies, genera (sing. genus), and finally species. Not all these subdivisions are usually employed in each case, but the majority are.

The coral known on the Great Barrier Reef as the branching ivory coral will be used to illustrate how this system of classification operates. The basic body plan of corals is a sac-like body with a central stomach cavity possessing an opening, the mouth, at one end. The mouth is surrounded by tentacles that bear microscopic structures called *cnidae* or *nematocysts*, which are used in prey capture. The body wall consists of three layers, the middle layer having a jelly-like appearance. All animals that possess cnidae and a basic body plan

The branching ivory coral, *Acrhelia horrescens*, a member of the family Oculinidae.

similar to that just described are placed in the phylum Cnidaria. Thus corals, jellyfish, hydroids, anemones, soft corals, sea-pens, sea-fans, and their kin are placed in this phylum. Members of the phylum that have a jellyfish (medusa) stage in their life cycle, such as jellyfish and hydroids, are placed in the subphylum Medusozoa, and those members which lack such a stage are placed in the subphylum Anthozoa. Corals do not have a medusa stage in their life cycle and hence are placed in the subphylum Anthozoa. Members of this subphylum may be placed in one of three classes depending on the arrangement of their tentacles and the way their stomach cavity, termed the *coelenteron*, is divided. If members have six (or multiples of six) unbranched tentacles and the coelenteron is divided by a number of paired partitions, they are placed in the class Zoantharia. Corals have these structural features and so are placed in this class, along with anemones, zoanthids, and their kin. Representatives of this class are then placed in one of four orders depending upon their possession of a collection of structural features that characterize a particular order. Since the outermost layer of their body wall secretes a hard limy skeleton, corals are placed in the order Scleractinia. Members of this order are then placed in one of five suborders depending on the nature of their tentacles and the arrangement of vertical radiating partitions known as *septa* in their skeletons. Study of the branching ivory coral found on the Great Barrier Reef would lead to its being placed in the suborder Faviina, individuals belonging to which possess more than two rings of tentacles around the mouth and have septa that are toothed. Features of the coral skeleton as outlined in chapter 5 are then used to subdivide the suborder into families. The branching ivory coral under consideration has the features possessed by members of the family Oculinidae. It could be placed in one of the two genera (*Galaxea* and *Acrhelia*) of this family that have been recorded from the Great Barrier Reef on the basis of whether it forms a hemispherical or lobed colony or whether it branches. Since it is a branching form, it belongs to the genus *Acrhelia*. Only one species, the species *horrescens*, belonging to this genus is known. Accordingly, the complete classification of the branching ivory coral is as follows:

Phylum	Cnidaria
Subphylum	Anthozoa
Class	Zoantharia
Order	Scleractinia
Suborder	Faviina
Family	Oculinidae
Genus	*Acrhelia*
Species	*horrescens*

When referring to any animal, it is not necessary to give each of these groupings. The last two groupings, the genus and species, suffice. Thus in zoological parlance the branching ivory coral becomes *Acrhelia horrescens*. The second part of the name is written with a small initial letter and both genus and species are italicized. Every species of animal known to science is given such a two-part scientific name, which is usually derived from Latin or Greek.

In the zoological literature there are written descriptions and figures of the known animal species, and it is possible for any zoologist with access to this literature to ascertain the scientific name for any species collected provided the species is known to science. Most museums, too, contain specimens of local animals complete with their correct scientific names, and it is possible to have animals identified (i.e., given their scientific names) by the museum authorities. It will be appreciated that common names conferred on animals may vary from district to district and from language to language. Hence it is essential that an agreed internationally recognized scientific name be conferred on each species of animal.

Botanists use the same system of classification and naming employed by zoologists. However, in place of phyla and subphyla they refer to divisions and subdivisions.

Some of the groups of animals found on the Great Barrier Reef have been little studied, and many contain undescribed species. At the present state of knowledge it is not possible to identify every species or even genus encountered on the Great Barrier Reef. However, for most groups it is usually possible to place the animal in its correct family. Consequently, the animals mentioned in this book are mostly dealt with at the family level. Another reason for adopting this approach is to keep the length of the book within reasonable limits. A common name, as well as the scientific name, is given for each family listed. After a study of relevant descriptions, diagrams, and photographs provided in the book, it should be possible for the reader to put the majority of animals encountered in their correct families. Some of the common genera belonging to each family listed are given to assist the reader in identifying specimens encountered on the Great Barrier Reef. A few groups of animals are so poorly known that they are dealt with at levels of classification above the family level.

5

The Reef Builders — Hard Corals

Animals known commonly as hard or stony corals are primarily responsible for the construction of modern coral reefs in that they initiate reef construction and provide the basic framework of reefs. However, the activities of marine algae (chapter 6) are essential for subsequent reef formation and stabilization. Technically, hard corals are cnidarians (Phylum Cnidaria) belonging to the class Zoantharia, order Scleractinia. Individual coral animals are called *polyps*. Although the polyps belonging to some species of stony coral occur singly (the solitary corals), those belonging to most species of reef-building corals occur in large groups known as colonies. A single polyp that has developed from a fertilized egg founds each colony, but the founding polyp soon gives rise to numerous other polyps by a process called *budding*. This is a form of asexual reproduction involving the partial or complete separation of a group of cells from existing coral tissue and the formation of a new polyp from the separated cells.

Essentially, each coral polyp has the form of a hollow cylinder, sealed at one end (the base) and bearing a number of tentacles surrounding an opening (the mouth) at the other. The tentacles are capable of extension and contraction. The region in the vicinity of the mouth upon which the tentacles are borne is called the *oral disc*. Preliminary digestion of foodstuffs taken in through the mouth occurs within the stomach cavity, or coelenteron. This cavity is subdivided by a series of radiating vertical partitions (see fig. 3) called *mesenteries*. These are attached above to the inner surface of the oral disc, but their lower margins are free. The cells of the vertical edge of each mesentery constitute the so-called *cnidoglandular band*, and many of these cells are responsible for secreting enzymes that initiate digestion of food. At the lower margin of each mesentery each band is attenuated to form a convoluted, whip-like *mesenterial filament*, which assists in

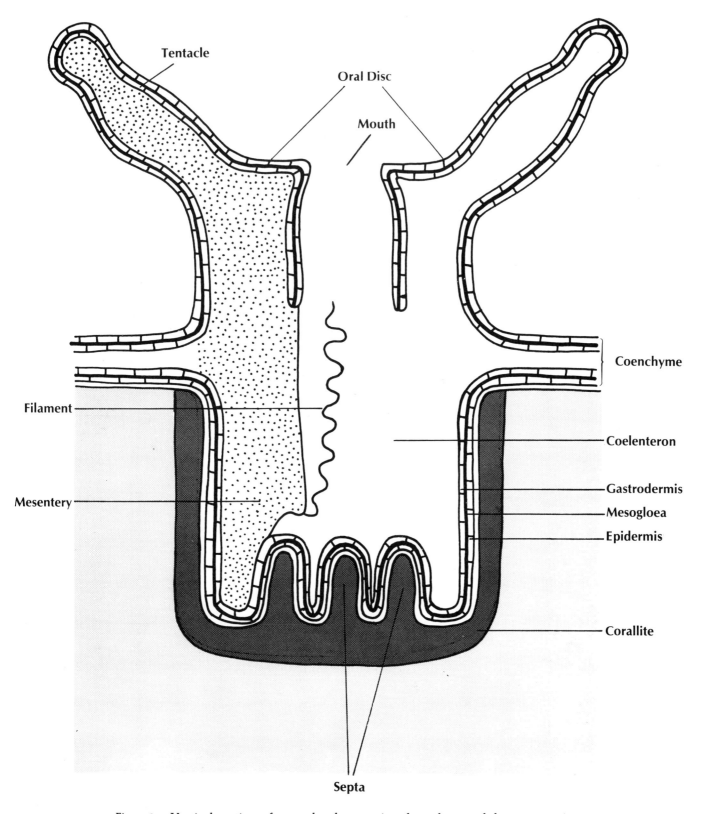

Figure 3. Vertical section of a coral polyp passing through one of the mesenteries.

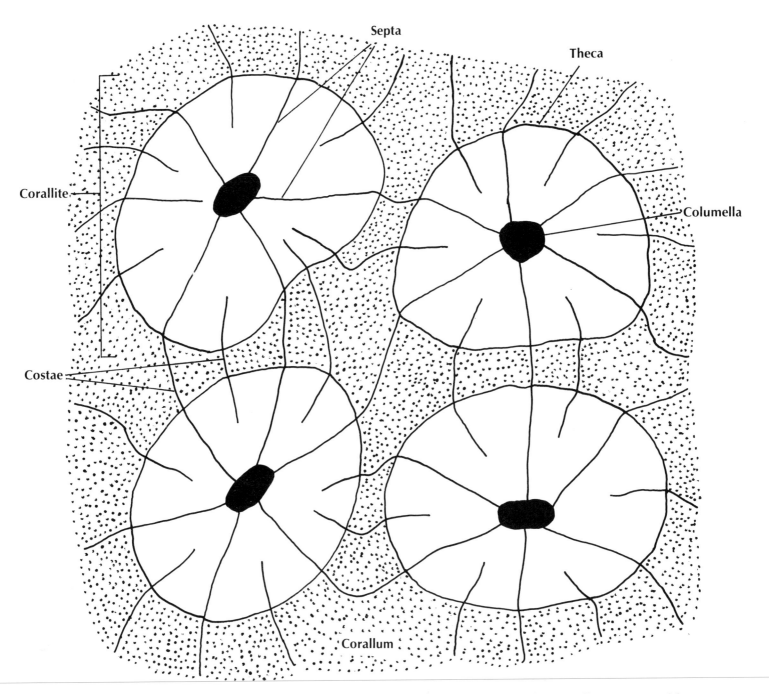

Figure 4. Portion of the surface of a corallum viewed from above and showing four corallites connected by costae. Note that some of the septa of each corallite do not extend as far as the central columella.

prey capture (since the tip can be protruded through the mouth) and assists also in subduing struggling prey brought into the coelenteron. A layer of cells (the *gastrodermis*) lining the coelenteron absorbs partially digested fragments of food, and digestion is completed in minute sac-like vacuoles within these cells. The cell layer on the outside of the polyp is called the *epidermis*. Cells belonging to this layer in the region of the polyp near the tentacles and on the tentacles themselves bear motile hair-like structures termed *cilia*, and frequently these cells also produce mucus. The gastrodermis and epidermis are separated by a third layer, the *mesogloea* which has a jelly-like consistency.

A protective skeleton of lime (calcium carbonate) called a *corallite*, which typically assumes the form of a cup with a number of radiating vertical partitions (called *septa*) arising from the basal plate of the cup, is secreted by regions at and near the base of each polyp. The polyp base is forced into folds by the septa, which are frequently fused at their inner ends to form a central axial structure termed the *columella* (see fig. 4). Continued secretion of calcium carbonate by basal regions of the polyp causes the septa to increase in height and push the polyp outwards within the tubular walls constituting the *theca* of the corallite (see fig. 5). At intervals, a partition forms at the outer ends of the septa and constitutes a new basal plate for polyp attachment. Thus the polyps are pushed outwards as the coral skeleton increases in size.

Individual polyps of a colony are interconnected by a lateral extension of the polyp walls called the *coenchyme*. This consists of the same cell layers (epidermis and gastrodermis) as the polyps and contains a cavity continuous with the coelenteron of each polyp. The lower surface of the coenchyme secretes that part of the skeleton occurring between adjacent corallites. Lateral extensions of septa called *costae* also occur in some species. In the branching corals belonging to genera such as *Acropora* and *Montipora*, the coenchyme is so thin that the coral skeletons appear exposed in life; in others, such as the brain corals, the coenchyme is quite thick. In a number of coral families the whole skeleton is much perforated, so that adjacent polyps are interconnected by way of these pores. These corals are known as the *perforate corals*, as opposed to the *imperforate corals*.

It should be noted that the coral polyps always remain on the surface of the coral skeleton (the *corallum*) and that they do not increase in size as the corallum increases in size. Although the average diameter attained by a coral polyp is only about 1 centimetre, the total skeletal material secreted by all the polyps and the coenchyme of a colony may be very bulky. Indeed, the colonies of some species of branching corals often form immense submerged forests, and single colonies of non-branching (termed *massive*) corals may eventually weigh several hundred tonnes. Colonies of these massive corals frequently have a hemispherical shape. However, the shape of a coral

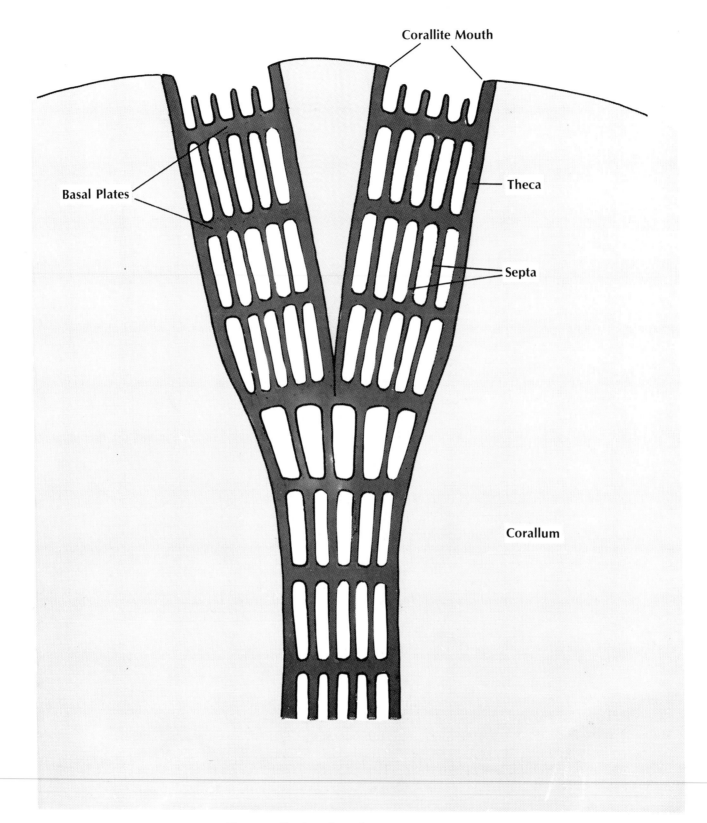

Figure 5. Section through two adjacent corallites.

colony varies greatly, not only from species to species but often also within the same species, some colonies showing subtle changes in form as a result of differences in environmental conditions to which each colony is exposed. Nevertheless, colonies belonging to each major group of coral usually have a characteristic shape. Differences in polyp size, in the ways in which budding occurs, and in the structure of the skeleton are principally responsible for differences among the major groups.

The polyps of some corals (e.g., the genera *Favia* and *Goniastrea*) are very large; those of others (e.g., the genus *Porites*) are small. Buds that give rise to new polyps may form in the coenchyme between pre-existing polyps and give rise to widely spaced polyps, as in the genus *Galaxea*. Buds arising on opposite sides of the oral disc (see diagram) may give rise to contiguous polyps, as in the genus *Favia*. If buds arise on the same side of the oral disc of a polyp, branching may occur, as in the genus *Acropora*. Alternatively, the polyps may be confluent and confined to depressed rows as in the "brain corals" exemplified by the genus *Platygyra*. In these corals the incomplete polyps in the depressed rows share a common fringe of tentacles and their corallites are confluent. Differences in the type of budding that occurs are of course reflected in the structure of the skeleton, which is used as the principal basis for classifying corals. In addition, in some groups of coral there are deletions from (e.g., loss of theca) or additions to (e.g., a double theca) the basic structure of the skeleton described earlier. In some groups, rods link the septa and may form the walls of the corallite.

The substratum, to which most reef corals attach, is semi-consolidated rubble overlying the limestone core of the reef, but there are some species, including many of the solitary corals (e.g., the mush-room corals belonging to the genus *Fungia*), that are free-living when adult.

Over three hundred species of coral occur in Great Barrier Reef waters. Most species found there belong to one of the families and genera of coral mentioned in the following list.

Families of Corals found on the Great Barrier Reef

Thamnasterids (Thamnasteridae) have minute corallites which lack thecae; costae extend between adjacent corallites. The small polyps bear less than twelve tentacles in a single ring. Only one living genus is recognized. Colonies of this genus form small rounded clumps or small clumps with stubby branches that bear irregular grooves. They occur on reef flats and in the back-reef areas on the Great Barrier Reef but appear to be somewhat rare. Colours exhibited are grey, brown, or purplish red.

Genus represented: *Psammocera*.

Astrocoeniids (Astrocoeniidae) have small corallites with prominent projecting septa and columellae. They are characterized by the possession of pillar-like structures that project from the surface of the corallum between adjacent corallites. Polyps rarely have more than twelve tentacles, which are arranged in a single ring. Only one living genus has been found in the Indo–West Pacific region. Small encrusting colonies belonging to this genus are occasionally found growing in reef crevices on the Great Barrier Reef.

Genus represented: *Stylocoeniella*.

Pocilloporids (Pocilloporidae) form branching or lobed colonies consisting of small, deep-set corallites which are usually arranged in rows. Each corallite possesses a columella, but the septa are often rudimentary. In the genus *Madracis*, which appears to be rare on the Great Barrier Reef the septa occur in multiples of eight or ten rather than multiples of six as in other corals. In the genus *Stylophora*, which is usually well represented on reef flats, reef slopes, and in lagoons, the short, slightly flattened branches of a colony are prickly to the touch because hoods arch over the openings of the corallites. In the genus *Palauastrea*, found in sheltered areas of fringing reefs, spines occur on the surface of the corallum between adjacent corallites. The genus *Seriatopora* is often referred to as "needle-coral" because some of the terminal branches of a colony are very fine. Colonies of *Seriatopora* are found in sheltered areas, particularly on reef flats. Species of *Pocillopora* sometimes occur commonly on reef flats and in lagoons. Pocilloporids range in colour from blue or purple to green, brown, and pink. The polyps are small and each bears a single ring of tentacles.

Genera represented: *Pocillopora, Seriatopora, Stylophora, Palauastrea, Madracis.*

Acroporids (Acroporidae). Small cylindrical corallites with up to twelve simple septa are present in the greatly perforated corallum of an acroporid, which has no columella. The polyps usually bear less than twelve tentacles arranged in a single ring. Members of this family are the dominant corals in most areas of the Great Barrier Reef. Numerous species of the genus *Acropora* occur there. These show great variation in growth form. Some form large branching colonies known as staghorn corals, some form low bushy clumps, some form platelike or tabular structures composed of interlocking branches, and a few are encrusting. Corallites protrude from the corallum, and in branching forms a single corallite may run the length of a branch and open at the tip while the other corallites are radially arranged. Colonies belonging to the genus *Montipora* usually form thin, leafy plates (sometimes arranged in conical stacks) or irregular encrustations; the surface of each corallum has a rough texture because projections arise between adjacent corallites. Likewise, numerous low spikes protrude from the coralla of colonies belonging to the genus *Astreopora*. The rounded openings of the corallites, which have short septa, also protrude from the coralla of the hemispherical colonies formed by this genus. The colours of acroporids range from purple and blue to green, yellow, brown, and pink.

Genera represented: *Acropora, Montipora, Astreopora.*

Agariciids (Agariciidae). In members of the family Agariciidae the thecae are usually absent or poorly developed and the fine septa extend between adjacent corallites as costae. Rods are usually present between adjacent septa. The polyps have more than two rings of tentacles. Colonies belonging to the genus *Pavona* are either encrusting or composed of clusters of small lobed or vertical plates. On close examination a starlike arrangement of the septa of each corallite will be apparent. Colonies are green or brown and occur on reef flats and reef slopes. Thin platelike colonies are formed by members of the genus *Leptoseris*. Concentric ridges involving systems of corallites occur in several regions of the plate. Colonies are found in shaded parts of the reef, particularly in caves and under overhangs. They are usually grey or greenish. In the genus *Gardinioseris*, colonies are encrusting or columnar. The surface of each colony is markedly striated because of the presence of parallel ridges and depressions. Colonies are brown, purple, and yellow and are found occasionally on reef flats and reef slopes. In the genus *Coeloseris* each corallite is defined by a wall (theca) and lacks a columella. Colonies are usually pale green, yellow, or brown and occur, sometimes commonly, on reef slopes. Colonies of the genus *Pachyseris* form thin, circular plates, the surfaces of which bear concentric ridges and valleys. The corallites are minute. Colonies average 20 centimetres in diameter and are grey or brown. They occur on upper reef slopes, particularly near surge channels, but are not commonly encountered.

Genera represented: *Pavona, Leptoseris, Gardinioseris, Coeloseris, Pachyseris.*

Siderastreids (Siderastreidae). The corallites of siderastreids are small and crowded with septa which bear serrations on their upper margins. Rods link adjacent septa and form the corallite wall. Costae are present. The small polyps have more than two rings of tentacles. Colonies belonging to the genus *Pseudosiderastrea* usually appear as thick, encrusting masses. The corallites have polygonal openings, and the septa

10

11

12

13

14

15

16

17

18

19

20

21

bear small spines. Colours exhibited are pale grey or pink. Rounded or encrusting colonies are formed by members of the genus *Coscinarea*. Low ridges surrounding groups of corallites are found on the surface of the corallum. Colonies range from brown to purple in colour and are usually found on reef slopes.

Genera represented: *Pseudosiderastrea, Coscinarea.*

Fungiids *(Fungiidae)* are largely non-attached corals that may be disclike or elongated. While most species are colonial, a few are solitary. The corallites are greater than 2 millimetres in diameter and have prominent septa which are united by rods and bear numerous perforations; costae are present. The polyps have more than two rings of tentacles. All fungiids are attached to the substratum by a stalk when young, but the stalk breaks in those species that are non-attached when adult.

The common "mushroom" corals belonging to the genus *Fungia* each consist of a solitary polyp between 5 and 15 centimetres in diameter. The corallite, which is usually somewhat oval in outline with a convex upper surface, has a large number of vertical radiating septa. Mushroom corals occur commonly on reef flats and are usually brown or greenish-brown in colour. Tentacles are usually retracted during daylight hours.

In the genus *Heliofungia* the solitary polyps are large (up to 20 centimetres in diameter). Their thick tentacles are up to 8 centimetres in length and are nearly always fully extended. They occur on reef flats and in lagoons.

Members of the genus *Cycloseris* are solitary non-attached corals that resemble *Fungia* but are only about 2 centimetres in diameter. A species of *Cycloseris* that is green, grey, or brown in colour is found on sandy areas in deeper water at the periphery of reefs.

The smallest representatives of the solitary fungiids belong to the genus *Diaseris*. They average only 1 centimetre in diameter. Each is flat and disc-shaped, although formed of several wedge-like segments. Specimens occur on sandy bottoms adjacent to reefs and have remarkable powers of locomotion that have resulted in the term "acrobatic coral" being applied to the genus.

Members of the genus *Lithophyllon* remain attached to the substratum when adult. They are colonial and have a foliate growth pattern. They occur in lagoons and other sheltered situations.

Representatives of the colonial fungiid *Podobacia* also remain attached to the substratum when mature. Colonies occur as sheets, which often assume a vaselike form. These are brownish and occur occasionally in lagoons and on sheltered reef slopes.

The colonial genus *Herpolitha* has an elongated, twisted shape (averaging about 25 centimetres in length) and is known commonly

Facing page
Illustration 10
Needle coral, *Seriatopora hystrix.*

Illustration 11
A forest of staghorn coral, *Acropora* sp.

Illustration 12
A tabular or plate coral, *Acropora hyacinthus.*

Illustration 13
Portion of a colony of *Astreopora myriopthalma.*

Illustration 14
Adjacent colonies of a species of *Montipora.*

Illustration 15
Part of a colony of a species of *Pachyseris.*

Illustration 16
A mushroom coral, *Fungia actiniformis.*

Illustration 17
Portion of a slipper coral, *Herpolitha limax.*

Illustration 18
Expanded polyps of portion of a colony of *Goniopora tenuidens.*

Illustration 19
Portion of a colony of the massive coral *Porites lutea.*

Illustration 20
The small expanded polyps of portion of a colony of *Porites lutea.*

Illustration 21
Portion of a colony of *Favites abdita* showing the large greenish retracted polyps.

as the "slipper coral". A deep groove runs longitudinally along the centre of the upper surface. Septa are prominent. The colony is free, brownish, and occurs in lagoons and in the deeper water at the edges of reefs.

Members of the colonial genus *Herpetoglossa* closely resemble those of *Herpolitha* but differ in septal characteristics. For example, the main septa of *Herpetoglossa* may run from the central groove to the perimeter

Expanded polyps of the ahermatypic coral *Tubastrea aurea*.

of the corallum, but those of *Herpolitha* never do so. Specimens of *Herpetoglossa* occur frequently in lagoons.

Members of the genus *Polyphyllia* are free-living and colonial. They resemble *Herpolitha* but are domed and appear smoother. Also, they lack a central furrow. Numerous corallite mouths are apparent in the corallum. This fungiid occurs in lagoons and on reef slopes and is brown in colour.

Colonies belonging to the genus *Halomitra* have a deep concavity in the undersurface and are often bell-shaped. There is a central depression from which septa radiate, but these septa pursue a sinuous and interrupted course.

Free-living colonial fungiids belonging to the genus *Parahalomitra* resemble an inverted dish and are known as "basket corals". Numerous corallite openings are apparent. Septa are well developed and give the corallum a rough appearance. The coral averages about 25 centimetres in diameter, is brownish, and occurs in lagoons and in deeper water at the periphery of reefs.

Members of the colonial genus *Sandolitha* have a similar appearance to those of the genus *Halomitra* but are more elongate. Also, the septa of *Sandolitha* have large serrations that are covered with granules and differ from those of *Halomitra* structurally.

Genera represented: *Fungia, Heliofungia, Cycloseris, Diaseris, Lithophyllon, Podabacia, Herpolitha, Herpetoglossa, Polyphyllia, Halomitra, Parahalomitra, Sandolitha.*

Poritids (Poritidae). Numerous contiguous corallites form the colonies of poritids. The septa are perforated by minute pores and some are linked by rods. The polyps have more than two rings of tentacles, which are capable of great extension. Colonies of the genus *Porites* exhibit a great variety of shape, but there is a tendency towards the formation of circular, flattened structures (micro-atolls) on reef flats and dome-like structures in deeper water. Some colonies form stubby branches. Sizes of colonies range from a few centimetres to over 5 metres in diameter. The openings of the corallites are very small, and colonies have a smooth appearance. Species belonging to this genus may be found in most areas of a reef and are often common. Colours range through green, grey, brown, pink, and mauve. The coralla of colonies of the genus *Goniopora* are rounded and resemble small colonies of *Porites*. However, each corallite of *Goniopora* has twenty-four septa compared with twelve in *Porites*. In living colonies the elongate polyps, which have twenty-four tentacles in a single ring, are nearly always extended, making identification easy. They are brown, green, or grey in colour. Colonies occur commonly on reef flats and reef slopes. Members of the genus *Alveopora* resemble *Goniopora*, but the colonies are very small and the corallites are relatively large. The septa arise from the walls rather than the floor of each corallite. Colonies occur on the reef slope and have a greyish colour.

Genera represented: *Porites, Goniopora, Alveopora.*

Faviids (Faviidae). The corallites of faviids are large and have prominent septa with serrations on their edges which project above the corallite mouth at their junctions with the thecae. The corallites have sturdy walls; however, in some genera, groups of corallites occur in series and lack internal walls. The polyps usually have more than two rings of tentacles. In the genus *Favia* the corallites are large (averaging 1 centimetre in diameter), with spherical or irregularly shaped surface openings. They are clearly separated one from another. Colonies are usually hemispherical, but sometimes encrusting, and average about 20 centimetres in diameter. Most are brown or green and are common on reef flats and reef slopes and in lagoons.

Colonies belonging to the genus *Favites* are similar in shape and size to those of *Favia.* However, the corallites share a common wall and are usually polygonal in shape. Polyps are brown, green, or brown with green centres. Colonies occur fairly commonly on reef flats and reef slopes and in lagoons.

In the genus *Hydnophora* the shared walls of adjacent corallites project from the corallum as cones, making members of this genus easy to recognize. Colonies are usually less than 20 centimetres in diameter and may be branching, rounded, or encrusting. They are coloured brown, grey, or green and occur on reef flats and reef slopes and in lagoons.

Small, rounded colonies are formed by representatives of the genus *Montastrea.* The corallites vary in size, have circular openings, are well separated one from another, and project slightly from the surface of the corallum. Costae are present. The brownish colonies occur on reef flats but are not commonly encountered.

Members of the genus *Plesiastrea* resemble those of *Favia* but the openings of the corallites are rounder. Also, very small corallites are found among the larger ones. Colonies are rarely more than 25 centimetres in diameter, are brown, and are found on outer reef flats, reef crests and upper parts of reef slopes.

Small, rounded colonies, rarely exceeding 20 centimetres in diameter, are formed by members of the genus *Cyphastrea.* The appearance of the corallites of this genus resembles those of *Montastrea;* however, granules occur on the surface of the corallum among the corallites in *Cyphastrea.* Colonies are brownish and occur, often in small clusters, on reef flats, reef crests, and upper reef slopes.

In the genus *Diploastrea* the septa of each corallite are thick peripherally and thin internally where they join a prominent columella. Very large dome-shaped colonies, usually pale cream in colour, are formed.

The colonies may occur in a variety of situations, ranging from the exposed reef front to protected back-reef areas.

Colonies belonging to the genus *Leptastrea* resemble those of *Montastrea*, but the corallites of *Leptastrea* are crowded together, conferring a honeycomb-like appearance on the corallum. Also, costae are lacking in *Leptastrea*. Colonies are brown or purplish and occur on reef flats and reef crests.

In the genus *Goniastrea*, groups of corallites are bounded by an outer calcareous wall which is shared by groups of adjacent corallites. Short, sinuous grooves where the polyps are located in life are thereby formed. Each polyp in a group has a separate mouth. *Goniastrea* species form hemispherical colonies averaging about 15 centimetres in diameter. The colonies are brown, green, or grey and occur commonly on reef flats and reef slopes and in lagoons.

Species belonging to the genera *Platygyra* and *Leptoria* constitute the so-called brain corals. In these corals, groups of corallites are linked in series and are bounded by an outer calcareous wall. This wall is shared by adjacent corallite groups. Thus a system of sinuous ridges and valleys is formed on the surface of the corallum. The polyps belonging to a series have a common mouth. Rounded colonies of *Platygyra* occur on reef.slopes and outer reef flats and in lagoons. They average about 2 metres in diameter and are coloured green, brown, or grey. Members of the genus *Leptoria* closely resemble *Platygyra* but have a continuous columella running along the floor of each sinuous groove. Colonies of *Leptoria* are green or brown and occur on reef flats and reef slopes and in lagoons.

Corals belonging to the genus *Oulophyllia* have a corallum with higher ridges and deeper and wider valleys than in the genera *Platygyra* and *Leptoria*, which they otherwise resemble. Colonies of *Oulophyllia* are light green or light brown and occur occasionally on reef slopes.

Colonies of *Echinopora* take the form of folded plates or branching structures averaging about 25 centimetres in diameter. The large projecting corallites have rounded openings. Spikes or ridges are found on the surface of the corallum among the corallite openings. Colonies are brown or green and occur commonly on reef slopes and occasionally in outer regions of reef flats.

Genera represented: *Favia, Favites, Hydnophora, Montastrea, Plesiastrea, Cyphastrea, Diploastrea, Leptastrea, Goniastrea, Platygyra, Leptoria, Oulophyllia, Echinopora.*

Trachyphyllids (Trachyphyllidae). The upper edges of most septa bear prominent lobes towards the centre of each corallite in members of the family Trachyphyllidae. Small serrations occur on septa at the margins of each corallite. Only one genus, *Trachyphyllia*, is represented on the Great Barrier Reef. It contains free-living colonial corals

composed of a small number of polyps. Colonies average 10 centimetres in diameter and are found on sand or among rubble near the bottom on reef slopes, particularly on the lee side of reefs. Colours exhibited are green, brown, reddish or grey.

Genus represented: *Trachyphyllia.*

Mussids (Mussidae) may be solitary or colonial and have very large fleshy polyps and correspondingly large corallites in the corallum. The septa exhibit markedly serrated margins, conferring a spiky appearance on the corallum. The polyps usually have more than two rings of tentacles. Mussid features are well shown by the domelike colonies of *Acanthastrea*, which attain a size of about 25 centimetres in diameter. Corallites of the genus *Lobophyllia* are large (averaging 3 centimetres in diameter), well separated from one another, and often protrude in stalklike fashion from the corallum, which may be 1 metre or more in diameter. A similar size is attained by colonies of the genus *Symphyllia*. In this genus the walls of groups of adjacent corallites fuse, producing a convoluted appearance reminiscent of brain corals. Small tufts of erect cylindrical corallites arise from the corallum in the genus *Blastomussa*. The colonial mussids occur in the outer zones of reef flats in lagoons, channels in back-reef areas, and on reef slopes. Colours are mostly greens and browns. Corals belonging to the mussid genera *Scolymia* and *Cynarina* are solitary. The corallite of *Scolymia* averages about 5 centimetres in diameter and resembles that of *Lobophyllia*. Species belonging to this genus are commonly found attached to cliff faces and to deeper sections of reef slopes. Polyps are usually coloured green or orange. The corallite of *Cynarina* is about 4 centimetres in diameter. The coral may be attached to the deeper reef slopes in protected areas or free on the sea-floor near reefs. The polyp is pale brown.

Genera represented: *Acanthastrea, Lobophyllia, Symphyllia, Blastomussa, Scolymia, Cynarina.*

Merulinids (Merulinidae). In the small merulinid family the corallites are always linked to form a series of rows which fan out towards the edge of the colony. The septa are thick and have jagged upper edges. The polyps have more than two rings of tentacles. In the genus *Merulina*, colonies usually occur as thin plates covered by radiating ridges. Raised growths often occur in central areas of the colonies. Usually colonies are brown, but occasionally they are greenish and are found on reef flats and reef slopes. The general appearance of the corallites in the genus *Clavarina* resembles that of the corallites of *Merulina*, but colonies of *Clavarina* form branching structures brown or grey in colour and sometimes more than 1 metre in height. They are found in lagoons and in back-reef areas but are somewhat rare.

Facing page
Large fleshy polyps belonging to a member of the family Mussidae (*Lobophyllia corymbosa*).

Small, rounded colonies of the genus *Scapophyllia* are found occasionally on reef slopes in waters of the Great Barrier Reef. They are usually grey or brown and resemble *Merulina* in the structure and arrangement of corallites.

Genera represented: *Merulina, Clavarina, Scapophyllia.*

Ivory corals (Oculinidae) form branching or hemispherical colonies characterized by the presence of the well-separated, round openings of the corallites which project from the corallum. The corallites have a spiky appearance because the septa project above the thecae of the corallites. Polyps with more than two rows of tentacles are present. In the genus *Galaxea*, colonies are small, usually hemispherical or lobed, with corallites about 5 millimetres in diameter projecting 5 to 10 millimetres above the corallum. Cream-coloured, green, or brownish colonies occur on outer reef flats and upper reef slopes but are not common. Only a single species of the genus *Acrhelia (A. horrescens)* is known. It resembles a branching form of *Galaxea*. Small clumps of this elegant coral occur on outer reef flats and upper reef slopes. Colonies are brown or grey.

Genera represented: *Galaxea, Acrhelia.*

The corallum of a hemispherical colony belonging to the faviid genus *Favia*. Individual corallites each with a series of radiating septa are apparent.

Pectinids (Pectiniidae) are colonial and have large polyps. Adjacent corallites fuse and have indistinct walls. The margins of the septa are irregularly toothed. Extensions of the septa (costae) are apparent in the intervals between adjacent corallites and confer a lined appearance on the corallum. Polyps have more than two rings of tentacles. Four genera belonging to this family have been recorded from the Great Barrier Reef. In the genus *Pectinia* the large fragile corallites are irregularly arranged, giving the corallum a leafy appearance which has led to its common name "carnation coral". Colonies are usually about 25 centimetres in diameter but may exceed 1 metre. They are brown or grey in colour and occur in lagoons and on reef slopes. In the genus *Echinophyllia* the colonies form thin sheets that are usually encrusting and have a rough appearance. The lines formed by the costae are prominent. Colonies are usually green or brown, occur on reef slopes and average about 20 centimetres in diameter. Corals belonging to the genus *Mycedium* resemble those belonging to the genus *Echinophyllia*, but the corallites open at an oblique angle to the surface of the corallum. Colonies of *Mycedium* are brown or green, average about 20 centimetres in diameter, and usually occur in the deeper waters of reef slopes. Colonies of the genus *Oxpora* consist of large, thin plates which may overlap. The corallites are well separated and each has a prominent columella. Perforations occur in the corallum in the spaces between adjacent corallites. Living colonies are brown, green, or reddish and occur in lagoons and on reef slopes.

Genera represented: *Pectinia, Echinophyllia, Mycedium, Oxypora.*

Caryophyllids (Caryophyllidae). Both solitary and colonial corals are included in the family Caryophyllidae. The septa are smooth and platelike. Polyps have more than two rings of tentacles. The corallites of the genus *Euphyllia* are elongate and occur singly or in rows. Their openings have irregular shapes. The prominent septa project above the openings. The polyps are large, with numerous tentacles. Colonies are usually grey or brown and occur on reef slopes and in lagoons. They sometimes exceed 1 metre in diameter. Only one species belonging to the genus *Catalophyllia*, which is closely related to *Euphyllia*, is known. Its corallites occur in rows in sinuous depressions. The polyps have fleshy grey tentacles and green oral discs. Large colonies are domed and up to 1 metre in diameter. They occur on reef slopes and in lagoons. Small solitary corals, only about 1 centimetre in diameter, are included in the genus *Heterocyathus*. Each coral is always associated with a gastropod shell containing a sipunculid worm (see chapter 9). The worm moves the coral about in the sand in the vicinity of reefs. Colonies of the genus *Plerogyra* have an appearance similar to those of *Euphyllia*, but the corallites of *Plerogyra* are united at their bases and have very large projecting septa. The greyish colonies occur chiefly on vertical faces or in caves and crevices in protected areas. In members of the genus *Physogyra*, which also resemble those of *Euphyllia*, the corallites are united at the tops of the thecae. Colonies are grey or brown and occur on reef slopes.

Genera represented: *Euphyllia, Catalophyllia, Heterocyathus, Plerogyra, Physogyra.*

Dendrophyllids (Dendrophyllidae). The corallites of colonial members of the dendrophyllid family are large, protuberant, and well spaced. Rods link adjacent septa. The corallum is very porous. The polyps have several rings of tentacles. Some genera do not have symbiotic algae in their tissues and are termed *ahermatypic.* Colonies of the genus *Turbinaria* occur as crenated plates, often with a vaselike appearance. The large, well-spaced corallites are confined to the upper surfaces of the otherwise smooth plates. Colonies are coloured brown, yellow, green, or grey and are found in lagoons and on the lower reef slopes. Corals belonging to the genus *Dendrophyllia* exhibit a treelike growth form, with branches growing from each side of the main stems. The corallites are large, and each has a prominent columella. Brown, green, orange, and black are among the colours displayed. These so-called "tree corals" grow on reef slopes in shaded situations such as caves and under overhangs. They are ahermatypic, as are corals belonging to the genus *Tubastrea.* These occur as clusters of tubular corallites growing from a common base and are found in similar habits to those occupied by *Dendrophyllia.* Colours shown are bright orange, yellow, and green. Members of the genus *Heteropsammia* are known as "button corals". They are either solitary or consist of colonies of a very few polyps. They are free-living, the base of each coral enclosing the tube of a sipunculid worm, which moves the coral about on the sandy bottom off the reef slope where it is occasionally encountered. Colours exhibited are brown, yellow, and green. Button corals are usually about 2 centimetres in diameter.

Genera represented: *Turbinaria, Dendrophyllia, Tubastrea, Heteropsammia.*

Physiology and Life Histories of Hard Corals

Various feeding methods are employed by coral polyps. One method is known as *tentacular feeding.* Polyps of most types of coral have retractile tentacles that are arranged in rows around their mouths (six to thirty tentacles per row depending on the species of coral involved). The tentacles are armed with batteries of minute organelles called *nematocysts* and *spirocysts.* Two types of nematocyst occur in corals.

Each is involved with the injection of a potent toxin into other animals, usually prey. There are spines associated with the hollow thread of these organelles. The spirocyst contains an unarmed thread which, when discharged, produces numerous long slender fibres that appear to entangle prey. Corals such as species of *Dendrophyllia*, which live in shaded areas on reefs, and large-polyped, reef-forming corals such as species belonging to the genera *Favia*, *Goniastrea*, and *Lobophyllia* feed by means of tentacles whenever the opportunity to do so is provided. Their prey is trapped and immobilized by the nematocysts carried by the long tentacles, which also convey prey to the mouth.

Another major method of feeding employed by corals is termed *ciliary-mucoid feeding*. The epidermis (outer covering) of corals contains cells that possess minute cilia. In most corals these cilia are abundantly represented and form ciliary pathways that run the length of the polyp. They may also run from base to tip of tentacles and to the mouth area. Mucus is secreted by many cells of the epidermis, especially cells near the mouth. Particulate material (minute animals, clumps of bacteria, and detrital matter) present in the water is enmeshed in the sticky mucus if the material impinges on the surface of a polyp. The material is then moved by ciliary currents to the tentacles, where sorting of the material leading to acceptance or rejection occurs. Material that is accepted passes by means of ciliary currents to the mouth, where it is swallowed; material that is rejected passes by the same means to regions where it can be ejected from the polyp. Ciliary currents are also involved in removing sediment from polyps, and they have this role almost exclusively in those species that feed primarily by tentacles. Species belonging to genera such as *Merulina* and many mushroom corals (Fungiidae) have tentacles that are too small to bring food to the mouth, and they rely heavily on ciliary-mucoid feeding of the type just described. Feeding of this type is also engaged in extensively by representatives of many genera of corals, including *Seriatopora*, *Stylophora*, *Leptastrea*, *Cyphastrea*, *Porites*, *Pavona*, and *Psammocera*.

Another type of feeding is by means of mesenterial filaments. As noted earlier, the free margins of mesenteries are thickened to form whip-like mesenterial filaments. These bear enzyme-secreting cells and nematocysts. The mobile filaments may be thrust through the mouth or, in some species, through permanent or temporary holes in the body of the polyp. Feeding by extrusion of mesenterial filaments is particularly common in species belonging to the families Mussidae and Faviidae. In some corals the filaments are used to stir up detritus in the vicinity of the corals and to trap particulate matter. Species of *Pachyseris* lack tentacles entirely. In this genus, particulate material enmeshed in mucus is moved by ciliary currents to the mouth of each polyp, where mesenterial filaments wrap around any struggling prey.

25

26

27

28

29

30

31

32

33

34

35

36

It has long been known that dissolved organic substances ranging from single amino acids and sugars to complex macromolecules are present in sea water. Corals certainly have the ability to take up organic substances directly from sea water, but the extent to which they engage in this type of activity generally is not known with certainty.

Yet another type of feeding involves the utilization by corals of materials produced by microscopic organisms called *zooxanthellae*, which live in the tissues (principally the gastrodermis) of corals. Zooxanthellae are the non-motile (encysted) stages of certain species of algae. Their association with corals is an example of symbiosis, where two organisms live in an association from which they derive mutual benefit. The algae are provided with living space and protection and a plentiful supply of basic nutrients such as phosphates and nitrates. The manner in which the coral polyps benefit is not so obvious, but there is now good evidence to suggest that they obtain part of their nutritive requirements from zooxanthellae. The algae possess chlorophyll pigments which enable them to use the energy of sunlight in the synthesis of organic materials. Some of the soluble products of this synthesis are released by the zooxanthellae, and some, at least, appear to be used in coral metabolism. However, the proportion of a coral's nutritive requirements that is provided by zooxanthellae is not yet known. It may be considerable, particularly in branching corals such as species of *Pocillopora*, where approximately half the biomass of the polyp consists of zooxanthellae.

As well as enabling them to cope more effectively with varying conditions of food availability, the abilities of corals to use several feeding methods and several types of food enable them to partition or share out the available food resources. Possibly large-polyped species specialize in plankton capture, small-polyped massive species specialize in ciliary-mucoid feeding, and branching acroporids that form canopies specialize in obtaining their nutrition from zooxanthellae.

Reef-forming corals do not grow below about 50 metres, and they flourish best in water shallower than 30 metres. It is probable that the depth to which these living corals grow is correlated with the light requirements of their contained zooxanthellae. As mentioned earlier, the symbiotic algae require light for photosynthesis. Although it appears likely that the zooxanthellae produce materials that provide nutrients for corals, they are of importance to corals in another major way. One of the structural features of reef-forming corals is their possession of heavy calcareous (limy) skeletons. It has been found that the amount of lime secreted by a coral colony varies over a twenty-four-hour cycle, much more being secreted during daylight than during darkness. Calcium uptake from sea water is fastest on a

Facing page

Illustration 25
A large hemispherical colony of the brain coral *Platygyra lamellina*. (The colony has been damaged in two places.)

Illustration 26
Portion of the surface of a colony of *Platygyra dadaelea*. The sinuous ridges and valleys characteristic of brain corals are well shown. The retracted tentacles of polyps line the valleys.

Illustration 27
Portion of the surface of a colony of *Oulophyllia crispa*. The mouths of individual polyps are apparent in the valleys.

Illustration 28
A colony of *Hydnophora exesa*.

Illustration 29
A portion of a colony of the massive coral, *Symphyllia nobilis*.

Illustration 30
A solitary coral belonging to the family Mussidae.

Illustration 31
Portion of a colony of *Merulina ampliata*.

Illustration 32
Portion of a colony of the ivory coral, *Galaxea fascicularis*.

Illustration 33
Portion of a colony of *Mycedium tubifex*.

Illustration 34
A colony of *Euphyllia* sp. showing the tubular corallites.

Illustration 35
A colony of *Tubastrea aurea* with most of the polyps retracted.

Illustration 36
Portion of a colony of a species of *Turbinaria* showing the well-spaced polyps.

clear, sunny day and is reduced by 50 per cent on a cloudy day and by 90 per cent in total darkness. In corals from which zooxanthellae have been removed, calcification rates are very low and independent of light intensity. It has been postulated that zooxanthellae facilitate deposition of calcium carbonate by participating directly in the chemical reactions leading to its formation or by producing organic material that acts as a framework on which the calcium carbonate is deposited. At any rate, corals containing zooxanthellae (the so-called *hermatypic* corals) are restricted to shallow water where sufficient light is available for photosynthesis by the zooxanthellae. Hermatypic corals are primarily responsible for reef building. Ahermatypic corals, since they do not possess zooxanthellae, are not restricted in their distribution by the need for light and may occur in very deep water (water over 5,000 metres in depth).

The daily variation in calcium carbonate deposition mentioned earlier leads to the presence of obvious bands interpreted as growth bands in the skeletons of some species of coral. J. W. Wells of Cornell University noted that there were about 360 bands in the space of a year's growth and suggested that the bands were daily growth increments. Interestingly, he noted that in several fossil corals from the Devonian period (some 360 million years ago) the number of fine growth bands within the annual increments approximated 400, while corals from the more recent Carboniferous period (some 320 million years ago) had a mean of 380. He interpreted these findings as implying that the number of days per annum had decreased progressively since the Devonian period. Probably the days had become longer because of slowing of the earth's rotation because of tidal friction. It would thus appear that some species of corals may be used as fossil clocks.

There is evidence that some species of coral appear to grow throughout life, while others may cease growing once they have reached a certain size. In 1890, William Saville-Kent measured three colonies at Thursday Island. The same colonies were subsequently measured by A. G. Mayer in 1913. A colony belonging to a species of *Symphyllia* had grown from 0.8 to 1.8 metres in diameter during this period, and a colony belonging to a species of *Porites* had grown from 5.8 to 6.9 metres in diameter. On the other hand, a colony belonging to a species of *Goniastrea*, which measured 2.4 metres in diameter in 1890, had the same diameter when measured in 1913.

Coral colonies are potentially long-lived; some may live for centuries. However, corals are subject to a number of destructive factors (see chapter 23), and some colonies may survive for only a few years. Also, growth of a coral colony could be retarded or checked completely by a number of factors, particularly by interactions with other species (competition and predation). Indeed, the initial rapid growth rate of a coral colony is frequently followed by a slowing down leading to an almost complete cessation of growth.

It is frequently stated that colour runs riot on a coral reef. Corals themselves contribute substantially to the colour displayed. Often corals adopt .the hue of their contained zooxanthellae, which are usually some shade of yellow, brown, or green. However, pigment cells containing black, red, or orange granules may be present in the epidermis, and different combinations of these coloured granules give rise to a wide range of tints. Sometimes different specimens of the same species of coral show marked differences in colour.

The reproductive organs of coral polyps occur on the mesenteries in the coelenteron. In some species only eggs or sperm are produced by individual polyps at any one time. In other species (e.g., *Pocillopora brevicornis*), individual polyps have been found to possess ripe eggs and sperm at the same time; self-fertilization is possible in such cases. Also, it is possible that polyps change sex as they age. In most species it is not known whether fertilization (union of egg and sperm) is normally external or internal. In some cases larvae resulting from fertilization are brooded within the polyp.

Reproductive activity has been found to be continuous throughout the year in some species but seasonal in other species. Sometimes (e.g., in *Pocillopora bulbosa*) the rate of release of larvae is affected by the phases of the moon, an example of *lunar periodicity*. Mature colonies of some species of coral are known to release thousands of larvae (called *planulae*) at a time.

Larvae just released swim upwards towards the light. Subsequently, before attachment, they change their behaviour and swim away from light towards the sea-floor. Apparently most larvae attach within two days of release from the parent polyps. Many appear to settle near their parents. Sometimes the larvae are released at low water in packets coated with mucus which adheres to objects in the vicinity of the parent coral. However, the larvae of some species are capable of remaining for months in the surface waters, and these are of importance with respect to the distribution of the species.

Little is known about how the larvae choose a place to settle. The presence of numerous predatory organisms makes settling a hazardous process. In some cases the presence of coralline algae appears to be a prerequisite for successful settling. Mortality in early life, particularly at the planula stage and during the period after settling, is especially heavy.

Both physical and biological factors affect the distribution of corals. Physical factors such as water temperature, salinity, degree of sedimentation, extent of wave action, and water depth play a major role in determining the broad distributions of corals, as discussed in chapter 23. However, biological factors such as competition and predation play a major role in determining the fine-scale distribution of corals as discussed in chapters 14 and 15.

6

The Reef Builders — Algae

Apart from a few species of sea-grasses (phanerograms) which occur in patches on some coral reefs, algae are the dominant plant forms present. Their abundance on any reef appears to be inversely related to the abundance of living corals. Because of the efficient feeding methods employed by corals, algal spores (the reproductive bodies of many algae) cannot settle and grow on living corals. Also, most corals have efficient methods for acquiring and holding living space, which prevent encroachment by established algae. Consequently algae are, on the whole, restricted to regions of a reef that are unfavourable for coral settlement and growth. For example, some species of algae are able to withstand the pounding surf and wave surge on exposed reef fronts. Algae are rapid colonizers of space vacated by living corals; indeed, dead coral skeletons and semi-consolidated rubble provide excellent substrates for algae. As most algal species require exposure to adequate light for photosynthesis, most are found in exposed situations, and only a few algal species occur under coral boulders, under overhangs, and in caves on reefs.

Despite these restrictions on their distribution, which are in part responsible for the marked zoning patterns exhibited by algal species living on reefs, algae are abundantly represented. It has been estimated that about 330 species of algae occur on the Great Barrier Reef. While some species are tiny and inconspicuous, other species form large, fleshy structures. Indeed, coral-reef algae exhibit an amazing variety of form. Also, despite the drab appearance of some common species, algae display a wide range of colour. Colour was in fact used as a basis for classifying algae by early naturalists. The principal algal groups found on coral reefs are discussed below.

Green Algae (Division Chlorophyta)

The division Chlorophyta is a large group of algae which includes unicellular as well as multicellular forms and numerous freshwater as well as marine representatives. The algal body, or *thallus* as it is known technically, exhibits a great variety of shapes in the different species. Their green colour stems from the presence of large amounts of chlorophyll located in structures called *chromatophores*. The multicellular marine species often assume striking shapes. Some form a bright green felt-like mass (e.g., species of *Chlorodesmis*) or green spheres (e.g., species of *Valonia*), and others resemble bunches of green grapes (e.g., some species of *Caulerpa*). *Codium spongiosum* forms large, solid, irregularly lobed, dark green masses, while *Boodlea composita* forms a light green, maze-like meshwork. Some stalked forms resemble parasols (e.g., species of *Acetabularia*). Some species are encrusted with lime. Indeed, the disclike or beadlike segments of species of *Halimeda* contribute significantly to the reef sediments. Skeletons of living corals are often penetrated by species of the boring green alga *Ostreobium*.

Some of the genera represented: *Boodlea, Caulerpa, Halimeda, Acetabularia, Valonia, Dictyosphaeria, Enteromorpha, Codium, Bryopsis, Ostreobium, Chlorodesmis.*

Blue-Green Algae (Division Cyanophyta)

Blue-green algae either are unicellular or form segmented filaments that are regarded as multicellular since adjacent segments (cells) have common end walls. They reproduce by fission or by fragmentation of filaments. Sometimes they contain cellulose in their walls and in this respect differ from bacteria, which they resemble in many other respects. Some species form macroscopic clusters of filaments that are attached to the substratum. Often these appear as threadlike growths. They are rapid colonizers of the skeletons of recently killed corals. Although they exhibit a wide colour range, the predominant colour of cyanophytes is blue-green because of the presence of a pigment called phycocyanin. Blue-green algae are regarded as being among the oldest and most primitive life forms on this planet.

Some blue-green algae have become associated with fungi to form lichens, of which there are some marine representatives. Blue-green algae are responsible for producing some potent toxins. Some species (e.g., *Entophysalis* and *Mastigocoleus*) penetrate the skeletons of dead corals.

Some genera represented: *Microcoleus, Schizothrix, Entophysalis, Hormothamnion, Mastigocoleus.*

Brown Algae (Division Phaeophyta)

All members of the division Phaeophyta are multicellular and range in size from microscopic forms to the giant kelps that attain heights of 30 metres or more. Such giants are not, however, found on coral reefs, although some brown seaweeds (e.g., species of *Sargassum* and *Cystoseira*) are among the tallest of the algae found on reefs. The common name applied to the group — brown algae — is not entirely appropriate, as some species are olive green. Even so, most are brownish, owing their colour to a pigment called fucoxanthin. The thallus may be a simple filament or it may be a complex branching structure. Many species possess strap-like structures resembling leaves. Also, some (e.g., *Sargassum* species) have gas-filled bladders that buoy up the alga. A few species (e.g., species of *Padina* and *Lobophora*) are fan-shaped. In *Turbinaria ornata*, the branches of the thallus resemble small trumpets with serrated margins. On some reefs the large, gas-filled sacs of *Colpomenia sinuosa* are prominent. Another two brown algae that are usually well represented on reefs are *Chnoospora implexa*, which forms a large spongy meshwork, and *Hydroclathrus clathratus*, whose strap-like thallus carries numerous large perforations and is aptly termed the wire-netting alga.

Some genera represented: *Padina, Cystoseira, Sargassum, Lobophora, Hydroclathrus, Turbinaria, Chnoospora, Colpomenia.*

Red Algae (Division Rhodophyta)

Many small to medium-sized seaweeds belong to the division Rhodophyta, most of which are multicellular and attached to the substratum. Most have elaborate thalli, which may be cylindrical, branched, flattened, foliaceous, or disc-shaped. The red colour, for which the group as a whole is noted in temperate waters, stems from the presence of a red pigment called phycoerythrin. However, many red algae occurring on the Great Barrier Reef are dark, sometimes blackish, because of the presence of other pigments, particularly phycocyanin. Perhaps it would cause less confusion if they were referred to as rhodophytes rather than red algae. Rhodophytes differ from other algae in their lack of motile sperm. Sperm must be carried to the eggs by water currents if fertilization is to occur.

In Great Barrier Reef waters, rhodophytes tend to be less conspicuous and to constitute a lower proportion of the total flora present than they do in temperate waters. Nevertheless, they are still well represented. Some species are short and form a fur-like covering on coral

37

38

39

40

41

42

43

44

45

46

47

48

rubble. Others (e.g., species of *Laurencia*) form fleshy branching structures. *Gelidiella acerosa* has a comb-like structure.

The cell walls of some rhodophytes have a coating of lime. Some form multi-branched clusters (e.g., species of *Amphiroa* and *Lithophyllum*). Others have a more encrusting habit (species of *Peyssonellia*, *Porolithon* and *Lithothamnion*); these are the so-called coralline algae, which play a major role in the consolidation of reef debris and in the stabilization of exposed regions of reefs.

Some genera represented: *Amphiroa, Gelidiella, Laurencia, Polysiphonia, Hypnea, Centroceras, Champia, Jania, Chondria, Lithophyllum, Lithothamnion, Porolithon, Corallina, Galaxaura, Amansia, Peyssonellia.*

Diatoms (Division Chrysophyta)

The photosynthetic structures possessed by members of the division Chrysophyta contain xanthophylls and carotenes and have yellow-green to yellow-brown colours. Diatoms are the most abundant marine representatives of this group of algae. Indeed, they are the most abundant component of marine plankton (see p. 000). They are unicellular or colonial organisms, each individual possessing glassy walls containing silica. The walls, which exhibit a great variety of shape and ornamentation, always consist of two halves that fit together like a box with its lid. Although essentially planktonic organisms, many occur on the surfaces of coral reef sediments.

Dinoflagellates (Division Pyrrhophyta)

Dinoflagellates are small unicellular algae characterized in free-living forms by the possession of two whip-like appendages, or *flagella*, of unequal length. The cell wall, when present, is composed largely of cellulose. Many species are found in marine plankton, some (e.g., species of *Noctiluca*) causing phosphorescence of the sea, others sometimes being present in such numbers as to colour the sea.

Some dinoflagellates live in an encysted state in the tissue of various animals, particularly corals, where they are known as zooxanthellae. Despite the presence of a cyst wall (periplast), the photosynthetic abilities of the encysted algae appear to be as great as in free-living motile forms.

Facing page
Illustration 37
The green alga, *Caulerpa racemosa.*

Illustration 38
The green alga, *Halimeda cylindrica.*

Illustration 39
The green alga, *Codium spongiosum.*

Illustration 40
The green alga, *Chlorodesmis fastigiata,* commonly known as turtle weed.

Illustration 41
The brown alga, *Padina gymnospora.*

Illustration 42
A brown alga, *Sargassum* sp.

Illustration 43
The brown alga, *Chnoospora implexa.*

Illustration 44
The brown alga, *Turbinaria ornata.*

Illustration 45
The blue-green alga, *Hormothamnion enteromorphoides.*

Illustration 46
The red alga, *Amansia glomerata.*

Illustration 47
The red alga, *Galaxaura* sp.

Illustration 48
The red alga, *Peyssonellia inamoena.*

Roles of Algae

Fixation of light energy by the process of photosynthesis is one of the fundamental roles played by coral reef algae and is discussed in chapter 15. While macroscopic algae are of great importance here, the part played by microscopic algae, particularly diatoms, as a source of energy and nutrients for other organisms in the coral reef community is considerable and should not be overlooked. Neither should the part played by algae that live in the tissues of animals. Their role in energy and nutrient provision in corals and in the calcification of corals has already been discussed.

Some algae elaborate powerful toxins, some of which are in the nature of antibiotics that are used in the holding or acquisition of living space. Others are in the nature of poisons. If ingested, they may cause serious injury or even death. However, some predators have evolved mechanisms for dealing with these toxins and even for converting them to their own use.

Some of the boring algae, such as species of *Ostreobium*, penetrate the skeletons of corals, weakening them and making them susceptible to the attacks of herbivorous parrot-fish.

Calcareous algae, whose remains dominate reef sediments, play major roles in reef construction (see chapter 7). Some types of calcareous algae also exert a stabilizing action on exposed windward sides of many reefs, enabling the windward side of a reef to act as a breakwater which in turn permits some reef growth to occur on the lee side. Calcareous algae tend to form a casing around the basal regions of corals, particularly branching corals. It is thought that this casing gives added strength to coral skeletons and helps to protect them from physical erosion and from the activities of boring organisms.

7

Reef Construction

While the commonly held view that corals provide the bricks and calcareous algae provide the mortar in reef construction is a simplistic one, there is ample evidence that calcareous algae stabilize the framework provided by corals, particularly when the upward growth of this framework reaches the zone where wave action becomes pronounced. Indeed, in the regions of a reef that are frequently exposed to pounding surf and wave surge, calcareous algae are the dominant organisms present. Their skeletons, which are composed of calcite (a crystalline form of calcium carbonate) appear to be harder and certainly less soluble than the aragonite (another crystalline form of calcium carbonate) of which the skeletons of corals are comprised. On exposed regions of the windward sides of reefs, calcareous algae form a smooth, hard surface to the reef front which provides an effective barrier to erosive forces.

Unfortunately, there is little information on the growth rates of calcareous algae, and the actual extent to which they contribute to the bulk of a reef at their site of growth is in dispute. Estimates of net calcification rates on both windward and leeward sides of reefs give values of about 4 kilograms per square metre per year. However, most if not all of the calcareous material produced each year on the windward side is removed as a result of the action of erosive agents linked with water movements. It would seem likely that outward growth on the windward side of a reef, if it occurs at all, is very slow and that the reef front is essentially static with constructional and erosive forces in equilibrium. However, this part of the reef acts as a breakwater, permitting reef construction to proceed on the lee side of the reef. Here corals can proliferate and calcareous sediments can accumulate to some extent.

Calcareous structures — which may be the walls of calcareous algae; the skeletons of corals or forams, or bryozoans, or sea-fans; the calcareous tubes of some worms; the shells of molluscs; the skeletons of barnacles and sea-urchins; or the skeletal spicules of soft corals, holothurians, and other organisms exposed when these organisms die — are all broken down to some extent by the actions of various physical and biological agencies (see chapter 23) to produce sediments. Among the principal destructive agencies operating on reefs are gales and the tropical storms known as cyclones. The mechanical force exerted by the waves and pounding surf generated by such disturb-

Facing page, above
Small colourful colonies of acroporid corals near the reef crest at Heron Island.

Facing page, below
Micro-atolls of species belonging to the genus *Porites*, on the reef flat at Low Isles. Black sea-urchins, *Diadema setosum*, are in evidence.

Below
The seaward slopes of Masthead Island showing the spur and groove system on the reef slope.

ances is sufficient to smash the skeletons of numerous shallow-water corals and to cause mass mortalities of associated organisms. Loose fragments of calcareous structures occurring in shallow water are abraded by being rolled about on reefs by wave action and tidal currents, and small particles are broken from them.

Some fishes are important agents in the production of calcareous sediments. Parrot-fish (scarids) have strong beaks which they use in abrading the skeletons of dead corals in order to obtain boring algae. They also abrade the surfaces of dead coral skeletons incidentally when grazing the algal turf growing on these skeletons. Some large wrasses (labrids) have been observed to bite off short pieces of branching corals, possibly in attempts to obtain invertebrates associated with the corals. Surgeon-fish (acanthurids) are the major eaters of coralline algae. Particles of calcareous material are not digested and pass right through the alimentary tracts of the fish. It has been estimated that reef fishes are responsible for depositing between 2,000 and 3,000 kilograms of calcareous material per hectare of reef per year. In addition, there are many organisms, including various worms, molluscs, and barnacles, that bore into calcareous skeletal materials, abrading particles in the process and thereby contributing to sediment production. Eventually fine calcareous particles are produced, giving rise to the so-called coral sand that covers large areas of some reefs.

Of course, calcareous sediments usually do not remain at the site of production. Apart from water movements, which are powerful agents for shifting sediments, all sediment-feeding animals of coral reefs are active in changing the position of surface sediments. On most coral reefs, holothurians are probably the most important sand deposit feeders. One common species, *Holothuria atra*, passes about 44 grams of sediment per day through its alimentary canal.

As the winds in the Great Barrier Reef area blow predominantly from the south-east, water movements across the reefs are mostly to the north-west. Actual measurements of water movements across reefs during rising tides and ten-knot south-easterly winds show water velocities of 25 to 50 centimetres per second — sufficient to move fine sediment. At times, winds are much stronger and the water movements across reefs generated show greater velocities and are capable of moving coarse sediments. (During cyclone disturbances, even huge coral boulders may be moved.) The sediments moved across reefs may accumulate in shallow water on the lee side of reefs. Alternatively they may be swept away from reefs and accumulate in deeper water. Their fate is determined by the interplay of water currents, water depths on the lee side of reefs, and the availability of sediment traps. These traps are formed by fragments of coral skeletons, skeletons of forams, and the calcareous discs of algae such as those of *Halimeda* being bound by coralline algae so as to form a semi-consolidated meshwork. The meshwork is usually caught up in the bases of corals, particularly branching corals, growing on the lee of a reef. Fine sediment is trapped in the meshwork and may fill the interstices of the meshwork. This process of accumulation and consolidation of calcareous material continues, and at an accumulation depth of about 5 metres the consolidated material is converted to reef limestone.

Reef construction as described cannot, of course, proceed above mean low water. This leads to the formation of a reef flat in the lee of the breakwater formed by the stabilized windward edge of a reef. In effect, once reefs grow up to the water surface, they grow downwind, as noted by P. J. Davies. However, the capacity for reef growth on the lee side appears to be limited and in many cases may have reached a state of equilibrium with destructive forces. On most reefs of the Great Barrier Reef the reef flat near the windward edge of the reef ranges from 100 to 400 metres in width. The present platform reefs of the Great Barrier Reef have grown on top of antecedent knoll-like structures, and these underlying structures strongly influence the shapes and sizes of the reefs. Many such reefs show downwind projections called cusps. Sometimes the area of shallow water substrate available for coral growth has been sufficient to enable these cusps to grow together and form a lagoon, thereby giving rise to the atoll-like platform reefs of the Great Barrier Reef. In other cases the presence of depressions on the surfaces of the antecedent knoll-like structures might have led directly to lagoon formation. The degree of infilling of each lagoon depends, among other factors, on the length of time the associated reef has been at the surface and subject to wave action. The shapes of reefs are also influenced by hydrodynamic conditions such as strength and direction of currents, tidal range, extent of wave action and by proximity of other reefs.

As discussed in chapter 3, the present reefs of the Great Barrier Reef have had a long and complex history. Their basements were constructed of limestone thousands of years ago, before the Pleistocene lowerings of sea-level exposed them to sub-aereal erosion. During these sea-level lowerings, their surfaces were sculptured by erosive forces. Then, as the seas finally returned some ten thousand years ago, the eroded reef cores were covered with water and provided solid substrates for the development of new coral reef communities. These reef communities grew vertically as the waters rose. The numbers, positions, shapes, and sizes of the new reefs were governed by the numbers, positions, shapes, and sizes of the old erosion surfaces from which the new reefs grew. Because the surfaces were often at different depths, the vertically growing reefs reached present sea-level at different times over the last six thousand years. Possibly a few "deep reefs" such as North-west Reef near Cairns are still

growing vertically towards the water surface, but the great majority reached the surface hundreds of years ago. When they neared sea-level they came under the influence of waves and currents which have further modified their shapes. Such a history accounts well for the numbers, present distribution, and variable appearance of the reefs.

It is not known whether overall reef growth in the Great Barrier Reef area before the arrival of Europeans was in a state of balance with destructive agencies. Probably it was. Certainly the structure of the existing reefs, the topography of the sea-floor among the reefs, and prevailing hydrographic conditions in the area would appear to preclude any marked increase in the numbers or sizes of the reefs in the immediate future.

Facing page, above
Tabular and branching species of *Acropora* in a drainage channel on the upper part of the reef slope at Tryon Island reef.

Facing page, below
A forest of branching *Acropora* species on the lee side of Tryon Island reef.

Above
Pools and drainage channels near the reef crest, Heron Island at low tide.

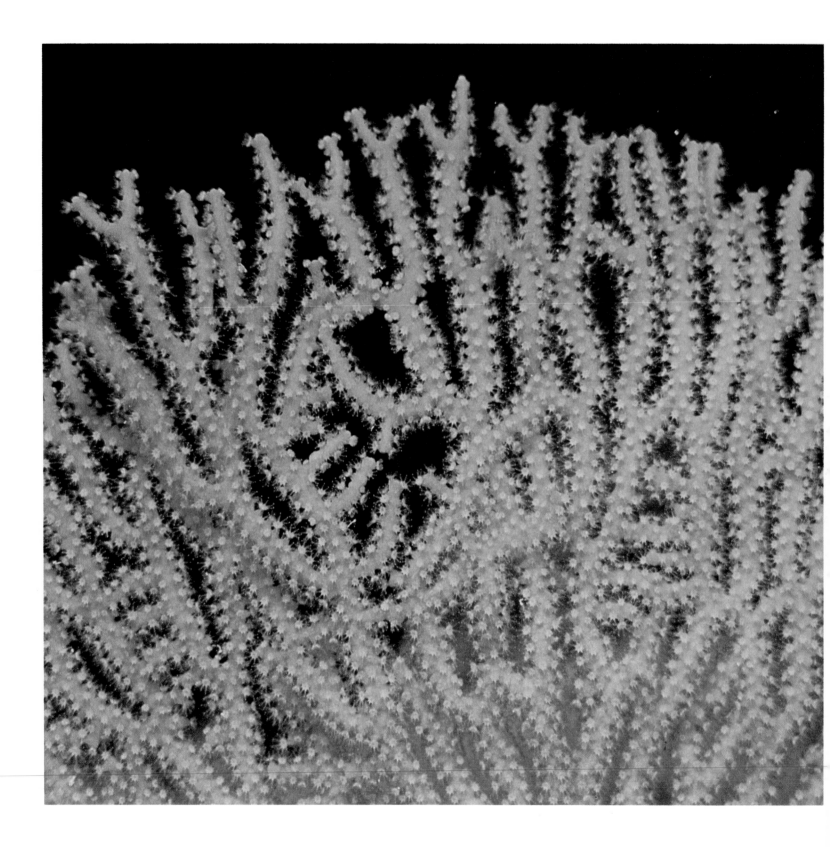

8

Other Attached Animals on the Reefs

As well as hard corals, numerous other animals are attached to the semi-consolidated rubble of the reef surface. Some of these — the tube-forming worms, the barnacles, and the bivalved molluscs — will be dealt with in subsequent chapters. Others are discussed below. Most of these animals are colonial, and many, like the hard corals, are cnidarians (Phylum Cnidaria).

Sea Anemones (Class Zoantharia, Order Actiniaria)

Anemones are cnidarians that resemble enlarged coral polyps with thick, muscular body walls. They occur usually as separate individuals lacking hard skeletal material. Tentacles, which may be pointed or bead-like, occur in rings around the mouth or cover the whole of the surface where the mouth occurs. The end opposite the mouth usually forms a sucker-like disc for temporary attachment to a solid object but is adapted for burrowing in some species. Injector type nematocysts (stinging capsules) on the tentacles are used to paralyse prey. In addition, another type of nematocyst, called a spirocyst, is present. When the coiled spirocyst thread discharges, it liberates an adhesive material from the tip of the thread. This adhesive material entangles and helps to inactivate prey and to bind it to the tentacles. Sometimes relatively large prey, including crustaceans and small fish, are caught. Some species of anemone appear to rely more on minute organisms and organic detritus as a food source than on sizeable prey, and these anemones employ ciliary-mucoid feeding methods similar to those employed by some species of coral. In some species of anemone the

Facing page
Part of a colony of a sea-fan belonging to the genus *Melithaea*.

56

57

58

59

60

61

62

63

64

65

66

67

sexes are separate; representatives of other species may be hermaphrodites. Asexual reproduction by fission or by budding from the basal disc occurs commonly in some species.

Numerous species of anemone representing several families occur in Great Barrier Reef waters. They are found in crevices, in rubble among living corals, on and under boulders, and burrowing in the sand on reef flats, reef slopes, and in the deeper waters on the edges of reefs. As is the case with many animal groups encountered on the Great Barrier Reef, few of the species of anemones found there have been identified. Some species show a great range of colour forms. While some species are small (only a few millimetres in diameter) others, such as *Stoichactis kenti*, may be up to 1 metre in diameter. A few, such as the fire anemone, *Actinodendron plumosum*, which is common on some fringing reefs, are capable of inflicting severe stings on humans.

Some of the genera represented: *Actinodendron, Paractis, Stoichactis, Radianthus, Cryptodendron, Calliactis.*

Zoanthids (Order Zoanthiniaria)

Most zoanthids are colonial forms resembling clusters of small anemones linked together and attached to the substratum by ramifying tubular structures called *stolons*. No skeleton is present. The individual polyps carry unbranched tentacles numbering six or, more usually, multiples of six. Paired partitions subdivide the body cavity of each polyp. Zoanthids occur in crevices on reef crests and are sometimes found on coral boulders. Occasionally they form large carpets on reef crests. They are noteworthy because individual polyps change sex as they age. Some polyps contain a powerful toxin.

Genera represented: *Palythoa, Epizoanthus.*

Cerianthids (Class Ceriantipatharia, Order Ceriantharia)

Cerianthids occur as single individuals each encased in a mucous tube (impregnated with detritus) that is buried vertically in the substratum. Each individual resembles an elongated anemone that possesses two rings of tentacles, those of the inner ring being shorter than those of the outer ring. Cerianthids are found among sand in back-reef areas and in the deeper water on the periphery of platform reefs in Great Barrier Reef waters. They are common in sandy areas of some fringing reefs but have been little studied.

Genus represented: *Cerianthus.*

Facing page

Illustration 56
The tentacles of a large reef anemone belonging to the genus *Physobrachia.*

Illustration 57
A colourful reef anemone.

Illustration 58
Some of the tentacles of an anemone, *Stoichactis kenti.*

Illustration 59
The stinging anemone, *Actinodendron plumosum.*

Illustration 60
A colony of anemones belonging to the family Hormathiidae.

Illustration 61
Colonies of the zoanthid, *Palythoa caespitosa.*

Illustration 62
The open mouths of zooids belonging to a species of the zoanthid *Palythoa.*

Illustration 63
Part of a whiplike colony of a species of black coral belonging to the genus *Cirrhipathes.*

Illustration 64
Expanded polyps of a colony of a clavulariid belonging to the genus *Clavularia.*

Illustration 65
The red skeleton of the organ-pipe coral, *Tubipora musica.*

Illustration 66
A telestacean, *Telesto* sp.

Illustration 67
The soft coral, *Lobophyton pauciflorum*, at Green Island.

Black Corals (Order Antipatharia)

Black corals form shrublike or whiplike colonies ranging from a few centimetres to over a metre in height. They are attached to the substratum by the main trunk. Individual polyps are small and resemble those of true corals, although their tentacles cannot be retracted. However, instead of a rigid calcareous skeleton, black corals possess a flexible skeleton of black or dark brown horny material. This will take a glossy polish and is used in the manufacture of so-called black coral jewellery. Black corals are found on reef slopes and in the deeper water on the edge of reefs in the Great Barrier Reef region. They appear to be more common in the waters off fringing reefs of some mainland islands than in the waters near platform reefs.

Genera represented: *Antipathes, Cirrhipathes.*

Stoloniferans (Class Alcyonaria, Order Stolonifera)

Stoloniferans form small colonies. Individual polyps each have eight feathery tentacles and arise from ramifying tubular stolons. Clavulariids and organ-pipe coral are stoloniferans.

Clavulariids (Clavulariidae). Large polyps, about 2 centimetres high, arise separately from ramifying root-like stolons in members of the family Clavulariidae. Each polyp has eight feathery tentacles. Calcareous spicules are present. Clavulariids are found in the deeper water around reefs, particularly on the bases of coral pinnacles found in back-reef areas.

Genus represented: *Clavularia.*

Organ-pipe coral (Tubiporidae). In the aptly named organ-pipe coral, individual polyps are accommodated in parallel calcareous tubes that are connected at intervals by calcareous shelves running at right angles to the tubes. The tubes are red and retain their colour when the large, greenish polyps die. Organ-pipe coral forms small colonies that are commonly encountered on reef flats of platform reefs.

Genus represented: *Tubipora.*

Telestaceans (Order Telestacea)

Colonies of telestaceans are formed as a result of elongate polyps growing up as stems from a root-like base. Numerous short lateral

68

69

70

71

72

73

74

75

76

77

78

79

polyps protrude from each stem. Each polyp has eight featherlike tentacles. Spicules are present in the body walls of the polyps. Frequently sponges become associated with the stems. Telestaceans are found in lagoons and in the deeper water around the edges of reefs. Only one family (Telestidae) of telestaceans appears to be represented in Great Barrier Reef waters.

Genus represented: *Telesto.*

Soft Corals (Order Alcyonacea)

Soft corals consist of colonies of polyps interconnected by canals which permeate a gelatinous matrix in which calcareous spicules are found. Each polyp has eight featherlike tentacles and can be withdrawn into the matrix. Soft corals are common on reef flats and back-reef areas of some reefs. They grow completely exposed, no doubt because of the need to expose the zooxanthellae present in their tissues to light. Soft corals will grow in situations subject to considerable wave action, although they may be excluded from such situations normally by hard corals. If hard corals are killed by natural disasters or by infestations of the crown-of-thorns starfish, *Acanthaster planci*, their dead skeletons are often covered by carpets of rapidly growing soft corals. At least four families of soft coral occur in Great Barrier Reef waters. These are alcyoniids, nephtheids, siphonogorgiids, and xeniids.

Alcyoniids (Alcyoniidae) form large, fleshy colonies. Frequently they are vase-shaped, often lobed, and sometimes branching. The elongate polyps are connected by a system of large and small canals and are embedded in a thick and tough coenchyme which bears numerous spicules. The basal stem of the colony is devoid of polyps. Alcyoniids are abundant on many reefs of the Great Barrier Reef, particularly on reef flats in the northern sector. Greens, yellows, and browns are the dominant colours. Some colonies are 1 metre across, and frequently the polyps expand during daylight hours.

Genera represented: *Sarcophyton, Lobophyton, Sinularia, Cladiella.*

Nephtheids (Nephtheidae) form branching tree-like colonies; the polyps are borne on the ends of the branches. They have non-retractile tentacles, and each has a long gastral cavity that ends blindly in the coenchyme. Only a few polyps are interconnected. Long spicules visible to the unaided eye project beyond the polyps, forming a spiny defence. Frequently the polyps are pink or brown, with the thick

trunk and branches of the colony much paler. Nephtheids are found commonly in lagoons and in the deeper water around reefs.
Genera represented: *Dendronephthya, Litophyton.*

Siphonogorgiids (Siphonogorgiidae) bear a marked resemblance to gorgonians (i.e., sea-fans and sea-whips; see below), the colonies being erect, branching, and generally fan-shaped. A core of large spicules is present in the larger stems. Siphonogorgiids occur in lagoons and in the deeper water around reefs.
Genus represented: *Cactogorgia.*

Xeniids (Xeniidae) usually occur as small colonies about 12 centimetres in diameter. Each colony comprises masses of large, cylindrical polyps which are non-retractile. The polyps arise from a relatively small mass of coenchyme. A system of canals in the coenchyme unites individual polyps. Spicules, when present, occur as minute spherical or ovoid bodies. Only a single pair of partitions is present in the body cavity of each polyp. Although the large tentacles open and close at intervals, xeniids appear to rely solely on their contained zooxanthellae for their nutritive requirements. Xeniids are usually bluish, greyish, or brownish and are common on reef flats in the Great Barrier Reef area.
Genera represented: *Xenia, Heteroxenia, Anthelia.*

Blue Coral (Order Coenothecalia)

In the blue corals the skeleton is massive and indigo blue in colour when freshly broken but tends to be greyish-blue normally. It is perforated by canals that interconnect the polyps, each of which has eight featherlike tentacles and eight partitions in its body cavity as in polyps of most families of soft corals. Blue coral is common in the northern part of the Great Barrier Reef. The order Coenothecalia contains only one family (Helioporidae) and one genus.
Genus represented: *Heliopora.*

Sea-Pens (Order Pennatulacea)

Sea-pens are colonies consisting of a large, highly modified central polyp which either gives off short polyps from its surface or gives origin to parallel side branches from which short polyps arise. The polyps each have eight featherlike tentacles. The expanded end of the central polyp anchors it in soft substrates. Calcareous spicules are

Facing page
Illustration 80
A blue calcareous bryozoan belonging to the Order Cyclostomata.

Illustration 81
A bryozoan, often known as lace coral.

Illustration 82
Another lace coral, the bryozoan, *Reteporella graeffei*.

Illustration 83
An unidentified orange bryozoan encrusting the undersurface of a coral boulder.

Illustration 84
The brachiopod, *Frenulina sanguinolenta*.

Illustration 85
A colony of vase-shaped sponges belonging to the genus *Haliclona*.

Illustration 86
A brown sponge belonging to the genus *Pericharax*.

Illustration 87
An encrusting sponge.

Illustration 88
An orange sponge.

Illustration 89
A colony of sponges.

Illustration 90
A hemispherical sponge.

Illustration 91
An encrusting sponge.

present. In some species the whole colony can retract below the surface of the sea-floor. Sea-pens, which range from a few centimetres to over a metre in length, are found in soft sediments associated with some reefs, particularly fringing reefs. Possibly several families are represented, but the Australian sea-pens are poorly known.

Genera represented: *Cavernularia, Pennatula.*

Sea-Fans and Sea-Whips (Order Gorgonacea)

The polyps and connecting tissues of members of the order Gorgonacea produce a skeleton which may be calcareous or composed of a horny material called gorgonin. The skeleton takes the form of an axial rod from which side branches bearing the polyps arise. In many species (the sea-fans) the side branches are extensive and in some cases interconnect. In others (the sea-whips) the side branches are minute. Colonies are firmly anchored to the substratum by one end of the axial rod. Individual polyps are small and closely resemble those of soft corals in structure. Many sea-fans and sea-whips are found commonly on reef slopes and in the deeper water around the bases of reefs, but members of the families Isididae and Plexauridae occur commonly on reef flats. Unfortunately, the sea-fans of the Great Barrier Reef area are poorly known, although several families appear to be represented. While some species show a great range of colour, yellows, browns, and reds predominate. Other organisms such as sponges and feather-stars frequently associate with gorgonians, as sea-fans and sea-whips are also known.

Some genera represented: *Subergorgia, Mopsella, Paramuricea, Primnoella, Isis, Melithaea, Juncella, Rumphella.*

Hydrozoans (Class Hydrozoa)

Among animals that possess nematocysts (the cnidarians) two basic forms occur. One is the polyp, which is a cylindrical animal with a mouth surrounded by tentacles at one end and a region modified for attachment at the other — the basic body form of anemones and individuals within a coral colony. The other basic body form is the medusa, which is bell-shaped or saucer-shaped and normally is not attached. This basic body form is possessed by the familiar jellyfish. There is a group of animals, the hydrozoans, that usually possess both polyp and medusa forms in their life history. Typically, these animals occur on reefs as fixed colonies of interconnected polyps. An outer

80

81

82

83

84

85

86

87

88

89

90

91

layer of tough, horny material usually invests the colony. In some species the polyps themselves lack a protective sheath of this horny material. In two families (Milleporidae and Stylasteridae) a calcareous skeleton is elaborated. The medusa form in hydrozoans is usually small and free-swimming and carries the reproductive organs. Larvae are produced from fertilized eggs, and these give rise to new polyps. Asexual reproduction is, of course, involved in colony formation.

Most attached hydrozoans are known as hydroids. Many of these form erect colonies, some of which are only a few millimetres in height, others of which are over 20 centimetres in height. The stinging hydroids, *Aglaeophenia cupressina* and *Lytocarpus philippinus,* have powerful batteries of nematocysts and can cause injury to humans (see chapter 19). Hydroids are commonly encountered growing on rubble or semi-consolidated debris on reef flats or under overhangs and in caves on reefs. As yet, not a great deal is known about the species occurring there.

Stylasterids (Stylasteridae) form small branching colonies in shaded situations on reefs, especially in caves and on the under-surfaces of overhangs on the edges of reefs. These hydrozoans are characterized by the presence in the calcareous skeleton of minute pores where the polyps are housed. They are usually brightly coloured, orange, blue, mauve, or pink being the colours commonly encountered. Stylasterids are common in their preferred habitat on the Great Barrier Reef.

Genera represented: *Stylaster, Distichopora.*

Fire corals (Milleporidae). In members of the hydrozoan family Milleporidae the interconnected polyps are embedded in a massive calcareous skeleton which may be erect and branching or flat and encrusting with lobes and buttresses. The colonies may be quite large and cover several square metres. They are typically of a yellow-brown colour and are readily recognized by the minute pores that accommodate the polyps. A tingling or burning sensation is usually perceived if one brushes against fire corals, and sometimes a rash appears on the skin at the point of contact with the coral. Fire corals are common on the Great Barrier Reef, particularly in drainage channels near reef crests.

Genus represented: *Millepora.*

Bryozoans (Phylum Bryozoa)

Until recent times there was a general belief that the bryozoan fauna of the Great Barrier Reef was sparse, since relatively few species had been recorded from coral reefs in the area. However, it is now known that the bryozoan fauna of these reefs is rich and diverse. Bryozoans are colonial animals, the colonies of different species showing a wide range of form and size. Some are plantlike, some form encrusting sheets or erect plates or gelatinous lobes, and some — the so-called "lace corals" — resemble small corals. This variation in form is reflected in the variety of materials used to construct the colonies, for some of the colonies are calcified or partially calcified, and others are constructed of a cuticular or a gelatinous material.

Individuals of a colony are called *zooids*. They are very small, millions of them being found in some colonies. Each zooid is usually urn-shaped but may be specialized for one of several functions. Most are involved with feeding, and these are characterized by the possession of a structure called a *lophophore*, which has a cluster of ciliated tentacles. The mouth is situated at the base of the cluster. Small organisms and organic detritus are brought to the mouth in water currents created by the cilia on the tentacles. The gut is bent upon itself, and the anus opens near the lophophore. Zooids may be modified for a variety of roles. Some do not possess a lophophore and act as regions for colony attachment, some act as stems to support the colony, and some act as brood chambers for the young. Other zooids are protective, and some are modifed for removing detritus and fouling organisms from the colony. These have a seizing apparatus resembling the beaked head of a bird. All zooids of a colony are interconnected and arise by asexual reproduction, budding from a free-swimming larva which develops from a fertilized egg. Some zooids in a colony may be male and some female.

On the Great Barrier Reef, calcareous encrusting bryozoans, often coloured pink, orange, red, or mauve, are abundantly represented around the bases and undersurfaces of corals, in the interstices of semi-consolidated rubble, on dead mollusc shells, under overhangs, on the walls of crannies and caverns, and on the undersurfaces of coral boulders. They are among the first macro-organisms to colonize freshly exposed surfaces on coral reefs. Obviously they play a major role in cementing together reef materials as well as contributing significantly to reef sediments. Other bryozoans form erect colonies in shaded areas, particularly on ledges and open spaces in back-reef areas. A few species grow in exposed situations. Erect and branching colonies often act as sediment traps, providing habitats for worms, crustaceans, and juvenile molluscs. Also, they provide food for a multitude of animals, particularly polychaete and nemertean worms (see chapter 9).

At least two hundred species, representing dozens of families, have been found on the Great Barrier Reef, and many more species remain

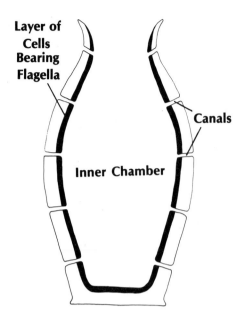

Layer of Cells Bearing Flagella

Canals

Inner Chamber

to be collected and identified. It would be premature to attempt to list the families of Bryozoa occurring there.

Some common genera represented: *Reteporella*, *Bugula*, *Watersipora*, *Celleparia*, *Fenestrulina*, *Rhynchozoon*, *Hippaliosina*, *Margaretta*, *Crepidacantha*, *Colletosia*.

Brachiopods (Phylum Brachiopoda)

Like bivalved molluscs, the soft parts of brachiopods are enclosed within a shell comprised of two calcified valves hinged together at one end. However, brachiopods are always attached to the substratum either by a stalk or by the cementing of one valve to the substratum. Internally, each valve is lined by a thin fleshy extension of the body called a *mantle*. In the mantle cavity is found a characteristic ringed or lobed lophophore, bearing ciliated filaments, which is a food-gathering and respiratory structure. A mouth is present near the lophophore and opens into a gut which lacks an anus. Sexes are usually separate, and there is a free-swimming larval stage. Brachiopods appear to be rather rare on the Great Barrier Reef. A few species (e.g. *Frenulina sanguinolenta*) have been found in the interstices of semi-consolidated rubble and live coral clumps on the reef flats of platform reefs. Species of the ducksbill brachiopod *Lingula* are found in soft sediments on some fringing reefs.

Genera represented: *Lingula*, *Frenulina*.

Sponges (Phylum Porifera)

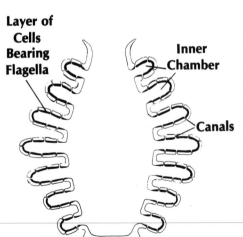

Layer of Cells Bearing Flagella

Inner Chamber

Canals

Although sponges are commonly encountered on the Great Barrier Reef, the species found there have been little studied. Those present consist basically of sheets of cells that cover the outer and inner surfaces of the sponge and which line the numerous canals and chambers that characterize sponge structure. Each of the cells lining the inner chamber or chambers (see fig. 6) bears a long, whip-like flagellum as well as a circlet of minute tentacles surrounding the base of the flagellum. The beating of flagella cause currents of water to be drawn into the inner chamber or chambers by way of the canals that open on the outer surface. Food particles present in the water currents are extracted by the minute tentacles. Between the outer and inner sheets of cells mentioned is a region where some free, mobile cells occur as well as skeletal material. In some sponges the skeleton is of calcium carbonate occurring as individual spicules or as a fused mass of spicules. In other sponges the skeleton is composed of spicules of silica associated with organic fibres termed *spongin*. In still others, silicious spicules and spongin fibres overlay a massive calcareous skeleton. Sponges are all attached to the substratum and show a great variety of external form. Some are vase-shaped, some form fingerlike growths, some are straplike, some form spheres, some form coral-like growths, and many form encrusting sheets. Most sponges are hermaphrodites, both male and female sex cells being produced. Fertilization results in the formation of a free-swimming larva that eventually settles and develops into a sponge. Sponges also reproduce asexually by budding off clusters of cells, called *gemmules*, which develop into new sponges after release from their parent and attachment to the substratum.

In Great Barrier Reef waters sponges occur in a bewildering array of colours on the undersurfaces of coral boulders, in crevices and caverns, and on vertical faces in deeper water on the periphery of reefs. They occur also round the bases of living corals in association with algae and in some cases in exposed situations on top of reef rubble and semi-consolidated debris. Numerous species are obviously present, but they are so poorly known that it would be futile to attempt to list the families represented. Some species produce powerful antibiotics.

Some genera represented: *Leucosolenia, Tethya, Ircinia, Myxilla, Phyllospongia, Neofibularia, Pericharax, Jaspis, Phakellia.*

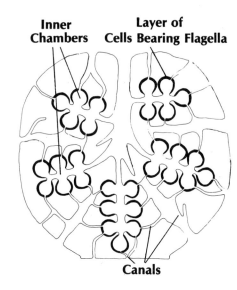

Figure 6. Vertical sections through generalized sponges. *Facing page, above:* A representative of species possessing a simple inner chamber. *Facing page, below:* A representative of species showing folding of the body wall. *Above:* A representative of species possessing a complicated system of canals and inner chambers.

Ascidians (Phylum Chordata, Class Ascidiacea)

Adult ascidians are vase-shaped animals attached at one end to the substratum. They occur as solitary individuals or as colonies. Each individual is enveloped by a tough *tunic* composed of fibres of a cellulose-like material called tunicin cemented together by other substances. Two openings in the tunic, called siphons, are associated with each individual. Water is drawn into one opening (the inhalent or *branchial siphon*) and passes to the anterior end of the gut (the pharynx) which has perforations called gill slits in its wall. Water passes through these slits into a cavity called the *exhalent chamber*, which opens to the exterior by way of the second siphon (the exhalent or *atrial siphon*). The water current itself is created by the beating of cilia on the gill slits. Food particles in the water current are ensnared in mucus secreted within the pharynx and pass to the stomach. From the stomach an intestine leads to the exhalent chamber.

Most ascidians are hermaphrodite, and the gonads also open into the exhalent chamber. Fertilized eggs usually give rise to a tadpole-like young, each of which settles on a surface after a short free-swimming existence and metamorphoses into a miniature adult. Asexual reproduction by budding is common in colonial species. The individuals of an ascidian colony, like those of a bryozoan colony, are known as zooids. Ascidians are well represented on the Great Barrier Reef, over two hundred species having already been found there. Most occur on rubble, particularly on the undersurfaces of dead coral boulders near reef crests. Many attach themselves to algae on reef flats, and some are found in dead mollusc shells. Numerous species occur in crevices, under ledges, in caves, and on vertical faces in deeper water on the edge of reefs. No doubt the list of ascidian species found on the reefs will be augmented considerably when these species are examined in detail. Ascidians show an amazing colour range, some species being spectacularly colourful. Families of ascidians found on the Great Barrier Reef are listed below:

Clavelinids (Clavelinidae) are colonial ascidians with relatively large zooids that often are semi-transparent. Frequently they protrude for much of their length from a common tunic, but in some species they are completely embedded in the tunic. Each zooid is divided into a thorax and abdomen. The branchial sac contains three to many rows of gill slits and is devoid of folds or longitudinal vessels. The gonad is confined to a loop of the gut in the abdomen. Atrial siphons are usually independent, but they may open into a common cloacal aperture in some species. Clavelinids occur under coral boulders, under overhangs, and in caves on reefs.

    Genera represented: *Podoclavella, Eudistoma, Sigillina, Clavelina, Sycozoa, Pycnoclavella.*

Polyclinids (Polyclinidae) form massive colonies with the zooids completely embedded in the gelatinous or "cartilaginous" tunic and grouped in various ways. Each zooid is elongated and divisible into a thorax, abdomen, and post-abdomen, the latter division containing gonads and heart. The branchial sac is small but contains more than seven rows of gill slits. Usually the atrial apertures form a common cloaca, but in some species they are free. The branchial siphons have six to eight lobes. Polyclinids are found under coral boulders on reef flats and exposed in the deeper water on the edges of reefs.

    Genera represented: *Polyclinum, Amaroucium.*

Didemnids (Didemnidae) are colonial ascidians usually forming flat encrusting sheets. Occasionally the colonies are globular. Frequently the common cloacal aperture shared by individual zooids of a colony is conspicuous, but the inhalent or branchial siphon of each zooid is more difficult to see because the zooids are minute. The branchial siphon has six lobes. Each zooid is divided into an anterior thorax containing the pharyngeal sac and a posterior region containing the gut and other organs. Tiny spicules, usually star-shaped, occur in the tunic. Didemnids, which are often brightly coloured, occur commonly under coral boulders on reef flats in Great Barrier Reef waters. They are also found exposed on reef flats either on coral rubble or associated with other organisms.

Genera represented: *Didemnum, Trididemnum, Lissoclinum, Diplosoma, Leptoclinides.*

Diazonids (Diazonidae). Most diazonids are solitary, although colonial species in which the zooids are embedded in a common tunic do occur. These colonial zooids do not share a common cloacal aperture. The elongated body of each zooid is divided into an anterior thorax, containing a branchial sac which possesses many rows of gill slits, and a posterior abdomen. The U-shaped gut is in line with the principal axis of the zooid, and the gonad is contained in the loop. Diazonids appear to be rare in Great Barrier Reef waters. However, at least one species of this family occurs under boulders on reef flats.

Genus represented: *Rhopalea.*

Perophorids (Perophoridae) are colonial ascidians with the zooids connected only by ramifying stolons. The branchial sac has numerous gill slits and usually possesses inner longitudinal vessels. The loop of the gut lies to one side of the branchial sac. One species belonging to this family has been observed under coral boulders on some reefs.

Genus represented: *Ecteinascidia.*

Ascidiids (Ascidiidae) are solitary, attached forms. The branchial siphon is usually eight-lobed and the atrial siphon six-lobed. Straight gill slits are present in the branchial sac, which possesses inner longitudinal vessels. The loop of the gut containing the gonad is to one side of the branchial sac. Members of this family are relatively large ascidians. They occur on the undersurfaces of coral boulders and under overhangs on reefs.

Genera represented: *Ascidia, Phallusia.*

Styelids (Styelidae). Members of the large family Styelidae may be solitary or colonial. The body is not divided into thorax and abdomen. The siphons have smooth edges or are four-lobed. The branchial sac has fewer than five folds on each side. Gonads are present on the body wall on both sides of the animal. Some of the colonial styelids, in particular, are brightly coloured. Styelids grow on and under coral boulders, under overhangs and ledges, and in caves on coral reefs.

Genera represented: *Botrylloides, Botryllus, Distomus, Polycarpa, Styela, Polyzoa, Cnemidocarpa, Chorizocarpa.*

Pyurids (Pyuridae) are solitary ascidians that frequently attain a large size. Usually the tunic, which is attached to the substratum, is leathery and tough and sometimes bears spines or tubercles. Both siphons have four lobes. In most species five or six folds are found in the branchial sac, which has small straight or spirally arranged gill slits. An obvious stomach associated with a lobed "liver" is present. One or more gonads are present on each side of the body. Pyurids are found attached to the undersurfaces of coral boulders and overhangs and in caves on reefs.

Genera represented: *Pyura, Herdmania, Microcosmus.*

Molgulids (Molgulidae) are solitary, usually spheroidal ascidians that are only occasionally attached to solid objects. Most live partially buried in the substratum. Frequently the tunic, which is usually translucent, carries fine processes to which sediment adheres. These processes act as anchors. Both siphons have six lobes. The gill slits in the pharynx are usually curved. Molgulids are not well represented on reefs of the Great Barrier Reef but are found commonly in soft sediments abutting on fringing reefs.

Genus represented: *Molgula.*

9

The Worms

Numerous worm-like groups of animals are found on reefs of the Great Barrier Reef. These groups are representative of some of the major subdivisions of the animal kingdom recognized by zoologists, and they differ markedly in bodily structure and function from group to group. However, they all have important roles to play in the coral reef community. Many are scavengers, breaking down organic detritus and recycling organic compounds. Others are active predators, feeding on small organisms. In turn they become prey for other animals. Generally, the worm-like animal groups found on the Great Barrier Reef have been somewhat neglected by zoologists.

Flatworms (Phylum Platyhelminthes)

Worms of the phylum Platyhelminthes are flat and usually thin. They have a distinct head that bears sense organs and a ramifying multibranched alimentary canal that has one opening serving as both mouth and anus. No respiratory structures, blood circulation, or body cavity are present. Most flatworms are hermaphrodites and have complex reproductive systems. Many are parasitic, the flukes and the tapeworms invariably so. These parasitic forms, found commonly in fish, turtles, marine snakes, birds, crustaceans, molluscs, and other animals often have several larval stages in their life histories, and the various larval stages may be found in different hosts. However, many flatworms are free-living, occurring under boulders and among rubble on reefs. Development in these forms may involve a larval stage or be direct.

Free-living flatworms are usually oval in outline, flattened, and often semi-transparent. They range in size from a few millimetres to over 5 centimetres in length, but the majority are less than 1 centimetre. Some of the larger ones found on reefs are brightly coloured. They move over surfaces with a characteristic gliding motion and can swim by making undulatory movements of the body margins. Flatworms all appear to be carnivorous, prey being enveloped by a tubular and muscular proboscis that can be everted through the mouth. The flatworms occurring in Great Barrier Reef waters are not well known. Numerous families are probably represented there.

Some genera represented: *Pseudoceros, Thysanozoon.*

Roundworms (Phylum Nematoda)

Roundworms are well known as parasites of humans and domestic animals. However, many free-living species are found on the sea-floor. Most are microscopic, being less than 2 millimetres in length, but they are probably the most abundant of the animals associated with sea-floor sediments, including those of coral-reef areas. The translucent and unsegmented body of a roundworm is cylindrical or spindle-shaped and covered with a ,tough cuticle. Bristles arise from the body surface in some species. At the anterior end is a mouth surrounded by lips. Also situated at the front is a pair of sense organs called *amphids*, which occur in pits. The sexes are separate, and the fertilized egg gives rise to juvenile worms that develop into adults after a series of moults. Roundworms exhibit a characteristic writhing motion which enables them to move among sediments. Many species ingest organic debris and associated micro-organisms and serve to decompose and recycle organic nutrients. Other species are actively predacious. All, of course, are themselves preyed on by a multitude of animals.

Ribbon-worms (Phylum Nemertea)

Ribbon-worms are elongate, unsegmented worms with an amazing ability to contort their muscular bodies. In some species the body is flattened, in others it is cylindrical. The head is not sharply marked off from the rest of the body and, although bearing eyes, is frequently difficult to distinguish. A mobile, tubular proboscis bearing one or more stylets and, in some species, capable of injecting venom is used

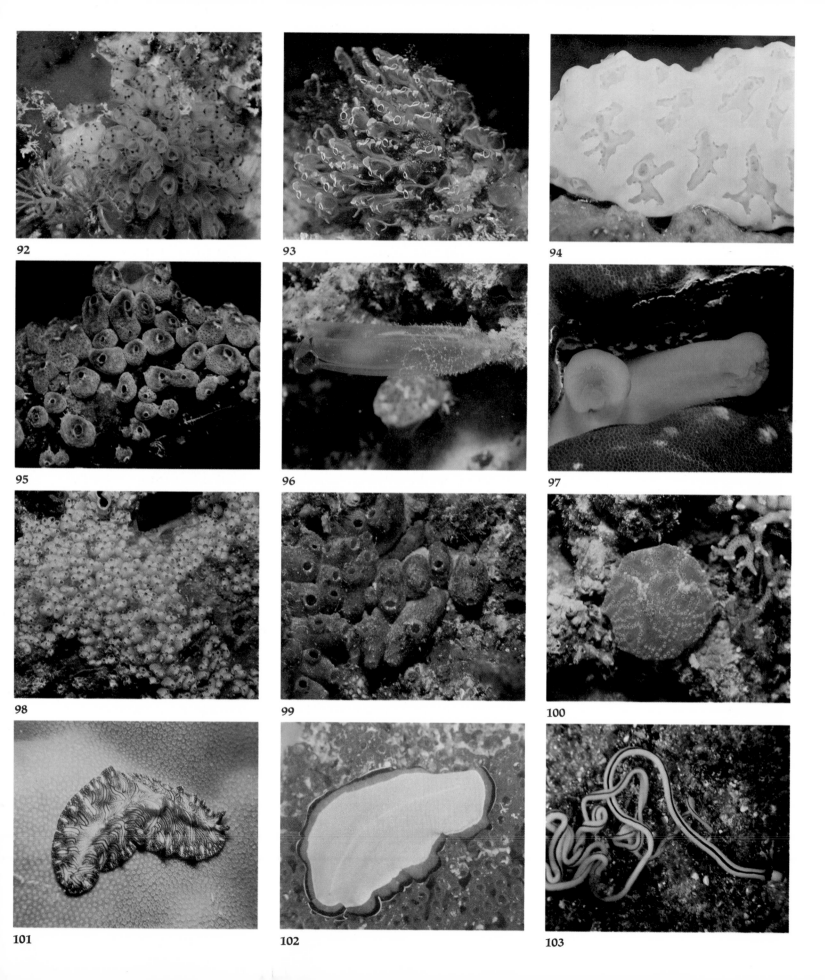

92

93

94

95

96

97

98

99

100

101

102

103

in the capture of prey. Sexes are usually separate, and in many species there is a free-swimming larval stage in the life history. Nemerteans are found among rubble and among algae on coral reefs. Some species are conspicuously marked and relatively large. *Baseodiscus quinquelineatus*, for example, carries five black lines on its body and may be over 50 centimetres in length. An orange species, *Gorgonorhynchus repens*, has a remarkable branched proboscis which writhes when shot out from the anterior end of the animal and looks like a mass of worms. Unfortunately, the ribbon-worms of the Great Barrier Reef area have received little attention from zoologists, and it is not known how many families are represented there.

Some genera represented: *Baseodiscus*, *Gorgonorhynchus*.

Peanut-Worms (Phylum Sipunculida)

The body of a peanut-worm is divided into a sac-like trunk (shaped like a peanut in some species) and a thinner tubular structure, the *introvert*, which is capable of great extension and which can be telescoped inside the trunk. The mouth is situated at the tip of the introvert, while the anus is placed towards the front of the trunk, the alimentary canal being bent upon itself. Sexes are separate. Development from the fertilized egg proceeds through a ciliated larval stage which is planktonic for a period. Peanut-worms are found under and among rubble, among algae, and burrowing in dead coral on reefs. The burrowers appear to extract organic material from material ingested whilst they are burrowing. Other peanut-worms collect detritus and minute organisms from surface films with the introvert which often carries ciliated tentacles.

Some genera represented: *Sipunculus*, *Siphonosoma*, *Aspidosiphon*, *Phascolosoma*, *Paraspidosiphon*.

Echiurid worms (Phylum Echiurida)

These are unsegmented finger-like worms that possess a broad extensible proboscis at the anterior end. The proboscis carries a ciliated groove on one side. A mouth is found at the junction of the proboscis with the trunk. Echiurids are not able to withdraw the proboscis into the body. The alimentary canal is long and coiled and the anal opening is found at the posterior end of the trunk which often carries rows of bristles. The sexes are separate, but in some species the male is much smaller than the female and is carried on or in her body.

Echiurids are occasionally found under rubble and in crevices in dead coral on reefs. They utilize the proboscis to feed on organic detritus and minute organisms in surface films. Echiurids found on the Great Barrier Reef have received little attention from zoologists.

Polychaete Worms (Phylum Annelida, Class Polychaeta)

Polychaetes are elongated worms that are typically segmented and marine. Indeed, they are probably the commonest group of macroscopic organisms associated with marine sediments. Some species burrow in the sediments; others live in the interstices of semi-consolidated sediments or among rubble or on the surface of sediments. Some species live in association with sedentary organisms. Hence it is not surprising that polychaetes are abundantly represented on coral reefs.

Usually the head of a polychaete consists of two regions, the *prostomium* and *peristomium* (see fig. 7). The prostomium is the more anterior region and often bears eyes and appendages that take the form of expanded flaps called *palps* which may be sensory or involved in feeding or both, and pointed structures called antennae which are always sensory. The peristomium is found in the vicinity of the mouth and often carries tentacles that are sensory and may also assist in food capture. Each of the segments of the body found behind the head region usually bears lateral appendages known as *parapodia*. Typically, each parapodium consists of an upper (notopodium) and a lower (neuropodium) branch, each branch bearing tough structures called *setae* (see fig. 8). These are often bristle-like but assume a variety of forms in different polychaete groups. Sometimes one or both branches of the parapodium possess feelers or gills or both. Frequently the anterior end of the digestive system (the pharynx) can be everted through the mouth to form a tubular structure that is often armed with jaws for seizing prey (see fig. 9). In some groups, the region of the body behind the head is obviously divided into an anterior thorax and a posterior abdomen. Normally the sexes are separate in polychaetes, and most species liberate eggs and sperm directly into the water. Developmental stages may occur in the plankton or on the sea-floor. A few species brood their young.

Some polychaetes construct tubes which are often membranous but in some groups are calcareous. The bodies of tube-dwelling polychaetes are often modified, parapodia being frequently reduced and gills and food-collecting tentacles being often enlarged.

Representatives of numerous polychaete families have been recorded from the Great Barrier Reef. These families, together with a

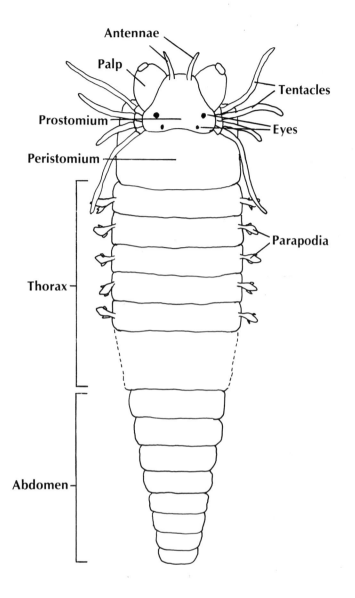

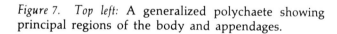

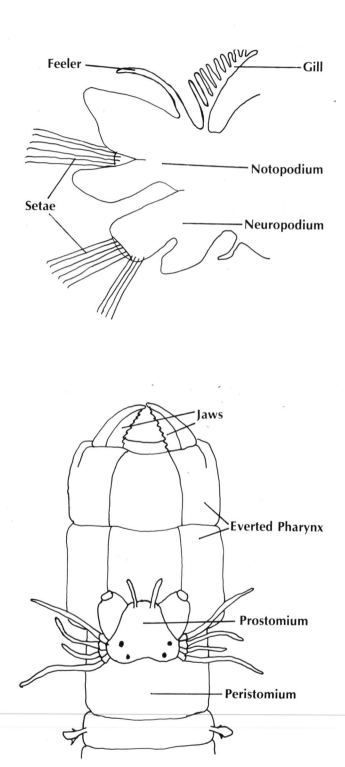

Figure 7. Top left: A generalized polychaete showing principal regions of the body and appendages.

Figure 8. Top right: A generalized parapodium of a polychaete.

Figure 9. Below: The anterior end of a polychaete showing everted pharynx with jaws.

brief description of the diagnostic features of each family, are listed below. However, the polychaetes of the Great Barrier Reef area are not well known. Representatives of additional families will undoubtedly be found there. At present it is not possible to list the genera represented.

Spionids (Spionidae). In the family Spionidae the prostomium is devoid of appendages. A pair or two groups of feeding tentacles occur on the peristomium. No jaws are present. Parapodia are usually well developed. Some spionids burrow into coral rubble and into mollusc shells on coral reefs. Others build tubes in the sand.

Chaetopterids (Chaetopteridae). The prostomium of chaetopterids carries a pair of short palps; the peristomium, a pair of tentacles. The body is divided into two or three regions. Each parapodium on the anterior region has only one branch, but there are two branches in the parapodia on posterior regions. Chaetopterids live in parchment-like tubes. On some fringing reefs and reef flats of platform reefs occurring near the Queensland mainland, the tubes of *Chaetopterus variopedatus* are often found. These are open at both ends, which project above the substratum. Water is drawn through the tube as a result of the movements of enlarged parapodia found near the middle of the worm. The water passes through a mucous filter secreted at the anterior end of the worm, and particulate material is filtered out. At regular intervals the particle-laden mucous filter is eaten and a new one secreted.

Capitellids (Capitellidae). No appendages are carried on the prostomium. The first and sometimes the second trunk segments are devoid of setae. Usually the setae of thorax and abdomen are obviously different. The lower portion of each parapodium is in the form of a transverse pad. Capitellids are threadlike and usually coloured reddish anteriorly. They are common in the interstices of partially consolidated rubble, under stones, and burrowing in coral sand on reef flats.

Bamboo-worms (Maldanidae). As their common name implies, bamboo-worms have elongated segments resembling those of bamboo stalks. Otherwise they resemble capitellids structurally and occur in similar habitats on coral reefs.

Scalibregmids (Scalibregmidae). The prostomium in members of the family Scalibregmidae is T-shaped or bifid and lacks appendages. Parapodia with upper and lower branches are present. The body is usually inflated anteriorly and usually has a wrinkled skin. Branching gills are often carried on the anterior body segments. Scalibregmids are found in sand under coral rubble on reef flats.

Opheliids (Opheliidae). In the family Opheliidae the prostomium is entirely devoid of appendages. Parapodia are poorly developed and carry only simple tapering setae. The body is usually short and often somewhat grublike. An unarmed eversible proboscis is present. Gills occur in some segments in some species. Opheliids are burrowers and occur in coral sand, especially around the bases of embedded rubble and in the interstices of coral rubble on reef flats.

Cirratulids (Cirratulidae). The prostomium is devoid of appendages. Grooved tentacles directed anteriorly arise from the peristomium or from one to several segments behind the peristomium, which is fused with two or more thoracic segments. Threadlike gills, or *branchiae*, are present on some segments. Cirratulids occur buried in sand or rubble or in the interstices of semi-consolidated rubble on reefs.

Paddle-worms (Phyllodocidae). Four or five antennae and small eyes are present on the prostomium, while four to eight tentacles arise from the peristomium in members of this family. An eversible proboscis, devoid of jaws, is used for food capture. The body is long and slender. Several species, many brightly coloured, belonging to this family have been observed on sand and among rubble on fringing and platform reefs.

Hesionids (Hesionidae) are short, flattened worms which carry two or three antennae on the prostomium and four to sixteen tentacles on the peristomium. An eversible pharynx, possessing jaws in some species but not in others, is present. The upper part of each parapodium (the *notopodium*) is smaller than the lower part (the *neuropodium*) but bears a long feeler. Hesionids are common in the interstices of dead coral clumps and under rubble on reef flats.

Nereids (Nereidae). Only two (sometimes one) antennae are found in nereids which have elongated, many-segmented bodies. Palps are present on the prostomium and four to eight feelers are found on the peristomium. The eversible pharynx is armed with a pair of jaws. Complex branches and feelers are associated with the parapodia. Nereids are found commonly in the interstices of coral rubble, under coral boulders, and among algae on reefs.

Glycerids (Glyceridae). Two pairs of antennae are borne on the markedly conical prostomium. The peristomium is devoid of feelers. The long pharynx, which is armed with four usually black jaws, is everted readily if glycerids are disturbed. Either the parapodia are all composed of upper and lower sections or they all have only one section. Glycerids are found among coral rubble. One species, *Glycera gigantea*, as the scientific name implies, is very large.

Syllids (Syllidae). Probably there are more species belonging to the family Syllidae on the Great Barrier Reef than belong to any other polychaete family. Syllids are small, usually threadlike worms that have three antennae and a pair of palps on the prostomium and four tentacles on the peristomium. An eversible pharynx, which is armed with teeth in some species but not in others, is present. Typically a prominent feeler is associated with the upper part of each parapodium. Syllids are abundant in the interstices of semi-consolidated coral rubble and in the bases of coral clumps on reef flats.

Fire-worms (Amphinomidae). One to five antennae, palps, and a backwardly directed sensory structure called a *caruncle* are present on the prostomium. Multi-lobed branchiae are associated with the upper portions of most parapodia. A roughened pad is present in the jawless pharynx. Spinose setae project in tufts from the parapodia. These setae are apt to penetrate and break off in the flesh of anyone handling the worms. There they cause intense irritation and often act as foci for infection. Large elongate specimens of the fire-worm *Eurythoe complanata* are found commonly under coral boulders on reef flats. Other long-bodied species of fire-worms occur among corals. Short-bodied, ovate fire-worms are also found on coral reefs, usually among and under rubble. Some fire-worms feed on corals.

Onuphids (Onuphidae). Seven antennae are found on the prostomium of onuphids. Jaws are present in the eversible pharynx. Sensory feelers are associated with the parapodia. Many onuphid species construct parchment-like tubes to which detritus often adheres. Others are burrowers. Most appear to be scavengers. Onuphids are found among coral rubble on reef flats.

Eunicids (Eunicidae). One to five antennae are carried on the prostomium. Several jaws are associated with the eversible proboscis. The upper portion of each parapodium is reduced to a sensory feeler and is associated with a many-lobed gill. Eunicids have been found in the interstices of semi-consolidated rubble and under coral boulders on reefs. Some species are large (over 1 metre in length in one case), and are active carnivores.

104

105

106

107

108

109

110

111

112

113

114

115

Lumbrinereids (Lumbrinereidae) carry no appendages on the prostomium. Several jaws are present in the eversible pharynx. The upper branch of each parapodium is absent or greatly reduced to form button-like structures. Lumbrinereids occur in the interstices of semi-consolidated rubble, in sand under coral boulders, and among the holdfasts of algae on reef flats.

Arabellids (Arabellidae) closely resemble lumbrinereids, differing mainly in details of their jaw apparatus. The two families occur in similar habitats on coral reefs.

Dorvilleids (Dorvilleidae). Two pairs of antennae are carried on the prostomium. Several jaws are present in the eversible proboscis. The upper portions of the parapodia are not as large as the lower portions, but both portions bear setae. Most members of the family are small. They have been found in the interstices of coral rubble.

Scale-worms (Polynoidae). A characteristic feature of the family Polynoidae is the presence of scales (elytrae) alternating with feelers on the upper surface of each segment. Three (sometimes one or two) antennae are usually present on the prostomium. Four jaws are found in the eversible proboscis. Scale-worms are usually flattened. Most are small to medium sized and are found on and under coral boulders. A few species live as commensals on other organisms, particularly echinoderms (see chapter 12).

Oweniids (Oweniidae). In members of the family Oweniidae the prostomium and peristomium are fused. The prostomium may be rounded or lobed or carry a crown of low tentacles. The anterior segments of the body are markedly longer than the posterior ones. Setae that take the form of small hooks occur densely in the lower part of each parapodium. Oweniids construct membranous tubes to which sand and shell fragments adhere. Usually only the anterior end of the tube projects from the sand and rubble in which the tube is buried or enmeshed. Species belonging to this family have been found in and among semi-consolidated rubble on reefs.

Flabelligerids (Flabelligeridae). In the family Flabelligeridae the prostomium carries lateral palps while the peristomium gives rise to filamentous branchiae. Both prostomium and peristomium can be retracted into the first three setae-bearing segments of the thorax. The body may be cylindrical or vasiform. Mucus that enmeshes sand grains and shell fragments is secreted by glands on the body surface. Consequently flabelligerids are often encased in sandy sheaths. They occur in and among rubble on coral reefs.

Facing page
Illustration 104
The bifid proboscides of two echiurid worms (*Bonellia viridis*) extending from a coral clump where the worms are hidden.

Illustration 105
A reef polychaete.

Illustration 106
The glycerid, *Glycera gigantea*, over one metre in length.

Illustration 107
The fire-worm, *Eurythoe complanata*.

Illustration 108
The setae of a fire-worm.

Illustration 109
A so-called sea-mouse, *Chloeia* sp.

Illustration 110
A scale-worm (Polynoidae) showing the overlapping scales (elytrae) on the upper surface.

Illustration 111
The spaghetti-worm, *Reteterebella queenslandiae*.

Illustration 112
An unidentified terebellid worm from Heron Island reef.

Illustration 113
The crown of tentacles belonging to a fan-worm of the genus *Sabellastarte*.

Illustration 114
The tentacles of a fan-worm, *Protula magnifica*.

Illustration 115
The calcareous tubes of specimens of the serpulid worm, *Filograna implexa*.

Terebellids (Terebellidae). The prostomium of terebellids has no appendages, but the peristomium bears numerous feeding tentacles that are usually long and highly contractile. Gills that are often markedly branched are found on the anterior segments. The parapodia of anterior segments of the body consist of upper and lower branches, but those of posterior segments consist of only one branch. Terebellids secrete mucous tubes to which sand, shells, and detritus adhere. On the Great Barrier Reef they are commonly found under coral rubble and around the bases of coral clumps. In some species (e.g., the so-called spaghetti-worm, *Reteterebella queenslandia*) the feeding tentacles often move actively over the surface of reef sediments, gathering organic detritus and minute organisms. In other species the tentacles filter particles from the water.

The spiral tentacles of a group of serpulid worms, *Spirobranchus giganteus,* protrude from their tubes which are embedded in coral. Most of the tentacles are blue in this group seen at Bowden reef.

Fan-worms (Sabellidae). A fan of tentacles is present at the anterior end of the cylindrical body in sabellids, which secrete non-calcareous membranous tubes into which they withdraw for protection. The tentacles are used to collect planktonic organisms and detrital material and are also used in respiration. The prostomium is fused with the peristomium. Only a few of the thoracic segments carry setae. This is often the case with the abdominal segments, but in some species many abdominal segments carry setae. The tentacles of fan-worms are often reddish or banded with red. Some bear eyes. Some species of fan-worms attain lengths in excess of 15 centimetres and diameters exceeding 1 centimetre. On the Great Barrier Reef, fan-worms are found attached to coral boulders and partially embedded in semi-consolidated rubble on reef flats.

Uncoiled calcareous tube-worms (Serpulidae). In members of the family Serpulidae a crown of tentacles used to collect food as well as for respiratory purposes surrounds the anterior end of the body. A calcareous tube, which may be straight or twisted, is secreted, and the animal withdraws into this when alarmed. The body of the worm is symmetrical. These tube-worms are common on and under coral boulders and slabs of beach rock on reef flats. One species, the so-called peacock-worm, *Spirobranchus giganteus,* is commonly associated with live corals, particularly species of *Porites* (see chapter 17).

Coiled calcareous tube-worms (Spirorbidae) closely resemble members of the family Serpulidae. However, their bodies are asymmetrical and the calcareous tubes secreted are coiled into a spiral. These tube-worms are found under boulders on the reef flat.

Oligochaete Worms (Phylum Annelida, Class Clitellata, Subclass Oligochaeta)

Oligochaete worms resemble polychaetes, but they are devoid of parapodia, the few setae they possess arising directly from the body wall. The most anterior region of the body, the prostomium, lacks appendages. Gonads are confined to a few segments, and all species are hermaphrodite. An egg case is produced by the glandular skin of a few segments. It is only in recent years that oligochaetes have been reported from any reef of the Great Barrier Reef. However, they appear to be quite common at Heron and Wistari reefs in the Capricorn group, and no doubt oligochaetes will be found elsewhere on the Great Barrier Reef.

Tubificids (Tubificidae) are small oligochaete worms whose gonads are found in segments 10 and 11 and receptacles for the receipt of sperm in segment 10. Tubificids burrow in coral sand near coral clumps.

Some genera represented: *Aktedrilus, Bathydrilus, Coralliodrilus, Heronidrilus, Limnodriloides, Phallodrilus, Jamiesoniella.*

Enchytraeids (Enchytraeidae). The gonads of enchytraeids are found in segments 11 and 12 and receptacles for the receipt of sperm in segment 5. These small worms burrow in sand near coral clumps.

Genus represented: *Grania.*

Phoronids (Phylum Phoronida)

A characteristic feature of the small group of wormlike animals called phoronids is the presence of a biolobed fan of tentacles surrounding the mouth at the anterior end of each individual. The posterior end is swollen. The gut is bent upon itself, and the anus also opens anteriorly. Each phoronid is housed in a chitinous tube into which it withdraws its anterior end and tentacles when disturbed. Mucus secreted by the tentacles ensnares organic debris and micro-organisms that are brought to the mouth by water currents created by cilia on the tentacles. Phoronids occur in sandy areas around the bases of corals and coral rubble on reef flats. Possibly only one species occurs there.

Genus represented: *Phoronis.*

Acorn-Worms (Phylum Hemichordata, Class Enteropneusta)

The body of acorn-worms is divided into the proboscis, the collar, and the elongate trunk. The anterior proboscis is a sensory and food-collecting structure, detritus and minute organisms being enmeshed in mucus and passed back by currents created by cilia on the proboscis to the mouth situated on one side of the collar. Gill slits which carry cilia occur in the pharynx region of the alimentary canal. Beating of these cilia causes water to be drawn into the alimentary canal through the mouth and to pass through the gill slits to the exterior. The current thereby created is involved with respiration. Acorn-worms occur in sandy regions of coral reefs, particularly in lagoons and back-reef areas.

Genus represented: *Balanoglossus.*

Facing page
The yellow spiral tentacles of this specimen of *Spirobranchus giganteus* project above the coral in which its tube is embedded.

10

The Crustaceans

The jointed-limbed, armoured crustaceans (Phylum Crustacea) form a large group of animals that are mostly marine. Many species are tiny and poorly known to the non-scientist since a microscope is required to discern their body structure. Others such as the crabs, crayfish, and prawns are relatively large and generally well known because they are edible.

Essentially, the segmented bodies of crustaceans are divided into a head region, a middle region called the thorax, and a posterior region called the abdomen (see fig. 10). However, in most species some of the anterior thoracic segments are fused with the head segments. The head usually bears two pairs of sensory antennae as well as eyes. A number of paired appendages, some of which arise from head segments and some from the anterior thoracic segments, surround the mouth and assist in manipulating food. Paired thoracic and abdominal appendages are also present. Each has an expanded structure called a *gill* associated with its base, which forks to give two branches. However, there is a great deal of variation in this basic structure, and the appendages may be modified for a number of functions, including walking, swimming, grasping, cutting, digging, and carrying. A tough cuticle secreted by the skin covers the animal. In addition, a fold of skin, often strengthened by the deposition of calcareous material and known as the *carapace*, frequently projects from hind regions of the head to cover part of the body of the crustacean; it is essentially a protective structure. A tail fan is usually associated with the tip of the abdomen. Sexes are usually separate, and a series of free-living, often planktonic, larval stages occur in the life histories of most species.

Crustaceans show an amazing variety of form, colour, and habits but are divided into a number of basic groups by zoologis s. Those groups found on the Great Barrier Reef are discussed below.

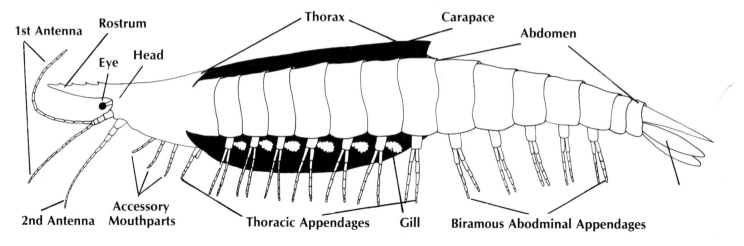

Figure 10.   A generalized crustacean showing principal regions of the body and appendages on one side. The carapace on the left side has been removed.

Water-Fleas (Order Cladocera)

Water-fleas are somewhat transparent animals, only a few millimetres in length, that swim by using enlarged second antennae (first antennae are absent). The thorax and abdomen are shortened and typically are enclosed in a bivalved carapace. The head, which usually carries a pair of eyes as well as paired antennae and mouth parts, is not so enclosed. A few pairs of appendages, each with a gill attached to the base, arise from the thorax. In many species these appendages assist in feeding by filtering minute organisms and suspended material from sea water, but in other species they are used to seize and hold prey organisms. Brood chambers, in which the young pass through various developmental stages, are formed under the abdomen in females. Water-fleas are often abundant in the plankton in the water mass covering coral reefs, and they provide food for a multitude of animals.

Ostracods (Class Ostracoda)

Ostracods, which range in length from less than 1 millimetre to over 2 centimetres, have a bivalved carapace joined at a hinge-line enclosing the whole body. Two pairs of antennae used in locomotion are found in the head region together with a single eye. Only two pairs of limbs are found on the thorax, and the short abdomen is devoid of appendages except for pointed structures at the tip. Several free-swimming larval stages occur in the ostracod life cycle.

Some ostracods are found in the plankton, but most are bottom-living forms found on, and burrowing in, sediments on coral reefs. Some are filter feeders, some feed on organic detritus, and some are active predators. In turn, ostracods become prey for other animals and are of importance in food webs on reefs.

Isopods (Order Isopoda)

Crustaceans belonging to the order Isopoda are flattened from back to front and are frequently ovoid in outline. They range from a few millimetres to a few centimetres in length. One, occasionally two, thoracic segments are fused with the head segments. Paired eyes and antennae are usually prominent in the head region. Each of the unfused thoracic segments bears a pair of walking legs. The abdominal appendages are flattened and often function as gills. Some isopods, the wood-lice, are terrestrial and are found on coral cays. Many (the shore slaters) are found along the shore-line, usually hidden under boulders. Numerous species occur on reef flats, in crevices, under coral boulders, and among algae. A considerable number of species are parasitic on fish and other crustaceans. Most of the free-living forms feed on organic detritus, but some feed on small organisms. Numerous species belonging to several families are to be found in the Great Barrier Reef region.

Copepods (Class Copepoda)

Although minute (ranging in size from less than a millimetre to a few millimetres), copepods are abundant in marine waters. They are cylindrical or pear-shaped, segmented animals and possess typical crustacean body divisions of head, thorax, and abdomen, although the head is fused with one or more thoracic segments. They do not have a carapace. Prominent antennae are carried in the head region and are often used to assist the biramous (two-branched) thoracic appendages in swimming. A single eye is usually prominent. Appendages are lacking on the abdominal segments except for a pair of pointed structures carried on the last segment. Sexes are separate, and one or two egg sacs are carried under the abdomen by females. Although most copepods are free-living, a number of highly modified parasitic species occur.

Copepods usually dominate the animal plankton in all seas and are present in the waters bathing coral reefs. Many species are herbivorous, preying on plant plankton; others prey on minute animal organisms in the plankton. Either way they are of great importance as intermediates in food webs. A surprisingly large number of copepod groups are bottom-dwellers, feeding on organic debris and minute organisms. They too have important roles in food webs in coral reef waters. Numerous copepod species belonging to dozens of families occur on the Great Barrier Reef.

Amphipods (Order Amphipoda)

Amphipods are compressed laterally, and most are small (less than a centimetre in length). They have no carapace. Paired sessile eyes are present. All except the first pair of thoracic limbs can function as walking legs. One or more pairs bear nippers. Usually the last three pairs of walking legs are directed backwards. The abdomen is not distinctly marked off from the thorax and carries appendages modified for swimming or jumping. Several species of amphipod found in upper regions of the sea-shore on coral cays and continental islands have these appendages modified for jumping and are known as sand-hoppers. Numerous species belonging to several families occur on reef flats among and under rubble and sheltering among algae and other organisms. Most feed on detritus, but a few are active predators. A few species are commensals, living in association with other animals.

Barnacles (Class Cirripedia)

Although barnacles are prominent on intertidal boulders, they are not well represented on reef flats, reef slopes, and back-reef areas of coral reefs. In all but burrowing and parasitic forms, a number of calcareous plates are found in the carapace. This encloses and protects the body, which has a reduced abdomen and appears to lack segmentation. However, six pairs of jointed appendages, called *cirri*, are usually present in the thoracic region and are used in feeding. Normally barnacles are attached to the substratum when adult as a result of the secretion of an adhesive substance by glands present on the first pair of antennae. The cirri reach upwards and kick planktonic food towards the mouth. Most species are hermaphrodite. The so-called goose-barnacles are attached to the substratum by a stalk; those attached directly to the substratum are known as acorn barnacles. Some barnacles are parasitic. Species of *Sacculina*, for example, are found as parasites in the abdomen of crabs and lose all semblance of typical barnacle structure when adult. Most goose-barnacles drift into coral reef areas attached to floating objects, but one species, *Ibla cumingi*, is found commonly attached to boulders on reefs. The acorn barnacle *Tetraclita vitiata* occurs in clusters on intertidal boulders; another acorn barnacle, *T. caerulescens*, is common in some regions. The acorn barnacle *Chelonibia testudinaria* is found attached to the carapace of turtles. Boring barnacles, *Stephanolepas muricata*, bore into these carapaces.

Mantis Shrimps (Order Stomatopoda)

Mantis shrimps attain fairly large sizes, with lengths ranging from 5 to over 30 centimetres. The head and only part of the thorax is covered by the carapace. Their common name derives from the structure of the claws on the second pair of thoracic legs, which are seizing organs that fold like a penknife and resemble the food-gathering limbs of a preying mantis. Mantis shrimps have a long, well-developed abdomen that terminates in a tail fan; swimming appendages occur on the abdominal segments. They can move with surprising rapidity and are active predators on a variety of animals, including worms and fishes. They occur commonly in pools and in crevices on reef flats and under boulders on reef crests.

Genera represented: *Gonodactylus, Odontodactylus.*

The Ten-Legged Crustaceans (Order Decapoda)

The order Decapoda is a large group which includes the prawns, shrimps, burrowing shrimps, crayfish, lobsters, hermit crabs, half-crabs and true crabs. In these crustaceans the head and thorax are fused and covered with a carapace that projects downwards. A pair of stalked eyes, usually separated by a forward projecting rostrum, two pairs of antennae and a pair of jaws (mandibles) are found in the head region. The first three pairs of thoracic appendages are modified as accessory mouth parts, while the last five pairs are variously modified for grasping and walking. Usually, pincerlike structures called chelae are borne at the tips of one or more pairs. Each chela is comprised of an expanded terminal segment (the hand) which is drawn out to form a fixed finger and an associated moveable finger. The hand is carried on the second segment of the appendage known as the wrist which may be jointed (see fig. 11) whilst the appendage itself is known, somewhat incongruously, as a cheliped. Gills are found on the thorax under the carapace. In most forms the abdomen is large and terminates in a tail fan. Paired biramous appendages are usually found on the abdominal segments and eggs are frequently attached to these appendages in females.

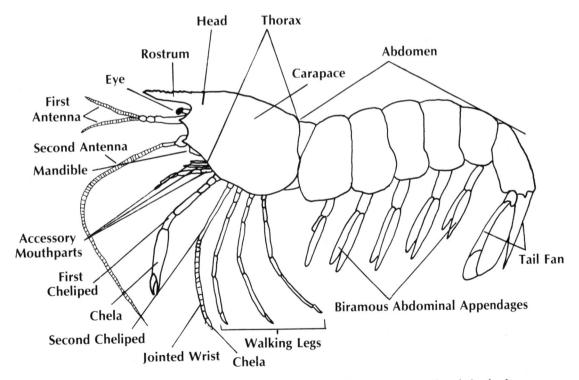

Figure 11.   A decapod crustacean showing appendages on one side of the body.

Prawns and Shrimps (Sub-Order Natantia)

Prawns and shrimps are swimming representatives of the decapod crustaceans, the abdominal appendages being developed principally as swimming organs. The rostrum is usually prominent. Often the body is laterally compressed and all abdominal segments are of a similar size. In general, the swimming decapods are called prawns if they are relatively large when adult and shrimps if relatively small. Technically, prawns release eggs directly into the surrounding water and possess three pairs of chelipeds (pincers), whilst female shrimps carry eggs on the abdominal appendages and shrimps of both sexes usually possess only two pairs of chelipeds. In addition, the plates on the sides of the second abdominal segment of shrimps overlap those of the first. Prawns are found in the deeper water off reefs of the Great Barrier Reef where they are fished commercially. However, they cannot be regarded as a major part of the coral reef fauna. On the other hand, shrimps are well represented on coral reefs. Some of them are spectacularly coloured and, collectively, they form a characteristic part of the coral reef fauna. The principal families of shrimp found on reefs of the Great Barrier Reef follow.

Palaemonid shrimps (Palaemonidae). In members of the large family Palaemonidae the second pair of chelipeds are generally longer and larger than the first pair, and the second joint or wrist segment is not subdivided into a number of smaller joints (annulations) as it is in some families. Mandibles are bilobed and the rostrum is long, laterally compressed, and serrated. The family is well represented on the Great Barrier Reef. Some species are free-living, but many live commensally in sponges, gorgonians, sea-anemones, corals, bivalves, feather-stars, sea-urchins and ascidians. One species removes external parasites from fishes after first attracting them by waving its antennae. This species and several others are strikingly coloured, but others are cryptically coloured. Frequently the colours of commensal species blend with those of their hosts.

Genera represented: *Periclimenes, Stegopontonia, Jocaste.*

Pasiphaeid shrimps (Pasiphaeidae) are remarkable for the imperfect development of some walking legs, while others are well formed. Usually the last three pairs of walking legs are slender, feeble, or imperfect. The rostrum is small or absent.

Genus represented: *Leptochela.*

Crangonid shrimps (Crangonidae). The first and second pairs of chelipeds are unequally developed in crangonid shrimps. Each of the chelae of the first pair possesses a mobile finger which closes against the anterior margin of the hand, the fixed finger being spinelike. Mandibles are simple, and the wrists of the second pair of chelipeds are never annulated. Several species belonging to this family are found in pools or burrowing in coral sand on reefs.

Genus represented: *Pontophilus.*

Gnathophyllid shrimps (Gnathophyllidae). The chelae of the second pair of chelipeds are much larger than the first in members of the family Gnathophyllidae. Some of the accessory mouth parts have broad platelike segments. These shrimps are spectacularly coloured. Some species live in association with sea-urchins. Species of *Hymenocera* are known to be starfish predators.

Genera represented: *Hymenocera, Levicaris, Gnathophyllum.*

Snapping shrimps (Alpheidae) derive their common name from the presence of a sound producing mechanism associated with the first pair of chelipeds, especially in the male. The chela of one member of the pair is enormous. A prominent peglike projection near the base of the moveable finger fits into a socket in the fixed finger. A loud sound is produced when the peg falls into the socket as the mechanism snaps shut. It is believed that the loud report frightens predators. Also, the jet of water displaced from the socket by the peg as it closes has been used to capture prey.

Each member of the second pair of chelipeds of snapping shrimps (alpheids) is long and slender and the wrist segment is subdivided by numerous joints. Usually the rostrum is short. Alpheids are common under boulders on reef flats of the Great Barrier Reef. Numerous species are represented. Some species are free-living. Others live commensally with sea-urchins, annelids, gastropods, and corals.

Genera represented: *Alpheus, Synalpheus, Athanus, Alpheopsis.*

Hinge-beak shrimps (Rhyncocinetidae). The family Rhyncocinetidae contains only one genus, *Rhynchocinetes.* It is characterized by the possession of a rostrum that is hinged to the front of the carapace and moveable in a vertical plane. The antennae are well developed and the eyes large. Colour patterns are complex and bilaterally symmetrical. Specimens are able to change colour to match the background. Some species are found in pools on reef flats. Other species appear to be associated with corals.

Genus represented: *Rhynchocinetes.*

Hump-backed shrimps (Hippolytidae). A characteristic feature of the family Hippolytidae is the presence of a distinct hump on the abdomen. The rostrum is usually long and conspicuous. The wrists of the second pair of legs are subdivided into a number of joints. Most members of the family are free-living and are found under coral boulders and in pools on reef flats. However, some live in association with sponges and anemones. Many are brightly coloured.

Genera represented: *Saron, Thor, Latreutes, Angasia, Hippolyte, Gelastocaris.*

Coral shrimps (Stenopodidae). Three pairs of chelipeds are present in members of this family of shrimps, the third pair being much longer and more robust than the others. Eggs are carried under the well-developed abdomen in females. One species, the banded coral shrimp (*Stenopus hispidus*), is noteworthy because of its habit of removing external parasites from fish which visit the "cleaning stations" that the shrimp sets up. Fish are attracted by the waving of the shrimp's antennae. The shrimps form enduring pair associations. They occur among coral in pools on reef flats and in caves along the margins of reefs.

Genera represented: *Stenopus, Microprosthema.*

The Walking Decapods (Sub-Order Reptantia)

In this group the thoracic appendages are well developed for walking whilst the abdominal appendages are usually poorly developed. The body is usually flattened from top to bottom. The rostrum is poorly developed and the first abdominal segment is smaller than the remainder.

Burrow-Forming Shrimps

Burrow-forming shrimps are walking decapods that are somewhat flattened from top to bottom and are specialized for a burrowing existence. The carapace is not fused with a plate in front of the mouth. Three pairs of chelipeds are present; those of the first pair are better developed than the others. The first abdominal segment is reduced, but the abdomen is elongated and symmetrical and ends in a tail fan.

Ghost shrimps (Callianassidae). The abdomen of ghost shrimps is only feebly calcified and often semi-transparent (hence the common name). It has only a narrow attachment to the thorax. The eyes are small and the first pair of antennae are elongated. The burrows of the common ghost shrimp, *Callianassa australiensis*, are abundant on intertidal sandy areas near mangroves where these encroach on fringing reefs or islands in Great Barrier Reef waters. Small mounds of earth are thrown up around the entrance to each burrow. Underground the burrows may form complex galleries. One of the chelae of the first pair of chelipeds in *C. australiensis* is enlarged and flattened and is used in burrowing. The species is often dug up and used for bait.

Genus represented: *Callianassa.*

Laemediids (Laemediidae) have a longitudinal hinge running along each side of the carapace which permits a flapping movement of the lower portion of the carapace on each side. This portion covers the gills and its movement helps to circulate water, which facilitates oxygenation of the water in the burrow. The bright pink species, *Laemedia healyi,* burrows deeply in mangrove regions and in channels draining these regions where they encroach on fringing reefs and islands in Great Barrier Reef waters. The chelae of the first pair of chelipeds are symmetrically enlarged. In this species the antennae are long, the eyes small, and the anterior surfaces of the limbs bear prominent bristles.

Genus represented: *Laemedia.*

Axiids (Axiidae) have a short carapace, a flattened rostrum, small eyes, and a long, soft abdomen. The tail fan has more segments than is usual in decapod crustaceans. A species of *Neaxius* frequently makes vertical burrows on reef flats of platform reefs and on fringing reefs. It is a scavenger.

Genus represented: *Neaxius.*

Crayfish, Lobsters, and Crabs

Members of the sub-order Reptantia found in Great Barrier Reef waters may be divided into three groups: (1) marine crayfish and lobsters; (2) hermit crabs, squat lobsters, porcelain crabs, and mole crabs; and (3) true crabs.

Marine Crayfish and Lobsters

Marine crayfish and lobsters are large walking decapods that have a heavily calcified carapace which is usually covered with spines. The tail fin is broad and well developed. These crustaceans are renowned throughout the world for their edible qualities. Marine crayfish and lobsters are placed in separate families.

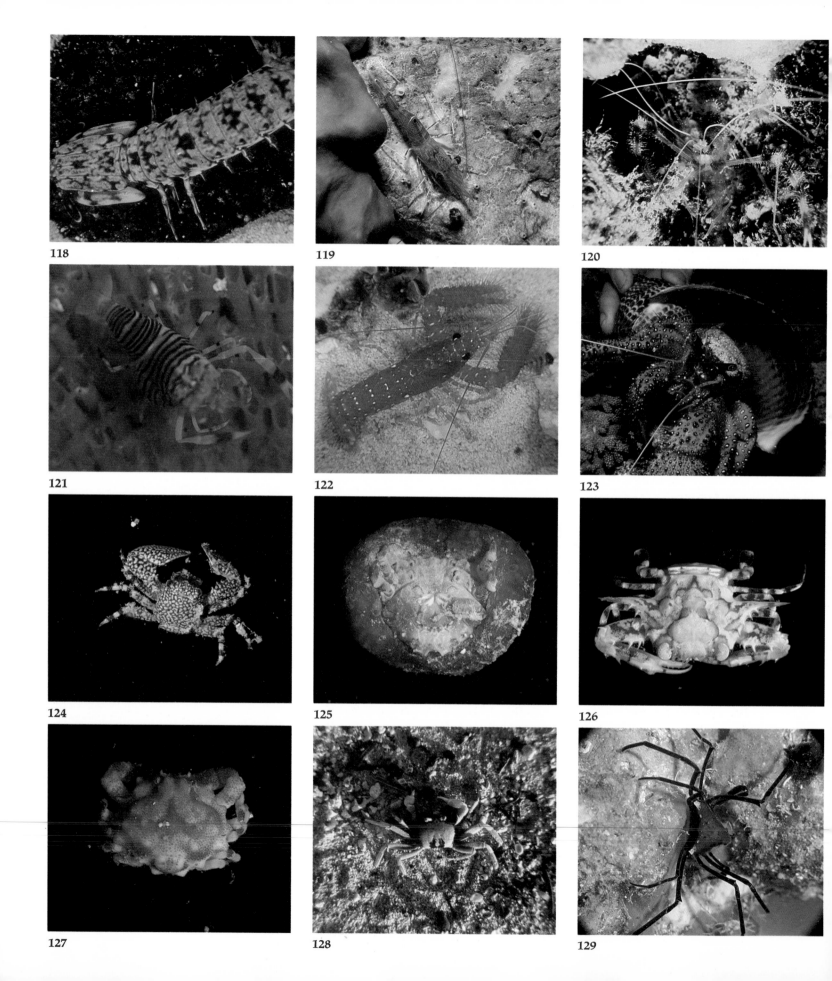

118

119

120

121

122

123

124

125

126

127

128

129

Marine crayfish (Palinuridae). The carapace of the marine crayfish is almost cylindrical and fused with a plate just in front of the mouth. The abdomen is large and flattened and terminates in a broad tail fan. No pincers are present, all of the legs having claws at the tips. Antennae are very long, usually much longer than the body of the crayfish. Marine crayfish are found under coral clumps in lagoons and back-reef areas. At least three species occur in Great Barrier Reef waters. They are highly prized as food but are rarely fished commercially.

Genus represented: *Panulirus.*

Lobsters (Nephropidae) resemble marine crayfish, but the cylindrical carapace does not fuse with the plate in front of the mouth. Another major difference is the presence of large nippers on the first pair of walking legs. The second and third pairs of walking legs also end in chelae. To date, only one species belonging to this family, which is well represented in the North Atlantic, has been found in Great Barrier Reef waters. It is a rather small representative, attaining a length of about 20 centimetres. It occurs in the deeper waters round the edges of reefs and is nocturnal.

Genus represented: *Enoplometopus.*

Hermit Crabs, Squat Lobsters, Porcelain Crabs, and Mole Crabs

Hermit crabs, squat lobsters, and porcelain and mole crabs are walking decapods in which the fifth pair of legs (and sometimes the fourth pair as well), are smaller than the others and are often hidden under the carapace. Pincers are present at the tips of the first pair of walking legs. The carapace does not fuse with the ventral plate in front of the mouth. In some representatives the abdomen is well developed but flexed under the carapace. In others it is soft and carries poorly developed or asymetrically developed appendages.

Hermit crabs (Paguridae). The large abdomen of hermit crabs is soft and spirally twisted so that it can be accommodated in the upper whorls of a discarded gastropod shell. Also, the tail fan appendages are modified for holding the abdomen inside the shell. The anterior part of the carapace is hard, and the eyes are borne on stalks. The chelipeds are large and frequently of unequal size, the larger being used to block the entrance when the crab withdraws into the protective gastropod shell that it acquires as a home. The first two pairs of walking legs are strongly developed, but the last two pairs are reduced. The anterior parts of the bodies of hermit crabs are usually hairy. Hermit crabs are found in many habitats on the Great Barrier

Facing page
Illustration 118
The mantis shrimp, *Gonodactylus graphurus.*

Illustration 119
A palaemonid shrimp.

Illustration 120
The coral shrimp, *Stenopus hispidus.*

Illustration 121
A gnathophyllid shrimp belonging to the genus *Gnathophyllum* living on the organ-pipe coral, *Tubipora musica.*

Illustration 122
The coral lobster, *Enoplometopus occidentalis.*

Illustration 123
The spotted hermit crab, *Dardanus megistos.*

Illustration 124
The half crab, *Petrolisthes lamarcki.*

Illustration 125
A sponge crab belonging to the genus *Petalomera.*

Illustration 126
A portunid crab (Portunidae).

Illustration 127
A leucosid crab (Leucosiidae).

Illustration 128
The ghost crab, *Ocypode ceratophthalma.*

Illustration 129
A false spider crab belonging to the genus *Halicarcinus.*

Reef and are particularly common among rubble on reef flats. One species, *Paguritta harmsi*, inhabits old worm tubes found in coral colonies.

Genera represented: *Paguritta, Aniculus, Clibanarius, Eupagurus, Calcinus, Pagurus.*

Land hermit crabs (Coenobitidae) resemble true hermit crabs but possess gill chambers that have a very rich blood supply and can utilize atmospheric oxygen. Some are able to remain out of water for months. However, they have gills and can make use of oxygen dissolved in sea water when required to do so. Most are nocturnal and live in burrows. One species, *Coenobita perlatus*, occurs on cays in the Swain Reefs area and in the Capricorn and Bunker groups, but land hermit crabs are not found elsewhere in the Great Barrier Reef area despite their abundance in other parts of the tropical Indian and West Pacific Ocean regions.

Genus represented: *Coenobita.*

Spotted hermit crabs (Diogenidae) are large (up to 20 centimetres in length) and have their entire body pigmented, unlike true hermit crabs whose anterior parts alone are pigmented. The prominent abdomen appears to be unsegmented. They frequently occupy discarded tun-shells (see chapter 11).

Genus represented: *Dardanus.*

Squat lobsters (Galatheidae). The oval carapace of members of the family Galatheidae bears a prominent pointed rostrum. The chelipeds are long and characteristically extend in front of the animal. The fifth pair of walking legs are reduced, and the tailed abdomen is flexed under the carapace. Species of squat lobsters found in Great Barrier Reef waters are small and usually occur as commensals on feather-stars.

Genera represented: *Galathea, Allogalathea.*

Porcelain crabs (Porcellanidae) have long antennae, prominent chelipeds which fold upon themselves like a penknife, and an abdomen which, although normally tucked under the carapace, bears a tail. In addition, the fifth pair of walking legs are greatly reduced. Porcelain crabs are generally small. Some live among the tentacles of anemones; others are free-living and are usually found under slabs of beach rock or under coral boulders on reefs.

Genera represented: *Petrolisthes, Neopetrolisthes.*

Mole crabs (Hippidae). The elongate carapace of mole crabs is oval in outline. The first pair of legs are unspecialized, but the second, third, and fourth pairs are specialized for shovelling, the last joint being curved and flattened. The abdomen is tucked under the body. Mole crabs swim backwards and can burrow rapidly; they spend much of their time just below the surface of the substratum.

Genus represented: *Hippa.*

True Crabs

True crabs are walking decapods that usually scuttle sideways. The body is flattened from top to bottom, and the carapace is fused with a ventral plate in front of the mouth. Antennae are small and the eyes are variously developed. Each of the first pair of legs bears a prominent pincer. The abdomen is reduced, flattened, and tucked under the thorax. Numerous species of true crab occur on the Great Barrier Reef.

Sponge crabs (Dromiidae) have a domed, furry carapace and a prominent abdomen. They cover their bodies with a piece of living sponge or with ascidians, leaving only the anterior parts exposed. Initially the covering material is cut and fashioned by the red-tipped chelipeds. It is held in position by the last two pairs of walking legs, which are modified for this purpose. Sponge crabs are found among rubble on reef flats.

Genus represented: *Petalomera.*

Spanner crabs (Raninidae). In members of the family Raninidae the carapace is elongated but the abdomen is not covered. The tip of each of the chelipeds resembles a spanner. Particularly is this so in the case of the large, reddish spanner crab (*Ranina ranina*) found on the Great Barrier Reef. This crab is usually found partially buried in coral sand with only the anterior region protruding. Water is drawn into the gill chamber through an opening found near the junction of the abdomen and thorax at the bases of the last pair of walking legs.

Genus represented: *Ranina.*

Cancrids (Cancridae). The oval or hexagonal carapace of cancrids is usually broader than it is long, with an arched and serrated anterior margin. The rostrum is very short or absent altogether.

Genus represented: *Kraussia.*

Swimming crabs (Portunidae). Members of the large family Portunidae have broad carapaces that are often elongated laterally and bear prominent spines. The fifth pair of legs are typically flattened to form paddle-like structures used for swimming and sometimes for burrowing. Some species, such as the blue swimmer (*Portunus pelagicus*), the blood-spotted crab (*P. sanguinolentus*), and the mud-crab (*Scylla serrata*), attain large sizes and are highly prized for their edible qualities. Other species are small and some are commensals. The harlequin crab (*Lissocarcinus orbicularis*), for example, lives on and in the bodies of holothurians. Its fifth pair of legs is not modified for swimming. Free-living members of the family occur in burrows or under coral boulders on reef flats of the Great Barrier Reef. Species of the genus *Thalamita* are among the commonest of crabs found on the reef flats.

Genera represented: *Thalamita, Portunus, Lissocarcinus, Caphyra, Scylla.*

Dark-fingered crabs (Xanthidae) constitute the largest family of crabs found on the Great Barrier Reef. A great variation in size, appearance, and habits is shown by the various species represented. Almost all have black tips to the chelipeds, which are always strongly developed. The carapace is broad, and the eyes are well separated. The abdomen is tucked under the body. In some species the carapace is smooth; in others it is knobbled. Some are highly coloured, some patterned, and others drab. Many species are nocturnal, but others move about actively during daylight hours. Their apparent freedom from pre-dation at such times may stem from the fact that many are highly toxic (see chapter 14). Some species live commensally with corals.

Genera represented: *Trapezia, Tetralia, Cymo, Domecia, Chlorodiella, Liomera, Actaea, Etisus, Eriphia, Lophozozymus, Ozius, Atergatis, Pilumnus.*

Pea crabs (Pinnotheridae) have membranous and globular carapaces. They usually live in association with other animals, such as bivalves and tube-forming worms, extracting a share of the minute organisms brought in with the water currents created by their hosts.

Genera represented: *Pinnixa, Xanthasia.*

Box and sand crabs (Calappidae). Water enters the gill chambers of box and sand crabs through a channel found below the eyes. The large, laterally compressed chelipeds can be folded snugly against the front of the body. In the box crabs (*Calappa* species) the slender walking legs can be folded under lateral expansions of the carapace. The right cheliped of box crabs carries a toothed structure used to open the shells of gastropods upon which the crab preys. Hermit crabs living inside empty gastropod shells also fall victim to box crabs, which are fairly common in shallow water on reef flats. In sand crabs (*Matuta* species) the carapace is almost circular in outline. The segments of the four walking legs are flattened and used for swimming or burrowing in sand. A pair of lateral spines are present. Sand crabs occur in sandy areas of reef flats.

Genera represented: *Calappa, Matuta.*

Pebble crabs (Leucosiidae). As with box and sand crabs, water enters the gill chambers of pebble crabs through a channel found below the eyes. Pebble crabs have a globular carapace which is somewhat pointed at the front, where the eyes and antennae are found. The chelipeds are well developed. These crabs occur among rubble in shallow water areas of reef flats.

Genera represented: *Philyra, Leucosia.*

Spider crabs (Majidae) have a carapace that is roughly triangular in outline. Their walking legs are long and slender, giving them a somewhat spider-like appearance. Water is taken into each gill chamber through a channel found at the base of each cheliped. Carapace and legs possess hair-like processes that assist in the attachment of sedentary organisms such as algae, which are placed in position by the chelipeds and which serve to camouflage the crab. Several species of spider crabs occur among algae and rubble on reef flats.

Genera represented: *Hyastenus, Camposcia, Oncinopus.*

Parthenopids (Parthenopidae) have a carapace that is triangular in outline and covered with protuberances. A characteristic feature of the chelae of this family is the possession of a moveable finger which is bent at an angle towards the side on which the fixed finger is found. Antennae are very slender and the eyes can be withdrawn into small circular orbits.

Genus represented: *Daldorfia.*

Stilt-eyed crabs (Ocypodidae). A characteristic of the family Ocypodidae is the presence of eyes on long stalks. The paired stalks originate near the centre of the anterior edge of the carapace, and each can be accommodated in a groove that runs along the anterior margin of the carapace. These crabs excavate burrows. Those of the ghost crabs (*Ocypode* species) are deep and found in sand well above the waterline on coral cays and beaches of continental islands. Other species belonging to this family occur among eel-grass when this occurs on reef flats. Members of this family can run with surprising rapidity. In the males of some species (e.g., fiddler crabs of the genus *Uca*), one or both of the chelipeds are considerably enlarged and used for courtship display or ritualistic fighting.

Genera represented: *Ocypode, Uca, Macrophthalmus.*

Shore crabs (Grapsidae) have a rather squarish carapace and powerful legs which enable them to scuttle around rocks and boulders along the shore-line, where they typically occur. The beach rock of some coral cays is a favoured habitat for species of *Grapsus.* Species of

Metapograpsus and *Sesarma* are common among mangroves, which occasionally invade reef flats.

Genera represented: *Grapsus, Percnon, Metapograpsus, Sesarma.*

Hapalocarcinids (Hapalocarcinidae) have a convex carapace which is twice as long as it is wide. The abdomen is wide and does not fold tightly under the carapace as in most crabs. In the female the abdomen forms a wide brood pouch for eggs and larvae. Males are tiny, being just over 1 millimetre in length. Adult crabs live in cavities in branching corals (see chapter 17). They feed on plankton carried to the imprisoned crabs by water currents created by the beating of special appendages.

Genus represented: *Hapalocarcinus.*

False spider crabs (Hymenosomatidae) are small, often strikingly coloured crabs that are usually found associated with algae. They resemble the true spider crabs in general appearance.

Genera represented: *Trigonoplax, Eulamena.*

Eumedonids (Eumedonidae) have a rhomboidal or subpentagonal carapace which is remarkably smooth.

Genera represented: *Ceratocarcinus, Eumedonus.*

Soldier crabs (Mictyridae). The bodies of soldier crabs are spherical and mounted on rather spindly legs. *Mictyris longicarpus*, the common soldier crab, is renowned for its habit of forming large groups or "armies" at low tide on sandy areas along the coastline. Some of these sandy areas abut on fringing reefs of the Great Barrier Reef.

Genus represented: *Mictyris.*

11

The Molluscs

Thousands of different species of mollusc occur in Great Barrier Reef waters. As a group, members of the phylum Mollusca are readily recognizable. They are soft-bodied forms which, apart from a few deep-sea species, show no trace of the segmentation so characteristic of polychaete and oligochaete worms and of crustaceans. Typically, the undersurface of the body possesses a muscular organ known as the *foot*, since it is usually used in locomotion (see fig. 12). The upper

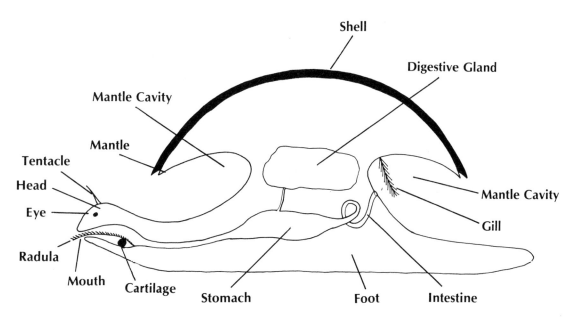

Figure 12. A section through a generalized mollusc showing typical molluscan features.

surface is covered by skin referred to as the *mantle*. A fold of the mantle projects round the mollusc like the eaves of a roof. Usually a protective shell, secreted by the mantle, is present. Gills occur in the space between the mantle and the foot, and in many species an edge of the mantle is drawn out to form one or two tubular structures known as *siphons*. A head which carries the anterior opening of the alimentary canal (the mouth) and which bears prominent sense organs such as eyes and tentacles in many species is situated anteriorly. The mouth opens into a chamber, the *buccal cavity*, where a typically molluscan structure occurs. This structure, the *radula*, resembles a flexible file that can be protruded through the mouth. The radula, with its numerous teeth, is pulled back and forth over a cartilaginous block situated in the floor of the buccal cavity. The tubular alimentary canal is associated with accessory structures such as a large digestive gland, which is frequently coiled. It and other internal organs such as the heart are housed in a region of the body known as the *visceral mass*. Often the alimentary canal is bent upon itself so that the anus opens anteriorly. The sexes are usually separate, and planktonic larval stages are usually found in the life cycle.

Chitons (Class Polyplacophora)

The chitons are characterized by the possession of a shell divided into eight overlapping valves which protects the upper surface of an animal that is usually markedly flattened (see fig. 13). An area of the mantle known as the *girdle* surrounds the eight valves. A broad, muscular foot is found on the lower surface of the animal. A groove separates the foot from the head, which lacks prominent sense organs but bears the mouth. Another groove separating the foot from the encircling mantle accommodates a number of gills. The anal opening is situated posteriorly in the mid-line. Sexes are usually separate, and there is a planktonic larval stage in the life history.

Many chitons are nocturnal, retreating to crevices and depressions in coral rubble and beach rock during daylight hours and emerging at night to forage for food. They use a well-developed radula to rasp algae from the substratum. A few species burrow into semi-consolidated rubble, presumably in a search for boring algae.

The families of chitons occurring on the Great Barrier Reef are listed below.

Cryptoplacs (Cryptoplacidae). In the family Cryptoplacidae the eight granule-bearing valves are reduced and separated one from another, but the girdle is large, fleshy, and covered with spicules. The various

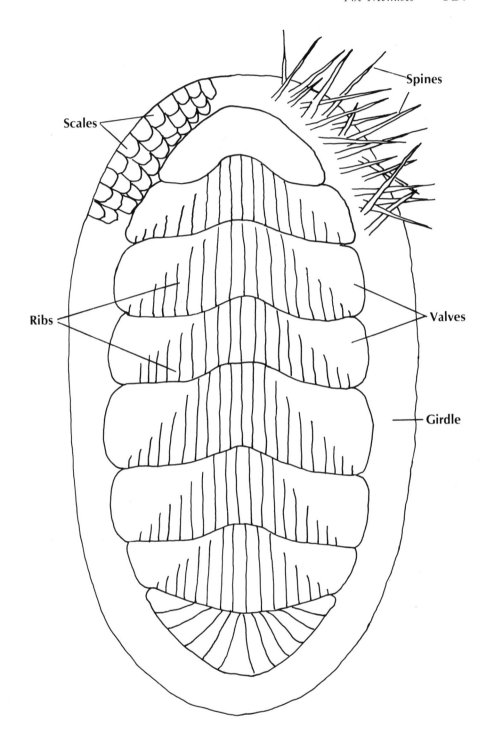

Figure 13. The upper or dorsal surface of a generalized chiton. Spines are shown on one part of the girdle and scales on another part.

species belonging to this family have a somewhat wormlike appearance. Specimens found on the Great Barrier Reef occur under coral boulders or in burrows in dead coral.

Genus represented: *Cryptoplax.*

True chitons (Chitonidae). Members of the large family of true chitons have comblike teeth on the insertion plates of the valves. The girdle is covered with scales or calcareous spines. Several species occur in Great Barrier Reef waters. Some of the larger species, including *Acanthopleura gemmata*, which attains a length of about 10 centimetres, occur in crevices or completely exposed on the upper surfaces of dead coral boulders.

Some genera represented: *Acanthopleura, Lucilina, Schizochiton.*

Callistochitons (Callistochitonidae). The anterior and posterior valves of callistochitons bear radiating ribs. The girdle is covered with scales. Specimens found on the Great Barrier Reef are usually small — only about 1 centimetre in length — and occur under coral boulders that are embedded in coral sand or rubble.

Genus represented: *Lophochiton.*

Gastropods (Class Gastropoda)

Figure 14. A gastropod mollusc showing external features.

Most gastropods have a well-developed head which bears prominent tentacles and eyes (see fig. 14). Much of the visceral mass, particularly the part that contains the digestive gland, is usually coiled into a spiral and accommodated in a single-chambered shell, which is also coiled. The shell is composed of a chitinous layer (the *periostracum*) on the outside and a calcareous layer on the inside. The periostracum and part of the inner calcareous layer are secreted by the edge of the mantle

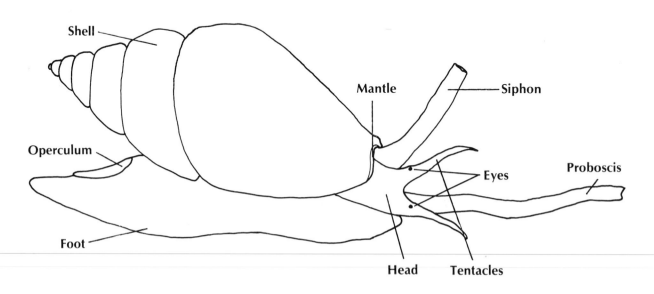

at the entrance to the shell. However, the whole surface of the mantle in contact with the shell secretes much of the calcareous material. Often the muscular foot, which is used both in locomotion and as an anchoring device, bears a structure known as the *operculum*, which can effectively seal the entrance to the shell. Structural features of the gastropod shell are depicted in figure 15. Reduction of the shell occurs in some species, and it is absent altogether in others.

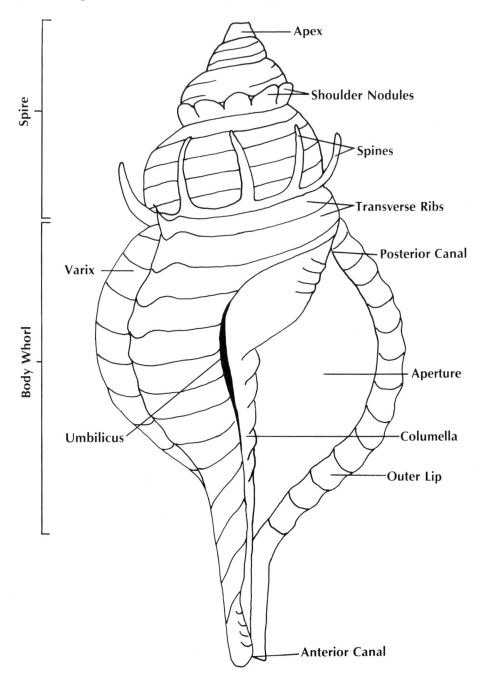

Figure 15. A generalized gastropod shell showing features used in descriptions of the shell.

In many species of gastropod a cavity, the *mantle cavity*, containing a gill or gills and an anal opening is situated above and behind the head as a result of the visceral mass twisting through 180 degrees above the foot. In others the mantle cavity is present on the right side as a result of the partial reversal of this process. In some species the mantle cavity has disappeared. Usually the sexes are separate, but some hermaphrodite species are found. After fertilization of the eggs, which may occur internally or externally, the eggs usually become enclosed in jellylike material.

Modifications of the foot or mantle edges or of both enable some gastropods to swim. In one large group of gastropods known as nudibranchs there is no shell and a mass of gills arises from an area on the upper surface of the animal. A few gastropods (the pulmonates) have a mantle cavity that can function as a lung, enabling them to breathe air.

Most of the gastropod families occurring on the Great Barrier Reef are discussed below. However, the list is incomplete, and representatives of additional families will undoubtedly be found there. Descriptions of the various families are usually based on features of the shell.

False limpets (Fissurellidae). The conical shells of false limpets usually have a hole at the apex of the shell or a marginal slit or notch at the anterior margin of the shell. In the shield-shells, the shell is partially or completely covered by folds of the mantle, but in other representatives of the family the conical shell encloses the soft parts of the animal. False limpets are herbivorous and are found on and under coral boulders.

Genera represented: *Scutus, Fissurella.*

Abalones (Haliotidae). The shell of an abalone is flat and coiled with a tiny spire and a greatly expanded body whorl. A row of holes occurs near the edge of the shell, and the rim is inturned. There is a nacreous lining to the shell. The animal that carries the shell is large in relation to shell size and has eyes, numerous tentacles, and a thick, muscular foot which adheres firmly to the substratum. Abalones are algal feeders. Several species occur on and under dead coral boulders and in crevices of reefs on the Great Barrier Reef. None of these grows as big as their southern relatives, which are exploited commercially for abalone meat. When breeding, reproductive products are shed directly into the water, where fertilization occurs. The larval stage is pelagic.

Genus represented: *Haliotis.*

Wide-mouthed shells (Stomatellidae) resemble small abalones, but the shells lack the row of perforations near the margin and are less flattened. At least three species belonging to this family occur in Great Barrier Reef waters.

Genera represented: *Stomatella, Stomatia, Pseudostomatella.*

Top-shells (Trochidae). Although the shells of members of the family Trochidae are often toplike, they are frequently twisted into a turban shape. The bulk of the shell is nacreous, but it is coloured and ornamented externally. Frequently the columella is notched. A thin, horny operculum is attached to the foot of the animal housed within the shell. Algae provide food for top-shells. Numerous species are found on the Great Barrier Reef, and they occur from the shores of sand cays to the deeper water at the edges of reefs. They range in size from tiny, almost microscopic forms to giants 12 centimetres or more in diameter such as the trochus shell of commerce (*Trochus niloticus*), which was formerly collected in large numbers and used in the manufacture of buttons. Some species shed eggs into the sea water, but others enclose the fertilized eggs in a gelatinous egg mass, where the early stages of development occur.

Some genera represented: *Trochus, Monodonta, Calliostoma, Clanculus, Chrysostoma.*

Turban-shells (Turbinidae). Usually the shell is turban-shaped and ornamented and coloured in various ways. The bulk of the shell is nacreous as in top-shells. Turban-shells can be distinguished from top-shells by the presence of a heavy, limy operculum, by the rounded aperture to the shell, and by the smooth columella. The opercula are often used in jewellery, and the shell of the giant green snail (*Turbo marmoratus*) — over 20 centimetres in length — is used in the manufacture of mother-of-pearl articles such as buckles and handles for utensils. Several species of turban-shell are found on and under coral boulders and among dead coral rubble on reefs. All species are herbivorous. Gelatinous egg masses are produced, and the young hatch as free-swimming larvae.

Genera represented: *Turbo, Astraea.*

Wheel-shells (Liotiidae) have small, flattened, turbanlike shells. An operculum which is partly calcareous and partly horny may block the essentially circular aperture to the shell. Wheel-shells occur under coral boulders and among algae on reefs but are not well known, probably because of their small size.

Genera represented: *Liotina, Liotia.*

Nerites (Neritidae). The shell of nerites has a large body whorl, a low spire, and a prominent columellar shelf adjacent to the semicircular opening to the shell. There is a heavy, limy operculum. Frequently nerites are gregarious and intertidal. During the day they tend to congregate in crevices and under dead coral boulders, but they move about actively at night. They feed on algae. Several species of nerite are found in waters of the Great Barrier Reef. Some species possess a planktonic larval stage, but in other species development is direct.

Genera represented: *Nerita, Neritina.*

Limpets (Patellidae). The soft parts of limpets are enclosed within conical shells that often have radiating ribs. A broad, muscular foot enables the limpet to adhere firmly to rocks. Limpets are essentially intertidal animals and in Great Barrier Reef waters are found on the surfaces of dead coral boulders, particularly those found on reef crests. They are herbivorous.

Some genera represented: *Patella, Cellana.*

Periwinkles (Littorinidae) are the highest climbers of the littoral molluscs and in Great Barrier Reef waters are found on dead coral boulders tossed up on coral cays, on beach rock, and on mangrove trees associated with some coral reefs. The shells are loosely coiled and the aperture is circular in outline. All periwinkles are herbivores and browse on algae.

Genera represented: *Nodilittorina, Littorina.*

Clusterwinks (Planaxidae). As the common name implies, members of the family Planaxidae are usually found in groups. They occur intertidally and are common on beach rock associated with coral cays. The shell is elongate and spirally ribbed with an elliptical aperture. Clusterwinks are herbivorous.

Genus represented: *Planaxis.*

Sundial-shells (Architectonidae). The characteristic shell of the family Architectonidae assumes the form of a flattened cone. The inner whorls of the shell can be seen through the widely open umbilicus. A horny operculum is present. Sundial-shells are carnivorous and in Great Barrier Reef waters are usually found in association with cnidarians, particularly zoanthids, upon which they feed.

Genera represented: *Architectonica, Philippia, Heliacus.*

Creepers (Cerithiidae) have solid, elongate, many-whorled shells. The aperture is ovoid, and there is a prominent, frequently upturned, anterior canal. The horny operculum has an excentric nucleus. Many species of creeper occur on coral sand and among coral rubble in Great Barrier Reef waters. Some species are moderately large (6–10 centimetres in length), others relatively small. Some are brightly coloured, and some bear nodules on the whorls. They feed on algae and micro-organisms found among detritus. Strings of eggs encased in gelatinous material are laid by females. Free-swimming larvae hatch from the eggs.

Some genera represented: *Clypeomorus, Rhinoclavis, Cerithium, Ischnocerithium.*

Mud whelks (Potamididae) have shells that resemble those of large creepers, but the anterior canal is short and the horny operculum has a central nucleus. As indicated by their common name, these molluscs live in muddy situations. In Great Barrier Reef waters such situations are found on several fringing reefs and on some platform reefs located north of Cairns. Mud whelks are usually exposed at low tide, when their jerky movements attract attention. They are edible; some species were consumed in large numbers by Aborigines, as evidenced by the abundance of their shells in middens found along the Queensland coast. Like creepers, mud whelks feed on algae and detrital material.

Genera represented: *Terebralia, Telescopium.*

Triphoras (Triphoridae). The shells of triphoras resemble those of creepers but are coiled to the left so that the aperture is to the left side of the long axis of the shell. Most species are small (less than 2 centimetres in length) and prey on sponges.

Genera represented: *Triphora, Notosinister.*

Worm-shells (Vermetidae). As the common name implies, members of the family Vermetidae have shells that resemble the calcareous tubes of some marine worms. Initially, the shell is spirally coiled, but as the animal grows the tubular calcareous material that is deposited may not associate with the spirally coiled material formed earlier but may become attached instead to the substratum, to corals, to sponges, or to the shells of other molluscs including those of other worm shells. The tube of one species of worm shell, *Vermetus maximus*, may attain a diameter of 3 centimetres and a length of over 20 centimetres. Members of the family filter minute organisms from sea water.

Genera represented: *Serpulorbis, Vermetus.*

Screw-shells (Turritellidae). Elongate, tapering, many-whorled shells resembling screws are characteristic of the family Turritellidae. The aperture is circular and the columella is smooth. Like members of the family Vermetidae, screw-shells are filter feeders.

Genus represented: *Turritella.*

Strombs (Strombidae) are among the most abundant, colourful, and spectacular of Great Barrier Reef molluscs. The porcellanous shells have a large body whorl, a prominent spire, and an elongated aperture. The

polished outer lip of the shell is frequently expanded and often carries projections. A characteristic notch through which the head and eyes may protrude is present near the anterior end of the outer lip. The elongated foot carries a curved, jagged-edged operculum. When thrust into the sand, this acts as an anchor and provides purchase during locomotion. The well-developed eyes are borne on stalks. Strombs are generally found on sand patches and among coral rubble on reef flats. They are primarily herbivores but to some extent are also scavengers. Eggs are laid in long, sand-encrusted tubes of jelly. The young hatch as free-swimming larvae.

Genera represented: *Lambis, Strombus.*

Wentletraps (Epitoniidae). The shell is many-whorled, frequently elongate, and often loosely coiled. Riblike structures called *varices*, which represent successive positions of the outer lip of the circular aperture, are usually prominent on the whorls. The wentletraps are carnivorous and are usually found in association with cnidarians, particularly anemones, upon which they feed. Eggs are laid in strings.

Genera represented: *Epitonium, Cirsotrema.*

Rissoids (Rissoidae). The large rissoid familiy comprises species that are usually very small. The shells are conical, often many-whorled. Apertures are rounded and often thickened. Sculpturing and colouring vary with the species. Rissoids are herbivorous and are often found living on algae growing on dead coral boulders.

Genera represented: *Moerchiella, Rissoina.*

Fig-shells (Ficidae). The thin shell of members of the family Ficidae bears a resemblance to a fig in shape. There is a large, spirally ribbed body whorl with a long tapering anterior canal, but the spire of the shell is almost non-existent. There is no operculum to block the large aperture to the shell. The foot is large, and the animal can move rapidly. The narrow head carries tentacles and eyes; the mouth is found at the tip of a long, extensible proboscis. Fig-shells feed on sea-urchins and other echinoderms. They are occasionally found in sandy areas on reefs.

Genus represented: *Ficus.*

Tun-shells (Tonnidae). The term *tun* is a reference to the fancied resemblance of tun-shells to the ancient vessels used for the storage of wine. Members of this family have thin shells which may attain large sizes. The body whorl is large and bulbous, and the aperture is large. The spire is short. There is no operculum. Prominent spiral ribs occur on the shell, which is covered with a thin periostracum. The animal moves over coral sand and rubble on a broad foot which is lobed anteriorly. Two prominent tentacles with eyes at their bases are borne

Facing page
The chromodorid, *Chromodoris coi.*

on the head. There is a long, cylindrical proboscis used when attacking bivalves and echinoderms on which they prey. When at rest, tun-shells lie buried in the sand with only the tip of their respiratory siphon visible. Tun-shells pass through pelagic larval stages.

Genera represented: *Tonna, Malea.*

Cowries (Cypraeidae). Numerous species of cowrie occur on the Great Barrier Reef. Cowries have a peculiar shell. During its development the body whorl comes to enclose the spire and the outer lip turns inward, giving rise to a long, narrow aperture. The body whorl in the vicinity of the aperture becomes flattened, and teeth form on the borders of the aperture. The mantle is reflected over the shell as two lobes, and constant rubbing by the mantle imparts a gloss to the shell which is usually prettily marked and coloured. The mantle carries tubular projections. There is a well-developed head which bears tentacles and eyes. Most cowries appear to be herbivorous, but some may browse on small animals found attached to coral boulders and rubble. Cowries are nocturnal, hiding during the day under coral boulders and in crevices. Egg capsules, each containing numerous eggs, are laid in a gelatinous mass under coral boulders. In some species there is a free-living larval stage which spends a few days in the plankton before settling; in other species development is direct. Cowries are much used as ornaments. Some of the so-called money cowries were used as a primitive form of currency by the inhabitants of some Pacific islands.

Genus represented: *Cypraea.*

Spindle cowries (Ovulidae) have shells that resemble those of cowries except that the anterior and posterior ends are usually drawn out and the mantle is usually flattened. Spindle cowries feed on soft corals and gorgonians, and frequently the shells have the same colour as the animal upon which they feed. Several species of spindle shell occur on the Great Barrier Reef.

Some genera represented: *Ovula, Volva, Primovula, Calpurnus.*

Trivias (Triviidae) resemble small cowries, but their shells can be distinguished from cowrie shells by the presence of fine ribs (extensions of the apertural teeth) which pass around the sides of the shell to link with a longitudinal groove on top of the shell. Some specimens are found on the undersurfaces of dead coral boulders, others are associated with living corals.

Genera represented: *Trivirostra, Ellatrivia.*

Sand-snails (Naticidae) have a smooth and globular shell with a large body whorl and a tiny spire. There is frequently an umbilicus near the semicircular aperture. The voluminous foot, which can expand to cover the shell, carries an operculum which may be calcareous or horny. Sand-snails are carnivorous, feeding principally on bivalves. They use their radula, aided by an acidic secretion, to bore through the shell of their prey, which is then partially digested before being removed from its shell. Several species of sand snail occur in sandy areas of reefs. All move just below the surface of the sand, and their tracks are readily visible when intertidal sandy stretches are bared at low tide. Some species lay eggs enclosed in collarlike ribbons which are impregnated with sand.

Some genera represented: *Polinices, Natica, Notocochlis.*

Tritons (Cymatiidae). The solidly built shells of tritons have varices (representing earlier positions of the margin of the aperture) on the whorls, which are usually spirally ribbed. There is a short anterior canal to the oral aperture. The outer lip is thickened and bears teeth. Ridges are usually present on the columella. A tough periostracum is present, and a horny operculum is borne on the foot. Tritons are found among corals and coral rubble. All are carnivorous, preying on different species ranging from echinoderms to ascidians. The shell of the giant triton, *Charonia tritonis*, grows up to approximately 50 centimetres in length; this species is one of the largest gastropods known. It preys on starfish and sea-cucumbers. Tritons lay their egg capsules on the undersurfaces of coral boulders.

Some genera represented: *Charonia, Lampusia, Distorsio, Ranularia, Septa.*

Dwarf tritons (Colubrariidae). The shells of dwarf tritons are elgonate and have high spires, with varices on the whorls. The rather narrow aperture has a short anterior canal and is notched at the rear. A horny operculum is carried on the foot. Representatives of the family are occasionally found on reefs, but little is known about their general biology.

Genus represented: *Colubraria.*

Frog-shells (Bursidae) differ from tritons in that they have a posterior canal to the aperture, and the heavy shells have a knobbly appearance suggestive of the warts on the skin of some frogs and toads. Some frog-shells grow to a large size — up to 30 centimetres in length. They occur among corals and coral rubble. All are carnivorous, some feeding on marine worms. Egg capsules are laid on the undersurfaces of coral boulders.

Some genera represented: *Bursa, Tutufa.*

131

132

133

134

135

136

137

138

139

140

141

142

Helmet-shells (Cassidae). The characteristic shells of members of the family Cassidae resemble ancient Roman helmets. The shells are solid and porcellanous with a globose body whorl and short spire. The aperture is long and narrow. It is bounded on one side by the thickened outer lip which is often toothed on its inner edge. The opposite lip of the aperture is often toothed and may border a shieldlike area which lies over the columella. The outer surfaces of the shells may be studded or smooth. The large muscular foot carries a horny operculum. A large head carrying tentacles with eyes at their bases is present. Several species occur in sandy regions of reefs. Echinoids (sea-urchins, sand-dollars and heart-urchins) form the prey of cassids. A paralysing toxin is produced within the salivary glands of cassids and squirted over echinoids encountered. The cassids then bore a hole through the hard corona of their immobilized prey and digest the soft parts. Normally, cassids burrow in the sand where their prey occurs. They are medium to large animals, and the shells of some have been used for carving cameos. Large egg masses containing numerous egg capsules are laid; a great part of development occurs within the capsules.

Some genera represented: *Cassis, Phalium, Cypraecassis, Casmaria.*

Thin-plated shells (Lamellariidae). Although the shells of members of the family Lamellariidae resemble those of sand-snails in shape, they are thin and fragile with a depressed spire, large body whorl, and large aperture. Moreover, they are normally concealed by the mantles. In one species occurring commonly on the Great Barrier Reef, the upper surface of the animal is covered with black, berry-like elevations and appears like some form of slug. Soft corals, hydroids, and colonial ascidians are among the prey taken by these carnivores.

Genera represented: *Lamellaria, Coriocella.*

Murex-shells (Muricidae) are among the most spectacular of coral reef gastropods. The shells have a prominent spire, and the whorls carry varices. These in turn carry spines, frills, or nodules. The aperture is ovoid, and the interior of the shell porcellanous. The anterior canal is well developed and frequently elongated. The outer lip of the aperture bears folds or teeth. A horny operculum is present. Numerous species, covering a range of sizes, occur on the Great Barrier Reef. All are carnivorous, and most appear to prey on other molluscs. These they attack by boring a hole in the shell of the victim. Acid secreted by glands in the foot assists in the boring operation, which frequently takes three to four hours to complete. A number of eggs are laid in each of several egg capsules by the female murex shell. The planktonic larval stage that hatches from the egg is usually of short duration.

Facing page
Illustration 131
A chiton, belonging to the family Ischnochitonidae.

Illustration 132
The abalone, *Haliotis asinina.*

Illustration 133
The encrusted shell of a trochid, *Tectus pyramus.*

Illustration 134
The base of a sundial shell, *Architectonica* sp.

Illustration 135
A creeper, *Cerithium novaehollandiae.*

Illustration 136
The spider stromb, *Lambis lambis.*

Illustration 137
A wentletrap, *Epitonium* sp.

Illustration 138
A fig-shell, *Ficus subintermedia.*

Illustration 139
The spotted cowry, *Cypraea vitellus.*

Illustration 140
Two egg cowries, *Ovula ovum.*

Illustration 141
The giant triton, *Charonia tritonis.*

Illustration 142
The red helmet, *Cypraecassis rufa.*

143

144

145

146

147

148

149

150

151

152

153

154

Some genera represented: *Murex, Chicoreus, Acupurpura, Homalocantha.*

Purples (Thaididae) are closely related to murex shells, but their solid shells have relatively shorter spires and larger body whorls. Also varices are absent and the anterior canal is usually short. The outer lip to the aperture may be strongly toothed. Numerous species, most of them intertidal, are found on reefs. Purples are carnivores; barnacles, molluscs, and coral polyps are among the prey taken. When molested, a purple fluid is usually released from a special gland; hence the common name of the family.

Some genera represented: *Thais, Mancinella, Morula, Drupa, Cronia, Drupella.*

Coral-shells (Magilidae). The common name applied to members of the family Magilidae stems from their close association with corals and other cnidarians, such as anemones. There is great variation in shell shape. The shells of some species have a low spire, a bulbous body whorl with a flaring outer lip, and a prominent anterior canal. They resemble turnips and are sometimes known as turnip-shells. The shells of other species have apertures that are extended to form tubes. After vacating the original shell, which becomes enclosed in the limy skeleton of the host coral, the animal moves along the tube so as to be close to its open end. It is believed that coral-shells feed on the tissues of their hosts. Although some species are enclosed by the skeletal material of corals, other species are found only on the outside of coral colonies.

Some genera represented: *Rapa, Coralliophila, Quoyula.*

Dove-shells (Pyrenidae) are small and have solid, prettily marked shells. The spire is usually prominent, the whorls smooth, and the aperture narrow. The columella is grooved, and the outer lip carries teeth on its inner margin. Dove-shells are found in sandy, algae-covered, and rubbly areas of coral reefs. Some species tend to cluster under and around dead coral boulders. They are herbivorous.

Some genera represented: *Pyrene, Mitrella.*

Dog whelks (Nasariidae). The shells of dog whelks are solid and ovoid with a moderately long spire. They have an oval aperture with an outer lip that is usually thickened and toothed. The anterior canal is widely open and there is usually a prominent callus on the columella. A horny operculum is carried on the muscular foot, which is forked at the front. The head bears prominent tentacles, and there is a well-developed proboscis. Most species are small (2–3 centimetres in length) and occur intertidally in sandy areas of reef flats. They

Facing page
Illustration 143
An operculum blocking the opening of the shell of a murex-shell, *Chicoreus ramosus.*

Illustration 144
A purple, *Morula spinosa.*

Illustration 145
A dove-shell, *Pyrene varians.*

Illustration 146
A harp shell, *Harpa articularis.*

Illustration 147
A mitre, *Vexillum patriachalis.*

Illustration 148
A volute, *Amoria maculata.*

Illustration 149
A baler, *Melo amphora.*

Illustration 150
Part of the shell of a textile cone, *Conus textile,* which is burrowing in the sand.

Illustration 151
A geographer cone, *Conus geographus.*

Illustration 152
An auger-shell, *Terebra subulata.*

Illustration 153
A turrid, *Lienardia* sp.

Illustration 154
A pale bubble shell, *Haminoea cymbalum.*

move just below the surface of the sand and the trails they make are readily seen. All are carnivorous. They frequently congregate around dead and decaying animals. Egg capsules are laid, and these give rise to larvae that spend long periods in the plankton.

Genus represented: *Nassarius*.

Buccinid whelks (Buccinidae). There is great variation in shell shape among members of the family Buccinidae. The shells are solid and usually carry ribs, nodules, or folds. The columella is usually smooth and there is a short anterior canal associated with the ovoid aperture. These whelks are carnivores, feeding mostly on other molluscs. A few species are scavengers. In Great Barrier Reef waters buccinid whelks occur in rubble areas, particularly near reef crests.

Genera represented: *Cantharus, Phos, Engina*.

Conchs (Melongenidae). The solid shells of conchs are large with an elongate spire (which often breaks off in large specimens), a smooth columella, and a prominent anterior canal which is open. A brownish periostracum covers the shell, and a large, horny operculum is borne on the foot. Conchs are among the largest of living gastropods. The shell of one species found in Great Barrier Reef waters, the false trumpet-shell (*Syrinx aruanus*) grows up to 60 centimetres in length and has been used for carrying water. Conchs are shallow water scavengers occurring occasionally on coral reefs. Large egg cases are laid by female conchs. That of the false trumpet-shell resembles an overgrown corn cob. Young hatch from the eggs as miniature conchs.

Genus represented: *Syrinx*.

Tulip-shells (Fasciolariidae). Members of the family Fasciolariidae usually have spindle-shaped shells with an elongated spire. The ovoid aperture has a prominent anterior canal which is narrow and open; it may be straight or curved. Coloured spiral bands are usually present on the shell whorls, which are often strongly ribbed and nodulose. A horny operculum is carried on the foot. Tulip-shells are found among corals and coral rubble. Several species occur in Great Barrier Reef waters. All are carnivorous, preying chiefly on other molluscs.

Some genera represented: *Pleuroploca, Latirus, Latirolagena, Peristernia*.

Olives (Olividae). The solid and highly polished shell has a large elongate body whorl and a short low spire. There are several plaits on the columella. The shell is prettily marked and much sought after by shell collectors. Olives are found in sandy areas and frequently move just below the surface of the sand with only the tip of the siphon visible. The broad, muscular foot partially covers the shell. Several species of olive occur in Great Barrier Reef waters. All are active

predators or scavengers, and some are several centimetres in length.
Genus represented: *Oliva.*

Harp-shells (Harpidae) are found occasionally on sand and coral rubble
or under stones on reefs. The elegant shell has a bulbous body whorl,
longitudinal ridges reminiscent of the strings of a harp, a short spire,
and a wide aperture. The animal has a small head with eyes borne on
long stalks and a broad muscular foot which is extended forward to
form a burrowing organ. Part of the rear end of the foot can break
off and is used to divert the attention of an attacker while the animal
makes good its escape. Harp-shells themselves are carnivorous.
Genus represented: *Harpa.*

Vase-shells (Vasidae). Two species belonging to the family Vasidae are
found commonly on boulders and among coral rubble on reefs of the
Great Barrier Reef. Their shells are solid and spirally shaped with a
narrow aperture, plaits on the columella, and nodules on the whorls.
Vase-shells are carnivores.
Genus represented: *Vasum.*

Mitres (Mitridae). The shell is elongate and tapers at either end. The
aperture to the shell is narrow and notched. No operculum is present
but there is a thin periostracum. There are strong folds on the columella. In some species the shell is smooth, in others it is strongly
sculptured. Numerous species are found in Great Barrier Reef waters.
Some occur under coral boulders and some among living corals; some
burrow in the coral sand. All are carnivorous and use a very long
proboscis to capture their prey. Some species exude a purplish fluid
when handled. Shell lengths of different species range from about 2
to 15 centimetres. Some species lay eggs in capsules under coral
boulders.
Some genera represented: *Mitra, Neocancilla, Vexillum, Cancilla,*
Strigatella, Pulchrimitra, Cylindromitra, Imbricaria.

Volutes (Volutidae) have shells with a large body whorl and short spire.
(In the baler or melon-shells, which belong to this family, the body
whorl is greatly swollen). Frequently the shoulders of the whorls are
smooth, but in some species they carry nodules or spines. The columella usually bears plaits. The exposed foot and siphon of a volute
are frequently brightly coloured. Numerous species of volute occur in
sandy areas of reefs. Some occur intertidally, and these burrow at low
tide. Many of these species are found in colonies. All volutes are
carnivores, preying principally on other molluscs. Their eggs are laid

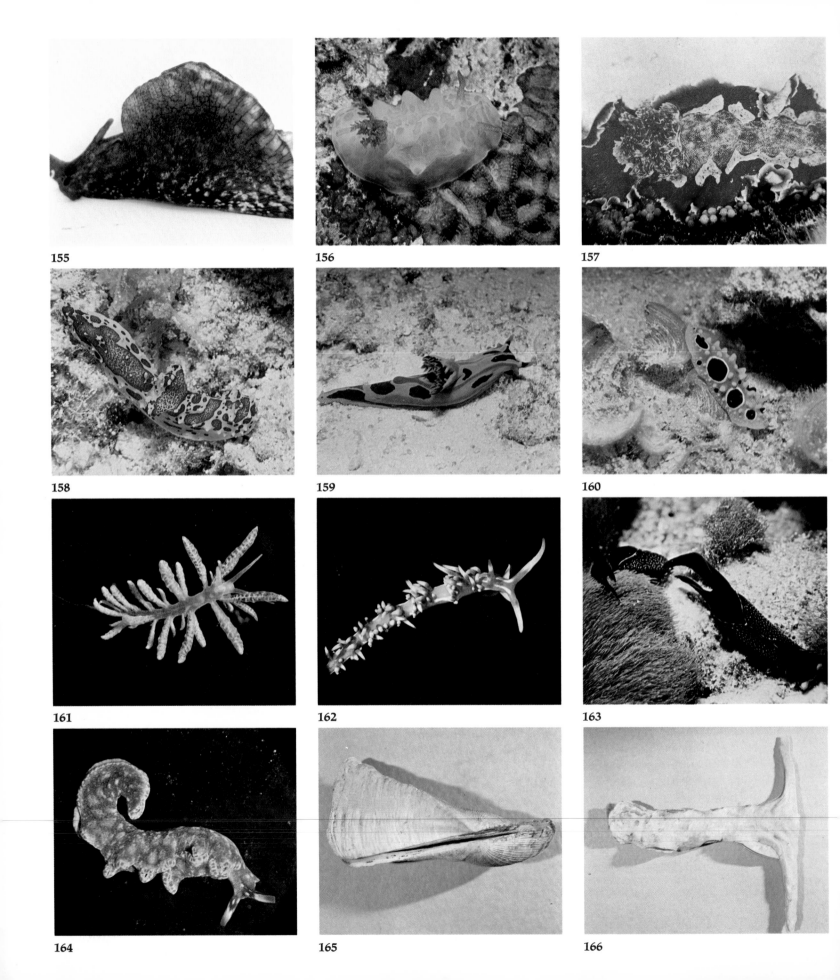

155

156

157

158

159

160

161

162

163

164

165

166

in cylindrical egg masses. The young hatch directly from the eggs as miniature adults.

Some genera represented: *Cymbiolacca, Melo, Amoria, Cymbiola.*

Cone-shells (Conidae). As the common name implies, members of the family Conidae have a shell that is basically conical. The spire is mostly low and pointed, the aperture usually narrow, and the columella smooth. Most species have shells that are solid and porcellanous and carry spectacular colour patterns. A periostracum frequently hides this pattern from view in some species. All cones are predaceous and have a remarkable venom apparatus (described in chapter 19) used primarily in the capture of prey. Most species prey on marine worms, some (possessing tent-like markings on their shells) prey on gastropod molluscs, and a few prey on small fish. Members of the latter group have been responsible for human injuries; indeed, one species, the geographer cone (*Conus geographus*), has caused several human fatalities. The animal crawls on a thick muscular foot. At the front a pair of eyes are borne on long stalks, and there is a prominent siphon. When feeding, a thin tubular proboscis is protruded from the narrow anterior end of the shell. A hollow harpoonlike radular tooth is held at the tip of the proboscis and thrust into the flesh of a victim. Venom passes through the tooth, which acts like a hypodermic needle. Numerous species of cone occur on the Great Barrier Reef. They are found in a wide variety of habitats, including crevices, under boulders, in the interstices of dead coral, and in sandy areas. Eggs are laid in flask-shaped capsules attached to the undersurfaces of coral boulders. Some species go through a planktonic larval stage, but other species develop directly.

Genus represented: *Conus.*

Auger-shells (Terebridae) are elongate, tapering, and many-whorled, with folds on the columella and a short anterior canal. A small operculum is carried on the foot. Several species occur in sandy areas of reefs, where their tracks are usually plentiful. Most species appear to prey on marine worms. Some species possess a venom apparatus akin to that possessed by Conidae, which assists in the capture of prey; other species lack a venom appartus. Eggs are laid in capsules, but larval development has not been studied.

Some genera represented: *Terebra, Hastula, Duplicaria.*

Turrid-shells (Turridae). Members of the family Turridae have elongate shells that are characterized by a slit in the upper part of the outer lip. They are predatory animals. A venom apparatus associated with the radular teeth is used in the capture of prey. Several species occur on

Facing page

Illustration 155
A sea hare, *Aplysia sowerbyi.*

Illustration 156
The dorid, *Halgerda aurantiomaculata.*

Illustration 157
The Spanish dancer, *Hexabranchus sanguineus.*

Illustration 158
A notodorid, *Notodoris gardineri.*

Illustration 159
A polycerid, *Nembrotha* sp.

Illustration 160
A phyllid, *Phyllidia ocellata.*

Illustration 161
An aeolid, *Phyllodesmium* sp.

Illustration 162
An aeolid, *Phydiana indica.*

Illustration 163
An aglajid, *Chelidonura inox.*

Illustration 164
An elysiid, *Elysia* sp.

Illustration 165
The twisted ark, *Trisidos yongei.*

Illustration 166
The hammer oyster, *Malleus malleus.*

the Great Barrier Reef, but their general biology is not well known.

Some genera represented: *Turris, Pseudodaphnella, Inquisitor, Lienardia.*

True bubble-shells (Bullidae) are relatively small molluscs. The smooth shell has a large body whorl, a sunken spire, and a wide aperture. It is marked in contrasting colours. Lateral lobes from the mantle partly enclose the shell. Several species occur on the Great Barrier Reef, where they are found mostly in sandy areas. They are herbivores.

Genus represented: *Bulla.*

Pale bubble-shells (Haminoeidae) resemble the true bubble-shells; however, the shell is thin and white or pale creamish, and the aperture extends above the body whorl. Species belonging to this family are herbivorous.

Genera represented: *Atys, Haminoea.*

Rose bubble-shells (Hydatinidae). The shell is thin and globular with a depressed spire, a large body whorl, and a wide aperture. In life the shell is partly hidden by pink, filmy folds of the mantle and foot, which give a fancied resemblance to the petals of a rose, hence the common name of the family. The foot is very large, and there is a large, shieldlike head bearing eyes and tentacles. At least three species belonging to this family occur on sandy areas of reefs. All are relatively large. They are active carnivores, preying on polychaetes. Strings of eggs encased in a gelatinous, fluted egg mass some centimetres in length are laid during the breeding season.

Genera represented: *Hydatina.*

Pupa-shells (Acteonidae) have solid shells with large body whorls, short spires, and elongated apertures. There are folds on the columella, and a horny operculum is carried on the foot. Several species occur on the Great Barrier Reef. All are small (less than 3 centimetres in length) and are found in sandy regions, particularly in lagoons and back-reef areas.

Genera represented: *Pupa, Acteon.*

Umbrella-shells (Umbraculidae). A shieldlike shell, ornamented only with concentric growth lines, is carried on the middle of the back of a large, sluglike animal. The shell has a fancied resemblance to an umbrella, hence the common name of the family. Wartlike protuberances cover the sides of the foot. A pair of prominent tentacles are borne on the head. There is a gill on the right side between the foot and the mantle.

Umbrella-shells occur on rubble subtidally but do not appear to be common on the Great Barrier Reef.

Genus represented: *Umbraculum.*

Side-gilled slugs (Pleurobranchidae) have soft bodies and usually lack a shell (however, a small internal shell is present in some species). A characteristic feature is a long, feathery gill on the right side between the foot and the mantle. Some species are large — about the size of a small dinner plate. Others are relatively small. Many are brightly coloured and marked. The Great Barrier Reef species are not well known, probably because they have not been sought by shell collectors.

Genera represented: *Pleurobranchus, Berthellina.*

Polybranchs (Polybranchiidae). Several rows of flattened protuberances adorn the upper surface of *Cyerce nigra*, the only representative of the family Polybranchiidae to be found in Great Barrier Reef waters. It is conspicuously coloured and feeds on the green alga *Chlorodesmis comosa*. A single pair of tentacles is carried on the head.

Genus represented: *Cyerce.*

Sea-hares (Aplysiidae) are large, sluglike animals with four tentacle-like structures on a prominent head. A pair of eyes lie at the bases of the posterior tentacles. The sac-like posterior region of the body may be drawn out to form a tail. Numerous small projections arise from the skin. The common name applied to the group stems from their fancied resemblance to a hare. Several species, some of them attaining lengths of 20 centimetres or more, occur on the Great Barrier Reef. In most species a small shell, frequently hidden by a fold of the mantle, is carried on the back of the animal. The shell usually overlies and protects a gill. A large fold of the mantle runs along each side of the animal in those species that are active swimmers. Sea-hares feed on algae. When disturbed, they often emit copious amounts of a reddish-purple fluid. Egg masses are laid in long, jelly-like strings.

Genera represented: *Aplysia, Dolabella, Dolabrifera.*

Dorids (Dorididae) are sluglike animals with no shell. They possess a cluster of feathery and retractile gills set in a cavity on the upper surface towards the posterior end of the body. The foot merges with a head anteriorly and a tail posteriorly. The head carries a pair of retractile tentacles and a pair of eyes. The upper part of the body (mantle) is separated from the foot and may bear papillae or thread-like processes. Several species are found in shallow water on reefs. Most species are several centimetres in length and feed on sponges.

Genera represented: *Asteronotus, Discodoris, Platydoris, Halgerda.*

Chromodorids (Chromodorididae) closely resemble dorids, but the tail usually protrudes beyond the mantle and they are usually vividly coloured. Numerous species occur on the Great Barrier Reef, from the intertidal zone to the sea-floor around a reef. Most appear to be sponge feeders. Coiled jellylike ribbons containing many eggs are laid during the breeding season.

Genera represented: *Chromodoris, Ceratosoma.*

Hexabranchids (Hexabranchidae). One large (up to 15 centimetres in length) species of hexabranchid, *Hexabranchus sanguineus*, is frequently seen on the Great Barrier Reef. It attracts attention because of its movements while swimming and its bright reddish colour, which cause it to be known locally as the "Spanish dancer". It differs from dorids in having a smooth mantle with extensive skirtlike edges that enable it to swim. Sponges and ascidians constitute its prey.

Genus represented: *Hexabranchus.*

Notodorids (Notodorididae) are sluglike and have no shell. A cluster of feathery gills is set in a cavity on the upper surface towards the rear end of the body, but these gills are not retractile. The mantle merges with the foot and shows no free edges. The body is hard and not very flexible. One large (up to 8 centimetres in length) species of this family, the yellowish *Notodoris gardineri*, is commonly found in association with a calcareous sponge on reefs. Otherwise the family does not appear to be well represented on the Great Barrier Reef.

Genus represented: *Notodoris.*

Gymnodorids (Gymnodorididae) resemble notodorids in structural features, but their bodies are soft and flexible. Several species occur on the Great Barrier Reef.

Genus represented: *Gymnodoris.*

Polycerids (Polyceridae) closely resemble gymnodorids; however, members of the two families can be distinguished by the marked differences in the structure of their radular teeth. Several species of polycerid, most of them brightly coloured, occur on the Great Barrier Reef. All polycerids appear to feed on branching bryozoans.

Genera represented: *Nembrotha, Tambja.*

Phyllids (Phyllidiidae). The sluglike shell-less phyllids are characterized by the possession of numerous gills occupying the space between the mantle and the foot. Protuberances arise from the mantle. The body is tough and somewhat rigid. Several species, some of them brightly coloured, occur on the Great Barrier Reef.

Genus represented: *Phyllidia.*

Flabellinids (Flabellinidae) have two pairs of solid tentacles on the head and rows of finger-like processes (*cerata*) on the back. There is no shell. They feed on hydroids. Stinging capsules from their prey are stored in the tips of the cerata and used in the flabellinids' own defence. Flabellinids are found under coral boulders or exposed on hydroids.

Genus represented: *Coryphella.*

Aeolids (Aeolidiidae). Like flabellinids, aeolids have two pairs of solid tentacles on the head and rows of cerata on the back and lack a shell. However, the cerata are generally more squat and more numerous in aeolids, several species of which are found on the Great Barrier Reef.

Genus represented: *Berghia, Phidiana, Phyllodesmium.*

Smaragdinellids (Smaragdinellidae) are sluglike animals with enlarged outgrowths (parapodia) from the foot that are inrolled, conferring on each animal a tubular appearance. A small shell is enclosed by the parapodia near the hind end of the animal. The head is devoid of tentacles. Smaragdinellids are herbivorous.

Genus represented: *Phanerophthalmus.*

Aglajids (Aglajidae) resemble smaragdinellids but have paired asymmetric projections at the rear end. Also, they are carnivorous. They occur in shallow water, usually in sandy areas.

Genera represented: *Aglaja, Chelidonura.*

Elysiids (Elysiidae). The sluglike elysiids carry a pair of tentacles on the head and have conspicuous parapodia which are held away from the body. They feed on algae in shallow water areas of reefs.

Genus represented: *Elysia.*

Siphon-shells (Siphonariidae). The shells of members of the family Siphonariidae resemble those of limpets, but they can be distinguished from limpets by the presence of a groove on the inside of the shell running from the apex to the margin. The groove accommodates the opening of a pulmonary cavity. This cavity is formed by the mantle and functions as a lung, enabling siphon-shells to breathe air. Hence it is not surprising that siphon-shells are intertidal animals found on the tops of dead coral boulders. However, small gills are present in the cavity, enabling the molluscs to extract oxygen from water when they are immersed.

Genus represented: *Siphonaria.*

167

168

169

170

171

172

173

174

175

176

177

178

The Bivalves (Class Bivalvia)

Members of the bivalve group of molluscs possess a calcareous shell that is divided into two valves which are hinged one to the other. The two valves enclose the laterally compressed body of the bivalve. An elastic ligament links the two valves at the hinge and is responsible for causing the two valves to spring apart (see fig. 16). Closure of the

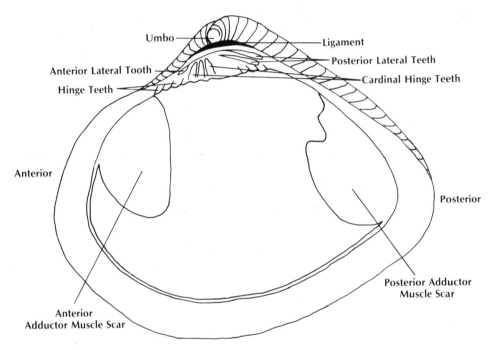

Figure 16. The inner surface of the right valve of a bivalve mollusc showing important structural features.

valves is accomplished by the action of muscles, the *adductor muscles*, which link the two valves. Frequently there are two adductor muscles (an anterior and a posterior), but in some families there is only one. A system of teeth and sockets into which the teeth fit is found at the hinge-line in most bivalves; this assists in keeping the two valves locked together. The valves may be patterned and ornamented in various ways in the different bivalve families. Features of the bivalve shell are used in the identification of these families. In describing bivalves, the hinge is regarded as being at the top; right and left valves correspond to the right and left sides of the observer when the bivalve is held with the hinge uppermost and the mouth of the animal directed away from the observer (see fig. 17).

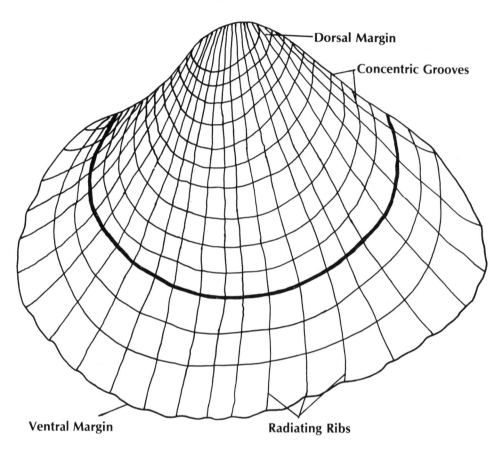

Figure 17.   The outer surface of a valve of a bivalve.

A lobe of the mantle lines the inner surface of each valve. In the space between the foot and the mantle on each side of the foot is a large gill. The gill filaments are interlinked in various ways and bear hairlike cilia, the beating of which creates water currents within the mantle cavities. Food organisms and particulate matter in the water are filtered by the gills, enmeshed in mucus, and moved to the mouth, which is situated anteriorly between a pair of sensory palps. The palps assist in sorting food materials brought to the mouth. In bivalves the head is not well defined and no radula is present. A pair of tubular siphons, one for the intake of water (the inhalent siphon) and one for the exit of water (the exhalent siphon) are found posteriorly. In burrowing forms the siphons may be very long. The foot in these forms is well developed and used in burrowing; in other forms it may be absent altogether. The visceral mass is found under the hinge. In many families glands on the foot secrete a mass of threads called a *byssus* which attaches the bivalve to the substratum or to other organisms. In some families the bivalve is attached by means of one of the valves. Many families have free-living representatives. Sexes are usually separate but some hermaphrodite species are known. Usually fertilization of eggs occurs in the external sea water, and there are free-living larval stages in the life history.

The families of bivalves occurring on the Great Barrier Reef are described below:

Nut-shells (Nuculidae) are regarded as among the most primitive of living bivalves. The shell is trigonal in outline. Numerous fine interlocking teeth are found in two series along the hinge-line. The two series are separated by a cartilaginous pit. The animal has a large foot and a pair of large lateral palps used in food collecting. Although a burrower, the nut-shell does not have siphons and the mantle lobes are free. One species of nut-shell (*Eunucula superba*), which attains a length of about 3 centimetres, occurs in sand on fringing reefs of mainland islands.

Genus represented: *Eunucula.*

Dog cockles (Glycymeridae). The shell is medium-sized, ranging from approximately 2 to 10 centimetres in length. Each valve is solid and almost circular. It may be smooth or strongly ribbed and is usually brightly coloured. Numerous prominent teeth form a curved row at the straight hinge-line. Dog cockles occur in coral sand patches on some reefs but only one species appears to be represented.

Genus represented: *Tucetona.*

Arks (Arcidae). Several species belonging to the large bivalve family Arcidae occur on the Great Barrier Reef. The shell is solid, usually covered with a hairy periostracum, and usually elongated posteriorly. Each valve is radially ribbed and has a prominent umbo (fig. 16) surmounting a long, straight hinge-line which bears numerous teeth. A black ligamentous area is found between the umbos. Arks are frequently found on and under coral boulders and among the bases of branching corals to which they are attached by a thread-like byssus. One species bores into coral skeletons.

Some genera represented: *Anadara, Trisidos, Cucullaea, Navicula, Ustularca.*

Mussels (Mytilidae). The shells are elongate and brown to purplish-black in colour and usually have a hairy periostracum. The hinge is poorly developed, but a strong ligament binds the two valves together. Strong byssal threads elaborated by many species serve to anchor specimens to coral boulders and to other shells. One species (*Lithophaga teres*) burrows into coral boulders.

Some genera represented: *Modiolus, Lithophaga, Septifer.*

Sponge fingers and hammer oysters (Vulsellidae). In representatives of the family Vulsellidae the hinge between the two valves of the shell is devoid of teeth. Each valve is elongated vertically — that is, from hinge to foot. As their common names imply, the shells of sponge fingers are fingerlike and associated with sponges, while each of the shells of hammer oysters has a remarkable resemblance to the shape of a hammer. Hammer oysters are occasionally found anchored to coral boulders by byssal threads.

Genera represented: *Malleus, Vulsella.*

Toothed pearl-shells (Isognomonidae) have a shell that is flattened and, although somewhat irregular in shape, is elongated vertically as in the Vulsellidae. However, the hinge bears flattened teeth. Each valve is rather flaky externally, and internally each has a nacreous lustre. Representatives of this family occur on coral reefs in crevices or against coral boulders. They are each attached by a byssus.

Genus represented: *Isognomon.*

Pearl-shells (Pteriidae). Members of the family Pteriidae have shells with a lustrous nacreous internal lining. Those of some species are thick and solid and are much sought after for use in the manufacture of mother-of-pearl articles. The two valves are joined at a long hinge-line. Each has a small anterior earlike projection and a greatly expanded (sometimes elongated) posterior projection. The outer surface of each bears concentric ridges as well as weak radial ribs and has a somewhat flaky consistency. Some coral reef species are attached to corals and coral boulders by a byssus, but others are found free as adults among coral rubble in the vicinity of reefs. One species bores into living coral.

Genus represented: *Pinctada.*

Razor-shells (Pinnidae). The shells are elongated and triangular in outline. Usually the inner surface is nacreous. The apex of the shell is buried in the substratum and anchored by byssal threads. Both valves are thin and brittle, and their sharp posterior edges protrude above the substratum. Cuts can be caused if these edges are trodden on — hence the name razor oyster. The species most commonly encountered among coral rubble on platform reefs is relatively small (about 10 centimetres in length) and does not pose a hazard to fossickers. Where mangrove areas intrude onto reefs, however, some of the large species of razor oysters, 25 centimetres and more in length, may be encountered.

Genera represented: *Atrina, Pinna.*

Scallops (Pectinidae). Perhaps the best known of all the molluscan families, scallops are found throughout the world. The valves are fanlike, carrying rayed ribs, and are often brightly coloured. One valve of the shell is usually convex and the other flat or slightly concave. Earlike projections (*auricles*) are present on either side of the hinge-line. Scallops can swim, hinge foremost, by clapping the valves together; they are also able to attach themselves to the substratum as a result of the production of byssal threads from the foot. There are prominent eyes, each with a well-developed lens, on the mantle edge. Some species are abundant and large and much sought after for food — the adductor muscle and gonad being eaten. However, species found on the Great Barrier Reef are rarely encountered and are often small. They are usually attached to coral rocks or rubble.

Some genera represented: *Gloripallium, Annachlamys, Comptopallium.*

Thorny oysters (Spondylidae). The shells of thorny oysters resemble those of scallops; however, one valve is usually attached to the substratum and is frequently cup-shaped, while the other valve is flat and seals the cup like a lid. The lid valve bears spiny projections from radiating ribs. Prominent interlocking cardinal teeth are carried on the hinge-line. In Great Barrier Reef waters thorny oysters are found attached to coral boulders and to reef crests.

Genus represented: *Spondylus.*

Plicate oysters (Plicatulidae) are small bivalves related to thorny oysters. One valve of their shell is attached to the substratum. The upper valve bears tile-like projections on radiating ribs. The hinge-line bears prominent teeth. Plicate oysters occur on reefs as oyster-like growths attached to dead coral.

Genus represented: *Plicatula.*

File-shells (Limidae). The two valves of the shell are white and similar in shape. They are fanlike and possess earlike projections on either side of the hinge-line. They are frequently radially ribbed and sometimes bear small thorn-like projections on the ribs. The animal is spectacular. It is orange or red, and long tentacles fringe the mantle. Some species are attached by a byssus to corals; others are free and can swim actively (see "Limas — Swimming Bivalves" in chapter 17). Species belonging to both groups occur on the Great Barrier Reef.

Genus represented: *Lima, Limaria.*

Jingle-shells (Anomiidae) are flattened shells characterized by a hole in one valve through which the partially calcified byssus passes and attaches the shell to a solid object. Both valves are thin, irregularly shaped, and translucent. Usually they are brightly coloured, often with orange tints. On the Great Barrier Reef jingle shells are found attached to coral boulders, to other molluscs, and, in regions where mangroves encroach on coral reefs, to the roots and leaves of mangroves. Artificial shell flowers are frequently made from the petal-like valves of jingle-shells.

Genera represented: *Patro, Enigmonia.*

Chamas (Chamidae). The two valves constituting the shell are unequal and often irregular in outline. One valve, which is often cup-shaped, is attached to the substratum, while the upper, flatter valve is free but fits snugly over the lower valve thereby enclosing the animal in a boxlike structure. Scaly or spiny projections are borne by the valves. Teeth are irregularly arranged on the hinge-line. Chamas are found attached to coral boulders or to crevices on reef crests in Great Barrier Reef waters.

Genus represented: *Chama.*

Oysters (Ostreidae). Because they are eaten with relish throughout the world, oysters are among the most widely known of bivalve families, and their somewhat irregular foliaceous shells with weakly developed hinges are a familiar sight in restaurants. Most species of oyster attach themselves to solid objects when adult. In Great Barrier Reef waters the purplish shells with their crenulated borders of one species, *Crassostrea amasa*, often cover the upper surfaces of coral boulders that are exposed at low tide on platform reefs. Other species, such as the large (20-centimetre diameter) hyotoid oyster (*Lopha hyotis*) occur on fringing reefs nearer the Queensland mainland. Oysters do not have an obvious foot. Peculiar sex changes occur in oysters, some species being alternately male and female.

Some genera represented: *Crassostrea, Lopha, Pycnodonte.*

Carditas (Carditidae) are rarely found on the Great Barrier Reef. The shell is medium sized, ranging usually from 2 to 6 centimetres in length, and has a yellowish periostracum. Each valve is somewhat elongated with rounded margins and scaly, radiating ribs. The hinge-line bears oblique interlocking teeth, usually two teeth on one valve and one tooth on the other. A byssus is often associated with the foot of the animal, attaching it to rubble and dead coral boulders on reefs. Carditas have no siphons. Some species brood their young.

Genus represented: *Cardita.*

Saucer-shells (Lucinidae) are medium to large, circular in outline, and flattish. Each whitish, somewhat chalky valve possesses fine concentric grooves as well as radiating grooves. There are two centrally placed *cardinal teeth* at the hinge of each valve, as well as an anterior and a posterior lateral tooth on the hinge of the right valve and corresponding depressions on the hinge of the left valve. A long ligament is present at the hinge-line. The animal has an elongate foot which it uses for burrowing in the coral sand among coral clumps on reefs.

Some genera represented: *Codakia, Epicodakia, Lentillaria.*

Heart cockles (Cardiidae) have swollen, frequently heart-shaped shells. Four teeth, two grouped centrally, are found on the hinge-line of each valve, which is usually radially ribbed. The ribs may have spines or scales. The valves are crenulated marginally and interlock. The animal has a large foot, which is used in burrowing, and a pair of short siphons. Heart cockles occur in coral sand on reefs. Most found there are approximately 4 centimetres in length.

Some genera represented: *Regozara, Fragrum, Corculum.*

Clams (Tridacnidae). Included in the family Tridacnidae are the largest of all living molluscs. The shells are large, solid, and porcellanous. Each valve has a number of radiating ribs that bear scales in most species. Large, irregularly arranged teeth are found on the hinge-line. Clams are among the most prominent of the bivalves found on coral reefs. Most occur among living corals. One common species, *Tridacna crocea*, bores into corals and dead coral boulders. Another, *Tridacna fossor*, nestles in shallow depressions, while other species, including the giant clams, lie free on their hinge. Members of this interesting family are described in detail in chapter 18.

Genera represented: *Tridacna, Hippopus.*

Venus-shell (Veneridae). Usually the shells of members of the large family Veneridae are strongly sculptured and bear striking colour patterns. The hinge is excentric and carries strong teeth. Three or four cardinal teeth are present on each valve, as well as a lateral tooth. An external ligament is present along the hinge-line, and there is a prominent lunule (area on the hinge-line anterior to the umbos). The animal possesses a strong muscular foot for burrowing, and the paired siphons are united along most of their length. Normally venus-shells burrow in coral sand and are found just below the surface. Several species, most of them rather large, are found on the Great Barrier Reef. They are edible and were much sought after by Australian Aborigines. In the North Atlantic a species of this family, *Mercenaria mercenaria*, is commonly known as a clam and is used for making clam chowder.

Some genera represented: *Periglypta, Ventricolaria, Glycodonta, Chione, Lioconcha, Costacallista.*

Tellens (Tellinidae) show great variation in shell size, shape, and ornamentation. Each valve is usually compressed and bears fine concentric grooves; sometimes it bears radial grooves as well. Often it is brightly coloured. Teeth on the hinge-line are weakly developed, and there is a conspicuous external ligament. The animal has long siphons and a broad foot and burrows deeply in coral sand. Several species occur on the Great Barrier Reef.

Some genera represented: *Tellinella, Laciolina, Scutarcopagia, Cyclotellina, Macoma, Phylloda.*

Trough-shells (Mactridae). The shell is usually swollen and frequently trigonal in outline. Two strong cardinal teeth and an anterior and posterior lateral tooth are carried on the hinge-line of each valve, which is smooth and concentrically grooved. The siphons are united. Some species occur in large numbers in coral sand on reef flats and lagoons of reefs.

Genus represented: *Mactra.*

Little wedge-shells (Mesodesmatidae). As the common name implies, the shells of members of the family Mesodesmatidae are small (2–3 centimetres long) and wedge-shaped. Each solid valve carries one cardinal tooth at the hinge-line and is smooth or concentrically ridged externally. The siphons are separated one from another. Specimens are usually found burrowing in coral sand intertidally. One species, *Atactodea striata,* is one of the commonest bivalves to be found on the Great Barrier Reef.

Genus represented: *Atactodea.*

Sunset clams (Psammobiidae). The shells of some sunset clams have rays of colour radiating from the low umbos, a feature that has given the group its common name. Generally the shells are elongate and compressed but gape posteriorly. A well-developed periostracum is present and a prominent external ligament occurs at the hinge-line. Hinge teeth are weakly developed. Concentric grooves are generally present on each valve, and the valves themselves are rather thin. Each animal has long siphons and a pointed foot. Several species, ranging usually between 3 and 6 centimetres in length, occur burrowing in coral sand on reefs.

Genera represented: *Gari, Asaphis.*

Finger oysters (Solenidae). The shells of finger oysters are elongate, thin, and open at one end (posteriorly). The valves can be straight-sided or curved and are usually smooth. A pair of cardinal teeth are found on the hinge-line, and an external ligament is present. A powerful cylindrical foot is used for burrowing. Finger oysters can burrow rapidly and deeply. They are occasionally encountered in sand on coral reefs (particularly fringing reefs) but are commonly encountered in muddy situations near mangroves when these occur on coral reefs.

Genera represented: *Solen, Ensiculus.*

Angel's wing shells (Pholadidae) burrow into rock, coral, and wood. They have swollen, elongated shells which gape at either end. Each valve is sculptured with fine concentric ridges and radiating lines, and the hinge carries a peg-like projection internally. The edges of the mantle are united, but an opening is left for the protrusion of the foot. The two siphons are united and elongated. One species, *Parapholas incei,* found on the Great Barrier Reef, bores into coral.

Genera represented: *Pholas, Parapholas.*

Ship-worms (Teredinidae). The bodies of members of the family Teredinidae are elongate and wormlike. However, a shell consisting of two small white valves is carried anteriorly, and two shelly extensions called *pallets* are carried posteriorly. A pair of long siphons are found between the pallets. Ship-worms attack wood; mangroves, coconut husks, logs, and timber (such as the hulls of boats) are attacked by these bivalves in Great Barrier Reef waters. They bore into wood by rotating the valves of the shell. The burrows excavated are lined with calcareous material, calcareous tubes being thereby formed. Some of those produced by the giant ship-worm, *Kuphus arenaria,* may be up to 2 metres in length.

Some genera represented: *Teredo, Kuphus, Bankia.*

Cephalopods (Class Cephalopoda)

The term *cephalopod* means head-footed, a reference to the belief that the tentacles surrounding the mouth of a cephalopod are derived from the foot of ancestral forms. The tentacles bear cuplike suckers, and the mouth is found anteriorly at the point of confluence of the tentacles (see figs. 18 and 19). A beak resembling that of a parrot protrudes from the mouth. Eyes bearing a remarkable resemblance to vertebrate eyes are found on the well-developed head. The body is bent upon itself, the anus opening anteriorly on the lower surface of the animal into a cavity formed by the mantle. Gills are also housed in this mantle cavity. Water passes into the mantle cavity by way of the anterior

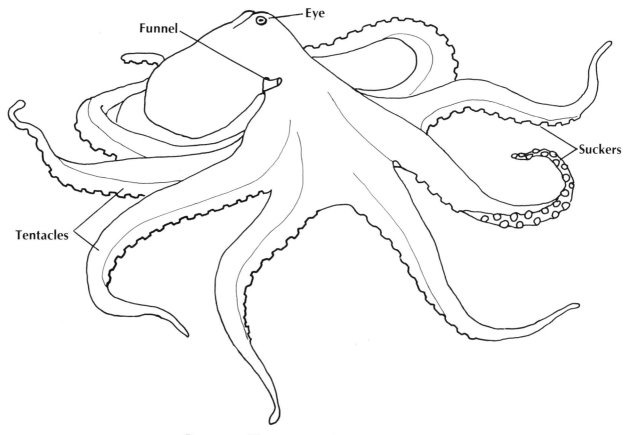

Figure 18. The upper surface of an octopus.

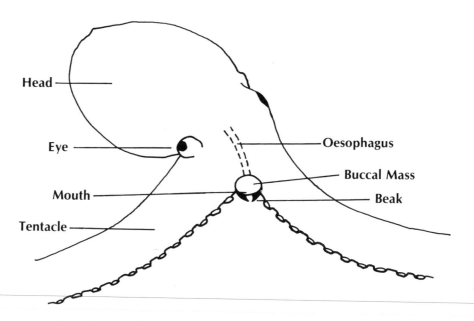

Figure 19. Lateral view of an octopus showing position of the mouth and beak.

edge of the mantle but passes out through an anteriorly directed tubular extension of the mantle known as the *funnel*. The walls of the mantle cavity are muscular, and water can be expelled with considerable force through the funnel, resulting in the cephalopod shooting backwards, a form of jet propulsion. A so-called ink sac also opens into the mantle cavity; its contents, when voided, cloud the water in the vicinity of the cephalopod, thereby assisting it to elude pursuers. Cephalopods have an amazing ability to change colour.

Prey is seized with the tentacles and bitten by the beak. Saliva, containing in many forms toxic material elaborated by modified salivary glands which open into the buccal cavity, passes into the puncture made by the beak and helps to inactivate prey. In some cephalopods found on coral reefs, the molluscan shell has been modified to form an internal supporting structure, but in others it is absent. Sometimes the supporting structure formed is chitinous and flexible and known as a *pen*; at other times it is calcareous and porous and constitutes the "cuttle-bones" washed ashore so frequently on beaches. The sexes in cephalopods are separate. Eggs are surrounded with jellylike material when laid, and development is direct.

At least three cephalopod families occur on the Great Barrier Reef.

Cuttlefish (Sepiidae) have a calcareous and spongy internal supporting structure. A long, narrow fin is found on each side of the body. Two of the ten arms are modified as tentacles for seizing prey, frequently fish.

Calamaries (Omnastrephidae) have a chitinous pen. The two fins may be broad and extend the length of the body, or they may be triangular and located at the opposite end of the body from the ten tentacles. Some species attain a large size. They prey principally on fish.

Octopuses (Octopodidae). The appearance of the eight-armed octopus is widely known. In Great Barrier Reef waters a large red and white species is common in lairs in coral on reef flats. These lairs are surrounded by the dead shells of molluscs that form a large part of its prey. The species is nocturnal. Other smaller species are also found on reefs.

12

The Echinoderms

Of the many types of invertebrate animal found on the Great Barrier Reef, few would be more conspicuous than the echinoderms. Their conspicuousness stems from their relatively large size, their peculiar body shapes, their usually striking coloration, and the fact that many species make little attempt to conceal themselves.

The term *echinoderm* means "spiny skinned", but not all echinoderms have spines. However, some basic features are shared by all. First, they are radially symmetrical animals, the principal organs of the body being repeated and arranged around a central hub like the spokes of a wheel. (Usually the radial symmetry is based on a five-rayed plan.) Consequently echinoderms have no front or hind ends and no right or left sides. The mouth provides a convenient reference point, and that surface where the mouth is found is called the *oral surface*. The opposite surface is the *aboral surface*. Secondly, echinoderms possess a skeleton of calcareous plates, or *ossicles*, embedded in the skin. Often the plates are large and prominent, but sometimes they are reduced to a collection of spicules. Spines, when present, are attached to the plates. Thirdly, echinoderms have a radially arranged *ambulacral system* composed of water-filled tubes which act as a hydraulic system to push out or retract tubular appendages called *ambulacra*. Sometimes these function in locomotion, when they are known as *tube-feet*, but they may have other functions; for example, they may assist in food collection, be involved in respiration, or act as anchoring devices. Typically the sexes are separate, and free-swimming larval stages occur in the life history of each species. Toxins are produced by many species.

Five major groups of living echinoderms are recognized by zoologists. These are the starfish (Asteroidea), brittle-stars

(Ophiuroidea), feather-stars (Crinoidea), sea-urchins (Echinoidea), and sea-cucumbers (Holothurioidea). In the starfish, brittle-stars, and feather-stars, the radial scheme of arrangement characteristic of echinoderms extends to the structures seen externally — in the arrangement of the arms, for example. In the sea-urchins and sea-cucumbers the radial scheme of arrangement is not obvious externally but can be clearly seen when these animals are examined internally.

Echinoderms are probably the best known (to zoologists) of all the major groups of animals found on the Great Barrier Reef, and it is possible to list most of the species that occur there. However, the list would be a long one. In the following account, the echinoderms of the Great Barrier Reef will be dealt with at higher taxonomic levels.

Feather-Stars (Class Crinoidea)

The central disc, called the *calyx*, of feather-stars is supported on a ring of jointed structures, termed cirri. Five segmented arms arise radially from the calyx. In most species the arms branch repeatedly, the final branches being elongated and tapering. Each arm segment gives rise to a pair of jointed appendages called *pinnules* conferring a feather-like appearance on the arm. The arms break easily, usually at special breaking planes called *syzygies* (see fig. 20).

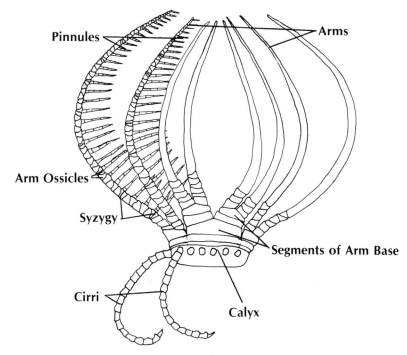

Figure 20. Diagram illustrating the principal features of the skeleton of a feather-star.

Both mouth and anus are found on the upper oral surface of the calyx, which is thus referred to as the tegmen. The cirri arise from the opposite, or aboral, surface. Ciliated grooves known as *food grooves* run along the oral surface of each arm from the arm tip to the mouth and are also found on some pinnules. Tubular ambulacra, which move actively, border the grooves, but these appendages are not involved in locomotion. Gland cells that occur in the covering of these ambulacra produce toxic material and mucus, used respectively to inactivate and to ensnare minute organisms present in the surrounding sea water. These organisms, enmeshed in mucus strings, are moved along the food grooves to the mouth by the action of cilia in the floor of each groove. Thus the ambulacra in feather-stars are used in food capture. Different species of feather-stars hold the arms in characteristic positions when feeding.

Powerful muscles link the arm segments and are responsible for the graceful movements of the arms involved in swimming. Attachment to the substratum is accomplished by the cirri. Calyx, arms, pinnules, and cirri are heavily armoured with calcareous plates. Large amounts of pigments are produced by most species of feather-stars, and they are frequently brightly coloured. Reproductive cells occur in specialized pinnules which break open to release the male or female sex cells. Fertilization occurs in the external sea water and gives rise to a pelagic larva. Subsequently this attaches to the substratum by a stalk. Eventually the developing feather-star breaks free from the stalk.

The families of feather-stars so far recorded from the Great Barrier Reef are listed below.

Comasterids (Comasteridae) form a large group in which the mouth with associated food grooves is near the margin of the tegmen. Also, the pinnules on the tegmen have their terminal segments modified to form a comb. A great variety of form and colour is shown by the many different species belonging to this family that are found on the Great Barrier Reef. During daylight hours most comasterids are found on the lower surfaces of coral boulders or in crevices around the edges of pools on reef flats or in the interstices of coral clumps in deeper water. At night they usually move to more exposed situations.

Genera represented: *Capillaster, Comatula, Comantheria, Comanthina, Comanthus, Comatella, Comaster.*

Zygometrids (Zygometridae). A breaking plane is present between the first two segments of each arm base in members of the family Zygometridae. The mouth is near the centre of the tegmen. Very few species belonging to this family have been found in Great Barrier Reef waters.

Genus represented: *Zygometra.*

Himerometrids (Himerometridae) possess a mouth near the centre of the tegmen and cirri that are compressed laterally and have pronounced keels. Also, the outer pinnules, at least, are cylindrical and have elongated segments. Ten or more arms are present; if there are more than ten, four ossicles are usually found between the first and second branchings of each arm base. Himerometrids are not well represented on the Great Barrier Reef.

Genera represented: *Himerometra, Amphimetra, Heterometra.*

Mariametrids (Mariametridae) resemble himerometrids with respect to the position of the mouth and the structure of cirri and pinnules. However, they always have more than ten arms, and only two ossicles are found between the first and second branchings of each arm base.

Genera represented: *Lamprometra, Oxymetra, Stephanometra.*

Colobometrids (Colobometridae). The outer pinnules of colobometrids are cylindrical and have elongated segments. The mouth is centrally placed. The cirri are not keeled, but each cirrus segment bears two or more spines or a serrated ridge.

Genera represented: *Oligometra, Colobometra.*

Tropiometrids (Tropiometridae). The pinnules of tropiometrids are all triangular in cross-section. The mouth is centrally placed. Only ten arms are present.

Genus represented: *Tropiometra.*

Antedonids (Antedonidae) have only ten arms. The mouth is centrally placed. The pinnules are all cylindrical or flattened with long segments.

Genera represented: *Antedon, Euantedon, Toxometra, Iridometra.*

Starfish (Class Asteroidea)

As the name implies, starfish usually have a conventional star shape. There is a central disc from which the arms radiate (see fig. 21). Most species have five arms, although some species have more. The central disc may be small or it may be extensive, and the arms may be relatively long or they may be short depending upon the species of starfish under consideration. The body surface of starfish is covered by a thin skin through which may be seen the outlines of calcareous plates (ossicles), which collectively comprise the skeleton. Sometimes the ossicles form a skeleton that resembles a cobblestone pavement, sometimes they form a reticulated structure, and sometimes they form

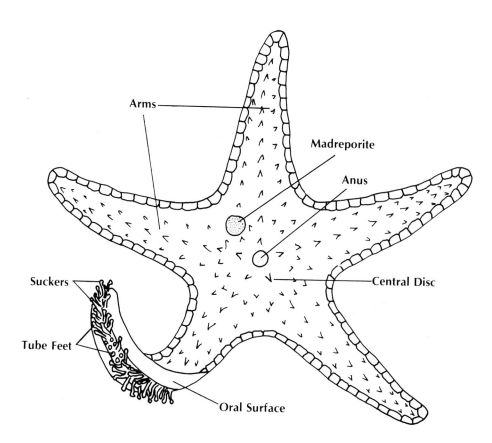

Arms

Madreporite

Anus

Suckers

Tube Feet

Central Disc

Oral Surface

Figure 21. Diagram of a starfish showing mostly the upper or aboral surface. One arm is twisted to show the tube feet on the lower or oral surface.

a structure resembling tiles on a roof. Projections of various kinds may arise from the ossicles, conferring on many species their characteristic appearance.

On the lower surface, which is the oral surface because of the presence there of the mouth in the centre of the disc, grooves run the length of each arm. Tubular structures (tube-feet) occur in rows in these grooves. Usually the tube-feet have suckers at their tips for adhering to objects. They are involved in locomotion. Each tube-foot is pointed in the direction in which the starfish is moving or intends to move. Then the tip of the tube-foot comes into contact with an object on the sea floor to which the sucker adheres. Muscles in the walls of the tube-foot then contract pulling the starfish towards the point of attachment. Of course, numerous tube-feet work in unison during locomotion. The hollow tube-feet are associated with the ambulacral system, the water-filled system of tubes that acts as a type of hydraulic system.

Starfish have the ability to evert their stomachs through their mouths and so envelop their prey. Digestive enzymes are poured over the prey, which is partially digested externally. The products of this

partial digestion then pass to the rest of the alimentary canal for
further processing. The food of starfish varies with the species involved and ranges from algae and micro-organisms to sponges, corals,
worms, crustaceans, molluscs, and even other starfish. Starfish are
often found near the ends of food chains, and many species are
regarded as key species (see chapter 15).

Most species of starfish have characteristic structures called
pedicellariae on the surfaces of their bodies. These are minute two-
jawed pincers used for seizing small organisms, particularly the larvae
of fouling organisms and those of parasites. Toxins usually present in
the skin of starfish ensure that they have few predators.

Starfish have great powers of regeneration, some species being able
to regenerate their whole body from a sizeable fragment. Some species
reproduce asexually by tearing across the disc, each half regenerating
the necessary structures. Other species reproduce asexually by breaking off one or more arms; the arms then regenerate a disc and other
arms. During the early stages of regeneration such individuals have
a comet-like appearance. The sexes are separate. Union of male and
female reproductive products occurs in the external sea water, giving
rise to pelagic larval stages.

Starfish families recorded from the Great Barrier Reef are listed
below.

Comb stars (Astropectinidae) have five moderately long arms and a small
central disc. Each arm is fringed with spines, giving it a comb-like
appearance. There are no suckers on the tube-feet. Comb stars are
found in the sandy areas of reefs. They burrow just below the surface,
their presence being indicated by star-like marks in the sand. They
are active at night and prey on invertebrates in the sand.

Genus represented: *Astropecten.*

Archasterids (Archasteridae) resemble comb stars; however, unlike comb
stars, their tube-feet carry suckers and the upper surfaces of their
arms are flat rather than arched. Archasterids are common on sandy
areas of reef in the northern half of the Great Barrier Reef. Males and
females pair when spawning.

Genus represented: *Archaster.*

Oreasterids (Oreasteridae) have large discs and short, usually tapering,
arms. In adult specimens of *Culcita novaeguineae*, the pin-cushion
starfish, the arms merge completely with the disc, giving the animal
a pentagonal shape. The disc and arms of oreasterids are flat below
but markedly arched above. Large tubercles or spines are often carried
by some of the plates forming the upper surface. In the genus
Choriaster, the plates are hidden by a thick skin. Some oreasterids,

such as species of *Culcita* and *Choriaster*, feed on coral polyps and hence are found frequently among corals on platform reefs. The brightly coloured *Protoreaster nodosus* is usually found on fringing reefs.

Genera represented: *Choriaster, Culcita, Protoreaster.*

Ophidiasterids (Ophidiasteridae). Members of the large family Ophidiasteridae have small central discs and usually five long, often

One end of the large sea-cucumber, *Thelenota ananas*, which is covered with pointed outgrowths.

somewhat cylindrical arms. They are often brightly coloured. Numerous species are found on the Great Barrier Reef. Frequently they lie fully exposed. Many feed on micro-organisms associated with algae. Some are able to reproduce asexually by breaking off an arm which gives rise to a new starfish. New individuals arising in this way are called "comet" forms.

Genera represented: *Leiaster, Gomophia, Linckia, Tamaria, Ophidiaster, Fromia, Nardoa, Neoferdina, Bunaster, Asteropsis.*

Asterinids (Asterinidae) have overlapping scale-like plates which usually bear small spines. Frequently they are flattened and often small. In most species the arms are short and the disc large. In Great Barrier Reef waters most asterinids are found on the undersurfaces of dead coral boulders.

Genera represented: *Nepanthia, Anseropoda, Tegulaster, Asterina, Disasterina, Patiriella.*

Echinasterids (Echinasteridae). One species of the family Echinasteridae, the reddish *Echinaster luzonicus*, occurs commonly on the Great Barrier Reef. Spinelets protrude through the skin covering the skeletal plates. Individuals have from five to seven arms. They are capable of reproducing asexually by splitting across the disc, then regenerating new arms.

Genus represented: *Echinaster.*

Crown-of-thorns starfish (Acanthasteridae). Only one species of the family Acanthasteridae, *Acanthaster planci*, occurs on the Great Barrier Reef. It has numerous arms and is covered with large venomous spines. It attains a very large size. This coral-eating species is discussed in chapters 23 and 25.

Genus represented: *Acanthaster.*

Valvasterids (Valvasteridae). One species, *Valvaster spinifera*, belonging to the valvasterid family has been found at the northern end of the Great Barrier Reef. It is characterized by the presence of huge pedicellariae on the upper marginal plates. The disc is extensive and prettily patterned. The five arms are triangular in shape.

Genus represented: *Valvaster.*

Asteriids (Asteriidae) are represented on reefs near the southern end of the Great Barrier Reef by the bluish *Coscinasterias calamaria*. The tube-feet are arranged in four rows. Usually more than five arms are present.

Genus represented: *Coscinasterias.*

Brittle-Stars (Class Ophiuroidea)

The arms of brittle-stars are sharply marked off from the central disc and are not confluent with the disc as in starfish. Also, the arms are segmented, and frequently spines arise from the sides of each segment (see fig. 22). Usually each arm segment is protected by an upper and lower arm plate and two lateral arm plates, one on each side. Powerful muscles link the arm segments and are responsible for the characteristic arm movements involved in the locomotion of brittle-stars.

Tubular structures homologous with the tube-feet of starfish are present in each segment, but they no longer function in locomotion. Instead, they have a sensory and food-gathering function and are known as tentacles. The grooves present on the oral surfaces of the arms of starfish are closed over in brittle-stars.

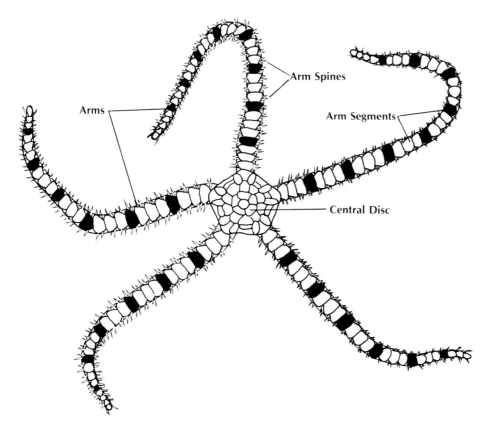

Figure 22.   The upper (aboral) surface of a brittle-star.

The mouth is in the centre of the lower surface of the disc and is associated with structures called teeth and with oral and dental papillae as depicted in figure 23. The upper surface of the disc is covered by a skin through which the plates of the skeleton may be visible. These are often scalelike and frequently bear granules or spines.

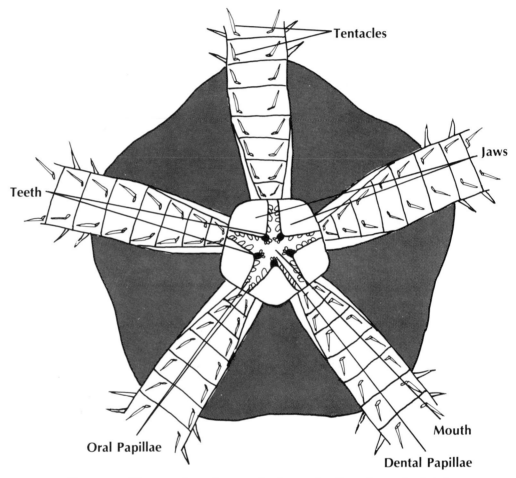

Figure 23.   The mouth region on the lower (oral) surface of a brittle-star.

As their name implies, brittle-stars break off arms readily. However, they have great powers of regeneration, and loss of an arm is only a temporary inconvenience. While some brittle-stars feed on detritus and micro-organisms, many are active predators, preying on small worms and crustaceans principally. Some species of brittle-stars have arms that branch, and they are known as basket-stars; the arms of most species, however, are unbranched.

The sexes of brittle-stars are separate, and in most species reproductive products are shed directly into the external sea water.

Fertilization gives rise to larval stages which are pelagic. A few species retain their young for various periods of time in special brood pouches.

Sometimes brittle-stars occur in large numbers and provide an important food for fish.

The families of brittle-stars recorded from the Great Barrier Reef are listed below.

Serpent-stars (Asteroschematidae) have very long arms covered with thick skin. The arms are able to coil vertically. Arm spines are confined to the lower surface of the arms. Barlike radial shields are present on the disc. Serpent stars occur entwined around the branches of black corals and gorgonians in the deeper waters around reefs.
Genus represented: *Astrobrachion.*

Basket-stars (Gorgonocephalidae). The arms of basket stars are branched and bear rows of hooks across their upper surfaces. At night, the basket formed of branched arms is held vertically and used to capture small planktonic organisms. During the day, basket-stars hide among sedentary organisms. Occasional representatives of this family are found in back-reef areas.
Genus represented: *Astrocladus.*

Spiny basket-stars (Euryalidae) have arms that branch repeatedly, and the upper surfaces of the arms and disc bear short spines. In Great Barrier Reef waters spiny basket-stars are often found on the branches of gorgonians.
Genus represented: *Euryale.*

Ophiomyxids (Ophiomyxidae). A thick skin covers the disc and arms of representatives of the family Ophiomyxidae. The arms are relatively short and unbranched. Ophiomyxids occur occasionally under dead coral boulders on reefs.
Genus represented: *Ophiomyxa.*

Ophiacanthids (Ophiacanthidae). In members of the family Ophiacanthidae a single pointed papilla (see diagram) is present at the apex of each jaw and three or more oral papillae on each side of each jaw. The arms, spines, and disc are frequently covered with thorny spinules. Representatives of this family appear to be rare on the Great Barrier Reef. However, as most species are small, being less than 6 millimetres across the disc, their presence on reefs may have been overlooked.
Genus represented: *Ophiacantha.*

181

182

183

184

185

186

187

188

189

190

191

192

Amphiurids (Amphiuridae). The presence of a pair of papillae at the apex of the jaw is a diagnostic feature of amphiurids. The disc is covered with scales, which bear spinelets in some species. Several arm spines are present in each arm segment. Numerous species occur on the Great Barrier Reef, and in some cases numerous individuals of a species aggregate. Some tend to burrow in coral sand under and among coral rubble, but many live in the interstices of semi-consolidated rubble or in association with sponges and algae.

Genera represented: *Amphioplus, Amphipholis, Amphiura, Ophiocentrus, Amphiodia.*

Ophiactids (Ophiactidae) have a single oral papilla at the apex of the jaw, separated by a gap usually from other oral papillae present on each jaw. Most species are small, less than 8 millimetres in disc diameter. They occur in association with sponges and branching corals and in the interstices of coral rubble. A few species have six or seven arms. Some species reproduce asexually by splitting across the disc, then growing new arms.

Genus represented: *Ophiactis.*

Ophiotrichids (Ophiotrichidae). A diagnostic feature of the large family Ophiotrichidae is the presence of a cluster of dental papillae at the apex of each jaw. Oral papillae are absent. Arm spines are usually prominent. The disc plates may be covered with spines or granules at the base. Numerous species, most of them prettily marked and some brightly coloured, are found on the Great Barrier Reef. Some of the larger species occur under coral boulders and some in crevices. Many of the smaller species associate with other organisms, such as sponges, coralline algae, and gorgonians. In some species such as *Macrophiothrix longipeda*, the arms are extraordinarily long and brittle.

Genera represented: *Ophiothrix, Macrophiothrix, Ophiogymna, Ophiomaza, Ophiothela.*

Ophiocomids (Ophiocomidae). Most species belonging to the family Ophiocomidae are large, attaining disc diameters in excess of 20 millimetres. They are characterized by the presence of a clump of dental papillae at the apex of each jaw and by prominent arm spines. Sometimes some of these arm spines are club-shaped, as in species of *Ophiomastix.* Two tentacle scales are usually present. In species of *Ophiocoma* the upper surface of the disc is covered with granules; in species of *Ophiarthrum* it is covered with a bare skin. In the genus *Ophiomastix* small spines are present on the disc. Ophiocomids are common on the Great Barrier Reef. Although most occur under dead coral boulders, some are found in crannies on the reef flat and others among the branches of dead and living acropores. Many are brightly coloured and prettily marked. They move actively when disturbed.

Genera represented: *Ophiarthrum, Ophiocoma, Ophiocomella, Ophiomastix.*

Ophionereids (Ophionereidae) are characterized by the presence of three upper arm plates in each arm segment, conspicuous arm spines that project sideways from the arm, and a single large tentacle scale on the lower surface of each arm segment. The disc is covered with fine scales. Oral papillae, but no dental papillae, are present. Most species found on the Great Barrier Reef are small, less than 10 millimetres in disc diameter.

Genus represented: *Ophionereis.*

Ophiodermatids (Ophiodermatidae). The arms of ophiodermatids are fused with the sides of the disc. The arm spines are small and pressed against the sides of the arm segments (except in species of *Ophiarachna*, where they are large and flaring). The disc is covered with granules. Oral papillae but no dental papillae are present. Some ophiodermatids are found under coral boulders; others, such as the large *Ophiarachna incrassata*, occur in pools.

Genera represented: *Ophiarachna, Ophiarachnella, Ophiopeza, Cryptopelta.*

Ophiurids (Ophiuridae) resemble ophiodermatids, but the disc is devoid of granules and is covered instead with scales or plates. Ophiurids are found under dead coral. When exposed, they tend to be inactive. Although most are dull coloured, some are strikingly marked. One species, *Ophioplocus imbricatus*, which possesses fragmented upper arm plates, is very common on many reefs.

Genera represented: *Ophiolepis, Ophioteichus, Ophioplocus, Ophiura.*

Sea-Urchins (Class Echinoidea)

In sea-urchins the plates of the skeleton have fused together to form a protective structure called a *corona*, which is globular or discoidal in shape. No arms are present (see fig. 24). Tube-feet in five double rows run meridionally from one pole to the other. Rows of plates known as *ambulacral plates* are perforated for the passage of tube-feet. Those plates occurring between the ambulacral plates are known as *interambulacral* plates. At one pole, which is usually pressed against the substratum, the mouth is found. Five white teeth (associated internally with a remarkable calcareous structure called Aristotle's lantern) protrude through the mouth, which is surrounded by a membranous area

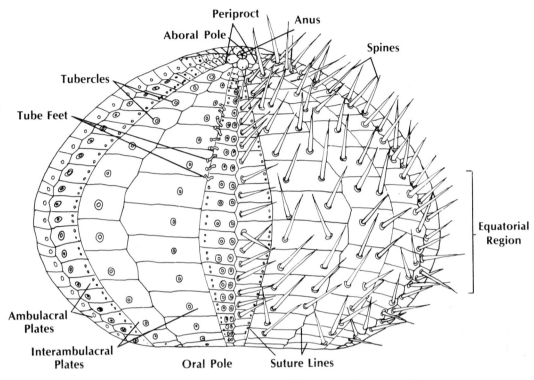

Figure 24. Diagram showing some of the external features of a sea-urchin. Spines have been removed from left side.

called the *peristome*. In the globular or regular sea-urchins the anal opening, surrounded by a membranous area called the *periproct*, occurs at the opposite pole. In the irregular sea-urchins (the heart-urchins and sand-dollars) the anus and periproct are displaced from this pole (see figs. 25 and 26).

Moveable spines, usually differentiated into large primary spines and smaller secondary spines, project from the plates of the corona. Each spine articulates with an elevation called a *tubercle*. Venom sacs may be present on the spines of some species. Three-jawed seizing organs (pedicellariae), which are attached to stalks, also arise from the coronal plates. The jaws of some types of pedicellaria are associated with venom glands. In the heart-urchins, belts of fine ciliated spines called *fascioles* occur.

The functions of the tube-feet vary. Some near the mouth have a sensory function. Others on the oral surface are involved with locomotion and with anchoring the sea-urchin. Those arising from the upper, or aboral, surface of the corona are involved with respiration; on the aboral surface of irregular sea-urchins they frequently form the outlines of petals, and the area involved is termed a *petaloid area*.

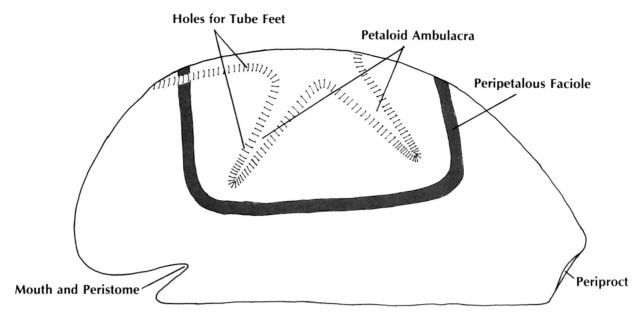

Figure 25.   A heart-urchin viewed from the left side.

Holes for Tube Feet

Petaloid Ambulacra

Peripetalous Faciole

Periproct

Mouth and Peristome

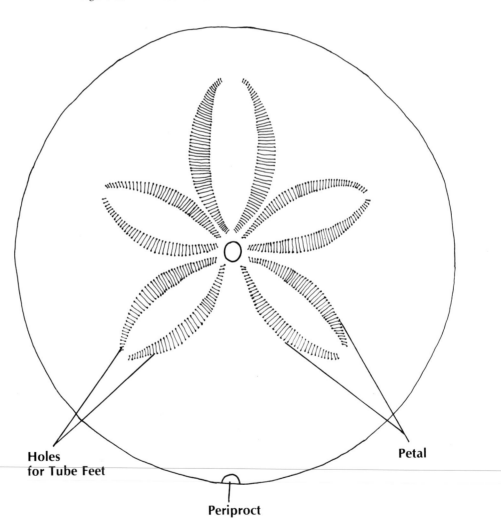

Holes
for Tube Feet

Petal

Periproct

Figure 26.   A sand-dollar viewed from the upper (aboral) surface.

Most sea-urchins feed on algal materal or detritus, but some will eat animal food. Large gonads, usually five in number, are found internally in the aboral half of the corona. The sex cells are released to the external sea water, where fertilization occurs, giving rise to pelagic larval stages.

Sea-urchin families recorded on the Great Barrier Reef are listed below.

Cidarids (Cidaridae). In cidarids the corona, apart from the peristome, is composed of rigid plates. The ambulacral areas bearing the tube-feet are narrower than the interambulacral areas. Each interambulacral plate bears a single large spine which is usually ringed with small flattened spines. The perforations in the corona for the passage of tube-feet form a single vertical series. The peristome is covered with flexible plates. Cidaroids are found among coral rubble and coral clumps in a variety of situations on coral reefs, but they appear to be somewhat rare in Great Barrier Reef waters.

Genera represented: *Eucidaris, Phyllacanthus, Prionocidaris*.

Echinothurids (Echinothuriidae). The hemispherical corona of echinothurids is flexible and flattens when removed from water. Plates cover some areas on the peristome. The spines are venomous and capable of inflicting painful wounds. Specimens occur under coral clumps in the deeper water at the edges of reefs in the Great Barrier Reef area.

Genus represented: *Asthenosoma*.

Needle-spined sea-urchins (Diadematidae). The plates of the near-spherical coronas of members of the family Diadematidae are covered with long, slender spines. However, the peristome carries only a few plates, which are usually devoid of spines. The spines are associated with toxic material and readily penetrate and break off in the flesh of a victim. Members of this family are commonly found among corals and coral rubble in pools on reef flats and reef crests and in back-reef areas. The spines are black and frequently over 20 centimetres in length in adult species of *Diadema*. In juveniles the spines are banded as they are in adult species of *Echinothrix*. Often needle-spined sea-urchins occur singly, but sometimes large numbers of specimens of *Diadema setosum* aggregate, with spines touching, in pools and in lagoons, particularly on reefs in the northern half of the Great Barrier Reef.

Genera represented: *Diadema, Echinothrix, Stomopneustes*.

Temnopleurids (Temnopleuridae). When the thin skin covering the corona of temnopleurids is removed, depressions or holes at the angles of the sutures between coronal plates are visible and the plates themselves

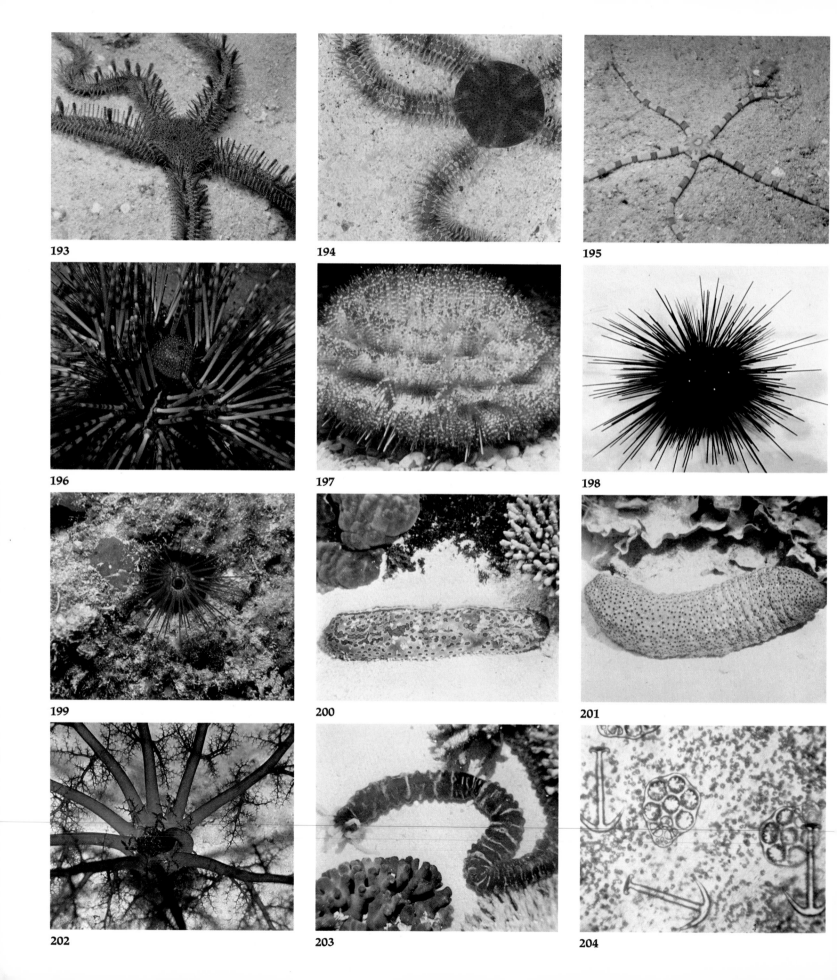

193

194

195

196

197

198

199

200

201

202

203

204

may carry depressions and ridges. Several species occur on the Great Barrier Reef, usually amongst algae in pools. Some species use algae to camouflage themselves.

Genera represented: *Mespilia, Salmacis, Temnotrema.*

Toxopneustids (Toxopneustidae). In toxopneustids no pits or depressions are found at the sutural angles of the coronal plates, which are also devoid of ridges. The equatorial region is circular or pentagonal when viewed from above. Deep gill clefts are apparent at the edges of the peristome. Dark, radially arranged stripes are visible on the coronas of some species. One type of pedicellaria that they possess bears venom glands. Toxopneustids are usually found among algal-covered rubble on reef flats.

Genera represented: *Tripneustes, Gymnechinus, Nudechinus, Lytechinus.*

Echinometrids (Echinometridae). Members of the family Echinometridae also have no pits or depressions at the sutural angles of the coronal plates, which are also without sculpturing. Gill clefts at the edges of the peristome are shallow, and frequently the equatorial region of the corona is oval in outline.

One species of this family, *Echinometra mathaei*, is probably the commonest sea-urchin to be found on the Great Barrier Reef. It occurs under slabs of dead coral or in shallow cuplike excavations in dead coral boulders in shallow water areas of the reef flat. It makes these excavations by abrading away limestone material with its stout spines. Usually the upper spines of this species are a uniform grey, but sometimes they have white tips.

The burrowing habit shown by *Echinometra mathaei* is taken further in another echinometrid called *Echinostrephus aciculatus*. The whole animal can be accommodated in deep pits that it makes in coral rocks. Normally this sea-urchin sits at the top of the pit with its vertically directed aboral tuft of purplish spines projecting. When disturbed, it retreats deep into the pit from which it is virtually impossible to dislodge. The species is commonly found in areas of dead coral boulders on reef flats.

Another echinometrid occasionally encountered on the reefs is the peculiar slate-pencil urchin (*Heterocentrotus mammillatus*) described in chapter 17.

Genera represented: *Echinometra, Echinostrephus, Heterocentrotus.*

Parasalenids (Parasaleniidae) resemble echinometrids, but the corona is flattened and the periproct carries few (usually four) plates. The large primary spines are encircled at their bases by white collars. Only one species of this family, *Parasalenia gratiosa*, has been found on the Great

Facing page
Illustration 193
The brittle-star, *Ophiomastix septemspinosa.*

Illustration 194
Ophiocoma variegata, one of the commonest brittle-stars found on reefs of the Great Barrier Reef.

Illustration 195
A brittle-star, *Ophiarachnella gorgonia.*

Illustration 196
The long-spined sea-urchin, *Echinothrix diadema.*

Illustration 197
The venomous sea-urchin, *Asthenosoma varium.*

Illustration 198
A long-spined sea-urchin, *Diadema setosum.*

Illustration 199
The burrowing sea-urchin, *Echinostrephus molaris.*

Illustration 200
The leopardfish, a sea-cucumber, *Bohadschia argus.*

Illustration 201
The sea-cucumber, *Stichopus variegatus.*

Illustration 202
The tentacles of the burrowing holothurian, *Neothyonidum magnum.*

Illustration 203
A synaptid sea-cucumber, *Synapta maculata*, Green Island reef.

Illustration 204
Microscopic spicules present in the skin of *Synapta maculata.* Anchor-shaped spicules are prominent.

Barrier Reef. It seems to be restricted to reefs north of Bowen. It usually occurs under coral boulders.

Genus represented: *Parasalenia.*

Echinoneids (Echinoneidae). The corona of echinoneids is hemispherical and the periproct has shifted from the centre of the aboral surface, where it is usually found in regular sea-urchins. The tube-feet are arranged radially in two parallel rows in each ambulacral area. Only one species, *Echinoneis cyclostomus*, is found on reefs in waters of the Great Barrier Reef. It usually occurs half-buried in coral sand under coral rubble.

Genus represented: *Echinoneis.*

Clypeasters (Clypeasteridae) have a flattened corona and a periproct near the margin of the disc. The tube-feet form distinct "petals" on the aboral surface. The small spines of the upper surface possess serrations near their tips. Clypeasters are occasionally found burrowing just below the surface in the coral sand of lagoons and back-reef areas of reefs.

Genera represented: *Clypeaster, Peronella.*

Laganids (Laganidae) are flattened sea-urchins which resemble members of the Clypeasteridae in most respects. However, the small spines on the upper surface have their tips expanded to form a crownlike structure. Laganids are common on or burrowing just below the surface of sandy areas of lagoons, reef flats, and back-reef areas of reefs in the northern half of the Great Barrier Reef area.

Genus represented: *Laganum.*

Loveniids (Loveniidae). The corona is heart-shaped and the ambulacral areas are petaloid in the family Loveniidae. A peripetalous fasciole (surrounding the petaloid area) and an inner fasciole (found inside the petaloid area) as well as a subanal fasciole (found below the anus) are present. Loveniids occur in burrows in the sand on some reefs.

Genus represented: *Breynia.*

Spatangids (Spatangidae). The corona in spatangids is heart-shaped and the peristome is anterior in position. The ambulacral areas are petaloid. A subanal fasciole occurs, but no peripetalous or inner fascioles are present. Spatangids occur in burrows in the sand on some reefs.

Genus represented: *Maretia.*

Brissids (Brissidae). Again the corona is heart-shaped and the ambulacral area petaloid. The petals are surrounded by a peripetalous fasciole, and a subanal fasciole is present. However, no inner fasciole is present. Brissids occur in burrows in sandy areas on some reefs.

Genera represented: *Brissus, Metalia.*

Holothurians (Class Holothurioidea)

Visitors to a coral reef are usually intrigued by sausage-like objects scattered, apparently at random, over the reef flat. The objects appear inert, frequently possess drab colourings, and are slimy to touch. The objects are animals called holothurians, or sea-cucumbers. If molested, they contract their body wall musculature and often void the major part of their internal organs through an opening, the cloaca, at one end of the body. At the opposite end of the body is a mouth surrounded by a crown of tentacles (see fig. 27). These sticky tentacles

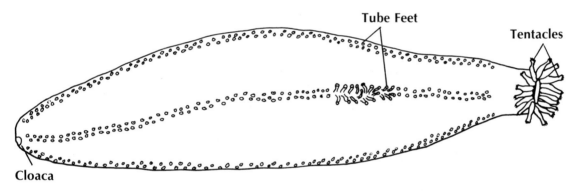

Figure 27. Diagram showing the general appearance of a sea-cucumber.

sweep the sand in their immediate vicinity. Particles of sand and detritus with associated bacteria and other micro-organisms adhere to the tentacles. The tentacles then convey adhering material to the mouth, where it is swallowed. Much of the material swallowed cannot be digested and is moulded into pea-size pellets which pass from the animal by way of the cloaca. It has been estimated that the population of approximately ten thousand holothurians inhabiting each hectare of a coral reef collectively pass about 150 tonnes of sand and other bottom material through their tubular digestive tracts each year. Obviously they play a major role in turning over surface sediments on a reef.

Water for respiratory purposes is pumped in and out of a cloacal chamber found at the hind end of the animal. The reproductive organs resemble a bunch of tubules and open anteriorly near the mouth. Sexes are separate, and reproductive products are shed directly into the sea water. Pelagic larval stages occur. Many holothurians reproduce asexually by breaking into two after a transverse construction appears which gradually deepens; the two halves regenerate the structures they lack.

Many species, when molested, throw out threads called *Cuvierian tubules* from the cloaca. The tubules elongate rapidly in sea water and often become intensely sticky. Their adhesive properties and strength are such that crabs and fish coming into contact with the tubules are often completely entangled. Even in some species where the tubules are non-sticky, they still have a defensive role. They contain toxic materials called *holothurins*. Any predator eating the wriggling worm-like tubules would be poisoned. Holothurins are also present in the skin of holothurians, which is usually thick and tough. Consequently holothurians, especially the larger species, have few predators. Some species of holothurian are chopped up by the indigenous peoples of certain Pacific islands and the pieces thrown into pools. Fish in the pools are poisoned by the holothurins liberated from the tissues and are rapidly inactivated, allowing their easy capture. Despite the presence of toxic material in their body walls, holothurians are collected and sold as *bêche-de-mer* which is regarded as a delicacy by many Asiatic peoples. They use the *bêche-de-mer* as a stock for soups and curries.

Within the body walls of all holothurians are microscopic spicules composed of calcium carbonate. These tiny spicules assume an amazing variety of form. Some are shaped like buttons with two, four, six, or eight holes. Others are shaped like open-weave baskets, some like rosettes, some like tables. Some have a simple rod-like shape, while others bear marked resemblances to miniature anchors or spoked wheels. The types of spicule present in a species are characteristic of that species. Pointed protuberances and tube-feet may project from the bodies of holothurians. The tube-feet are of course involved in locomotion and also serve as anchoring devices. The shape and number of tentacles, presence or absence of tube-feet, and number and position of the gonads allow ready separation of the holothurian families found in Great Barrier Reef waters. Identification of generic and specific rank is based primarily on the type of spicule present. Holothurian families recorded from the Great Barrier Reef are listed below.

Holothuriids (Holothuriidae). Dozens of species belonging to the family Holothuriidae occur on the Great Barrier Reef. Many attain large sizes, have thick body walls, and lie exposed on the reef flat. Others are

found under coral boulders. The oral tentacles are leaf-shaped. Tube-feet are present. Internally a single tuft of genital tubules occurs.
   Genera represented: *Actinopyga, Bohadschia, Holothuria.*

Stichopodids (Stichopodidae). Several species of large holothurians belonging to the family Stichopodidae occur on the Great Barrer Reef. Usually they lie fully exposed. Long tubercles project from their thick body walls. Tube-feet are present, and the oral tentacles are leaf-shaped as in holothuriids. Genital tubules are present in two tufts interally in stichopodids and this feature, plus differences in the types of spicule present in the body wall, allow separation of the two families.

Cucumariids (Cucumariidae) have ten bush-like tentacles and are often pentagonal in cross-section. Although common on the sea-floor between reefs of the Great Barrier Reef, cucumariids are not well represented on the reefs themselves.
   Genera represented: *Pentacta, Cucumaria.*

Phyllophorids (Phyllophoridae) have more than ten bush-like tentacles and are generally found under coral boulders and amid rubble on reefs. Large numbers of individuals may be found clustered together.
   Genera represented: *Afrocucumis, Actinocucumis, Phyllophorus.*

Synaptids (Synaptidae) are worm-like holothurians that lack tube-feet. In their skins characteristic spicules in the form of minute anchors are found. Synaptids are frequently found in coral pools on reef flats of the Great Barrier Reef. Some are very long, over a metre in length, but other species attain lengths of only a few centimetres.
   Genera represented: *Euapta, Opheodesoma, Polyplectana, Synapta, Synaptula.*

Chiridotids (Chiridotidae) are worm-like holothurians that have characteristic spicules in the form of miniature wheels in their skins. They have no tube-feet. Most species are found burrowing in coral sand or under dead coral.
   Genera represented: *Chiridota, Polycheira.*

13

Coral Reef Fishes

Coral reef fishes exhibit an apparently infinite variety of shape, size, colour, and habits. Some move slowly in silent procession over and around coral clumps, some maintain station above them, some dart in and out among the coral branches, while others flaunt their brilliant colours as they perform intricate manoeuvres in the vicinity of corals. Other fishes may be seen peering out from among coral branches or cradled in their interstices. Many of these fishes are intimately associated with particular coral clumps and rarely venture far from their protection. Others, particularly larger predatory fishes, have more extensive home territories or ranges that they patrol periodically. However, all these fishes return to the same site on the reef and may be said to be site-attached. Still other fishes, especially schooling species, regularly use the shelter of coral clumps, ledges, overhangs, and crevices but do not invariably return to the same sites. Some fishes travel in the waters among reefs, seeking out the shelter of the reefs by day, by night, or at longer intervals. Still others are only casual visitors to coral reefs. All these fishes, however, must be regarded as part of the coral reef community at any one time.

Despite the great diversity of shape and size exhibited, the general appearance of fishes is well known. Two basic groups occur on coral reefs. Members of one group, which contains the sharks and the rays, possess cartilaginous spinal columns, while members of the other group, which contains the bony fishes, possess bony spinal columns. The sharks and the rays possess a series of gills and gill slits (fig. 28) and their skins are covered with minute tooth-like scales. Bony fishes possess gill covers (opercula), scales and fins supported by bony rays (fig. 29).

In the following pages the principal families of fishes occurring on the Great Barrier Reef are discussed briefly.

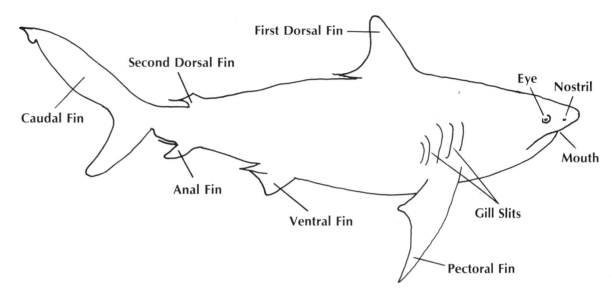

Figure 28. *Top:* Diagram illustrating the principal external features of a shark.

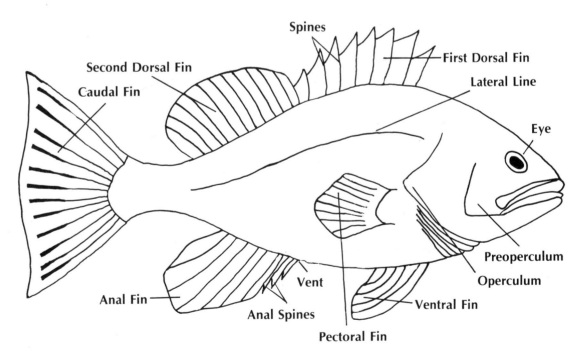

Figure 29. *Bottom:* Diagram illustrating the principal external features of a bony fish.

The Sharks and Rays (Class Chondrichthys)

Catsharks (Orectolobidae) are small to medium-sized and are restricted to shallow areas of the reef, particularly the reef flat. They are nocturnal and hide by day among dead or living corals or in crevices and holes in the reef. At night they move over the reef in search of their prey, which consists of invertebrates and small fish. Their teeth are small, and they are not regarded as dangerous to man. If carelessly handled, however, they can cause lacerations. Most species found in Great Barrier Reef waters are marked with spots and/or bands.

Some genera represented: *Orectolobus, Hemiscyllium, Stegostoma, Brachaelurus, Eucrossorhinus.*

Hammerheads (Sphyrnidae). The grotesque, flattened, and laterally expanded head of hammerhead sharks is responsible for their common name. They attain a large size and are known to have attacked humans. Occasionlly they are found in the deeper water off reefs, where they prey on fish.

Genus represented: *Sphyrna.*

True sharks (Carcharinidae). The Carcharinidae are medium to very large sharks, some of which are of danger to man. Some species (whaler sharks) are often found lying on sand in back-reef areas or lagoons during the day. They occasionally invade the reef flat area on night-time high tides. The common black-tip shark (possessing black tips to all the fins) is a member of this family and moves into shallow water on reef flats with the flooding tide. Other species (e.g., tiger sharks) tend to frequent deeper water near reefs.

Genera represented: *Carcharhinus, Galeocerdo, Scoliodon, Negaprion.*

Smooth dog sharks (Triakidae) are small to medium-sized sharks, which are easily recognized by the white tips to the dorsal and caudal fins. They have small teeth and do not attack humans. They appear to be territorial on reefs, where they feed on crustaceans and small fish. Frequently they shelter beneath ledges or in caves.

Genus represented: *Triaenodon.*

Fiddler rays (Rhyncobatidae). The pectoral fins of fiddler rays are fused with the flattened head, and the gill slits are on the lower surface as in stingrays, but the body is elongated as in sharks. The teeth form a crushing plate, well suited to dealing with the molluscs and crustaceans that constitute the prey. Fiddler rays are found on sand in

Facing page
The blue angel fish, *Pomacanthus semicirculatus.*

shallow water on reef flats or in the deeper waters of lagoons. They are harmless to humans and are considered good eating.

Genus represented: *Rhynchobates.*

Stingrays (Dasyatidae). Several species of stingray occur in Barrier Reef waters. These flattened fish are found in sandy areas, where they hunt invertebrates for food. Sometimes they partially bury themselves in sand. The whip-like tail carries one or more venomous spines.

Genera represented: *Dasyatis, Taeniura.*

Eagle rays (Myliobatidae). The large eagle rays often occur in schools near the surface, where they present a spectacular sight as they appear to fly through the water by using their pectoral fins as wings. They have a tapering snout and a long, thin tail carrying from two to six barbed spines. The teeth are flattened plates curved outwards towards the mouth and admirably suited to crushing the bivalve molluscs upon which these rays feed.

Genus represented: *Aetobatus.*

Manta rays (Mobulidae) are discussed in chapter 18.

Genera represented: *Manta, Mobula.*

Electric rays (Torpedinidae). The tail of electric rays, also called numbfish, is thick and short. Paired electric organs formed of specialized muscle tissue lie behind the eyes, and the ray is capable of delivering powerful electric shocks of about 200 volts. It is found occasionally on reef flats at the southern end of the Great Barrier Reef. During daylight hours it lies buried in sand.

Genus represented: *Hypnos.*

The Bony Fishes (Class Osteichthys)

Sprats (Clupeidae) form large schools in shallow water around reef edges. These small fish feed on plankton and are themselves preyed on by a variety of carnivorous fishes.

Genera represented: *Spratelloides, Harengula.*

Milkfish (Chanidae) are herring-like fish that grow to over a metre in length. They are greenish above and silvery below. Occasionally they are found on reef flats, where they feed on algae. Milkfish are raised in ponds in many Asian countries.

Genus represented: *Chanos.*

Lizard-fish (Synodontidae) are small carnivores that bury themselves in the coral sand or hide under coral boulders until prey approaches, when they dart from cover and seize the other fish. They have large mouths and sinuous, lizard-like bodies with cryptic colour patterns.
Some genera represented: *Synodus, Trachinocephalus, Saurida.*

Catfish (Plotosidae) are elongate fish with a fin-fringed, tapering tail and four pairs of whiskerlike appendages (barbels) on the snout. They possess venomous fin spines and are discussed in chapter 19. Juveniles occur occasionally in large schools on reef flats.
Genus represented: *Plotosus.*

Moray eels (Muraenidae) constitute a large group of medium to large eels. They are often boldly patterned and coloured. During daylight hours most species are found in holes in coral or under coral boulders. At night they emerge to hunt their prey. Most feed on fish.
Some genera represented: *Echidna, Siderea, Gymnothorax, Uropterygius.*

Snake eels (Ophichthyidae) are elongated with pointed tails free of fins. The tail is used for burrowing into coral sand, where many hide during the day. They actively hunt their prey (fish) at night.
Some genera represented: *Myrichthys, Leiuranus, Muraenichthys.*

Conger eels (Congridae). The family Congridae contains large eels that are cylindrical anteriorly. They have well-developed pectoral fins. Dorsal and anal fins extend to the tail. They live in crevices in coral, from which they emerge at night to hunt prey.
Genera represented: *Conger, Ariosoma.*

Long toms (Belonidae). The jaws of the elongate long toms carry needle-like teeth and are attenuated to form a long beak. Dorsal and anal fins are set well back near the tail. They often occur in large schools in coral reef waters. Small pelagic fishes form their prey. Frequently they skip along the surface of the water, propelling themselves with the tail fin.
Some genera represented: *Strongylura, Tylosurus, Lhotskia.*

Garfish (Hemirhamphidae) are elongate fish whose lower jaw is extended to form a pointed beak. Garfish tend to school and are herbivorous. Often they feed on algal material floating at the surface of the water.
Genera represented: *Hemirhamphus, Hyporhamphus, Euleptorhamphus.*

Flying-fish (Exocoetidae) are capable of aerial gliding for long distances by extending their large wing-like pectoral fins. They become

206

207

208

209

210

211

212

213

214

215

216

217

airborne as a result of a rapid beating of their caudal fins. They feed on plankton in surface waters and are frequently seen near reefs.

Genera represented: *Exoceotus, Cypselurus.*

Squirrel-fish (Holocentridae). Although squirrel-fish can often be seen peering out at the human intruder from among the branches of branching corals, they spend most of the day resting and are essentially nocturnal feeders. Like many nocturnal fishes, they have large eyes. Several species occur on the Great Barrier Reef. All are small, rarely exceeding 20 centimetres in overall length, and all are some shade of red. Their stout fin spines, spikes in the head region, and rough scales make them difficult to handle.

Some genera represented: *Holocentrus, Myripristis, Ostichthys.*

Flutemouths (Aulostomidae) are elongate and yellowish in colour and have tubular snouts through which they suck in smaller fish. They often use larger fish as cover when stalking prey, and they move in reverse readily.

Genus represented: *Aulostomus.*

Hairtailed flutemouths (Fistularidae). Small schools of hairtailed flutemouths are often encountered on reef slopes. They have elongate bodies and long tubular snouts through which they are able to suck in crustaceans and small fishes. The tail has a whip-like extension.

Genus represented: *Fistularia.*

Sea-horses (Syngnathidae). The family Syngnathidae contains the bizarre sea-horses and pipe-fish. They are protected by rings of bony armour. The small dorsal fin is the major organ of propulsion. Sea-horses usually swim with the long axis of the body held vertically. The tails of sea-horses are prehensile and they frequently attach to algae growing on dead corals. Eggs are carried by males. Several species of pipe-fish occur on reef flats. Some species occur in the intestines of holothurians.

Some genera represented: *Hippocampus, Choeroichthys, Corythoichthys, Doryrhamphus, Runcinatus, Micrognathus, Yozia.*

Hardyheads (Atherinidae). Occasionally, myriads of hardyheads form dense shoals in lagoons and in shallow waters near coral cays. At such times the waters may be dark with these small, silvery fish. They are plankton eaters and are themselves eaten by numerous predatory fishes.

Genera represented: *Pranesus, Hypoatherina.*

Mullets (Mugilidae). At least four species of the familiar mullet occur

Facing page
Illustration 206
The epaulette catshark, *Hemiscyllium ocellatum.*

Illustration 207
The tasselled wobbegong or catshark, *Orectolobus ogilbyi.*

Illustration 208
A whaler shark, *Carcharhinus ahenea*, beached at Tryon Island, Capricorn Group.

Illustration 209
A small blue-spotted ray, *Taeniura lymna.*

Illustration 210
A white-spotted fiddler ray, *Rhynchobatus djeddensis* on sand, Heron Island reef.

Illustration 211
A lizard-fish, *Synodus englemani.*

Illustration 212
A moray eel, *Gymnothorax tessellatus.*

Illustration 213
A squirrel-fish, *Holocentrus ruber.*

Illustration 214
The tubular snout of a painted flutemouth, *Aulostoma chinensis.*

Illustration 215
A pipe-fish, *Choeroichythys suillus.*

Illustration 216
A narrow-barred Spanish mackerel, *Cymbium commersoni*, brought ashore at Heron Island.

Illustration 217
A school of black-spotted trevally or dart, *Trachinotus bailloni.*

in small schools on reef flats and lagoons in Great Barrier Reef waters, where they feed on detritus associated with the coral sand.

Some genera represented: *Liza, Mugil, Myxus, Crenimugil.*

Mackerels (Scombridae). Many of the mackerel family are large, surface-swimming predators. They occur in schools near reefs and are much fished commercially in Great Barrier Reef waters (see chapter 22). They are elongate, streamlined fish with characteristic finlets in the tail region.

Some genera represented: *Scomberomorus, Grammatorcynus, Euthynnus.*

Marlins (Istiophoridae) are very large fish with an upper jaw that is extended into a long bill. They are pelagic and are found frequently near the outer reefs of the Great Barrier Reef, where they are fished for sport. They are discussed in chapter 22.

Genera represented: *Makaira, Istiompax, Istiophorus.*

Trevally (Carangidae) usually occur in large schools. They have characteristic forked tails and are laterally compressed. Usually they have a silvery sheen and small scales. All are swift predators, some preferring surface waters near reefs and others the sandy floors of reef lagoons. Several species occur in the waters of the Great Barrier Reef, and numerous common names such as jacks, darts, horse-mackerel, and kingfish have been conferred on the different species.

Some genera represented: *Carangoides, Caranx, Gnathanodon, Scomberoides, Trachinotus.*

Silver-biddies (Gerridae) are small, silvery fish found in shallow, sandy areas particularly on reef flats near coral cays. Usually they occur in small schools. They have a tubular, protrusible mouth and feed principally on crustaceans. Frequently they will swim right up to people wading in shallow water near cays and nibble exposed parts.

Genus represented: *Gerres.*

Cardinal-fish (Apogonidae) usually occur in small groups near or hidden in the interstices of coral heads. They are small carnivores and tend to be nocturnal. The body is elongate, the head relatively large with a protruding lower jaw, and there are two dorsal fins. The scales are usually prominent. Numerous species occur in Great Barrier Reef waters. Most are red or reddish.

Some genera represented: *Paramia, Cheilodipterus, Siphamia, Apogon, Pristiapogon, Apogonichthys, Gronovichthys.*

Coral cods (Serranidae) are medium to large predators with large mouths and protruding lower jaws. They tend to be solitary and territorial.

During the day most are somewhat sedentary and rest on their pectoral fins under coral clumps or in holes in the coral. However, some, such as the groper and the so-called coral trout, make swift rushes from their lairs at passing prey during daylight hours, and most can be enticed from their hiding places by suitable bait. They are premium food fish much sought after by anglers. At night most emerge from their daytime refuges and move over the reef flat. Most of the coral cods are camouflaged with disruptive coloration.

Some genera represented: *Cromileptes, Plectropoma, Variola, Cephalopholis, Promicrops, Epinephelus, Grammistes, Pseudochromis, Anyperodon, Diploprion.*

Dottybacks (Pseudochromidae) are small, carnivorous fish with an extensive dorsal fin. They are usually brightly coloured and associated with coral.

Some genera represented: *Pseudochromis, Dampieria, Pseudogramma.*

Butterfly perch (Anthiidae) are small, carnivorous fish that often have filamentous tails. In males the anterior dorsal spines often have filaments as well. Butterfly perch occur in small groups associated with corals on reef slopes. They are usually brightly coloured.

Genus represented: *Anthias.*

Moonfish (Menidae) are laterally compressed and extremely deep-bodied. They occur in small schools in the deeper water of reef slopes.

Genus represented: *Mene.*

Roundheads (Plesiopidae) are small, carnivorous fish associated with corals. They have relatively large, rounded heads and elongate, laterally compressed bodies. Posterior regions of the dorsal and anal fins are elongated and the caudal fin is rounded. Several species occur in Great Barrier Reef waters.

Some genera represented: *Plesiops, Assessor, Calloplesiops, Paraplesiops.*

Bullseyes (Priacanthidae) are a small group of medium-sized, laterally compressed fish. They are reddish and have large, dark eyes, a protruding lower jaw, and small scales. They are nocturnal predators and shelter among the branches of coral colonies during the day.

Genus represented: *Priacanthus.*

Snappers (Lutjanidae) are moderate to large, elongate fish that usually occur in small schools on the sea-floor in the vicinity of reefs. During the day, they generally lie close in to reefs and reefal shoals, but at night they tend to spread out over the sea-floor, where they feed on crustaceans and small fish. Numerous species exist in Great Barrier

218

219

220

221

222

223

224

225

226

227

228

229

Reef waters; several species, particularly the so-called red emperors and hussars, are prized by anglers.

Some genera represented: *Lutjanus, Caesio, Symphorus.*

Monocle and threadfin bream (Nemipteridae) are solitary, often colourful fish that are usually associated with coral heads. They resemble snappers but have no teeth on the roof of the mouth. They range in size from small to moderately large and prey on fish and crustaceans.

Some genera represented: *Scolopsis, Monotaxis, Pentapodus, Pentapus, Gymnocranius, Nemipterus.*

Sweetlip emperors (Lethrinidae). Like their close relatives, the snappers, the sweetlip emperors tend to aggregate in a resting condition near coral clumps during the day. At night they move out over sandy areas in search of prey, usually small fish, crustaceans, and molluscs. They are deep-bodied fish with pointed heads and protuberant lips. Unlike the snappers, they have no scales on the major part of the head region. They are excellent food fish and are among the commonest fish caught by anglers on the Great Barrier Reef.

Genera represented: *Lethrinus, Lethrinella.*

Javelin-fish (Pomadasyidae). Often grouped with the snappers, javelin-fish have prominent anal spines, a feature that has given rise to their common name. They are usually associated with corals. Some species have thick lips.

Some genera represented: *Pomadasys, Plectorhynchus, Spilotichthys.*

Silver bream (Sparidae) are medium-sized fish with a typical bream shape. They occur as isolated individuals or in small schools in sandy areas, particularly in lagoons and back-reef areas, where they prey on crustaceans and molluscs.

Some genera represented: *Argyrops, Rhabdosargus, Mylio, Acanthopagrus.*

Batfish (Platacidae). The aptly named batfish have laterally compressed bodies that are almost circular in outline. The dorsal and anal fins are greatly extended, particularly so in juveniles. They are frequently seen in the vicinity of coral pinnacles on reef slopes.

Genus represented: *Platax.*

Whiting (Sillaginidae) are found on sandy areas, particularly in lagoons, in Great Barrier Reef waters. They prey on worms and crustaceans.

Genus represented: *Sillago.*

Sweepers (Pempheridae) are small, laterally compressed fish, with an

Facing page

Illustration 218
The five-lined cardinal-fish, *Paramia quinquelineata.*

Illustration 219
A coral trout, *Plectropoma maculatum.*

Illustration 220
A spotted coral cod, *Epinephelus* sp.

Illustration 221
A red-bellied fusilier, *Caesio chrysozonus.*

Illustration 222
A juvenile red emperor, *Lutjanus sebae.*

Illustration 223
A sweetlip-emperor, *Lethrinus chrysostomus.*

Illustration 224
A hump-headed batfish, *Platax batavianus.*

Illustration 225
A group of butterfly-fish (*Chaetodontidae*).

Illustration 226
The high-finned butterfly-fish, *Coradion altivelis.*

Illustration 227
A blue angel-fish, *Pomacanthus semicirculatus.*

Illustration 228
An anemone-fish, *Amphiprion akindynos*, nestling among the tentacles of an anemone.

Illustration 229
Two damsel-fishes (*Pomacentridae*).

elongated tail region. They have large eyes and upwardly directed mouths. At times they occur in large shoals in shallow water on reef slopes.

Genera represented: *Leptobrama, Pempheris, Parapriacanthus.*

Drummers (Kyphosidae) are small to medium-sized fish, oval in outline and possessing a single dorsal fin. The mouth is terminal. Drummers feed on algae. They usually occur in small groups in rubble areas on reef flats and in lagoons.

Genus represented: *Kyphosus.*

Goatfish (Mullidae) are small to medium-sized and have a pair of barbels below the head which are used to probe the coral sand for the crustaceans and worms upon which they prey. Usually they occur in small groups. Several species are found in Great Barrier Reef waters. Most are reddish.

Some genera represented: *Upeneus, Mulloidichthys, Parupeneus.*

Butterfly-fish (Chaetodontidae) are small (rarely more than 15 centimetres in overall length), laterally compressed fish that are always closely associated with branching corals, particularly in shallow water areas such as reef flats. Indeed, some species feed on coral polyps, although most appear to prey on small invertebrates, such as small worms and crustaceans, found among the coral branches. A protuberant snout tipped with a small mouth containing comb-like teeth assists in this mode of feeding. Usually they occur singly or in pairs, and the manner in which they hover over coral clumps is reminiscent of the fluttering of a butterfly, hence their common name. The majority are strikingly coloured in shades of yellow, white, and orange. A dark stripe usually runs through the eye region and often there is a dark "eye-spot" on either side of the trunk, as there often is on the wings of a butterfly. Most seem to be associated with particular coral clumps. When disturbed, they plunge into their coral home and wedge themselves among the branches by erecting their fin spines. They are then very difficult for predators to dislodge. Dozens of different species of butterfly-fish occur on the Great Barrier Reef. Some of these species are very wide-ranging, occurring throughout the Indo–West Pacific area.

Some genera represented: *Chaetodon, Parachaetodon, Gonochaetodon, Forcipiger, Chelmon, Tetrachaetodon, Anisochaetodon, Coradion, Heniochus.*

Angel-fish (Pomacanthidae) are closely related to butterfly-fish but differ from them structurally by the possession of a prominent spine on the preoperculum (see fig. 29). Angel-fish are among the most beautifully marked and brilliantly coloured of all coral reef fishes. Moreover, they tend to change colour and pattern as they mature, so a magnificent array of colour and pattern is exhibited by them. Although well represented, fewer species of angel-fish than butterfly-fish occur on the Great Barrier Reef, and from the standpoint of numbers of individuals, angel-fish appear to be much less numerous there than butterfly-fish. Both groups are closely associated with corals and have similar habits, but angel-fish tend to attain larger sizes than butterfly-fish.

Some genera represented: *Euxiphipops, Pomacanthus, Centropyge, Dischistodus, Chaetodontoplus, Pygoplites, Glyphiododontops.*

Damsel-fish (Pomacentridae), also known as demoiselles, are small, brightly coloured fish that are associated with branching corals. Dozens of species occur in Great Barrier Reef waters, and these display a wide range of colour; greens, blues, and yellows appear to predominate. Some species (e.g., the common humbugs) are cross-banded. Although damsel-fish sometimes occur as solitary individuals, they are usually found in small groups, hovering over their chosen coral colony and ever ready to dash into the protective branches of the colony if danger threatens. Their scales are large and extend onto their cheeks and opercula. They are territorial and omnivorous.

Some genera represented: *Dascyllus, Pomocentrus, Abudefduf, Stegastes, Chromis, Acanthochromis, Cheiloprion, Daya.*

Anemone-fish (Amphiprionidae). As their name implies, anemone-fish are always associated with anemones. Several species occur on reefs of the Great Barrier Reef. Anemone-fish are small and usually reddish, dark orange, or blackish, with one or more transverse bands of white. Further information on anemone-fish will be found in chapter 17.

Genera represented: *Premnas, Amphiprion.*

Wrasses (Labridae) are among the most spectacularly coloured and numerous of all reef fishes. They range in size from the large hump-headed maori wrasse, which may attain a length of 2 metres, to the diminutive cleaner-fish discussed in chapter 17. They tend to be elongate, with thick lips and large scales. The front teeth are often tusklike, and for this reason labrids are often referred to as tusk-fish. These teeth, which are frequently greenish or pale blue, are adapted for seizing invertebrates such as crustaceans and molluscs. However, wrasses are partly herbivorous. Most species occur singly or in pairs, but some species school. Although bright green is a common colour in labrids, almost every tint of the spectrum is represented among the numerous species found on the Great Barrier Reef. Even within the one species there may be marked variation in colour, depending on the age and sex of the individual examined.

230

231

232

233

234

235

236

237

238

239

240

241

Some genera represented: *Labrichthys, Choerodon, Cheilinus, lepidaplois, Cheilio, Thalassoma, Labroides, Conus, Anampses, Lienardella, Lepidaplois, Halichoeres, Bodianus, Stethojulis, Hemigymnus.*

Parrot-fish (Scaridae) have teeth that are fused to form powerful beaks, hence the common name. The beaks are used to bite off pieces of algae and to scrape off algal turf from dead corals. In the process, some calcareous material is also removed from the coral skeletons. This material passes through the alimentary canal of the fish, which thereby assist in the degradation of the skeletons of dead corals. Parrot-fish are not entirely herbivorous; some invertebrates such as molluscs and crustaceans are also eaten. Sometimes they scrape living corals in their attempt to capture burrowing or partially protected invertebrates, and such scrape marks are not uncommon on massive corals such as species of *Porites*. Parrot-fish are medium to large fish related to wrasses. They have large scales and, like their avian counterparts, exhibit gaudy colours. Green, red, brown, and blue are the dominant colours in the several species that occur in Great Barrier Reef waters. Actually, most red and brown individuals are females or young males, whereas green or blue individuals are old males. Parrot-fish feed during the day and rest at night. Individuals of some species aggregate in large schools when feeding. Frequently wrasses and rabbit-fish join the schools, which move slowly over the reef flat. One of the most spectacular sights in coral reef waters is that of the exposed tails of parrot-fishes feeding in shallow water. The brilliantly coloured tails glisten in the tropical sun as they appear to wave leisurely to the human observer.

Some genera represented: *Scarus, Leptoscarus, Chlorurus, Calotomus, Scarpos, Bolbometopon.*

Barracudas (Sphyraenidae) are fierce carnivores that tend to move in packs in mid-water around reef slopes. They are large, elongate, torpedo-like fishes with forked tails and two dorsal fins. The large mouth is armed with large conical teeth.

Genera represented: *Agrioposphyraena, Sphyraena, Sphyraenella.*

Smilers (Opistognathidae) are solitary and territorial, living in burrows in the sand, often among rubble, from which they make short dashes to capture passing prey. They are discussed in chapter 17.

Genera represented: *Opistognathus, Merogymnus.*

Blennies (Blenniidae) belong to a large group of small sedentary fishes. Most occur in tide pools or in crevices in coral. When disturbed, they shelter under pieces of dead coral or wriggle deep into the interstices in coral. They are agile and can flip high into the air and wriggle from

Facing page

Illustration 230
The harlequin tuskfish, *Lienardella fasciatus.*

Illustration 231
The blue parrot-fish, *Scarus microrhinos.*

Illustration 232
An orange coral goby (*Gobiidae*).

Illustration 233
A scaled blenny (*Tripterigiidae*).

Illustration 234
The gold-spotted rabbit-fish, *Siganus chrysospilos.*

Illustration 235
The moorish idol, *Zanclus canescens.*

Illustration 236
A dragonet (*Callionymidae*).

Illustration 237
A reef flathead, *Platycephalus laevigatus.*

Illustration 238
A scorpion-fish, *Parascorpaena picta.*

Illustration 239
The wedge-tailed trigger-fish, *Rhinecarpus echarpe.*

Illustration 240
The cowfish, *Lactoria diaphana.*

Illustration 241
A three-bar porcupine-fish, *Dicotylichthys punctulatus.*

one pool to the next at low tide. They are carnivorous, and many species have large canine teeth. In some species the fangs are grooved and associated with a venom apparatus. Usually they are cryptically coloured, but a few species are brightly coloured. Numerous species occur in the Great Barrier Reef region.

Some genera represented: *Petroscirtes, Dasson, Meiacanthus, Alticus, Salarias, Negoscartes, Istiblennius, Halmablennius, Exallias, Escenius.*

Dragonets (Callionymidae). The scaleless bodies of dragonets are cylindrical. Two dorsal fins, longer in the male, are present. The caudal fin is broad and rounded. The eyes bulge upwards and protrude when the dragonet buries itself in the sand for concealment.

Genera represented: *Callionymus, Synchiropus, Dactylopus.*

Gobies (Gobiidae) are another large group of small, sedentary fish. The anterior position of the ventral fins is a feature used to distinguish them from blennies. In gobies the ventral fins are fused to form a sucker with which they cling to objects on the reef. They are frequently found on the bottom of pools, but some are found in the interstices of corals. While most are cryptically coloured, some have bright colours.

Some genera represented: *Paragobiodon, Gobiodon, Ctenogobius, Asterropteryx, Eliotrioides, Amblygobius, Eviota, Pridepis.*

Scaled blennies (Tripterygiidae) are blenny-like fish but differ from blennies in the possession of three dorsal fins and a scaled body. They occur in crevices in dead coral and in surge areas near reef crests.

Some genera represented: *Tripterygion, Norfolkia, Vauclusella.*

Clingfish (Gobiesocidae) are small goby-like fish that have a sucker on the belly region and a single dorsal fin. The sucker enables them to cling to pieces of dead coral and other objects in regions where there is considerable surge and strong currents. One species is found in association with feather-stars.

Genus represented: *Lepadichthys.*

Rabbit-fish (Siganidae). Several species of the herbivorous rabbit-fish occur on the Great Barrier Reef. The highly coloured species tend to occur singly and to maintain territories, whereas the more drab species tend to form schools and to associate with schooling parrot-fish. They are moderate-sized fish with oval, laterally compressed bodies. Fin spines are prominent and venomous. Siganids are active only during the day; at night they sleep in exposed situations with the venomous fin spines erected.

Genera represented: *Siganus, Lo.*

Messmate-fish (Carapidae) are thin, elongate fish that live in association with sea-cucumbers and bivalve molluscs and are discussed in chapter 17.

Genera represented: *Onusodon, Carapus.*

Surgeon-fish (Acanthuridae) are laterally compressed and have one or more lancet-like spines at each side of the butt of the tail, which accounts for their common name. (Some species have a hornlike structure above the snout and are known as unicorn-fish.) All have minute scales, a continuous dorsal fin, a continuous anal fin, and a body that is usually oval in outline. They are all herbivorous. Some species are among the most strikingly coloured of fishes found on the Great Barrier Reef. The more brightly coloured species tend to maintain territories, while the less conspicuous ones tend to school.

Some genera represented: *Acanthurus, Zebrasoma, Ctenochaetus, Callicanthus, Naso.*

Moorish idols (Zanclidae). Only a single species belonging to the Zanclidae is known, but it occurs throughout the tropical Indo–Pacific area. It is a small fish with a body that is almost circular in outline. The long, pendant-like dorsal fin and the poster colours of this fish make it a favourite subject for photographers and illustrators of books. It is a relative of surgeon-fish and like them is essentially herbivorous.

Genus represented: *Zanclus.*

Left-handed flounders (Bothidae) are small, bottom-dwelling flatfish. The left side is uppermost, and both eyes are on this side in adults. The dorsal fin extends onto the head region. These fish are cryptically coloured.

Genus represented: *Bothus.*

Soles (Soleidae) are small flatfish which lie with their right side uppermost in sandy areas on reef flats. They are cryptically coloured and difficult to distinguish. Pectoral fins are lacking.

Genera represented: *Achirus, Pardachirus.*

Flatheads (Platycephalidae). As the name implies, members of the family Platycephalidae have greatly flattened heads, which bear spines and bony ridges. They are medium-sized fish that lie partially buried in sand on the reef awaiting the approach of their prey.

Some genera represented: *Platycephalus, Inegocia.*

Flying gurnards (Dactylopteridae) are blunt-snouted fish characterized by their enormous pectoral fins, which can be used for gliding if the

fishes are disturbed in shallow water on reef flats. Specimens of these ornate fish up to 40 centimetres in length have been observed.
Genus represented: *Dactyloptaena*.

Scorpion-fish (Scorpaenidae) are small to medium-sized fish and noted for their possession of venomous spines (see chapter 19). Some, such as the zebra-fish, are brightly coloured, but the majority are well camouflaged. They occur in rubble patches on reef flats and under ledges on reef slopes. The head possesses spiny protuberances, and the mouth is large. Most species are sedentary and solitary and lie in wait for their prey, usually small fish and crustaceans. Scales and fin spines are well developed.
Genera represented: *Pteropterus, Pterois, Brachirus, Scorpaenoides, Sebastapistes*.

Stonefish (Synanceiidae) are scaleless and have large heads possessing deep concavities and bony protuberances. They have large pectoral fins that are used to make excavations in sand or rubble. They lie partially buried and waiting for their prey to come within range. The dorsal fin spines are associated with venom glands, and the venomous nature of these fish is discussed in chapter 19.
Genus represented: *Synanceia*.

Sucker-fish (Echeneidae) are elongate fish characterized by the presence on top of the head of a sucking disc formed from a modified first dorsal fin. The sucker is used for attachment to large animals such as sharks, mantas and turtles.
Genera represented: *Echeneis, Remora*.

File-fish (Aluteridae) are a group of small to medium-sized fish possessing minute scales bearing small spines which make them rough to the touch, hence the common name. The body is oval to circular in outline and laterally compressed and carries an erectile dorsal spine. They are often brightly coloured, and most species are regarded as poisonous. Many are considered to be herbivorous, but some are known to feed on zoanthids. They occur on reef flats and reef slopes.
Some genera represented: *Cantherines, Oxymonacanthus, Pervagor, Alutera*.

Trigger-fish (Balistidae). The anterior dorsal fin of trigger-fish consists of three spines, the first of which is stout and can be locked in an erect position. As well as tough shieldlike scales, these fish have very powerful jaws and are able to attack spiny sea-urchins and the venomous starfish *Acanthaster planci*, in addition to various crustaceans. Some species have elaborate colour patterns. The flesh of most trigger-fish is considered to be poisonous.

Some genera represented: *Abalistes, Canthidermus, Pseudobalistes, Balistoides, Balistopus, Melichthys, Rhinecanthus, Rhinecarpus.*

Boxfish (Ostraciontidae). The head and trunk of boxfish are encased in bony armour, and only the tail and fins are free to move. They possess beaklike teeth and feed on algae. Some (the so-called cowfish) have a pair of horns projecting forwards from the head. Many are attractively coloured, and most occur in shallow water on the reef flats. They exude toxic material from the skin.
Genera represented: *Ostracion, Lactoria.*

Puffer-fish (Tetraodontidae). As the name implies, puffer-fish are able to inflate their bodies. This is done by swallowing water or air. They are small to medium-sized fish that prey on a variety of invertebrates, including starfish. The teeth are fused to form a beak, and they lack fin spines and ventral fins. Usually they occur singly on the reef flat and reef slopes. Some species are brightly coloured. Most are extremely poisonous.
Some genera represented: *Arothron, Canthigaster, Gastrophysus.*

Porcupine-fish (Diodontidae). Although porcupine-fish are able to inflate themselves by swallowing water or air, they differ from puffer-fish in that they are covered with spines. However, like puffer-fish they are poisonous. They are small to medium-sized and are found on reef slopes.
Genera represented: *Diodon, Cyclichthys.*

Frogfish (Batrachoididae). When captured, frogfish emit croaking noises, a peculiarity that has given rise to their common name. They possess a large upturned mouth and projections from the skin which resemble algal growths. They make excavations in coral sand and rubble and lie with only their head exposed. Only one species has been found on the Great Barrier Reef. This species is not venomous, as are many of its relatives elsewhere.
Genus represented: *Holophryne.*

Angler-fish (Antennariidae). The first spine of the dorsal fin is elongated and carries a fishing lure. This is waved about to attract small fishes upon which the angler-fish preys.
Genus represented: *Antennarius.*

It will be appreciated from the foregoing account that most of the major groups of tropical marine fishes occur on coral reefs. Moreover, several species belonging to each major group are usually represented. Sometimes many thousands of individuals of the one species are found on reefs. In some cases they occur in such profusion that the diver cannot see past them. However, there is a limit to the standing crop of fish that a coral reef can support; it has been estimated that a standing crop of 2,000 kilograms of fish per hectare would be the maximum maintained by most coral reef fish communities. Even so, visitors to coral reefs often wonder why so many different kinds of fishes are present. Possible reasons are discussed in chapter 16.

Almost every conceivable habitat on coral reefs is occupied by fish: coral clumps, pools, sandy areas, rubble patches, reef flats, lagoons, reef crests, reef slopes, etc. — all have their complement of fish. It is a feature of coral reef fishes that many species are site-attached. For example, butterfly-fish, damsel-fish, and angel-fish adhere to their chosen coral clumps and rarely stray far from them. Many representatives of the larger species, such as the coral cods, have larger territories and will move away from the crevice or hole in the reef that is their resting place. However, they usually return to their resting place after their excursions. Some species move around reefs in schools; parrot-fish, some wrasses, surgeon-fish, and rabbit-fish would come into this category. It is not known whether these schools move from one reef to another, but it is suspected that they do not and that each school may in fact remain in a particular area of one reef. Possibly some species of the larger fishes found in deeper waters around reefs, such as the snappers, do move among reefs; this would appear to be true for many species of the larger pelagic predators, such as the mackerels. However, coral reef fishes, on the whole, tend to be territorial and to remain throughout their lives on the reef where they settled as juveniles. This fidelity to a particular reef raises problems about how fish share out among themselves the available resources of living space, food, and shelter and about how they maintain population numbers on isolated reefs considering that most fishes release their sexual products directly into the water and fertilization is external. These problems are discussed in later chapters.

Many visitors to coral reefs wonder why so many coral reef fishes are so strikingly coloured. It is believed that because there are so many species of fish on coral reefs, characteristic colour patterns are required for intraspecific and interspecific recognition. Also, males can frequently be distinguished from females by marked and subtle differences of colour or colour pattern. Then too, the background colours of corals and other sedentary organisms on coral reefs are often bright. Drab colours may not provide very effective camouflage in such situations.

14

How Living Space Is Shared on Coral Reefs

Living Places on Coral Reefs

Almost every conceivable habitat is used by coral reef organisms. Many animals live attached to the reef and freely exposed, as in the case of most corals, soft corals, gorgonians, and the like, which require light for their contained zooxanthellae. Other attached animals that do not require light frequently live on the undersurfaces of dead coral boulders, under overhangs, and in crevices and caves. All these attached animals provide protection for a host of other organisms such as worms, small crustaceans, molluscs, and fish. The degradation products (e.g., dead coral boulders, coral sand) of calcareous organisms also provide habitats for other organisms found on, in, and under boulders and on or burrowing in coral sand. On most reefs there are large areas of loose or semi-consolidated coral rubble that form a haven for numerous species, particularly nocturnal species that hide there during daylight hours. Also, the whole coral reef structure attracts pelagic fishes and casual visitors, such as turtles, sharks, manta rays, and mackerel. Then there are highly specialized species that live in association with other species in various ways.

In the water over and around a reef planktonic organisms occur. These are organisms that drift with the water currents. Many float passively, others move about in an apparently haphazard fashion. Both plant (phytoplankton) and animal (zooplankton) species are represented in the plankton. Most are small. Some species are permanent members of the plankton and their presence near a reef would be purely incidental. Other species are temporary members of the plankton and their presence may be directly linked with the coral reef community since the eggs and young of coral reef species may be well represented among the planktonic forms. The planktonic phase in the life cycles of these coral reef species is a dispersive phase permitting the colonization of new habitats. Then too, some coral reef species, particularly small crustaceans, rise from the reef during darkness and feed in the water column over the reef. They return to sheltered sites on the reef at dawn. Planktonic species provide food for a multitude of reef animals.

Stationariness

Algae that grow attached to the substratum are termed *sessile* algae. Many animals, too, are fixed to the substratum for all their adult lives and may be regarded as sessile animals. All these sessile organisms — algae, corals, hydroids, soft corals, gorgonians, anemones, sponges, ascidians, and so forth — provide the basic living cover of coral reefs. Numerous animals are said to be *sedentary* rather than sessile. They are in physical contact with the substratum, and although they are able to move about they rarely move far from their chosen habitat. Many species of gastropod, echinoid, and holothurian certainly fall into this category, and many other species of invertebrate, including brittle-stars, feather-stars, starfish, crabs, and worms are essentially sedentary. Many of these sedentary invertebrates are closely associated with the sessile coral reef organisms. Then there are *site-attached* or territorial animals. These animals are able to swim above the substratum but possess home ranges or territories to which they adhere. Many coral reef fishes come into this category. Sessile, sedentary, and site-attached organisms show varying degrees of stationariness, a strategy adopted by the majority of coral reef animals during their adult lives.

What is the advantage of being stationary? Each coral reef is usually an isolated structure with a surface area that is very limited when compared with the areas provided by many other marine habitats. However, it provides shelter and food in abundance. Consequently, suitable living space is at a premium, and competition for that available is intense. If a space is vacated, it will soon be occupied by another individual of the same or of a different species. Hence most coral reef animals adhere to particular sites on a reef so long as those sites remain suitable for their particular mode of life.

Of course, stationariness has disadvantages. In particular, sessile and most sedentary organisms cannot escape predators by moving away. Site-attached animals can move, but usually if they move out of their home range or familiar territory they enter the territories of other animals and expose themselves to a higher risk of predation. Also, stationary animals are in danger of being settled on by the larvae of sessile organisms, invaded by micro-organisms, and threatened by the growth of neighbouring organisms that tend to encroach on their territories. They have adopted one or more of a number of different strategies to cope with these hazards. Many have elaborated noxious or toxic chemicals to deter predators and competitors from molesting them. For example, 73 per cent of 429 species of exposed invertebrates found commonly on the Great Barrier Reef and representing four phyla (sponges, cnidarians, echinoderms, and ascidians) were found recently to be toxic to fish. Some species, although non-toxic themselves, mimic toxic species and are thereby afforded protection. Other species have developed specialized anatomical, morphological, physiological, and behavioural defences. Some have adopted specialized habitats where they find protection. Others have specialized in the production of large numbers of offspring and the possession of rapid regeneration times, so that although many fall victim to predators or pathogenic micro-organisms or parasites, a few always survive to continue the species.

Competition for Living Space

The presence of other organisms may limit the distribution and abundance of some species through competition. Such competition may occur among the members of one species or among the members of different species that eat the same types of food and live in the same sorts of places. While food for most species appears to be readily available on coral reefs, living space does seem to be a limiting factor. Indeed, competition for space upon which to settle and grow is intense on coral reefs. As already noted, the reefs of the Great Barrier Reef are limited in extent and the number of suitable living spaces available to an animal is finite. Various strategies have been developed by animals to acquire and hold space. Among the most important of the strategies adopted by sessile organisms are rapid colony formation and regeneration, *overgrowth* and *allelopathy*; in addition, corals show *overtopping* and *aggressive extracoelenteric feeding* and some possess *sweeper tentacles*. Among the mobile animals, some individuals often drive others from a particular site by aggressive behaviour. Such behaviour is shown by many fishes and crabs in particular.

Overgrowth

Some sponges appear able to overgrow many other sessile animals in their vicinity. Several other organisms with a spreading or encrusting growth habit, such as some soft corals and zoanthids, are also able to overgrow other organisms. Some probably use toxic secretions to assist them in the overgrowing process.

Allelopathy

Some reef organisms are limited in their distribution by toxic secretions produced by other organisms. Toxic secretions are commonly produced by terrestrial plants to prevent other organisms from invading their tissues, settling upon them, or encroaching on their living space. Penicillin produced by a terrestrial fungus is a well-known example of a toxin that prevents micro-organisms from invading the tissues of the fungus, and use has been made of its antibiotic properties in medicine. Likewise, many sessile coral reef organisms produce antibiotic substances.

Algae belonging to many species produce antibiotics, some of which are very potent. Many species of sponge produce antibiotic substances, and in some cases there is a zone of antibiosis around the sponge that effectively prevents other organisms from growing on the sponge or encroaching on its living space. Similarly, many species of gorgonians, soft corals, anemones, zoanthids, and ascidians produce antibiotics. Complicated competitive networks of species based on antibiotic interactions are believed to exist and are currently being unravelled by coral reef biologists. The extent to which hard corals produce antibiotics has not been investigated, but some species appear to do so. Some of the antibiotics elaborated by coral reef organisms have been isolated and chemically characterized and are finding a use in human and veterinary medicine.

Overtopping

Branching corals generally grow rapidly. Some species tend to form canopies and to overtop and shade out other species. Corals, of course, require light for the photosynthetic activities of the symbiotic zooxanthellae contained in their tissues. Such overtopping may lead to the deaths of shaded colonies or portions of colonies in deeper regions of reefs.

Aggressive Extracoelenteric Feeding

The polyps of many species of hard coral are able to protrude long nematocyst-laden mesenterial filaments through their mouths or through special holes in their body wall. Any fleshy areas of other species of coral within reach of the filaments are attacked and digested. There is a hierarchical ranking with respect to this method of feeding, subordinate species of coral being attacked by those species above them in the hierarchy. This method of feeding enables dominant species to extend their living space at the expense of subordinate species. However, the dominant aggressive species are usually slow growers, while the less aggressive subordinate species are usually rapid growers. Also, some of the subordinate species may produce antibiotics or may possess sweeper tentacles (see below). In effect, a balance is struck and no single species of coral becomes an absolute dominant over the whole reef area.

Sweeper Tentacles

A few species of coral have been observed to produce elongate tentacles known as sweeper tentacles. These appear to be primarily defensive structures which prevent the mesenterial filaments of aggressive species from coming into contact with the tissues of the colony from which the sweeper tentacles arise and prevent other species from overtopping or encroaching on the colony.

Symbiosis, Commensalism, and Parasitism

Many animals have effectively reduced competition for substratum by living in intimate association with other animals of a different species. The term *symbiosis* is frequently used to describe the cohabitation of different species of animal. If one of the symbionts derives energy from the other it is usually termed a parasite. If a symbiont derives energy from sources other than its partner it is called a commensal. Commensalism and parasitism are encountered frequently among coral reef animals. Corals, for example, act as hosts for a variety of commensal animals, including shrimps, crabs, copepods, barnacles, worms, molluscs, and fish. Sometimes the associations are very specific, as in the association of anemone-fish with anemones. It is believed that the number of parasitic species found on coral reefs exceeds the number of free-living species present.

15

How Nutrients Are Shared on Coral Reefs

Sources of Energy and Nutrients

An ecosystem of the kind constituted by the Great Barrier Reef can function only by maintaining a flow of energy and raw materials required by living organisms to build and maintain their structures and to perform their various living functions. The source of energy is solar radiation, and energy flow begins with its fixation by plants. Light energy is fixed by the process of photosynthesis and is then used to build up carbohydrates from carbon dioxide and water obtained from the surroundings of the plants along with such other materials as nitrates and phosphates. Some of the carbohydrates synthesized are then broken down again to carbon dioxide and water, and part of the energy released during this breakdown is used to synthesize proteins and nucleic acids and other vital compounds. Synthesis of proteins requires a source of nitrogen (e.g., nitrates), and synthesis of nucleic acids requires a source of phosphorus (e.g., phosphates). The bodies of plants are eaten by animals or decomposed by micro-organisms such as bacteria; hence, plants provide a source of energy and raw materials — that is, a source of food for other organisms. Plants are therefore regarded as the primary producers of food and constitute the first food, or *trophic* level in any ecosystem. The energy and raw materials stored by plants are passed through the ecosystem in a series of steps of eating and being eaten known as the *food chain*. Herbivores (animals that eat plants) are the primary consumers in the ecosystem; then come the carnivores that prey on herbivores. In addition to this food chain there is a separate chain of detritus feeders which decompose dead plant and animal material and permit essential raw materials to be recycled through the system.

In practice, the situation is usually more complex than that just outlined. Some animals will eat both plants and animals and are known as omnivores. Some animals are predominantly detritus feeders, feeding on detritus and associated micro-organisms. There are carnivores that prey on other carnivores or on omnivores or on detritus feeders or on combinations of them. Hence it is possible to describe various *food webs* for a particular ecosystem. See figure 30 for a generalized food chain.

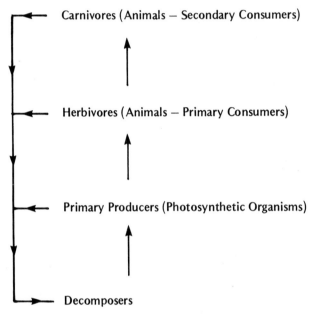

Carnivores (Animals — Secondary Consumers)

Herbivores (Animals — Primary Consumers)

Primary Producers (Photosynthetic Organisms)

Decomposers

Figure 30. Diagram of a generalized simple food chain.

Primary production in the coral reef ecosystem is remarkably high owing to the activities of photosynthetic plants such as calcareous algae, zooxanthellae in the tissues of corals and other sessile animals, macroscopic algae, and microscopic algae. Even in areas of coral sand and rubble the intensity of photosynthesis is high because of the activities of green micro-algae and diatoms. All this contrasts with the comparatively low primary productivity usually exhibited by the community of organisms present in the oceanic waters surrounding coral reefs. Tropical waters generally are poor in dissolved nitrates and phosphates. This raises the question of how the high rates of primary production on coral reefs, which have been aptly described as oases in the oceanic desert, are maintained.

It would appear that bacteria on coral reefs provide an effective mechanism for the retention in the coral reef system of much of the energy captured by plants and for the retention and recycling of nutrients such as phosphates and nitrates. Lagoon waters of coral reefs often contain as many as a thousand bacterial colonies per millilitre, but it is in the dark, internal spaces of the meshwork of dead coral skeletons and other materials found at many locations on reefs that the highest bacterial counts are obtained. The surface area of these internal spaces may exceed the horizontal area of a reef by a factor of three. It is in these internal cavities of a reef that the bulk of mobile reef invertebrates are concentrated during daylight hours. It is here that the bulk of encrusting invertebrates are also found. The materials that pass through the alimentary canals of the animals present in the internal spaces of the reef, as well as the remains of dead organisms that lodge there, make these spaces areas of organic enrichment ideal for the culture of bacteria. The ability of bacteria to grow and multiply on substrates rich in organic material leads to a rapid breakdown of the dead bodies of reef organisms or parts of them, and of the waste products such as faecal material and of secretory products such as mucus produced by living organisms. Bacteria and bacterial clumps are eaten by the multitude of filter feeding, suspension feeding, and detritus feeding animals (these include representatives of most groups, including corals) found on reefs, and in this way essential nutrients are retained and recycled within the reef community. In addition, bacteria are able to utilize significant amounts of dissolved organic matter present in incoming oceanic sea water and hence capture nutrients from external sources for use by the reef community.

As will have been apparent from earlier discussions of the food and feeding methods of the various groups of organisms found on coral reefs, feeding mechanisms of many different kinds are employed. Sessile organisms usually feed on small objects, and they depend on one or more of a varied group of filtering and trapping devices; some are able to absorb dissolved food materials directly from external sea water. Mobile organisms are usually able to pursue their prey, and they frequently feed on relatively bulky objects using piercing, cutting, and grinding mouthparts. Reef organisms may be placed in many different types of food web, as exemplified by figure 31.

As a group, the coral reef fishes are peculiar because of the great preponderance of carnivorous species. There are in fact over three times as many carnivorous as herbivorous species. Parrot-fish and surgeon-fish are perhaps the commonest of the herbivorous fishes, but rabbit-fish, some damsel-fish, and some blennies are important. Although there are no phytoplankton feeders among the coral reef fishes, zooplankton feeders are well represented. Small plankton feeders such as sprats (Clupeidae), hardyheads (Atherinidae) and

A FOOD WEB

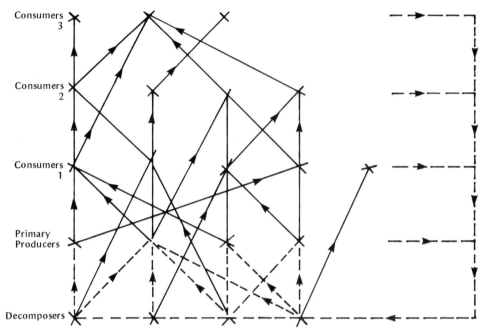

Consumers 3

Consumers 2

Consumers 1

Primary Producers

Decomposers

Figure 31. The primary producers are photosynthetic organisms. The arrows indicate the direction of the flow of food materials. Solid lines indicate predation (the eating of whole organisms or parts thereof). Broken lines indicate the absorption of decomposition products or metabolic products.

sweepers (Pempheridae) sometimes form huge schools. Butterfly perch (Anthiidae) and damsel-fish (Pomacentridae) also feed on zooplankton.

Many of the larger carnivorous fishes are opportunistic, taking the commonest prey available. Some, however, are highly specialized feeders, as in the case of the parasite-eating fish such as *Labroides.* Some fishes are omnivorous. Some damsel-fish, squirrel-fish, angel-fish, file-fish, boxfish, puffer-fish, wrasses, trigger-fish, and garfish would fall into this category. A few species, including mullets and some blennies, feed on detritus.

Predation

Much of the behaviour of animals is directed towards obtaining food and avoiding being eaten. Predation is the eating of one individual of a species, the prey, by an individual of another species, the predator. Sometimes the predator feeds on a variety of prey species, sometimes on only one or two. Each prey species in turn may be fed upon by many predatory species or by only one or two. The prey may be a food plant, in which case the predator is a herbivore, or it may be a herbivore and the predator a carnivore; or both prey and predator may be carnivores.

Naturally it is advantageous to an organism to develop defences against predation. Defences take many forms. Many animals have developed anatomical defences in the form of thick skeletons. Notable examples here are corals and molluscs. Coral polyps retract into the shelter of their corallites when molested. Bivalve molluscs, such as clams, close the two valves to their shells when danger threatens. The shells of gastropods may be very solid (e.g., the shells of *Trochus niloticus* and *Cassis cornuta*) and would defy the attempts of most predators to crush them. Other animals, such as sea-urchins, have evolved movable spines as protection. Some fishes, such as the box-fish, are encased in bony armour. The electric ray (*Hypnos monopterygium*) has evolved a mechanism for delivering a powerful electric shock to potential predators.

Some animals rely on speed and/or manoeuvrability to outpace and elude predators. Many fishes and many members of the peculiar group of crustaceans known as stomatopods are extremely fast and elusive. Flying-fish are able to leave the water entirely and glide through the air when pursued by predators. The cephalopods (octopuses, calamaries and cuttlefish) are noted for their ability to produce a dark cloud of ink when alarmed and to use the cloud as a "smoke-screen" in order to make good their escape.

Many animals have evolved powerful chemical defences. Some elaborate noxious or distasteful substances, called noxins, which result in their being repellent or unpalatable to potential predators. Some fishes, such as the coral cods known as soapfish, boxfishes, and some gastropod molluscs, secrete noxious substances when molested. Some holothurians deposit filaments containing noxious substances in their vicinity to deter would-be predators. Certain sponges and many other sessile species secrete noxious or toxic substances or both into their immediate environment apparently to deter other species from attacking them. Others have potent poisons in their tissues which render them virtually immune from predation. Some fishes, some crabs, most holothurians, most starfish, and some molluscs, soft corals, and anemones rely on this strategy. Still others are venomous. They have elaborated potent toxins in association with an apparatus — the venom apparatus — capable of delivering the toxin. Many fishes — such as scorpion-fish, rabbit-fish, catfish, and stingrays, as well as some sea-urchins — have elaborated venoms that are used solely in defence. Other venomous animals, such as cone-shells, use their venoms primarily in offence but may use them defensively if molested. A specimen of *Conus geographus*, for example, has been observed to harpoon and kill a mollusc-eating eel which attacked it (see colour plate). An animal may take its prey's defence mechanism and use it for its own protection. Certain species of nudibranch (sea-slug) prey on hydroids but do not digest the prey's nematocysts; these pass through the walls of the alimentary canal to the skin of the mollusc, where they are used for the mollusc's defence.

Many animals, notably bottom-dwelling fishes, have a cryptic coloration and colour pattern. They blend with their surroundings, making themselves very difficult for predators to detect. In some cases, as with many fishes and cephalopods, they are able to change colour to blend with their surroundings. Some species, such as some scorpion-fish, angler-fish, sea-horses, some crabs, and some gastropods, show contour obliteration — they have developed specialized projections from their bodies that disrupt the outline of their bodies. On the other hand, a few animals appear to advertise their presence. These may be venomous species with striking colour patterns, such as zebra-fish or some of the rabbit-fish. Then too, some species of butterfly-fish habitually display the large eye-like spots on their sides. These spots are used in conjunction with appropriate behaviour patterns. For example, some chaetodontids swim backwards, displaying their large eye-spots until disturbed, when they dash forward to cover.

Some animals actively camouflage themselves. Decorator crabs (e.g., *Petalomera lateralis*) hold algae and sponges trimmed to size over their carapaces. Sea-urchins often hold algae over their upper surfaces.

Still other animals rely on habitat selection to minimize predation. They live in crevices and interstices in living and dead coral or under coral boulders and overhangs. Some are buried in sand or live in holes in the sand. Some live in the discarded shells of molluscs (e.g., hermit crabs). Some seek shelter by close association with animals that have powerful defences against predation (e.g., hermit crabs that place anemones on the shells they inhabit). Examples are provided by the various anemone-fish that live among the stinging tentacles of anemones, the messmate-fish that live in the alimentary canals of toxin-producing holothurians, and the gall crabs that imprison themselves among coral branches. Parrot-fish form mixed feeding schools with wrasses and rabbit-fish. The latter have venomous spines, and it is thought that their presence in the schools deters predators from attacking the schools.

Then there are animals that might be termed tribute payers. Only part of their bodies is usually predated. Sponges, corals, soft corals, and many other sessile and colonial organisms fall into this category. They are able to regenerate those portions of their bodies damaged by predators. Some non-sessile animals also come into this category. One or more arms of brittle-stars may be snapped off by predatory fishes, but the arms rapidly regenerate. The appendages of crabs have breaking

242

243

244

245

246

247

248

249

250

251

252

253

planes — special regions where limbs break off when grasped by a predator; again the missing limbs are quickly replaced. Sometimes, as with *Acanthaster planci,* half the body of the animal may be eaten by a predator (e.g., the giant triton, *Charonia tritonis*) but the other half of the body may escape and regenerate missing parts. Such an animal is potentially immortal. Nereid worms are able to break off and later regenerate tails. Flatworms (polyclads) are able to regenerate much of their bodies.

In order to enhance their success as predators and to counter the defence mechanisms developed by prey forms, predators have specialized in several directions. Some, like many fishes, have concentrated on speed and manoeuvrability in order to capture prey. Many have developed powerful biting mouth parts. Large tiger sharks, for example, can readily bite right through the carapace of a turtle, large maori wrasses can bite through the branches of branching corals, and eagle rays can crush the heavy shells of bivalves without difficulty. The abrading radula of the larger baler shell in capable of boring through the valves of reef clams (*Tridacna maxima*).

Some have developed counter measures against the toxins elaborated by some prey forms and can detoxify or tolerate these compounds. Some have themselves elaborated potent venoms to inactivate their prey. The cone shells (*Conidae*) for example, use a remarkably sophisticated venom apparatus to immobilize their prey. On the basis of type of animal preyed upon, the cone shell family can be divided into three groups. The biggest group feeds on worms of various kinds. A large group, characterized by the presence of tent-like markings on the shell, feeds on other molluscs. The third group, which is the smallest, feeds on fishes. Interestingly, the venoms elaborated by each group appear to be specific for the type of prey. Thus the venoms of the fish-eating group will paralyse fish and other vertebrates (including humans) but will not paralyse molluscs or worms, those of the mollusc-eating group appear specific for the neuromuscular systems of molluscs but have no obvious effects on vertebrates or worms, while those of the worm-eating group do not affect vertebrates or molluscs but will render the movements of worms inco-ordinate.

Some predators have acquired a cryptic coloration. This and other forms of camouflage they might exhibit — for example, counter-shading and contour obliteration — assist them in stalking prey or render them difficult to detect by potential prey approaching them. Behaviour patterns that are of advantage in capturing prey — for example, the ability of stonefish to remain motionless until the unsuspecting prey is within range and then to leap upwards and engulf the prey — have been developed.

Predation may play an important role in regulating the numbers of individuals of a species present on a reef. Individuals belonging to some species are present in very large numbers and frequently produce enormous numbers of larvae. If these numbers were allowed to increase unchecked, the available food supplies and living places on a reef could be swamped by the new recruits to the population. Predation is usually most intense on the eggs and larval stages of coral reef species.

Sometimes predators are generalists and will accept a wide variety of prey, although they may exhibit a preference for one or a few kinds. To some extent they may be regarded as opportunistic. On occasions, most carnivorous reef fishes sampled have been found to have eaten a particular type of prey which may be present for a time in abundance. Some small reef crustaceans and worms occasionally aggregate in large numbers for breeding purposes and they are then taken by numerous carnivores. Some species of small fish school in large numbers and are prime target for carnivorous fish. Large numbers of larvae of some reef species are released at particular seasons or at particular phases of the moon, and they are then eaten by numerous predators. When large numbers of nestling turtles take to the water after hatching, they run the gauntlet of most of the larger reef predators; fish such as cods almost all contain hatchling turtles at such times.

On the other hand, as a result of the development of increasingly efficient methods of capturing prey and of increasingly sophisticated defence mechanisms against predation, many of the predator-prey relationships found among coral reef organisms are highly specific and probably represent co-evolved relationships. For example, the crown-of-thorns starfish, *Acanthaster planci*, which preys on corals possesses a highly specialized enzyme system for wax digestion which enables it to utilize the wax called cetyl palmitate which is found in abundance in corals. The giant triton, *Charonia tritonis*, is able to deal with the highly toxic *saponins* produced by starfish (including the crown-of-thorns starfish) and by holothurians upon which it preys. The presence of these saponins probably protects the starfish and holothurians against predation by other species who are not able to detoxify or tolerate these substances. Other species of triton feed apparently specifically on sea-squirts (ascidians). Venomous sea-urchins belonging to the genus *Diadema* are preyed on by the gastropod molluscs known as giant helmets (*Cassis cornuta*) and occasionally by file-fish, both of whom are able to cope with the venomous spines of the sea-urchins. Some species of sundial-shell eat the poisonous zoanthid *Palythoa caespitosa* with impunity. Likewise the egg cowry (*Ovula ovum*) is able to eat the polyps of the poisonous soft coral *Sarcophyton trocheliophorum*, and spindle cowries belonging to the genus *Volva* can cope with the powerful antibiotics produced by the fan corals (gorgonians) on which they feed. Sponges are not generally eaten because many contain or exude toxic materials. However, some species of fish, including some butterfly-fish (Chaetodontidae), file-fish (Aluteridae), puffer-fish (Tetraodontidae), and boxfish (Ostraciontidae), will eat sponges. They tend to eat small pieces of several species of sponge and presumably dilute the toxins of the antibiotic species in this way. Some nudibranch molluscs are able to deal with some of the toxins elaborated by sponges. It seems likely that particular species of nudibranch can deal only with specific toxins produced by one species or a group of closely allied species of sponge. In these ways the very specific predator-prey relationships that are characteristic of coral reef communities may be established.

A zebra-fish, *Pteropterus antennatus*, sheltering in a cave. The bold patterns and colours are an example of warning colouration.

Day and Night Feeders

As far as fish are concerned, there are myriads of variously coloured and patterned sea-floor feeders (parrot-fish [Scaridae], surgeon-fish [Acanthuridae], butterfly-fish [Chaetodontidae], wrasses [Labridae], etc.) and schools of plankton feeders (damsel-fish [Pomacentridae], hardyheads [Atherinidae], etc.) that are active during the day. At the same time, large predators such as trevally move over the sandy areas, and others such as barracudas cruise the reef edges, while schools of snappers and sweetlip emperors mill about slowly in their daytime resting areas in the deeper water near reefs. Other predators, such as cods and trout, lurk in their daytime resting places in crevices and holes in the coral.

For about twenty minutes after sunset the waters over and around a reef appear deserted. Then the night-feeding fishes become active. At night fewer species are active than are active during the day. No grazers such as parrot-fish, surgeon-fish, or rabbit-fish feed at night. Indeed, all species feeding at night are active predators. The snappers and sweetlip emperors seen in daytime resting schools near reefs spread out singly, the snappers hunting over the sea floor out from reefs while the sweetlip emperors frequently move into the shallower lagoons and sandy areas of reefs. Eels leave their lairs and move out over the reef flat, as do some of the big serranids — cod, trout and groper. A few species of soldier-fish and javelin-fish become active near coral clumps, and a number of species of cardinal-fish move into midwater at night.

Parrot-fish usually sleep at night in a hole in the coral enveloped in a loose cocoon of mucus that they secrete. Sand and weeds adhere to the cocoon. Wrasses, too, appear to sleep at night and often spend the night half buried in sand or in crevices in coral. As noted earlier, rabbit-fish sleep at night with their venomous fin spines extended. Small coral-associated fishes that are active during the day retire deep into the interstices of coral clumps at night.

Many invertebrates become active at night. For example, molluscs such as chitons, cones, and strombs emerge from their daytime hiding places and move out over the reef in search of food. Octopuses move from their lairs out over the reef flat. So too do many worms and crustaceans of various kinds. Feather-stars emerge from crevices and under boulders, where they have sought cover during daylight hours, and extend their arms so as to begin feeding. Their abundance on reef flats at night is surprising in view of the difficulty one has in locating them during the day. Brittle-stars also are active at night.

16

Why There Are
So Many Species

It is a feature of the coral reef communities of the Great Barrier Reef that they exhibit a tremendous species richness. A bewildering array of different kinds of alga, coral, fish, crab, starfish, mollusc, (and other animal groups) meets the gaze of the casual observer. The task of identifying each species of animal and plant present is a formidable one. The fauna and flora of the reef at Heron Island, where a research station is located, have been studied intensively over the last thirty years. The specific composition of some groups such as the algae, echinoderms, corals, and fishes found in the Heron Island reef is now reasonably well known, but future discoveries will undoubtedly result in additions to the species list for each group. At least 38 species of starfish, 32 species of brittle-star, 25 species of sea-urchin, 36 species of holothurian, 27 species of feather-star, 107 species of coral, and 931 species of fish have been observed on the reef at Heron Island, which extends over an area of approximately thirty-six square kilometres. Thirty-four species of Conidae (a single family of molluscs) have been observed there, and the total number of molluscan species present on Heron Island reef probably rivals the number of fish species present. Of course, many other major groups, such as sponges, soft corals, gorgonians, hydroids, anemones, worms, bryozoans, ascidians, and crustaceans, occur on this reef, and the total number of species present must be very large indeed.

Why are so many species found on the Great Barrier Reef? This question has taxed the minds of many biologists. One reason is that the Great Barrier Reef is located in the tropics. It is well known that species richness increases with decreasing latitude and that the most diverse systems — the wet rainforest on land and the coral reef in the sea — occur in the tropics. This is not surprising, because solar energy flow, upon which all life depends, is essentially constant at low latitudes and physico-chemical conditions prevailing there are predictable and favourable for most marine species. Another reason is that the Great Barrier Reef lies near the centre of the vast Indo–West Pacific region. This region contains the greatest number of species of any marine biogeographical region. Species richness is greatest near the centre of this region, possibly because of the extensive shallow water areas found there that favour the growth of hermatypic corals, and there is an attenuation of species to the east and to the west.

Then there is the past history of the coral reef community to consider. It is the oldest ecological community in geological history and has undergone evolution during a period of about two thousand million years. Representatives of most major groups of marine plant and animal occur on coral reefs, and there has been ample opportunity for specialized forms adapted to the special conditions found on coral reefs to evolve there or migrate there. What are these special conditions? First and foremost is the restricted living space available on coral reefs and the intense competition for this space. This in turn has led to the dominance of sessile, sedentary, and site-attached species on coral reefs and the development of specialized strategies to acquire and hold space. Also, it has led to the occupation of almost every conceivable habitat provided by coral reefs. In effect, there has been a fine partitioning of the available space among the species present.

Stationariness has necessitated the development of powerful defences against predation. Some of these defences are morphological, some anatomical, some physiological, some chemical, and some behavioural. Some animals rely on the choice of specialized habitats to minimize predation. All these defence strategies involve specialization. Likewise, there appears to have been a co-evolution of specialized predators who can counter the defences of the specialized prey forms. All this has led to a fine partitioning among numerous species of available food resources. In some cases the same food resources are used by two or more species but at different times.

The fine partitioning of available space and food resources noted has enabled numerous species to coexist on coral reefs and accounts for much of the species richness observed on coral reefs. Also, it has led to the existence of many highly specialized species, many of which appear to be somewhat rare. This raises the question of population sizes attained by reef animals.

Population Sizes — "Common" and "Rare" Species

As far as the macroscopic organisms found on coral reefs are concerned, it will be apparent, even to the casual observer, that some species are common while other species appear rare. Some species of staghorn coral (*Acropora*) for example, normally cover large areas of reef flats or reef slopes, while other species of coral are restricted to small patches on reef flats or slopes and still others occur usually as isolated scattered colonies. Likewise, as any shell collector knows, some gastropods, such as the jumping stromb (*Strombus luhuanus*), the ring cowrie (*Monetraria annulus*), or the flavid cone (*Conus flavidus*), are encountered frequently, while others, such as the cameo helmet (*Cypraecassis rufa*) and the ringed cowry (*Cypraea argus*) or the geographer cone (*Conus geographus*), are rarely encountered.

Population sizes are regulated by numerous factors. To some extent the sizes of the populations of different species present on a coral reef are governed by the overall area of the reef and its general topography and geographic position. In some Great Barrier Reef species (for example, *Thelenota ananas, Tridacna gigas*) there is an attenuation in numbers with increasing latitude. In some cases there is a longitudinal gradient, the numbers of individuals of a species varying according to proximity to the Queensland mainland. To some extent population sizes depend on the availability of the preferred habitat of the species under discussion, and to some extent population sizes depend on the availability of food and on the numbers of other organisms present that compete for food and living space. To a large extent, population numbers depend on the pressure exerted by predators.

It is a feature of those coral reef communities which are rich in species, such as those of the Great Barrier Reef, that fluctuations in population densities of the species present are well buffered. They are regarded as biologically accommodated communities, with biological interactions such as predation and competition playing a major role in determining community structure and in regulating the population densities of the individual species present.

Rarity

It is possible that in some species rarity is a consequence of intense predator pressure or paucity of suitable living space or a combination of both. Usually the rarer species are long-lived and have low rates of recruitment to their breeding populations. They are usually highly specialized. Perhaps specialization has made some of them so successful and increased their chances of survival to such an extent that they would overwhelm organisms upon which they prey if their populations were not regulated at low density. Some of them may produce numerous offspring but their populations are regulated by predators that are specialized to deal with them at one or more stages of their life history.

Then again, some species may have adopted rarity as a strategy that enables them to minimize competition for food and living space, to minimize predation, and to minimize invasion by parasitic forms. Their populations may be regulated by the production of relatively few offspring. At any rate, the existence of numerous rare species contributes substantially to the species richness of coral reef communities.

Opportunism

As opposed to rarity, some species appear to have adopted commonness as a life strategy. They have high recruitment rates, are usually short-lived, but produce numerous offspring at short intervals. The offspring are readily available to colonize any suitable areas of reef that are vacated by other animals, and they have an important role to play in ecological succession.

Although the environment of the coral reef community is generally benign (violent fluctuations in physico-chemical conditions being rare), occasionally disturbances do occur. Cyclonic storms, for example, periodically cause destruction of sessile and associated species at some locations on reefs. These habitats are quickly populated by opportunistic pioneer species which flourish for a period and are then supplanted by later colonists that are usually specialized for existence in such habitats. This variation in space occupancy with time — ecological succession — contributes significantly to the diversity of species present in the reef community. It also raises questions concerning the longevity of coral reef animals.

Longevity

Perhaps the greatest disadvantage stemming from rarity is the difficulty for sexually reproducing individuals to find a mate and breed successfully. Longevity would increase the chances of finding a mate and, if reproductive potential were unimpaired, of breeding successfully. Most of the rare coral reef animals that have been investigated appear to be long-lived. So too are many colonies of animals found on coral reefs. For example, judging by their sizes and known growth

Facing page
Ascidians, *Pycnoclavella detorta*, attached to the shells of a coxcomb oyster, *Lopha hyotis*, at Wistari reef.

rates, many colonies of massive corals found on the Great Barrier Reef must have survived for decades, possibly for hundreds of years. It would appear that colonies of many branching species also have the potential to survive for decades, but for corals growing in some areas subject to frequent disturbance — for example, shallow water areas near the reef crest — this potential is rarely realized. Most opportunistic species of coral, such as *Pocillopora damiconis*, appear to be short-lived. This raises questions about the recruitment of coral reef animals.

Reproduction and Recruitment of Coral Reef Animals

As already noted, many species belonging to the coral reef community are sedentary, highly specialized, long-lived, and numerically rare. In some species, problems arise in respect of finding a mate. As well, most reef organisms release sexual products directly into the water or have one or more larval stages in their life history, or do both. Because of the large number of filter-feeding and plankton-feeding animals found on reefs, eggs and larvae are subject to intense predation if they remain in immediate proximity to these animals. But if they pass to the oceanic waters surrounding reefs, which are usually separated from one another by stretches of water of considerable extent, there is still the problem of how to recruit new individuals of each species on the reef from which the eggs and larvae have come.

Many species of coral reef animal have solved the above problems by engaging in asexual reproduction during part of their life history. It is a feature of coral reef communities that the major groups of sessile animals are colony formers. Hard corals, soft corals, hydroids, zoanthids, gorgonians, sponges, and compound ascidians all fall into this category. In each case the larva derived from a fertilized egg settles and then gives rise to new individuals by budding, a process of asexual reproduction discussed earlier when dealing with corals.

In a number of animal groups found on coral reefs, asexual reproduction occurs by fission. An individual splits into two equal or unequal parts, and each part gives rise to a new individual. In some species of holothurian, for example, asexual reproduction occurs commonly by transverse fission. The orginal front end then forms a new hind end and the original hind end forms a new front end. *Holothuria atra*, one of the commonest holothurians on reef flats, usually reproduces in this way. Some starfish, such as species of *Linckia*, commonly cast off an arm which then grows a central disc and other arms. While these are forming, the starfish has the appearance of a comet. Some other species of starfish split across the centre of the disc, each half then regenerating the missing parts of its body. Brittle-stars, sipunculid worms, and the large polychaete worm group known as syllids also reproduce by fission.

Some species of branching corals, notably *Acropora aspera, A. hebes*, and *A. robusta*, reproduce asexually by fragmentation. This occurs when they are subject to excessive wave action as occurs during cyclones. Small fragments become wedged in crevices and give rise to new colonies. This type of reproduction enables them to colonize suitable space which becomes available outside their normal breeding season.

Some animals occur in pairs when adult. For example, the gastropod *Conus geographus* usually occurs in pairs, as does the starfish *Archaster laevis* and many fishes. Other animals aggregate for reproductive purposes. For example, the normally rare and cryptic crown-of-thorns starfish aggregates at breeding time, presumably to ensure fertilization of eggs released by females. Some worms aggregate in enormous number for breeding purposes.

Some fishes living in small groups have the ability to change sex. Notable examples are found among wrasses, parrot-fish, and anemone-fish. The change can be either from female to male or the reverse. In parrot-fish and wrasses, individuals born as females may subsequently change to males, but in many species of these fishes, there are, as well, males that are born as males and which do not change sex. The females mate chiefly with larger, older males. Frequently these large males are territorial and develop specialized structures and colorations for display purposes and for aggression. Females usually change into males when they become large enough to compete successfully for females. In anemone-fish the position is reversed, and it is the large females that control sex change in the smaller males by aggressive dominance. Presumably the ability to change sex is an adaptation to living in small, isolated groups.

In corals, eggs and sperm are produced (often at different times) within the one polyp and, of course, the presence of numerous polyps in a colony ensures fertilization of eggs. In some corals and their allies, such as the zoanthid *Palythoa*, polyps change sex as they age, being first female, then hermaphrodite, then male. In some corals, larvae are often brooded in the polyp. In at least one species of *Goniastrea*, the fertilized egg masses enmeshed in sticky mucus are released and these adhere to objects in the vicinity of the parent. The most widely distributed coral reef sea-squirts (ascidians) are viviparous. Indeed, in some species (didemnids) the larvae metamorphose within the parent colony, which disintegrates and is replaced by the young.

In many species of coral reef mollusc the eggs and young do not leave the reef where their parents occur. Numerous species of mollusc lay egg masses in strings or capsules which are frequently attached to the undersurfaces of coral boulders or to other objects — even to the shells of other individuals of the same species. In several groups, development is direct and the young hatch as miniature adults. However, in other groups there is a pelagic larval stage or stages of variable duration.

Some wrasses and anemone-fish make nests for their eggs and young. Blennies and gobies usually attach their eggs to empty mollusc shells and guard their young when they hatch out. Some cardinal-fish (Apogonidae) brood their young in their mouths. Many rabbit-fish (Siganidae), trigger-fish (Balistidae), and puffer-fish (Tetraodontidae) lay eggs attached to objects on the reef, and some guard their young when they hatch. On the other hand, many of the larger coral reef fishes — coral cods (Serranidae), trevally (Carangidae), silver-biddies (Gerridae), snappers (Lutjanidae), etc. — aggregate on outer reef crests and slopes and release their sexual products directly into the sea water. Smaller coral reef fishes such as parrot-fish, wrasses, goatfish, and surgeon-fish make rapid dashes to the surface, where they release their sexual products and then descend rapidly to the protection of the reef.

In many cases larvae, when released from eggs, spend only a short period in the plankton. Sponge larvae spend only a few hours, as do most coral reef ascidian larvae. Those of most reef-building corals frequently spend only one or two days in the plankton. It is possible that the ebb and flow of the tides serve to keep short-term larvae in the vicinity of the reef where they originated and that such larvae are released at times when oceanic surface currents wane. However, some larvae are able to survive long periods in the plankton if suitable substratum on which to settle is not readily available. Indeed, some larvae may normally spend weeks in the plankton, during which time they may be carried hundreds of kilometres in surface currents. Such long-lived larvae are essential to the dispersal of reef species. A common strategy among species with pelagic eggs and larvae is the timing of spawning to coincide with ebbing spring tides so as to ensure transport of eggs and larvae away from the reef where they originate. Possibly this strategy underlies the phenomenon of lunar periodicity in breeding, which involves spawning in the vicinity of spring tides which occur around the full or new moon.

Most species that produce larvae that spend long periods in the plankton produce enormous numbers of eggs. No doubt this strategy ensures that some larvae will survive the vicissitudes of a long planktonic existence and find a suitable place to settle. Opportunistic species such as the coral *Pocillopora damicornis* produce larvae at frequent intervals throughout the year. Most other species, particularly the highly specialized and rare species, have restricted breeding seasons.

17

Strange and Specialized Animals

Specialization

As far as most coral reef animals are concerned, their life strategies are directed principally towards acquiring and holding suitable living space on a reef, obtaining adequate food, defending themselves against predators and harmful micro-organisms, parasites, and fouling organisms, reproducing themselves, and coping with competitors for their living space, their food, and sometimes their partners in reproduction. Many coral reef animals have adapted to life on a coral reef by specializing in some way or ways. Some animals, as we have seen, have specialized in the production and use of toxins to acquire and hold living space, to defend themselves against predators and harmful organisms, and to obtain prey. Other animals have specialized anatomical, morphological, physiological, or behavioural features which assist them in pursuing their life strategies. Still others have specialized in the colonizing of particular habitats where they are afforded protection from predators and for which there is little competition from other species; many of these are commensals. Then there are species that have specialized in the almost continuous production of large numbers of offspring so that although many may fall victim to predators, some will survive and be ready to colonize any living space that becomes available on reefs; these are often termed opportunistic species.

Examples of some of the highly specialized animals found on coral reefs will be given in this and the following two chapters.

Anemone-fish

Anemone-fish of the genus *Amphiprion* are noted for their habit of living in association with certain anemones. Indeed, they are never encountered without their anemone hosts by which they are certainly afforded protection. When danger threatens, anemone-fish quickly flee to the sanctuary of the tentacles of their host. At night too, they settle deep among the tentacles and remain there until dawn. Experiments have revealed that while numbers of adult anemone-fish per anemone remain stable, numbers of juveniles present fluctuate considerably. It would appear that juveniles are frequently chased away from the protective anemones and devoured by carnivorous fishes. The availability of anemones appears to be a major factor limiting the size of anemone-fish populations. Anemone-fish do not roam far from their hosts and have a small feeding territory. Although some specimens of anemone-fish may obtain part of their nourishment by feeding on material ejected from their host, it would appear that they feed primarily on benthic algae and planktonic crustaceans such as copepods.

While there is some evidence that anemone-fish will protect their hosts from the attentions of anemone-feeding fishes such as certain butterfly-fish of the genus *Chaetodon*, and while some anemone-fish under aquarium conditions have been observed to carry food to the tentacles of their host, the benefits that the anemone receives from the association have not been clearly defined.

Male and female anemone-fish appear to form permanent pairs. Spawning seems to occur at monthly intervals throughout the year. The eggs are laid by females in nests which are small areas of bare coral rubble rock from which algae has been removed by paired fish and which are in reach of the anemone's tentacles. The eggs adhere to the bare rock while they develop. After hatching, larvae may spend some time in the plankton. Very small (6 to 8 millimetres long) post-larval fish colonize host anemones. The manner in which they acclimatize to the nematocyst-laden tentacles of the host has been the subject of much research. Apparently a change occurs in the external mucous coat of the fish which raises the threshhold for nematocyst discharge. Hence the fish do not trigger firing of the nematocysts.

Limas — Swimming Bivalves

Small bivalves known commonly as swimming limas are frequently found under dead coral boulders on sand flats and in sandy gutters on reefs. Some occur in "nests" formed of coral sand and shell fragments woven together by a sticky mucous material. When disturbed, the bivalves swim with a fluttering motion as a result of clapping together the two valves of their shells and expressing water from between the valves — a form of jet propulsion. Their glistening white shells are often fringed with brilliant red tentacles; hence they make a spectacular display when swimming. The tentacles are sticky and tend to break readily. Specimens found on the Great Barrier Reef belong to the genera *Limaria* and *Lima*.

Gall-Crabs

The gall-crab, *Hapalocarcinus marsupialis*, remains in the one position on the surface of living coral belonging to the family *Pocilloporidae* for a period long enough for the coral skeleton to grow around it and produce a gall in which the crab subsequently lives. Female specimens of the gall-crab are slightly larger than a pea in size and have a soft exoskeleton. Lateral extensions of the abdomen form a pouch that shelters developing eggs. The males are much smaller than the females and, although they live separately from the females, also inhabit galls in coral.

Life Inside a Holothurian or a Pearl Shell

Members of the family Carapidae, known as messmate-fish, are small, slender fish that live in association with starfish, holothurians, or large bivalve molluscs. They shelter in the intestine or mantle cavity of their host, which they enter tail first. Generally the head and anteriorly placed cloacal vent remain exposed. Periodically they leave their host to search for food. Eggs, when laid, are embedded in a mass of slime.

Carapus homei is a transparent bluish or reddish species with dark crossbands that lives in the intestines of holothurians. It grows up to 20 centimetres in length. *Onusodon margariferae* is a species that lives in the mantle cavity of pearl oysters and related bivalves. Sometimes the fish becomes encased in mother-of-pearl secreted by its host.

The Smile on the Face of the Tiger

One of the most remarkable fishes to be found in the Capricorn group of coral reefs is the harlequin smiler, *Merogymnus eximius*. It attains a maximum length of about 40 centimetres, but most specimens encountered are between 20 and 30 centimetres in length. The upper surface is a golden brown colour, and the sides of the trunk carry large circular yellow spots on a brilliant blue background. Both the abdomen and head are lilac, and the dorsal fin is banded with purple. The operculum is daubed with blue. The head and eyes are unusually large and the lower jaw gapes widely, revealing needle-sharp teeth. The gaudy raiment and the fixed gape have given rise to the common name applied to the fish, harlequin smiler. The body of the fish is scaleless and slimy to the touch.

A burrow is excavated by the fish in the sand of the reef flat and the fish enters the burrow tail first. It is solitary and rarely strays far from its burrow. Indeed, it spends much time in a vertical position peering from its burrow and sometimes popping in and out like a jack-in-the-box. Its eyes appear able to swivel in all directions.

If a small fish strays within striking distance, the smiler will suddenly leap from its burrow and pounce upon it, engulfing it in its huge mouth.

Sea-Snakes

Except for having a flattened, paddle-like tail, sea-snakes resemble land snakes in general appearance. However, they possess several physiological adaptations for a marine existence. Opening under the tongue is a gland that secretes excess salt which enters their body in food and drink. Compared with terrestrial snakes, they have an increased lung volume and an increased capacity for storing air. Also, many species are able to take up oxygen from sea water through the skin. Such respiratory adaptations enable most species to remain submerged for periods of half an hour to an hour and some species for periods up to two hours. The maximum depth to which sea-snakes dive is approximately 100 metres. They are essentially shallow-water animals.

Most sea-snakes are fish-eaters, but some feed exclusively on fish eggs. Eels are taken avidly by some species. Large prey is subdued by the injection of a potent venom produced in venom glands and delivered by paired fangs as in land snakes. Sea-snake venom is active against mammals (see chapter 19). In their turn, sea-snakes are preyed on by sea eagles and sharks. Tiger sharks, in particular, prey heavily on sea-snakes.

Sometimes sea-snakes spend extended periods lying at the surface, and occasionally they aggregate in large numbers at the surface, presumably for breeding purposes. Their distribution on the Great

Barrier Reef is patchy. Some reefs, particularly reefs in the Swain Reefs area, carry large numbers of sea-snakes belonging to several species. On other reefs they are rarely encountered. It is suspected that sea-snakes move from one reef to another, but much remains to be discovered about this and other aspects of their life history.

Two families of sea-snake, both occurring in Great Barrier Reef waters, are known, phylum Chordata, class Reptilia.

True sea-snakes (Hydrophiidae) have valves in the nostrils which close when the sea-snake dives. They are completely marine and never come onto land. They give birth to live young. It is believed that they have evolved from a group of Australian snakes known as elapids. About fifty species of true sea-snake are known, and several of them occur on the Great Barrier Reef.

Some genera represented: *Aipysurus, Astrotia, Emydocephalus, Hydrophis, Lapemis.*

Sea kraits (Laticaudidae) lay terrestrial eggs and must leave the water to reproduce. Also, some seek intertidal rocks or shrubs and debris on land near the strand line for basking purposes during the day. About five species of sea krait are known.

Genus represented: *Laticauda.*

The Colourful Peacock-Worm

The peacock-worm, *Spirobranchus giganteus,* is commonly associated with so-called micro-atolls of the coral genus *Porites* and also with some species of branching corals belonging to the genus *Acropora.* A calcareous tube is secreted by each peacock-worm and is usually deeply embedded within the host coral, only the dumb-bell–shaped entrance of each tube being exposed. The feeding tentacles of the worm are arranged in two spirals. Those of different individuals show an amazing range of colour. The rapidity with which the tentacles can be withdrawn is remarkable.

The Pincushion Starfish

Adult specimens of the pincushion starfish, *Culcita navaeguineae,* are almost pentagonal in outline and swollen to such an extent that they bear little resemblance to a starfish if viewed from their upper surface. However, five radiating grooves accommodating tube feet and a mouth at the confluence of the grooves will be revealed if the lower surface of the animal is examined. The species attains a large size — up to 40 centimetres in diameter — and has a remarkably thick body wall which contains numerous calcareous plates and is covered with large granules. Its upper surface is usually a mosaic of yellow, orange, and brown blotches. The pincushion starfish is found mainly on reef flats and in lagoons where it feeds on branching corals.

The Slate-Pencil Urchin

The primary spines of the slate-pencil sea-urchin, *Heterocentrotus mammillatus*, are remarkably large and bear a resemblance to the implements used last century in many schools for writing on slates. Secondary spines are much shorter structures with flattened tips. No doubt the spines provide a formidable armour against most potential predators.

Communication among Different Species in a Coral Colony

It has been shown recently that at least some of the fishes (members of the family *Gobiidae*), crabs (*Trapezia* species), and shrimps (*Alpheus* species) residing in a coral colony (*Pocillopora damicornis*) can communicate one with another by a system of signals. The signals include shivering movements in the case of the fishes and cleaning activities on the part of the shrimps. The signalling system ensures that the residents do not attack one another. However, they will attack intruding fishes, crustaceans, and shrimps of the same species and probably many intruders belonging to other species. Certainly resident crabs have been observed attacking the tube-feet of crown-of-thorns starfish that climbed onto their coral host.

The Sonar Specialists

Schools of marine mammals known as dolphins appear to stay in the vicinity of particular reefs. They are noted for their habit of riding the bow waves of boats moving through waters near these reefs, and the sight of the glistening backs of dozens of dolphins arching from the water is a memorable one. Dolphins attain a length of 2.5 metres and have an elongated beak-like snout armed with pointed teeth and a prominent dorsal fin. They are swift swimmers, the powerful tail with its horizontal flukes being the organ of propulsion. Dolphins have many specialized features, but their ability to use underwater sound to locate distant objects is remarkable. Underwater sounds are emitted in pulses and focused on a distant object by a mass of fatty material found in the forehead. Sound reflected from the object is received by areas of thin bone and fatty tissue found on each side of the lower jaw. These areas then transmit a signal by way of the middle ear to the brain. Apparently dolphins are able to determine the sizes as well as the locations of objects by using their sonar system. The manner in which the fatty material mentioned is involved in this system is under scrutiny with a view to advancing sonar technology.

Cleaners

Fish known as cleaners set up "cleaning stations" at various points on a coral reef. A variety of fishes is attracted to these stations by the peculiar oscillatory swimming movements of the cleaners, which are brightly coloured wrasses (Labridae). A common cleaner-fish on the Great Barrier Reef is *Labroides dimidiatus*, which bears prominent longitudinal stripes. This species removes ectoparasites and diseased tissues from fish visiting its cleaning stations. Remarkably, the fish being cleaned will hold open mouth and gill covers to facilitate the work of the cleaners. The latter are seldom, if ever, eaten.

L. dimidiatus is a diurnal fish and, as evening approaches, it will burrow into the sand and produce a mucous envelope in which it remains until sunrise.

A blenny belonging to the genus *Aspidontus* has a similiar coloration and size to *Labroides dimidiatus*. Moreover, it swims in a manner characteristic of the cleaner-fish which it mimics. When a fish presents itself for cleaning, however, the impostor darts in and tears pieces of skin from the surprised victim.

The Spanish Dancer

One of the most flamboyant displays provided by an animal found on the Great Barrier Reef is provided by the so-called Spanish dancer, *Hexabranchus sanguineus*. This large (up to 20 centimetres in length) nudibranch mollusc swims by undulating movements of voluminous flaps arising from the body above the foot. Much of the body is scarlet, and when the animal is swimming these flaps appear to billow and twirl like the skirts of a female flamenco dancer. As the mollusc effectively advertises its presence, it is not surprising that it possesses a chemical repellent to which sharks and fishes show aversive behaviour.

Making Both Ends Part

The commonest holothurian found on reef flats in Great Barrier Reef waters is the black species, *Holothuria atra*. At times, specimens are observed that have constrictions near the centre of the body. Subsequently the two halves separate. The front half develops a new hind end, and the other half develops a new front end. This is an example of asexual reproduction and leads to a rapid increase in numbers of the resident *H. atra* population of a reef. Holothurians generally have remarkable powers of regeneration. When molested, many species will void most of their internal organs, but these can be replaced within a few weeks.

18

Giants and Pygmies of the Reef

Giant Clams

Among the largest invertebrates that have ever existed are the giant clams belonging to a family of bivalve molluscs known as the Tridacnidae. All of the six known species of this family occur on the Great Barrier Reef. However, one species, *Tridacna crocea*, is relatively small and rarely attains a shell length in excess of 15 centimetres. It is found in burrows in dead coral boulders on reef flats. In many cases the free margins of the shell valves lie flush with the surface of the boulders, giving the appearance of wavy lines. Another species, *Tridacna maxima*, is one of the commonest members of the reef-flat community throughout the Great Barrier Reef area. Its fleshy mantle, which is normally exposed between the two valves, shows an amazing variety of colour from specimen to specimen. Indeed, these clams are regarded by many casual visitors to the reef flat as one of the most attractive animals to be found there. Another species, *Tridacna squamosa*, which occurs commonly in the northern sector of the Great Barrier Reef, attains a size similar to *T. maxima* (about 40 centimetres in shell length) but can be readily distinguished from it by the leaflike scales on the ribs of each valve. Both species are attached to the substratum by gelatinous strands.

The remaining three species of giant clam are not attached to the substratum but rest on the hinge-line between the two valves of each shell, their great weight effectively maintaining them in position. One of these species, *Hippopus hippopus*, has a peculiar hoof-like indentation in the valves which has given rise to its common name, the horseshoe clam. It attains a shell length of approximately 45 centimetres. The

next largest is *Tridacna derasa*, which attains a shell length of approximately 50 centimetres and which occurs on outer reefs, particularly the reefs of the Swain Reef complex. The largest of the giant clams is *Tridacna gigas*, which occurs principally in the northern half of the Great Barrier Reef. Its normal maximum length is about 1 metre, but larger individuals do occur. Indeed, the shell length of one specimen from Sumatra was recorded as 4 feet 6 inches (137 centimetres), and the two valves constituting the shell weighed 507 pounds (230 kilograms).

Specimens of *T. gigas* lie with the two valves of the shell agape and the fleshy mantle, usually coloured green or brown, exposed. In the tissues of the mantle are symbiotic unicellular algae, the zooxanthellae. Part of the energy of solar radiation impinging on the mantle is used by these algae to produce organic compounds, some of which are liberated by the zooxanthellae and provide food for the clam. Interestingly, in the mantle of the clam there are lens-like structures which appear to concentrate light for the zooxanthellae. A proportion of the zooxanthellae appear to be farmed directly as food. Some nutriment is derived from planktonic organisms filtered from sea water by the gills, as in bivalves generally, but the zooxanthellae provide the bulk of the clam's nutritive requirements.

Giant clams are hermaphrodites and liberate eggs and sperm into the water. After fertilization of the eggs, larvae are formed which spend about ten days in the plankton before settling on the reef and metamorphosing into juveniles, each approximately 0.2 of a millimetre in diameter. It is estimated that each adult produces about ten million eggs a year, but recruitment appears to be low. Certainly, small juvenile clams are hard to find.

It is possible that large clams may be well over a hundred years of age, but nobody knows for certain. Under normal conditions adult mortality appears to be very low, and no natural predators are known for *T. gigas* and *T. derasa*.

Manta Rays

One of the most spectacular sights to be seen by divers in Great Barrier Reef waters is a large manta ray as it propels itself through the water like some huge bird by slowly flapping its pectoral fins. These relatives of the more familiar stingrays may attain a width of 5 metres and a weight of 750 kilograms in the case of *Manta alfredi*. They are usually coloured blue-black above and whitish with dark blotches below. The mouth is situated between a pair of head fins which project like horns and have given mantas their alternative name — devil

Facing page
The exposed edge of the fleshy mantle of the common reef clam, *Tridacna maxima*.

rays. Actually the head fins serve to guide a stream of plankton into the mouth, which is held open while the animal swims. The plankton is sieved from the water entering the mouth before the water passes out of the mouth, or buccal cavity, through five gill slits set on the lower surface. It is strange that such a large animal feeds exclusively on plankton.

The related pygmy manta, *Mobula diabolus*, which attains a width of nearly 3 metres, is also found in Great Barrier Reef waters. It differs from its larger relative in that its head fins curve outwards and its mouth is on the lower surface of the body.

Although mantas possess a whip-like tail with a small fin near its base, the tail carries no venomous barb. Mantas are harmless, despite their appearance, and it is a thrilling experience to grasp the leading edge of the pectoral fin and hitch a ride on one. Some care is necessary, however, as mantas are capable of jumping clear of the water and crashing back again with a mighty splash. Frequently when a manta swims near the surface, the tips of its two triangular pectoral fins project from the water, which the casual observer nearby may mistake for two sharks.

Groper

Among the largest inhabitants of reefs of the Great Barrier Reef is the giant groper, *Promicrops lanceolatus*. Specimens up to 3 metres in length and almost 300 kilograms in weight have been recorded. Large specimens often take up residence in caves in the reef or in old wrecks, from which they make feeding forays. At high tide they may wander over the reef flat. Adult groper are drab olive green, yellowish, or blackish-grey, but young groper are golden yellow with dark crossbands.

Groper are believed by many to be potential man-eaters. Certainly large specimens have huge heads and cavernous mouths and are voracious feeders. Their jaw musculature is powerful. The present author recalls one that took a bait set for a shark at Centipede Reef. The baited hook was attached to one end of a line which was secured at the other to a floating four-gallon drum. The hooked groper took the drum in its huge mouth and mangled it. However, there are no well-authenticated records of groper having launched an unprovoked attack on humans in Great Barrier Reef waters. They are curious and will sometimes swim slowly towards divers. Some have become tame and are regarded as pets. Ulysses is the name given to a groper that lives at Beaver Reef. It will rise to the surface to take pieces of fish proffered by the crews of boats visiting the anchorage at the reef.

Although they are notoriously difficult to capture by hook and line because of their large size and their habit of quickly returning to the protection of caves and overhangs after grabbing a bait, groper have frequently been the targets of spear-fishermen. On some reefs the numbers of sizeable specimens have been greatly depleted as a result. This is to be regretted, because groper undoubtedly have a part to play in regulating the numbers of other species found on reefs. For example, juvenile specimens of crown-of-thorns starfish, *Acanthaster planci*, have been found in the stomachs of two specimens. Large groper may be very old. Some have been known to local fishermen for decades. One such was "Powerhouse", who, before being blown up by vandals, resided at the entrance to the main channel leading into the lagoon at Lady Musgrave Reef and was estimated to be over 270 kilograms in weight. When adult, the coloration of groper serves as a very effective camouflage. The present author, thinking it was part of the reef, actually stepped onto a very large specimen lying in shallow water at Kangaroo Reef. The groper squirmed a little but otherwise seemed unaffected by the experience.

The Humpback Whale

Prior to the 1950s humpback whales (*Megaptera novaeangliae*) were a common sight in waters of the Great Barrier Reef area as they moved north or south on their annual migration between the Antarctic waters and the tropics, where their calves were born. Groups of these marine mammals (Class Mammalia, Phylum Chordata), averaging about 14 metres in length, would spend long periods in the channels between reefs. The humpback's head is remarkably broad and flattened, with the eyes set at the angle of the jaws. Baleen plates hang from the roof of the mouth on either side of the central palate and are angled from the front to the back of the mouth. The baleen plates act as a sieve, filtering pelagic crustaceans from sea water as the whale swims along with its mouth partially open. The pectoral flippers are extremely long and act as stabilizers. The great horizontal tail flukes are the organs of propulsion. The skin along the lower surface is ridged longitudinally, and on the upper surface is a hooked dorsal fin. The blubber at the base of the fin is thickened; this and the way the species bends its body sharply as it dives are responsible for the common name of this whale. Usually it is black on the upper surface and white on the lower surface. When sounding, the humpback usually stays submerged for six to seven minutes. It then takes about seven to ten breaths before sounding again.

During the 1950s, whaling stations were set up on the New South

257

258

259

260

261

262

263

264

265

266

267

268

Wales and Queensland coasts, and humpbacks were harpooned in their thousands during their migrations along the coast. This slaughter was in addition to what occurred in the Antarctic as a result of the activities of whaling ships. It has been estimated that in the early 1960s, when the whaling stations on the eastern Australian coast closed, only two hundred humpback whales remained in these waters. There are indications that today, some twenty years later, numbers are increasing. However, the lone silhouette of a distant humpback such as one occasionally sees today in Great Barrier Reef waters bears witness to the cupidity of humans.

Turtles

Five species of turtle occur in waters along the coast of eastern Queensland. Turtles belong to the class Reptilia of the phylum Chordata. The leathery turtle, *Dermochelys coriacea*, is pelagic and does not occur on reefs of the Great Barrier Reef. The other four species belong to the family Cheloniidae, and all may occur on these reefs. Members of this family have shells formed of strong but flexible bony plates which are overlaid by horny scutes. The upper part of the shell is called the carapace and the lower part of the plastron; these are streamlined and usually flattened. Turtles are strong swimmers. A pair of front flippers which move in unison like oars propel them through the water. A pair of rear flippers act as rudders.

The green turtle, *Chelonia mydas*, attains a length of approximately 130 centimetres over the carapace and a weight of 180 kilograms. As indicated by the common name, this turtle is greenish in colour. It has a domed carapace and large scales on the front flippers. When adult it is primarily a vegetarian but frequently eats jellyfish and, in captivity, will accept a diet of fish.

The loggerhead turtle, *Caretta caretta*, has a large head which is broad at the rear. The carapace and flippers are reddish brown and the plastron yellow. It is smaller than the green turtle when adult, attaining a maximum weight of about 70 kilograms. Although it will sometimes eat algae, it is basically carnivorous, feeding on fish, crabs and other crustaceans, molluscs, sponges, and jellyfish. The powerful jaws are capable of biting through a clam shell almost a centimetre in thickness.

The hawksbill, *Eretmochelys imbricata*, is omnivorous when adult, feeding on jellyfish, ascidians, and algae, and also on molluscs and crabs. Its curved, beaklike upper jaw is well suited to removing molluscs and crabs from nooks and crannies on coral reefs. Except in very large adults and in juveniles, the scutes overlap like shingles on a roof.

Facing page
Illustration 257
An anemone fish, *Amphiprion akindynos*, nestling among the tentacles of a reef anemone.

Illustration 258
The file shell, *Limaria fragilis*, with tentacles frilling the valves.

Illustration 259
A sea-snake on Big Sandy reef, Swain Reef complex.

Illustration 260
The pin-cushion starfish, *Culcita novaeguineae*.

Illustration 261
The slate-pencil sea-urchin, *Heterocentrotus novaeguineae*.

Illustration 262
A cleaner fish, *Labroides dimidiatus*, removing parasites from the jaws of an eel.

Illustration 263
The giant clam, *Tridacna gigas*, with valves agape and mantle edge exposed.

Illustration 264
The grotesque head of the giant manta ray, *Manta alfredi*.

Illustration 265
A groper, *Promicrops lanceolatus*, speared by divers, a fate that has overtaken many of the large fishes found on reefs of the Great Barrier Reef since the introduction of spear guns and SCUBA.

Illustration 266
A loggerhead turtle, *Caretta caretta*, excavating a pit in coral sand prior to digging a chamber for the receipt of eggs.

Illustration 267
A hawksbill turtle, *Eretmochelys imbricata*, resting under a coral ledge on Peart reef.

Illustration 268
Large forams, *Marginopora vertebralis*, lying on the green alga, *Halimeda macroloba*.

Radiating marks of red, brown, yellow, and black are found on the carapace scutes. These constitute the tortoiseshell of commerce, and the species has in the past been exploited for this product. Maximum recorded weight is about 137 kilograms, but most adult specimens encountered nowadays are much smaller.

A greatly flattened carapace is a characteristic of the flatback turtle, *Chelonia depressa*. It can also be readily distinguished from other species by the numerous small scales present in the centre of the front flippers. It attains a length of about 1 metre and a weight of about 75 kilograms. Although it nests on the Queensland mainland opposite the reefs of the Bunker Group, it does not appear to have been reported from coral reefs. However, it may have been confused with other species.

It is a feature of the life history of turtles that they undertake lengthy migrations; the purpose of these migrations is unknown. Adult green turtles tagged at Heron Island while nesting subsequently made their way to various points on the Queensland coast, to New Guinea, and even to New Caledonia. Adult loggerhead turtles tagged at Heron Island have subsequently been sighted at Cape York and the Trobriand Islands north of New Guinea. A small proportion of tagged turtles return to the same beach to breed in subsequent nesting seasons.

All species of turtle lay eggs. Mating occurs at the water surface before the nesting season. Males can be distinguished by their large tails. Only the females move onto land to construct nests, as described in chapter 20.

Although their large size renders adult turtles immune from predation by most fishes, they are sometimes attacked by large sharks, particularly tiger sharks. Many turtles have lost part or all of a rear flipper as a result of such attacks. On land, turtles are rather shortsighted, since their eyes are adapted for underwater vision. They possess a keen sense of smell and are very sensitive to vibrations.

Turtles have been observed to sleep after wedging themselves under coral ledges. It is not known how long turtles live under natural conditions. In the case of the green turtle, about eight years elapse between hatching and breeding. They are surprisingly fast swimmers and can dive for extended periods.

Forams

Microscopic single-celled animals placed by zoologists in the class Rhizopoda of the phylum Protozoa abound on the Great Barrier Reef. However, there are a few members of the group that are sufficiently large to be seen by the unaided eye; indeed, although many are only 1 millimetre or so in diameter, some range up to 2 or 3 centimetres in diameter. Apart from their unusually large size, these protozoans are characterized by the possession of a calcareous skeleton called a *test*. This encloses most of the living material (protoplasm) but often possesses pores through which fine strands of living material may pass in order to anchor the animal or to engulf minute food particles when the animal is feeding. These protozoans belong to the order Foraminifera and are known commonly as forams.

There is great variation in the appearance of the test from species to species. It may be spherical, disc-shaped, star-shaped, rod-like, or even spirally coiled. Frequently it is delicately sculptured. Living forams are found on coral rubble and attached to algae on most parts of reef flats of the Great Barrier Reef. Billions of their dead calcareous tests make up a large proportion of the so-called coral sand found on reefs, and, of course, forams are prominent in the sediments in the deeper water near reefs. Specimens of a large disc-like foram belonging to the genus *Marginopora* and abundant on the sandy beaches of coral cays are often collected, dyed, and threaded together to form necklaces for the tourist trade. Forams are eaten by a multitude of small animals and also by larger ones such as holothurians.

Rotifers

Rotifers are microscopic unsegmented animals belonging to the phylum Rotifera. Their usually elongate bodies are divided into head, trunk, and short foot or long stalk, depending on whether the rotifer is a free-swimming or attached form. A characteristic structure called a wheel organ is present on the head. This organ consists of one or more rings of hair-like cilia, and the manner of their beating makes it appear that the organ rotates. For this reason rotifers were long known to the early microscopists as "wheel animalcules". As well as being responsible for locomotion in free-swimming forms, the wheel organ creates a current that brings particulate matter, including minute organisms, to the mouth in both free-swimming and attached forms. The mouth is situated just behind the wheel organ. Some species have an eversible pharynx which assists in food capture. Rotifers are commonly found on reef flats. Several families are probably represented, but they have been little studied.

19

Dangerous Animals Found on Coral Reefs

BITING AND SLASHING ANIMALS

A few coral reef animals which possess biting mouthparts or slashing structures can inflict injury on humans.

Sharks

Of all dangerous marine animals, sharks are the most widely feared. Many of the larger sharks have the speed, power, and dental equipment to be man-eaters. On occasions they become so with gruesome results. However, they rarely attack humans, although presented with ample opportunities to do so. Particularly is this so in Great Barrier Reef waters, where confirmed attacks on humans are remarkably few. The reasons for this are obscure but may be connected with the abundance of natural prey in reef waters as well as the clarity of these waters.

The small epaulette shark (*Hemiscyllium ocellatum*) is commonly encountered on reefs. During the day it hides under coral clumps but moves about actively at night, even in very shallow waters. If picked up it will contort itself violently and will bite if given the opportunity to do so. Fortunately its teeth are not sharp, as they are adapted for crushing its invertebrate prey. Nevertheless, extensive lacerations can be caused. Likewise, the common black-tip shark (*Carcharinus spellanzani*) will bite in self-defence if cornered. It will grow to about 2 metres in length and is characterized by the black tips to all fins.

This shark moves onto reef flats on the flooding tide and will often investigate people who are wading on a flat. Many a novice reef fossicker has been terrified by the sight of a black-tipped dorsal fin cutting the water near by. Although the white-tipped shark (*Triaenodon apicalis*) attains a length in excess of 2 metres, it is timid and will move away from the human intruder.

Sometimes the small (up to 2 metres in length) graceful shark (*Carcharinus amblyrhynchoides*), one of the so-called whaler sharks, will show aggressive behaviour towards humans. It will make agitated movements which could be interpreted as threat behaviour, and it is possible that these sharks are, at times, territorial. Sometimes they lie about in groups on the coral sand of lagoons and back-reef areas. They are a nuisance to reef fishermen, as they are attracted by the struggles of hooked fish, most of which are deftly removed from the hooks. Another whaler shark found in the vicinity of reefs of the Great Barrier Reef is the bronze whaler (*Carcharinus alenea*). It attains a length of approximately 3 metres, and although there are no well-authenticated records of unprovoked attacks on humans by this shark in Great Barrier Reef waters, it has caused casualties elsewhere and must be regarded as a dangerous shark. It often invades reef flats on high tides at night, when it will readily take set baits of stingray flaps.

Tiger sharks (*Galeocerdo cuvier*) are sometimes encountered in the deeper waters near inner platform reefs and are not uncommon in the waters around outer reefs. They possess a formidable dental armature, attain lengths of up to 7 metres, and have been involved in human fatalities. Obviously they should be treated with care. They have been observed to prey on adult turtles in reef waters and, as noted earlier, are capable of biting right through the carapace of these armoured reptiles. However, they will not attack humans as a matter of course. They are attracted to areas near reefs where rubbish is frequently dumped, a practice that should be discouraged.

Occasionally the easily recognized and dangerous hammerhead shark (*Sphyrna lewini*) is found in waters near reefs, and there have been occasional sightings of large white pointer sharks (*Carcharodon carcharias*), a confirmed man-eater, in waters near reefs. However, white pointers appear to be infrequent visitors to the reefs.

Surgeon-fish

Surgeon-fish (Acanthuridae) have a sharp lancet-like spine or spines at the base of the tail on each side. If molested, they lash with the tail and are capable of inflicting severe lacerations on the unwary handler. Despite statements that surgeon-fish are not venomous, it is suspected that, in some species at least, toxic material is associated with their tail spines.

Eels

Most eels found on reefs have sharp teeth and a wide gape and should not be handled. Some of the larger ones are aggressive and somewhat unpredictable. They should always be treated with caution.

The Giant Toado

The giant toado (*Gastrophysus scleratus*) grows to about a metre in length and is greenish in colour. It has massive teeth, which are like the beak of a parrot, and powerful jaw muscles. Its ability to bite through the shank of a fish hook is well known. Less well known is its ability to amputate toes. In 1980 several children were attacked, probably by the same specimen of giant toado, in shallow water in the Shute Harbour area. Toes were deftly removed by the toado, which instituted a reign of terror among children in the area before it was caught.

First aid treatment for lacerations and trauma caused by biting and slashing animals involves the minimizing of further bleeding and the institution of measures to relieve shock as in the case of road accident victims. (It should be noted that severe injuries can also result from falling or being thrown against hard corals.)

VENOMOUS ANIMALS

These elaborate toxic material in association with an apparatus that is capable of injecting the material into a victim.

Scorpion-fish

Although a number of groups of fish found on coral reefs are venomous, the most dangerous belong to, or are closely allied to, the group known generally as scorpion-fish. Venom glands are associated with the bony spines that support the dorsal anal and ventral fins of these fish. Many are sluggish bottom-dwellers and lie apparently motionless among coral rubble or seaweed. Usually a protective camouflage renders them inconspicuous in their natural surroundings.

Stingings result from contact with their venomous spines, which are used only in defence.

Stonefish

Undoubtedly the most dangerous of the so-called scorpion-fish are stonefish, so named because of their resemblance to weed-covered stones. Stonefish may attain a length of more than 30 centimetres and a weight of several kilograms. The head region is characterized by the presence of bony eminences, deep hollows, and fleshy outgrowths. Wartlike bumps stud the trunk, which is often covered with a coating of slime to which algae and other organisms adhere. Normally stonefish lie partly embedded in sand amidst rocks or coral rubble and are exceedingly difficult to detect. At low tide they may be covered by only a few inches of water or even be completely exposed to the atmosphere.

A pair of venom glands is associated with each of the thirteen large bony spines supporting the dorsal fin which runs along the midline of the upper surface of the trunk. Stingings usually occur as a result of a barefooted person, or a person wearing inadequate footwear, treading upon the raised spines. Stonefish will take a bait, and stingings have also resulted from careless handling of captured fish, the flesh of which is edible. In order to prevent stingings from stonefish and scorpion-fish with similar habits, one should never venture onto coral reefs without adequate footwear. Captured stonefish may be held safely by the gills if necessary.

Zebra-fish

Not all fish of the scorpion-fish type conceal themselves in the way just described. Zebra-fish (also known as butterfly cod or lionfish) advertise their presence. Several species exist, and they are among the most gaudy and ornate of fishes, possessing long, lacy fins, peculiar outgrowths in the head region, and bright colour patterns. Pools and submarine caverns are their usual habitats, but they are also found among wharf piles and in the vicinity of old wrecks. They swim slowly about, apparently patrolling their territory, and they usually show little fear of man. The human intruder is tempted to reach out and grasp such an elegant fish in order to examine it more closely. Such an act would be regretted immediately, for needle-sharp spines with which venom glands are associated are concealed within all the fins except the huge pectoral (shoulder) fins and the tail fin. Moreover, the long dorsal spines are directed towards the hand that reaches towards the fish and, suddenly, the fish will jab at the hand and try to drive home its venom-laden spines. A net should be used if these fascinating fish are to be captured.

Immediate and intense pain is a feature of stings from stonefish, zebra-fish, and other fish of the scorpion-fish group. Pain associated with stings from stonefish and zebra-fish is often excruciating and, if the stings are untreated, may last for days. Stonefish stings are the most dangerous, possibly because more venom is introduced into wounds caused by the spines than is the case with stings from other fish. At any rate, stonefish stings are usually accompanied by swelling of the part affected, irregular breathing, a marked lowering of blood pressure, and sometimes partial paralysis. Frequently recovery from the effects of an untreated sting is long delayed, and ulceration and atrophy of tissues in the affected limb might occur. Washing of the wound with hot water is helpful, and in the case of stonefish stings, the irrigation of the wound with dilute acids (e.g., vinegar) or dilute oxidizing agents such as potassium permanganate will destroy the toxicity of venom present in the wound. An antivenom available from the Commonwealth Serum Laboratories, Melbourne, has proved remarkably effective against stonefish stings, and there is a strong possibility that it will prove to be effective against the stings of other scorpion-fish.

Rabbit-fish

Several species belonging to the family Siganidae occur in Great Barrier Reef waters. Some species (e.g., *Siganus lineatus, S. oramin*) commonly school with various species of parrot-fish near reef crests. Others (e.g., *L. vulpinus*) tend not to school. These rabbit-fish are also known commonly as "happy moments" because of their ability to cause pain. They possess a venom apparatus that consists of dorsal, anal, and ventral fin spines and twin venom glands associated with each spine.

Catfish

Another group of venomous fishes occurring on coral reefs are catfish, so called because of the barbels surrounding the mouth, which are reminiscent of a cat's whiskers. Their venom apparatus consists of three serrated spines — one on the upper surface at the leading edge of the dorsal fin and one at the leading edge of each pectoral fin. Cells, some producing venom and others producing mucus, surround the spines. Should one of the spines penetrate the flesh of a victim, the skin surrounding the spine tears away, liberating a venom-laden mucus which is introduced into the wound. If a spine penetrates deeply and breaks off it may be difficult to remove because of its serrated edges.

Catfish belong to two major groups — those with eel-like tails and those with forked tails. The former appear to be more venomous than the fork-tailed group. Stings received from the striped eel-tailed catfish (*Plotosus lineatus*) are particularly severe. These fish occur in large shoals which sometimes assume the form of a large ball that seems to rotate slowly in the water of the reef flat. The skins of catfish are scaleless, but very slimy and slippery, which makes them difficult to handle. Care should be exercised to avoid contact with the spines when removing them from hooks or nets.

Intense pain is felt almost immediately after being stung and the pain may persist for many hours. Swelling and discoloration in the area of a wound made by a spine often occurs and, in a severe stinging, swelling of the whole limb may ensue. The victim may suffer shock. Secondary bacterial infection of wounds is common, and some wounds take weeks to heal. First-aid treatment involves washing the wound with hot sea water followed by a mild antiseptic.

Stingrays

Stingrays belonging to several species occur on the Great Barrier Reef. These flattened animals are bottom-dwellers. Some may bury themselves partially in the coral sand, but the experienced eye can detect their characteristic outline. They range in size from a few centimetres to, in the case of a large coachwhip ray, well over a metre across. The venom apparatus takes the form of a serrated barb (or barbs) situated on the whip-like tail of the ray. In some species the barb occurs about two-thirds of the distance from the base to the tip of the tail. In others it is nearer the base of the tail. The barb is grooved on opposite sides, and in the grooves the skin that covers the barb is thickened because of a proliferation of venom-producing and mucus-producing cells.

Rays use their venom apparatus defensively if captured, trodden on, or otherwise molested. At such times a ray will lash vigorously with its tail and seek to drive its venom-laden barb into the flesh of its tormentor. As the barb is strongly serrated, it may break off and remain in the wound. Cases have been reported where barbs have been driven right through the leg or foot of a victim. Of course, the degree of penetration of the spine varies according to the species and size of ray involved. Species with spines nearer the tip of the tail can use their venom apparatus more effectively than those with spines nearer the base of the tail and, usually, the larger the ray, the stronger and larger the spine and the more powerful the lash of the tail. The skin surrounding the spine is frequently left as a bag in the puncture caused by the spine.

Rays will take a bait and are often caught by anglers. The hauling of a ray into a small dinghy is not usually appreciated by the other occupants of the dinghy, and unless the flesh of the ray is particularly prized, it would seem preferable to cut the line once a hooked ray is identified. Many stingings have resulted not only from careless handling of captured rays but from accidentally treading or jumping on buried rays. As well as mechanical injury (lacerations, etc.) caused by the passage of stingray spines through flesh, injuries inflicted by stingrays are accompanied by severe pain. Swelling of the part affected occurs and, in severe cases, victims may exhibit convulsive spasms. Stingray wounds should be washed immediately with cold salt water, an effort should be made to remove any foreign material in the puncture, and then the part affected should be immersed in water as hot as can be tolerated without injury for thirty minutes to one hour. Surgical removal of barbs which have broken off in wounds may be necessary.

Cone-shells

One group of molluscs known as cones (Conidae) has developed a remarkably sophisticated venom apparatus. This consists of a minute hollow harpoon held at the free end of a tubular and mobile proboscis which resembles a miniature elephant's trunk. The harpoon functions as a hypodermic needle, being associated with a syringe-like structure which is filled with venom (see fig. 32). Venom is forced through the harpoon when it is thrust into the flesh of a victim. Although the shells of a few species of Conidae are subcylindrical or ovoid in outline, most are conical. The shells are usually solid and porcellanous and bear striking colour patterns (sometimes obscured in life by a thin layer of brownish material — the periostracum). Dozens of species occur on coral reefs, and they are eagerly sought by shell collectors. Cones are active mainly at night. During the day they usually hide in crevices or bury themselves in coral sand, often under pieces of coral rubble.

All cones are carnivorous and use their venom apparatus to immobilize their prey. The various species may be divided into three groups according to the prey taken: one group preys on worms of various kinds, another preys on other molluscs, and a third preys on fish. Cones may use their venom apparatus defensively, and the

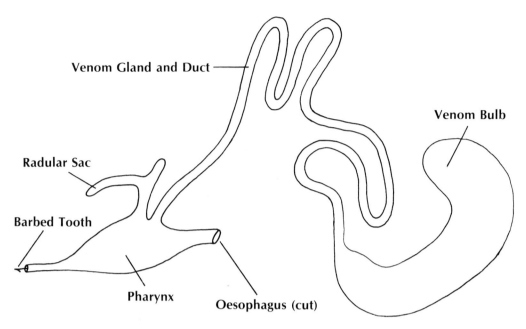

Venom Gland and Duct

Venom Bulb

Radular Sac

Barbed Tooth

Pharynx

Oesophagus (cut)

Figure 32. Diagram illustrating the principal regions of the venom apparatus of a cone-shell (F. *Conidae*).

venoms of the fish-eating cones are toxic to all backboned animals (vertebrates), including man. As far as man is concerned, the most dangerous species are the geographer cone *(Conus geographus)* and the tulip cone (C. *tulipa*). The former has been responsible for several fatalities, and both species have caused serious injury. The only other species that are of potential danger to man are the striated cone (C. *striatus*) and the magus cone (C. *magus*). However, many cones are capable of stinging man, and all cones should be handled only by the blunt end of the shell and dropped smartly if the tubular proboscis appears within striking distance. Visitors to reefs should learn to identify the geographer and tulip cones.

Victims of cone stingings usually feel a sharp sting as the harpoon is thrust into their flesh. A sting by one of the fish-eating cones can affect vision, hearing, and speech, and the victim may become partially or completely paralysed. A sting by worm-eating or mollusc-eating cones may cause pain, swelling, and discoloration of the area near the puncture. First-aid treatment involves removal of the harpoon, if it is visible, and thorough washing of the wound. Artificial respiration may be necessary if the victim experiences difficulty in breathing. A compression bandage as used in the treatment of snakebite may be useful to slow the transport of venom from the point of entry to other parts of the body.

Starfish

Only one starfish, the large, many-armed crown-of-thorns starfish, *Acanthaster planci*, is dangerous to man. Its upper surface is covered with long spines that can readily penetrate human skin. Toxic material is produced by the thin skin covering the spines, and this material is introduced into punctures made by the spines. Pain is immediate, severe, and prolonged. Swelling of the region affected occurs, and victims may vomit for prolonged periods. Any pieces of spines that have broken off in these punctures should be carefully removed. Thorough washing or irrigation of the punctures helps to remove toxic material. Penetration of spines into joints is especially dangerous as it may lead to immobilization of the joint.

Bristle-worms

Contact with the bristles or setae of the bristle-worm *Eurythoe complanata* causes pain, local oedema, and swelling of joints within a few hours. Blood-filled blisters form at the sites where bristles have penetrated the skin. The swelling recedes within a few hours, but healing of blisters is not complete for three to four weeks. The bristle-worm is common under coral boulders on reef flats and should never be touched with bare hands.

Sea-urchins

Some sea-urchins are venomous. Large, long-spined sea-urchins belonging to the genera *Diadema* and *Echinothrix* have sharp and brittle spines which readily penetrate and break off in the flesh of a victim. Toxic material is associated with the thin skin covering the spines and is thereby introduced into the tissues of the victim. This material causes prolonged pain and local swelling of the part affected. These sea-urchins are found in pools on reef flats, particularly in the vicinity of reef crests.

Another venomous sea-urchin found on the Great Barrier Reef is *Asthenosoma varium*. This species has prominent skin sacs covering its spines and is found in crevices and under ledges in the deeper water at the edges of reefs. When the spines penetrate the skin of a victim, the skin sacs rupture, discharging their contents into the punctures made by the spines. Pain is immediate and intense.

Stinging Hydroids

Two species of hydroid growing in Barrier Reef waters are capable of causing painful stings. These are *Aglaeophenia cupressina* and *Lytocarpus philippinus*. *Aglaeophenia cupressina* grows as large fern-like fronds on top and sides of coral boulders on reef flats. *Lytocarpus philippinus* is a more delicate hydroid. Both have batteries of large nematocysts, the threads of which are capable of penetrating human skin. Prolonged pain and swelling of regions affected may ensue. Treatment involves the application to the area stung of protein precipitants such as alcohol, dilute acids, or commercial preparations such as "Stingose".

Fire Corals

The fire corals belonging to the genus *Millepora* are not true corals despite their heavy, limy skeletons. Actually, they are closely related to hydroids and are known as hydrozoan corals. The polyps possess tentacles that are well armed with nematocysts. These fire if a victim brushes against the tentacles and the nematocyst threads penetrate the skin and toxin is injected. Pain is immediate and severe but can be relieved by the application of alcohols, dilute acids, aluminium sulphate, or "Stingose".

The Fire Anemone

The fire anemone, *Actinodendron plumosum*, is a potent stinger. It occurs more commonly on the fringing reefs of continental islands than on the off-shore platform and ribbon reefs. Stings from this animal are extremely painful. They should be treated similarly to stings from hydroids and fire corals.

Sea-Snakes

All sea-snakes are venomous and should not be handled. Fortunately those found in Australian waters are not aggressive. Nevertheless, most produce extremely potent venoms in venom glands associated with fangs in the mouth. Envenomation occurs in the same manner as with land snakes and treatment is similar (involving the immediate application of a compression bandage if a limb is involved). An antivenom effective against the venom of sea-snakes is available in Australia.

TOXIN-EXUDING ANIMALS

These release toxic materials continuously or intermittently into their immediate environment.

Sponges

Not all sponges can be handled with impunity. A flattish and brown encrusting sponge called *Neofibularia irata* occurs on the Great Barrier Reef. This species exudes a thick mucus which causes dermatitis on contact. Possibly other sponges and some soft corals and anemones found in the area also exude toxic mucus which causes dermatitis. Contact with such species should be minimized.

Holothurians

Toxic material is present on the body surfaces of many species of holothurians. If holothurians are handled and the toxic material transferred to the cornea of an eye, serious injury may be caused.

POISONOUS ANIMALS

Some animals elaborate a toxin in specific tissues or in the tissues generally. The toxin is not exuded or associated with an apparatus capable of injecting it. It must be ingested by an animal in order to exert its toxic actions. Potential predators soon learn to avoid poisonous organisms, and the species as a whole is thereby afforded protection against such predators.

Zoanthids

The zoanthid *Palythoa tuberculosa* contains a potent toxin, toxic by ingestion or inhalation in humans. However, the amount of toxin present varies from colony to colony and in some cases from region to region of the same colony. It has been found that toxicity is related to the presence of eggs in a polyp. The polyps change sex as they age. They are first female, then hermaphrodite, then male. The marked variation in toxicity displayed by this zoanthid stems from the uneven distribution of female polyps in a colony and to the seasonal changes that occur in their relative abundance. There is no known antidote for the toxin.

Anemones

The anemone *Rhodactis howesi* is extremely toxic when ingested. Many Pacific Islanders make soup or bouillabaisse consisting of mixed invertebrates collected from reefs. Occasionally one or more specimens of *Rhodactis howesi* are included and the results are invariably serious, often fatal. The toxin is a neurotoxin. No specific antidote is known.

Holothurians

As mentioned in chapter 12, in some regions of the Pacific, such as Guam and the Marianas, the indigenous people have for long captured fish by crushing holothurians (e.g., *Bohadschia argus* and *H. atra*) and throwing the crushed material into pools on reef flats. Toxic substances are leached from this material, and within a short time fishes in the pools leave their hiding places and attempt to escape. However, their movements rapidly become enfeebled and they are readily captured. The toxic materials responsible are known as holothurins.

Holothurians collected for human consumption are normally boiled before being eaten, and this boiling removes the toxic material. If not boiled, it would be ingested with disastrous results. The toxic material blocks nervous conduction and has a number of other physiological actions.

Crabs

Several species of crab found on the Great Barrier Reef elaborate toxins in their tissues and are poisonous if eaten. Although no human poisonings stemming from the ingestion of crabs from the Great Barrier Reef have been reported, some of the species occurring there have caused fatalities in other parts of the Indo–West Pacific region. These species include *Atergatis floridus, Lophozozymus pictor, Eriphia sebana, Daldorfia horrida,* and *Carpilius maculatus.* Other poisonous species of crab may occur on the Great Barrier Reef and it would be wise to refrain from eating any crabs from coral reefs.

Puffer-fish

Members of the puffer-fish group are able to inflate themselves by taking in water or air. Toadoes and porcupine-fishes belong to this group. Some of their tissues contain a potent toxin called tetrodotoxin, which is toxic upon ingestion. The toxin blocks nerve conduction and contraction of many types of muscle. The ingestion of puffer-fish can result in fatalities. Indeed, in Japan, where puffer-fish are eaten, there are many fatalities each year. Specially trained cooks prepare puffer-fish, called *fugu,* for human consumption in special restaurants. Much of the toxic material is eliminated during this preparation. The *fugu* is considered to be a delicacy and by some to be an aphrodisiac. However, if not properly prepared, it could constitute a last supper. Sharks and some large fishes such as mackerel appear to be able to eat puffer-fish with impunity.

Ciguatera

The term *ciguatera* is applied to a type of food poisoning stemming from the ingestion of certain fishes found on coral reefs or in the vicinity of coral reefs. Species of fishes that have been eaten with impunity for years may suddenly become toxic. The toxic material is initiated by a dinoflagellate called *Gambierdiscus toxicus,* which becomes associated with stalked algae growing on dead corals and is passed to large carnivores through a food chain involving herbivorous fishes. The most poisonous fishes are the large predators at the ends of food chains. The toxic material is cumulative in fish. Unfortunately, it cannot be removed from the flesh of a fish by washing, and it is stable at cooking temperatures and after prolonged refrigeration or drying. There is no way of detecting if a fish is carrying the toxin except by feeding some of it to an animal such as a cat and observing signs displayed.

The poisoning is characterized by gastro-intestinal and neurological manifestations. Signs and symptoms usually appear within two to four hours after ingesting a fish. Nausea and vomiting occur. A tingling or numbness occurs in the face, mouth, throat, hands, and feet. Hot objects may feel cold and cold objects hot. Frequently there is severe headache, dizziness, and muscle pains. Itching and increased sweating are common. Vision may be impaired. The symptoms may persist for weeks. In fatal cases, symptoms become progressively more

Facing page
Illustration 269
A reef stonefish, *Synanceja verrucosa.*

Illustration 270
A stinging hydroid, *Lytocarpus philippinus.*

Illustration 271
A soft coral, *Sarcophyton trocheliophorum,* that exudes toxic material.

Illustration 272
The poisonous shawl crab, *Atergatus floridus.*

Illustration 273
A poisonous xanthid crab.

Illustration 274
A holothurian, *Holothuria leucospilota,* that exudes toxic material when molested.

severe and dyspnoea and convulsions often occur, ending in respiratory failure and cyanosis. Obviously medical attention should be sought in severe cases.

Fortunately, ciguatera has not been as serious a problem in Barrier Reef waters as it has in other coraliferous parts of the Pacific Ocean. Fish from areas where there has been extensive coral destruction should perhaps be avoided and very large predatory fishes should not be eaten.

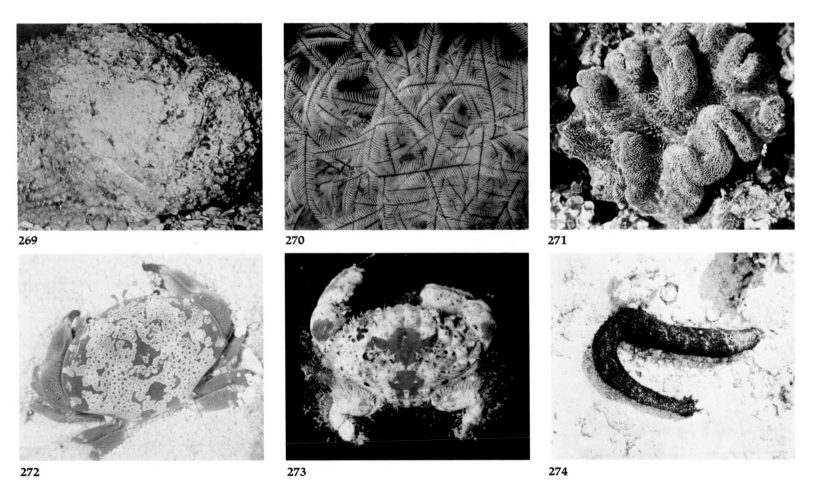

269

270

271

272

273

274

Flora and Fauna of Islands in the Great Barrier Reef Region

As noted earlier, islands in the Great Barrier Reef region are either rocky continental islands, volcanic islands, or cays formed of coral sand or coral shingle or a mixture of both. Continental islands are detached pieces of the adjacent Queensland mainland separated from the latter by bodies of water as a result of "drowning" of the coastline; their flora and fauna are basically similar to the flora and fauna of the adjacent mainland, discussion of which is beyond the scope of this book. The sand and shingle cays are formed on coral reefs; their fauna and flora will be discussed.

Sea birds find the sand and shingle cays of the Great Barrier Reef convenient resting and nesting areas. Their droppings form a primary layer of organic material, paving the way for colonization of the cays by plants. As well as providing vital nutrients for plants, the humus helps to retain fresh water falling as rain on the cays. Even so, the first plant colonizers must be very tolerant of salt because of the large amounts of salt spray in their environment. Also, they must be able to cope with high temperatures and desiccation as well as with substratum instability, as the surface sand of the cay is moved about by winds. Coarse grasses and creepers are usually the pioneer colonists on sand cays. The vegetation on many sand cays does not appear to be able to develop further.

Among the shrubs and trees, the primary colonizer is the casuarina (*Casuarina equisetifolia*). It is restricted to the strand line, but, once established, it affords protection for shrubs such as the tournefortia (*Messerschmidia argentea*), with its silvery leaves, and for the shiny green-leafed *Scaevola serica* and for other trees such as the strap-leafed *Pandanus tectorius*, with its segmented orange fruits and characteristic prop roots. Sometimes the pandanus trees dominate the forest, as at

Wilson Island in the Capricorn group. A further accumulation of organic matter — fallen leaves and guano formed from bird droppings — produces conditions favourable for the development of pisonia trees (*Pisonia grandis*). These trees attain a considerable height (up to 20 metres) and possess buttress roots and large, pale green leaves. They have great powers of regeneration, fallen branches often giving rise to new trees. During cyclones, almost every leaf may be stripped from the branches, but within a few weeks their foliage is as luxuriant as ever. Their fruit is sticky and adheres to the legs and feathers of birds, which thereby assist in propagating the tree. However, birds sometimes become so entangled in the sticky fruits that they are unable to fly. Some islands, such as Heron Island, Masthead, and North West Island in the Capricorn group, carry dense pisonia forests. A few other species of tree, such as the fig *Ficus opposita*, occur naturally on cays, and a number of species, including coconut trees, have been introduced by humans.

On some shingle cays mangrove forests have become established. These have a terrestrial flora and fauna similar to those of mangrove forests on the adjacent mainland.

View across the Wilson Island reef flat at high tide. The island is formed by an aggregation of coarse rubble some of which is visible in the foreground.

Birds of the Great Barrier Reef Islands

On approaching a coral cay in Great Barrier Reef waters, the human intruder often puts to flight clouds of sea birds that wheel and dip overhead while emitting raucous cries of alarm. Noddies, terns, boobies, and shearwaters are among the most abundant of the birds encountered. Many of the species seen actually nest on the cays. Nesting species include eight species of tern, two species of noddy, one species of gull, three species of booby, one species of shearwater, two species of frigatebird, one species of tropicbird, one species of petrel, and one species of pelican.

The number of species nesting on a particular cay is usually related to the state of its vegetation cover. On unvegetated cays only two or three species of sea bird (usually terns, noddies, and sometimes boobies) will breed. On cays where there are grasses and succulents but no trees, up to seven breeding species may be encountered. On cays with trees, any of the twenty species of sea birds mentioned above may nest. Up to eleven species have been reported nesting on the same cay. However, there is a marked tendency for the breeding activities of particular species to be concentrated on particular islands. In addition to the sea birds, a variety of land birds, including reef herons, sea-eagles, ospreys, pigeons, doves, oystercatchers, rails, kingfishers, honeyeaters, woodswallows, currawongs, and silvereyes, may nest on cays carrying trees.

Apart from nesting species, many other species of sea bird and land bird are migrants or occasional visitors to coral cays; the complete list of birds that have been seen on these cays would be a long one. In general, the nearer the island to the mainland the greater the number of visiting species from the mainland. Both sea birds and land birds may be present on continental islands, the actual species present depending on such factors as latitude, size, distance from mainland, type of soil, type of vegetation, and type of predator, if any, present.

Sea birds are responsible for transporting organic matter from the marine environment to the islands and hence play a major role in the cycling of plant nutrients from the sea to the islands. Indeed, the development and maintenance of vegetation on small islands depends primarily on the activities of these birds. Migratory species and birds that visit islands from the mainland help to disseminate many plant species.

The families of sea birds that nest on islands in the Great Barrier Reef area and a few of the interesting families of land birds that nest there are discussed below.

Terns, noddies, and gulls (Laridae) are mostly small to medium-sized, gregarious birds with webbed feet, which frequent islands and adjac-

Facing page
Strand-line vegetation on the beach at Heron Island. Casuarinas (*Casuarina equisetifolia*) occur on the strand-line.

Nesting crested terns, *Sterna bergii*, at Michaelmas Cay.

ent waters in the Great Barrier Reef area. Terns are slender birds with narrow wings and pointed bills. They also have forked tails, a feature that has caused them to be known as sea-swallows. Usually they are dark coloured on the back and head and white below. They tend to hover over their prey, which is usually fish or squid, before plunging down on it. They breed in colonies. Eggs are laid on the ground, and nests are usually little more than a few scrapings. The young are fed with fish or squid carried in the beaks of the parents.

Noddies are medium-sized birds with dark plumage except for the head, which is paler, often white. They have pointed bills and wedge-shaped or slightly forked tails. During the breeding season they aggregate in large numbers on coral cays. The common noddy (*Anous stolidus*) usually nests on the ground in a roughly made nest, but the white-capped noddy (*A. minutus*) makes a nest in a shrub or tree. The nests are formed of grasses and leaves cemented with excreta. Only one egg is normally found in each nest. The young are fed on fish and squid regurgitated into their gullets by their parents. Large colonies of nesting noddies are noted for the din made by the nesting birds and by the almost overpowering stench of guano in their vicinity.

The gull found commonly in Great Barrier Reef waters is the silver gull (*Larus novaehollandiae*). It is mainly white with grey upper parts. The heavy bill is hooked at the tip. Bill and legs are red in adults. The wings are long and the tail wedge-shaped. Gulls are notorious scavengers and almost omnivorous. They will take the young of other birds if given the opportunity. Also, they will prey on hatching turtles. They usually nest on the ground on islands. Two or three eggs are laid. The adults regurgitate food near their chicks, which then pick up the food.

Genera represented: *Sterna, Anous, Larus.*

Shearwaters and Petrels (Procellariidae). Shearwaters derive their name from their habit of tipping the water as they glide and bank near waves. They are birds of the open ocean, feeding predominantly on small pelagic animals such as squid and crustaceans and usually coming ashore only to breed. They require a small runway to take off. The bill is long and curved near the tip. Nostrils are located in a tube divided by a partition and located above the bill. The wings are long and narrow and angled forwards. When they come ashore for breeding purposes, they usually aggregate in large colonies. The species that nests commonly on islands in the Great Barrier Reef area is the wedge-tailed shearwater (*Puffinus pacificus*). It is medium sized (about 45 centimetres in length) with dark plumage. Burrows, which may be several metres in length, are usually dug when nesting, and the single egg is laid near the end of the burrow. During the nesting season some coral cays are honeycombed with burrows. Walking is hazardous at such times, for it is easy to break through the coral sand overlying the burrows, which are often a metre below ground. One bird stays on the nest during the day and is fed regurgitated fish, squid, and crustaceans caught by its partner. Later, both partners feed their chick. During the nesting season, nesting shearwaters — or muttonbirds, as they are known locally — fill the night air with their mournful, wailing cries. At times the birds appear to wail in unison, and sleep comes fitfully to the human who is not accustomed to the din.

Petrels, too, are birds of the open ocean and although several species have been observed in the Great Barrier Reef region only one species, the Trinidad petrel (*Pterodroma arminjoniana*) has been

A baby green turtle, *Chelonia mydas,* emerges from the egg.

observed to breed there. Compared with their close relatives, the shearwaters, petrels have shorter and stouter bills and longer tails.

Genus represented: *Puffinus, Pterodroma.*

Boobies (Sulidae), also known as gannets, are large birds with wingspans of 1.5 metres or over. They lack the usual nasal opening, but the mouth is extended back beyond eye-level and the extension functions as a nostril. They have heavy, pointed bills with a small, terminal hook. The neck is short, the wings are long and narrow, and the tail is long. The throat and part of the face are devoid of feathers and coloured. Their principal food is fish, which they capture by diving vertically from a height of 20 metres or more and seizing the fish during their plunge. Chicks are covered with fluffy down, and as they mature they often seem larger than their parents.

Genus represented: *Sula.*

Frigatebirds (Fregatidae) are medium-sized birds with long wings and a forked tail. They are skilled fliers and spend long periods in flight above the sea, eating and drinking while on the wing. Plumage is mostly black with some white patches. The males have red throat pouches, which can be inflated like balloons. They may scoop fish and squid from the water with their heavy, hooked bills, but often they force other sea birds to disgorge food by swooping on them repeatedly while they are in flight. Such acts of piracy are responsible for their common name. They occasionally alight in trees, only then using their small legs and feet. They nest in shrubs on islands, usually stealing nesting material from other birds. Only one egg is laid.
   Genus represented: *Fregata*.

Tropicbirds (Phaethontidae) are fairly large, pelagic birds characterized by the presence in mature birds of two long tail streamers arising from the middle of the wedge-shaped tail. They feed by diving on fish and squid from heights of approximately 14 metres and seizing their prey with their stout, pointed bills. Often they fly high, gliding for extended periods.
   Genus represented: *Phaethon*.

Reef herons (Ardeidae) are commonly found on islands and nearby reefs in the Great Barrier Reef area. They are fairly large birds (about 60 centimetres in length), with long necks, long pointed bills, and long legs. They occur in two colour phases, a white phase and a grey phase. During spring and summer, graceful plumes adorn the neck, breast, and back of breeding birds. Nests are made of twigs and are found usually in low shrubs. They may contain from two to five greenish eggs. Reef herons usually feed singly or in pairs at low tide. A variety of reef animals is captured for food. Reef herons fly with their heads retracted and their long legs extended. They usually utter raucous croaks when disturbed.
   Genus represented: *Egretta*.

Sea-eagles (Accipitridae). The white-breasted sea-eagle (*Haliaetus leucogaster*) is a large bird (up to 1 metre in length) with a wingspan that frequently exceeds 2 metres. It possesses a large, hooked beak and powerful talons. Although mostly white, it has a grey back and wing covers. Sea-eagles are mostly solitary, but are seen in pairs when nesting. They flap and soar on their upswept wings above islands. Their large nests are made of branches lined with twigs and usually placed in a forked tree. Sometimes the nests are constructed on the ground, as is one at One Tree Island. Nests may be used repeatedly, and as material is added to them each breeding season they become very large. Sea-eagles eat a wide variety of animals, which may be alive or dead when taken. The remains of fish, sea-snakes, and other birds have been seen at their nesting sites.

Genus represented: *Haliaetus.*

Ospreys (Pandionidae). The osprey (*Pandion haliaetus*) is a moderately large bird with a wingspan of 1.75 metres. The head and underparts are white, and the upperparts are brownish-black. The feet are adapted for seizing and holding fish, the talons being large and sharp and the toes possessing spiny projections. The legs are very muscular. Ospreys plunge into the water feet first from a considerable height in order to capture fish in their talons. When in flight, the wings are arched. Ospreys are found on many of the continental islands and wooded cays in the Great Barrier Reef region. They construct large nests of twigs and seaweeds. Sometimes the nests are placed in trees, sometimes on the ground.

Genus represented: *Pandion.*

Rails (Rallidae). One representative of the rail family is common and breeds on many wooded cays and continental islands; this is the banded rail (*Rallus philippinensis*), a medium-sized bird resembling a speckled and banded bantam. It spends the major part of its time on the ground. As the bird moves among the undergrowth, its small tail flicks up and down continually. It has strong legs and is a powerful runner. Although reluctant to fly, it will do so when necessary. It lays five or six eggs in a grasslined nest, usually sited under a grass tussock. Sometimes banded rails occur in groups, but usually they are solitary. They feed predominantly on insects and seeds.

Genus represented: *Rallus.*

Pigeons and doves (Columbidae). A number of pigeons and doves occurs on wooded cays and continental islands in Great Barrier Reef waters. One pigeon, the Torres Strait pigeon (*Ducula spilorrhoa*) is of particular interest. It is a large white pigeon with black flight feathers in the wings and a black tip to the tail. It moves southward across Torres Strait from Papua New Guinea in August and breeds commonly on islands in the northern part of the Great Barrier Reef area. At daylight it flies to mainland localities to feed on fruits and berries. Towards dusk it returns to the islands, flying low near the water in small groups that, from a distance, resemble fluttering white butterflies. In the past it was abundant, thousands of the pigeons occurring in huge flocks — but its numbers have been greatly reduced, apparently as a result of hunting. Nests are large platforms of twigs and are usually placed in trees.

Doves (*Geopelia humeralis*) nest commonly on many wooded cays and continental islands.

Genera represented: *Ducula, Geopelia.*

Turtles nesting on coral cays

Two species of turtle, the green turtle (*Chelonia mydas*) and the logger-head turtle (*Caretta caretta*), breed on some of the Great Barrier Reef islands. The cays of the Capricorn and Bunker groups and cays in the Swain Reefs area at the southern end of the Great Barrier Reef and cays at the northern end, such as Raine Island, are sites for some of the most important green and loggerhead turtle breeding grounds. Hawksbill turtles breed on some of the islands in the Torres Strait region just outside the Great Barrier Reef area.

Breeding female turtles normally emerge from the water at or just before high tide and under cover of darkness. They have difficulty in moving their ponderous bulk on dry land, and their progress up the beach is slow. It is also punctuated by numerous halts in order to breathe. Their great weight, unsupported by water, makes breathing difficult; consequently, progression stops and the head is lifted at intervals while air is exhaled from the lungs and fresh air taken in. Breathing is accompanied by throaty noises interpreted as sighs by many human onlookers. Nesting turtles also appear to be weeping, since there is a copious secretion of highly saline fluid from ducts which open near their eyes. Special glands that remove excess salt from the bodies of turtles produce the fluid that passes to the ducts.

The green turtle progresses on land by means of a rowing action involving the flippers, which move in unison and effectively drag and push the large body over the sand. On the other hand, the loggerhead turtle moves with a quadrupedal gait, its body being lifted above the sand, and the movements of members of each pair of limbs alternate; also, the right front flipper and left rear flipper move together, as do the left front flipper and the right rear flipper. Differences in the locomotion of these two species of turtle are reflected in the differences in the tracks they make on the beaches.

After moving up the beach to a point above high-tide level, turtles seek a suitable spot for nest construction. When a selection is made, the front flippers of the green turtle are angled so that they dig into the sand, which is flung backwards to form mounds at the side of the body. The rear flippers, working independently, push these mounds further to the rear. Digging is continued for about twenty minutes until a large pit in the sand, about 40 centimetres deep, is formed. Then the front flippers cease digging movements and the rear flippers change their action. They each become curved like a cupped hand and work alternately to scoop out a hole under the tail. This hole is the egg chamber, and it is excavated to a depth of about 40 centimetres below the pit accommodating the turtle's body. White, spherical eggs, each about 4 centimetres in diameter, with soft, flexible shells covered with mucus, are then laid. About 110 such eggs are normally laid, the actual number varying with the size of the turtle, among other factors. Very large turtles may lay up to 200 eggs. After egg-laying is completed, the eggs are covered with sand swept in by the rear flippers working alternately. As the egg chamber fills with sand the sand is patted down by the rear flippers. Then the front flippers recommence rowing movements, digging out sand in front of the turtle and filling in the body pit as the turtle slowly moves forward. After filling in the body pit, the turtle soon makes its way back to the water. About three hours are usually spent out of the water while nesting.

Each female green turtle normally comes ashore at least three times and occasionally as often as six times during the nesting season, which in the Capricorn and Bunker groups extends from late October to mid-February. However, three or four years will elapse before the female lays again.

The rate of development of the eggs varies directly with temperature in the immediate vicinity of the eggs. Normally hatching occurs about eighty days after the eggs are laid. About 88 per cent of the eggs give rise to hatchlings almost simultaneously. However, all the hatchlings remain in the nest for a short period. Then, usually at night, they emerge *en masse*. Hatchling green turtles are blackish above and white below, with an overall length of about 6 centimetres. (Loggerhead hatchlings are brown on both upper and lower surfaces.) Turtle hatchlings each possess an innate behaviour pattern which dictates that they move towards a light horizon. In effect, this behaviour pattern ensures that they move towards the water, unless they are distracted by artificial lights. Both green and loggerhead hatchlings move with a quadrupedal gait, and they move surprisingly quickly. Unless an obstacle or a predator is encountered, they reach the water within minutes after emerging from their nest.

Unfortunately for the hatchlings, predators abound. On the beaches, large ghost crabs (*Ocypode ceratophthalma*) wait to seize them with their pincers and drag them to their burrows where they are devoured piecemeal. If the hatchlings encounter beach rock or rubble patches near the waterline, they run the risk of being captured by the large red-eyed crab, *Eriphia laevimana*. If they make their dash for the water in bright moonlight, they must run the gauntlet of gulls (*Larus novaehollandiae*) that patrol the beaches when the moon is full. The gulls swallow the hatchlings whole and have ravenous appetites. Then, should the hatchlings be lucky enough to reach the water, they must swim across the reef flat where a large number of predatory fishes await their arrival. No doubt the greater the number of hatchlings that move down the beach and swim across the reef flat the greater the chance of some surviving. Probably, if their numbers

Facing page
Illustration 279
Hatchling green turtles, *Chelonia mydas*, that have just emerged from the egg chamber are intent on reaching the water.

Illustration 280
Two wedge-tailed shearwaters (*Puffinus pacificus*) nesting.

Illustration 281
A white-capped noddy (*Anous minutus*) on its nest in a pisonia tree.

Illustration 282
A banded rail, *Rallus philippinensis*.

Illustration 283
A reef heron, *Egretta sacra* (white phase) perched on top of a pisonia tree.

Illustration 284
A brown booby (*Sulu leucogaster*) on nest, Fairfax Island.

279

280

281

282

283

284

exceed a critical level, most predators will be satiated or engaged in eating captured turtles and many hatchlings will escape. Also a very dark night would assist the hatchlings to elude their predators. Sometimes the hatchlings emerge during daylight hours when their numbers are decimated by gulls.

Once they have crossed the reef flat the hatchlings head for the open sea. What happens to them after this stage is a mystery, for the smallest green turtles seen on reefs of the Great Barrier Reef are three to four years old and too large and well protected for most reef predators, except the larger sharks, to tackle. The unprotected hatchlings are pelagic and must be carried by surface currents. Perhaps they hitch a ride on floating seaweeds. One was found on seaweed drifting some miles from Heron Island in 1965. It is possible that they drift

A pandanus tree, *Pandanus tectorius*, with fruit at Tryon Island.

with currents in the Coral Sea area until they are sufficiently large to return to reefs without the risk of immediately being seized by a predator. Green turtles do not breed until they are almost eight years old.

The nesting behaviour of the loggerhead turtle is similar to that of the green. However, only about fifty eggs are laid, and loggerheads usually nest nearer the water than green turtles do. The relative proportions of green and loggerhead among nesting turtles on a cay in the Capricorn group varies, depending on the cay under consideration. At Wreck Island the nesting turtle population is half green and half loggerhead; at Heron Island, loggerheads constitute only 15 per cent of the nesting turtle population; while at North-West Island, nesting loggerheads are very rare. Of the other species of turtles found in

Queensland waters, the hawksbill turtle nests on islands in Torres Strait and the flatback at Mon Repos Beach on the mainland near Bundaberg. The leathery turtle does not appear to nest in Queensland waters.

Other Terrestrial Animals

A few birds and mammals such as domestic fowls, goats, cats, and rats have unfortunately been introduced to some coral islands since the advent of humans, and probably the ants and spiders found on some islands have had a similar origin. One Tree Island in the Capricorn group is noted for its centipedes.

Vegetation at Masthead Island. The tall trees in the background are pisonia trees (*Pisonia grandis*).

21

Island Tourist Resorts

Most tourist resorts in the Great Barrier Reef area are situated on rocky continental islands. While many of these islands have fringing reefs where corals and a variety of associated coral reef animals and plants are to be found, they are many kilometres from the platform and ribbon reefs where the coral reef communities are best developed. Frequently, their marine fauna and flora are dominated by rocky shore species or by species found commonly on muddy or sandy substrates. Only two large tourist resorts, Green Island and Heron Island, are situated on platform reefs. However, the continental island tourist resorts have attractions of their own. A brief description of Great Barrier Reef tourist resorts, listing some of their interesting features is given in the following pages.

Lizard Island

Lizard Island is the northernmost of the Great Barrier Reef tourist resorts, being situated on a rocky island approximately a hundred kilometres north of Cooktown. The tourist resort is small but well appointed. There is also a small research station on the island. It was from the high peak on the island that, in 1770, Lieutenant James Cook saw ribbon reefs stretching away to the north and to the south and realized for the first time during his epic voyage of discovery that the Queensland coast was protected by huge masses of coral. The island was named after the monitor lizards that are common there. Coral colonies are scattered around the perimeter of the island and in some places, especially on the windward side, form fringing reefs carrying luxuriant coral. There is also a flourishing coral reef community in a lagoon that extends between Lizard Island and two adjacent islands. Lizard Island itself is about fifteen kilometres from the nearest ribbon reef. An airstrip providing access from Cairns directly or via Cooktown has been built on the island.

Green Island

The tourist resort of Green Island is situated on a coral cay approximately twenty-seven kilometres east of Cairns. The small, densely vegetated sand cay surmounts portions of a platform reef about six square kilometres in area. Unfortunately, the hard coral cover of the reef was devastated in the early 1960s by the crown-of-thorns starfish and again in the period 1979–81, after considerable recolonization of the hard coral had occurred. Even so, the underwater enthusiast will find it a memorable experience to don face mask and snorkel and view the damage caused by the crown-of-thorns starfish to the hard coral cover of the reef flat. Care should be taken to avoid treading on the venomous spines of the starfish; signs have been erected on the beach of the cay warning visitors of this danger. To some extent the loss of the bulk of the hard coral cover has been compensated for by the prolific growth of soft coral. Many visitors find the beds of soft corals, which move gently in water currents, of particular interest. Glass-bottomed boats are available for viewing the reef flat organisms.

Interesting features of this resort are the underwater observatory, situated on the jetty, and Marineland Melanesia, situated on the cay itself. From the observatory the visitor looks out on the animals found on the reef flat. In Marineland Melanesia the visitor looks into aquaria where marine specimens are held; large crocodiles are also housed there. Green Island has had a long and interesting history which is recorded on a notice board near the tourist accommodation on the island. The island is readily accessible from the mainland port of Cairns; large launches and a fast hydroplane are used to transport visitors, and a seaplane also makes several flights a day. Consequently there are numerous day trippers to the island.

Dunk Island

The Dunk Island tourist resort is located on a densely forested continental island only five kilometres from the mainland. Most of the island is a national park comprising tropical rainforest and associated animal life. The terrestrial animals and plants have great potential interest for the tourist, and the tourist resort on the island has capitalized on this interest by providing walking tracks and by making the blue Ulysses butterfly its symbol. Accommodation units are inconspicuous and blend well with their lush tropical surrounds. Beaches are extensive, and there is a fringing reef on the eastern side of the island where corals and interesting marine organisms can be viewed. The island is approximately twenty-eight kilometres from the nearest platform reef, but trips to platform reefs can be arranged. Access to Dunk Island itself is provided by air from Townsville (there is an airstrip on the island) and by launch from Mission Beach on the near-by mainland.

Bedarra Island

Bedarra island is a small continental island only five kilometres from Dunk Island and the same distance from the mainland. It has been the site of a small, privately run tourist resort; at the time of writing tourist facilities at the resort were being upgraded. Bedarra Island is about thirty-two kilometres from the nearest platform reef of the Great Barrier Reef.

Hinchinbrook Island

A tourist resort is sited at Cape Richards near the north-eastern tip of Hinchinbrook Island, which is a large (684 square kilometres), unpopulated continental island lying only a few kilometres from the coast between Cardwell and Ingham. Cape Richards itself is about twenty-six kilometres east of Cardwell. Hinchinbrook is reputed to be the world's largest island national park. It possesses some fascinating rainforests, mangrove flats, high mountains, a rich fauna and flora, and some spectacular views. A series of beaches and headlands are found on the eastern side, and on the western side the famous Hinchinbrook passage separates the island from the mainland. Access is provided by seaplane and by boat. A few coral clumps are found on rocks, and the island is approximately twenty-eight kilometres from the nearest platform reef.

Orpheus Island

Orpheus Island is a continental island in the Palm group and lies some eighteen kilometres off the coast near Ingham. A tourist resort, formerly run as a small private venture but at the time of writing being upgraded, is situated on the western side of the island. A small research station owned and operated by James Cook University is also situated on the island. A complex system of ridges, bare on the eastern side but covered with scrub on the western side, runs the length of the island. There is a well-developed fringing reef on the island which was regarded as one of the best shell-collecting localities on the Queensland coast, and despite over-collecting, many interesting species of mollusc are still common there. Numerous species are represented among the corals present. However, the crown-of-thorns starfish has been active in the area. The nearest platform reef lies some twenty-eight kilometres to the north-east. Orpheus Island is accessible by launch from Lucinda, a mainland port.

Magnetic Island

Magnetic Island is a large continental island eight kilometres from Townsville. Several tourist resorts are located on the island, which has some attractive scenery, including beach-lined embayments, rocky headlands, and boulder-strewn hills. Scattered coral clumps are found in some of the embayments, but much of the coral that formerly flourished in some bays has been killed by siltation. Magnetic Island is approximately fifty-one kilometres from the nearest platform reefs.

Hayman Island

The tourist resort on Hayman Island is the largest of the Great Barrier Reef resorts and is well appointed. It is situated on the western side of Hayman Island, which is one of the islands of the Cumberland group. The island is approximately twenty-nine kilometres east of the mainland. In parts, Hayman Island is densely wooded and rises steeply. The terrestrial flora and fauna are particularly interesting. There is an extensive fringing reef on the southern and eastern sides of the island and other fringing reefs on near-by islands. These reefs carry many species of coral and associated fauna and flora and have much of interest for the naturalist and casual visitor. The platform reefs of the Great Barrier Reef are, at their closest twenty-nine kilometres to the east of the island. However, trips can be arranged to these platform reefs from the resort.

South Molle Island

Another continental island in the Cumberland group, South Molle borders Whitsunday Passage and lies about eight kilometres from the coast in the Proserpine region. The island is densely wooded in parts and there are extensive graded walking tracks. Oysters are to be found on intertidal rocks, but coral clumps are few. The resort is readily accessible to day trippers. It lies approximately sixty-five kilometres from the platform reefs of the Great Barrier Reef.

Hamilton Island

Hamilton Island is another of the Cumberland Islands, lying about thirteen kilometres from the mainland in the Proserpine region. The nearest platform reef is approximately sixty-four kilometres distant.

Long Island

A picturesque island in the Whitsunday group of the Cumberland Islands, Long Island lies about seven kilometres from the coast in the Proserpine region. The resort blends well with the environment. It is serviced by helicopter and launch. Only a few coral clumps will be found in the immediate vicinity of the island, which is situated some sixty-six kilometres from the platform reefs of the Great Barrier Reef.

Daydream Island

Daydream Island is situated in the Cumberland Islands near the Whitsunday Passage and is only five kilometres from the mainland. It is a continental island about 10.5 hectares in area. The resort is arranged around a free-form, salt-water swimming pool which is claimed to be the largest in the Southern Hemisphere. There is also an extensive palm-fringed beach of coral sand. Access to the island is by helicopter and boat. Only scattered clumps of coral are found in the immediate vicinity of the island, which is approximately fifty-six kilometres from the platform reefs of the Great Barrier Reef.

Lindeman Island

Another island in the Cumberland group of continental islands, Lindeman Island is situated about seven kilometres from the nearest point on the mainland. It is about 800 hectares in extent and was one of the first islands on the Great Barrier Reef to operate as a tourist resort. The accommodation units are sited on the side of a hill, and a small cable car helps to provide access. There is a well-developed fringing reef skirting the island, where coral colonies and their associated fauna and flora can be seen. Lindeman Island is approximately sixty-seven kilometres from the nearest platform reef. Access to the island is provided by plane and launch.

Brampton Island

Brampton Island is about 500 hectares in area and lies about twenty-five kilometres off the mainland coast to the north of Mackay. The tourist resort is situated on flat ground near the narrow channel separating Brampton Island from the neighbouring Carlisle Island, which rises to a high peak and is densely forested. There are numerous low ridges on Brampton Island which provide good vantage points for viewing the surrounding islands and the mainland coastline. Sandy beaches and scattered clumps of coral will be found around the island. Brampton Island is about fifty-seven kilometres from the nearest platform reef.

Wild Duck Island

Wild Duck Island is a continental island sited some eighteen kilometres north-west of the nearest point on the coast in the Broad Sound region. At the time of writing, a tourist resort was under construction on the island, which is some 110 kilometres from the nearest platform reef.

Great Keppel Island

A continental island located in the Yeppoon area, approximately thirteen kilometres from the nearest point on the mainland, Great Keppel Island possesses extensive beaches, rocky headlands, scrub-covered mountains, and an underwater observatory. Unfortunately, some of the beds of branching coral that formerly flourished near the island have been killed in recent years. However, others still remain for viewing by underwater enthusiasts. The platform reefs of the Great Barrier Reef are some seventy-seven kilometres distant.

Heron Island

The resort of Heron Island is sited on a coral cay, 18 hectares in extent, which, in turn, is situated on a platform reef approximately 27 square kilometres in area. Because of its distance from the mainland (approximately sixty kilometres), the waters around the island are free of mainland drainage and are of exceptional clarity. Protection was conferred on the fauna and flora of the reef some twenty years ago, with the result that most species of marine animal and plant occurring in the southern region of the Great Barrier Reef will be found there. Also, fish do not flee at the first sight of a human intruder as they so often do on reefs where spear-fishermen hunt fish regularly. Several species of birds, particularly noddies and shearwaters, breed on the cay, and it is also an important breeding area for green and loggerhead turtles. A world-famous research station, constructed originally by the Great Barrier Reef Committee but now owned and operated by the University of Queensland, is also located on the island.

Lady Elliott Island

The southernmost island in the Great Barrier Reef area, Lady Elliott Island is a true coral cay lying some eighty-two kilometres from the mainland coast near Bundaberg. The cay, which bears a lighthouse, is situated on a platform reef which carries luxuriant coral. Accommodation in the form of huts and tents in which visitors camp is provided on the island. Access is by plane from Maryborough.

22

Fishing, Reef-Walking, and Diving

Amateur Fishing

Most fish taken by amateurs in Great Barrier Reef waters are taken by the owners of small boats and their friends who accompany them on trips of short duration from mainland localities to offshore reefs. Usually these trips are made when reasonably calm conditions prevail and, of course, are more frequently made at weekends and public holidays than at other times. Thousands of speedboats with high-powered outboard motors and capable of completing the journey to many of the offshore reefs within two to three hours are kept at mainland localities west of the reefs. It has been estimated that approximately four hundred speedboats from Cairns and fifty from Innisfail visit reefs seaward from these localities each weekend when weather conditions are favourable; probably hundreds of speedboats from other mainland localities also visit reefs of the Great Barrier Reef at such times. In addition, small charter vessels (ranging from twelve to thirty metres in length) operate from most ports along the mainland coast and from tourist resorts. Many of these are hired by parties of fishermen for trips to reefs. Consequently, when the weather is favourable, thousands of amateur fishermen will be found testing their skill in Barrier Reef waters.

Newcomers to the ranks of amateur fishermen in these waters are invariably surprised by the type of fishing gear employed. Usually nylon monofilament lines ranging from 20 to 40 kilograms breaking strain are used, because the reef fish caught attain relatively large sizes and it is frequently necessary to prevent such powerful fish from darting into coral clumps when hooked; coral clumps, particularly branching corals, have a marked propensity for snagging and entangling fishing lines, much to the annoyance of fishermen. Hooks used are large, generally 6/0 to 9/0, because most reef fish sought by fishermen have surprisingly large mouths. As many of the larger predatory fishes normally caught also have teeth that are large and sharp, fishermen often use wire traces with the hooks. Sinkers used vary in weight and type with locality and the species of fish sought. A common rig is a line with a pendant-type sinker weighing from about 110 grams to 450 grams at the end of the line (some old-timers prefer railway dog-spikes) and two hooks, each attached to about half a metre of secondary line (often lighter than the main line) and mounted on the main line at intervals of half a metre above the sinker. However, some fishermen prefer a running sinker and a single hook at the end of the line, and, of course, there is the usual variation in fishing tackle and rig depending on the preferences and idiosyncrasies of individual fishermen.

Bait usually comprises sizeable (e.g., 3 cm x 10 cm) slices of fish flesh, although whole fish (e.g., pilchards, known commonly as "blueies") have found favour with some fishermen as bait for some species of fish, particularly coral trout. Choice of fishing site depends on such considerations as species of fish sought, weather conditions, state of tide, and season of the year. Some fishermen prefer to anchor in the lee of a reef and fish in back-reef areas among coral pinnacles, while other prefer to anchor on the seaward slopes of the weather side of a reef. Many fishermen search (often with echo sounders) for areas of rubble and/or coral in deeper waters near reefs; others prefer to fish while drifting in the channels among reefs. A few of the more adventurous types troll with artificial lures close to reef crests or fish in lagoons at night with a floating bait.

Numerous species of the larger reef fishes, most of which are carnivorous and will take a bait, are captured by line fishermen. The commoner types taken are coral trout and coral cods (Serranidae), sweetlip emperors (Lethrinidae), snappers (Lutjanidae), and wrasses (Labridae). Although well aware that the following statement will be hotly debated, it is the writer's experience that fishing in Great Barrier Reef waters does not require a great deal of finesse. The larger fishes usually grab the bait and attempt to swallow it in its entirety as quickly as possible. On finding themselves hooked they usually make a dash for the shelter of the nearest coral clump. It is merely necessary to check their headlong rush and haul them in rapidly before their struggles attract the attention of large predators such as sharks or groper. Many fishermen use gloves to prevent nylon lines cutting their fingers during the frantic dashes for cover made by hooked fish. Captured fish are usually skinned and filleted — these treatments requiring a certain amount of skill and experience as well as a sharp knife.

287

288

289

290

291

292

Professional Fishing

Because of obvious difficulties attending the use of nets in waters where coral abounds, professional fishermen operating on reefs of the Great Barrier Reef have, of necessity, relied on line fishing. Before the 1970s, hand-lining with gear similar to that used by the majority of their amateur counterparts produced catches of coral reef fishes sufficient for most to make a reasonable living after defraying the not inconsiderable costs involved in purchasing, equipping, and maintaining a small (usually about thirty to forty metres in length) diesel-powered boat carrying a freezer compartment for holding the fish caught while at sea. Some of the more enterprising fishermen carried one or two small dories on their fishing vessels. The dories were used in trolling for coral trout, a premium food fish that usually commanded a high price. In most cases the catch was ultimately sold through government-controlled Fish Board depots set up at major ports along the Queensland coast. The principal reef fishes caught were coral trout and coral cods, sweetlip emperors, and snappers.

During the 1960s and 1970s, spear-fishing became a more efficient method of catching reef fish than hand-lining and was engaged in by a number of professional and semi-professional fishermen. Parties of spear-fishermen using face mask and snorkel or scuba gear and operating from small dories would move systematically round the edges of reefs spearing most of the large site-attached fishes encountered. Sharks attracted by the slaughter were quickly dispatched by the use of "bang-sticks" — spears with bullets or shotgun cartridges that fire on impact cradled at their tips. The catches were usually filleted and sold as "fillets of reef fish" through Fish Board outlets. Unfortunately, this method of fishing for reef fish appears to have been too efficient; many reefs have been almost denuded of their populations of large, site-attached fishes. Indeed, the Queensland government recently thought it necessary to legislate for the banning of the use of scuba in conjunction with spear-guns for the capture of reef fish. As a result of this overfishing, as well as the deleterious effects on reef fish stemming from marked alterations in coral reef ecology caused by population explosions of crown-of-thorns starfish, commercial fishing in some sections of the Great Barrier Reef for reef-associated fish has declined markedly in recent years, particularly in the region between Cooktown and Bowen.

Trolling for mackerel and other pelagic fishes in offshore waters near the Great Barrier Reef has occupied the attention of professional fishermen for decades. The chief fish captured is the narrow-barred Spanish mackerel, *Cymbium commersoni*, which attains a length of 2.5 metres and a weight of 60 kilograms. Usually fish weighing between 4.5 and 11.5 kilograms are taken by the professional trollers, along with other mackerels and tunas.

Boats used by mackerel fishermen are generally twelve to fifteen metres long. They are taken to sea, usually for short periods of two to three days, at intervals during the mackerel season, which lasts from May to September. Nylon cord lines are used for trolling. These are linked to ten-metre traces of piano-wire or "Allbright" wire, which is separated by a swivel from a stainless steel spoon lure or a baited gang hook rig (three to four 6/0 hooks linked together). Garfish or blue pilchards are commonly used for bait. The nylon cord line is tied to a railing or cleat by means of speargun rubber, which absorbs the shock of a fish striking the lure or bait. Gloves are usually worn by the fishermen, and the powerful fish are hauled into the boat as rapidly as possible.

About half the annual intake of finned fish passing through Fish Board depots in north Queensland consists of mackerel. However, the annual catch has declined markedly (along with catches of most other species of fish) since the period 1966–68, when annual catches of mackerel in excess of 400,000 kilograms were recorded.

Big-Game Fishing

Since 1966 Cairns, in north Queensland, has become the centre for an industry based on the black marlin, *Makaira indica*. Big specimens, exceeding 450 kilograms in weight, of these pelagic fish occur in the deep water just seaward of the outer edge of the ribbon reefs lying north of Cairns. Of course, smaller specimens occur there and on the landward side of the reefs as well, but it is the large marlin that lure big-game fishermen from all parts of the world to Cairns for the so-called marlin season, which is short, lasting from September to November inclusive. This short season is dictated by the migratory habits of the black marlin, which appear to move eastwards out into the Coral Sea during the remainder of the year.

In 1967 only three game-fishing boats operated from Cairns, but by 1980 there were approximately a hundred in the area. Most now operating are small "day boats" about eight to twelve metres long and characterized by their flying bridges and long white outrigger poles arching towards the stern of each boat. Two expensive game rods are secured to the gunwales, and loops of heavy lines (usually 59 kilogram breaking strain) run from the rods to the outrigger poles, where they are each held by a peg. From the peg, each line trails behind the boat, one either side of the wake. When a fish strikes the baited hook at the end of a line, the peg at the outrigger pole snaps, this being the signal for the fishermen to snatch the appropriate rod and leap into the game-fishing chair mounted on the deck in the stern well. Tussles with large marlin can last well over an hour and require a lot of skill and endurance on the part of the fisherman. Only about 5 per cent of marlin caught are killed and weighed. The remainder are released, some being tagged before release. Usually the "day boats" involved in game-fishing return to port at the end of a day's fishing, but some are associated with luxuriously appointed mother ships that anchor in the shelter of reefs and provide first-class food and comfortable sleeping quarters for the big-game fishermen.

It is apparent that the big-game fishing industry based at Cairns has a turnover of millions of dollars. However, its economic base may not be very secure. Costs involved in purchasing and equipping a game-fishing boat are high, as are operational costs. Fuel costs in particular have increased markedly in recent years; so too have the salaries of crews. Most of the game-fishing boats are owned by fishing enthusiasts who offer their boats for charter to help offset annual operation costs. Although charter fees are high, the marlin season is brief. It would probably be advantageous to all concerned if the black marlin season could be extended by locating new fishing grounds in the Coral Sea or if other species of game-fish, such as the blue marlin, *Makaira nigricans*, could be fished. Marlin have of course, been sighted at many places long the length of the Great Barrier Reef, and it is possible that other big-game fishing centres will be established elsewhere. However, there are reasons for believing that the future of big-game fishing in Barrier Reef waters is not particularly promising. In recent years it has become apparent that Japanese long-liners, using set lines up to fifty kilometres in length, are capturing thousands of marlin annually in the Coral Sea region. (In one year more marlin than tuna were caught by the long-liners.)

Reef-Walking

At low tide it is possible to walk among reef-flat corals on many reefs and to examine corals and other elements of the fauna and flora of these reefs. Indeed, the low water levels on reef flats at periods of low tide often facilitate location and examination of many interesting specimens, some of which (e.g., some crabs) are only active at low tide. Particularly is this so during low tides at night. The reef-walker should wear adequate footwear (gym-boots that protect the ankles are favoured by many) and socks to prevent abrasion of the feet by coral sand. Appropriate clothing should also be worn to guard against over-exposure to the tropical sun. At all times care should be exercised to avoid cutting oneself on sharp coral skeletons. Whenever possible, it is preferable to walk on coral sand rather than on coral itself. When visiting a reef at night, waterproof torches should be carried and arrangements made for a light to be positioned at the point to which it is intended to return. It is surprising how many reef-walkers manage to lose their bearings on a reef flat at night. This can be quite disconcerting when the tide begins to rise. Of course, reef-walking can only be undertaken when tides are favourable. Spring tides are obviously preferable to neaps. Sunny days and a lack of surface ripple caused by wind facilitate viewing of reef-flat organisms. Reef-walking should begin about an hour before the predicted time for dead-low water and terminate about an hour and a half after this time. Allow adequate time to return to base; some reefs have a raised rim to the reef flat, and the reef flat will flood suddenly on the rising tide.

Diving

In order to see most reef-flat animals engaged in their normal activities, to see the inhabitants of deeper water at the reef perimeter, and to appreciate fully the beauty and mystery of a coral-reef community, it is necessary to view this community when it is covered by water. A glass-bottomed viewing box held in the hand or inserted into the hull of a boat will permit glimpses of submerged reef organisms. However, if one can swim, there should be no hesitation about equipping oneself with a face mask and snorkel in order to view reef-flat organisms. The dangers involved are negligible. Moreover, if flippers are used it is possible, after a little practice, for most people to view animals in the deeper water around the edge of a reef in perfect safety provided a few simple precautions are taken.

First, do not dive alone. Have an understanding with your partner or partners that you are going to keep an eye on each other and that you will stay in a particular area for an agreed length of time. Secondly, wear an inflatable safety vest and have a boat readily accessible. Remember that most of the offshore reefs of the Great Barrier Reef are more than twenty kilometres from the Queensland mainland. If you are swept away from a reef, a long swim may lie ahead before you are picked up or reach any land. Thirdly, keep within hailing distance of your partners, and don't lose sight of them or your boat. When you are in the water, your range of vision above water as well as below is restricted. It is easy to lose oneself among coral outcrops if no high reference points are available. Fourthly, test the strength of water currents before you swim away from your boat. Tidal currents on a reef vary in strength with the state of the tide and the point reached in the tidal cycle, with reef configuration, with the proximity of other reefs, and with the latitude of a reef. Also, surface currents near reefs wax and wane and sometimes even change direction according to wind movements and season of the year. Currents with strengths up to 8 knots have been found in some reef areas. Fifthly, coral skeletons can inflict deep lacerations if you are flung against them, so avoid areas of heavy wave action near reef edges.

Scuba diving is a sport that has become very popular in recent years, and Great Barrier Reef waters have a special attraction for scuba divers. Despite popular belief, these waters are among the safest in the world for scuba diving if a few extra precautions are taken. In addition to those mentioned above when using face mask and snorkel, take care not to hook your scuba gear on branching corals. Also, take extra care to avoid diving too deeply for too long a time. Reef waters are often crystal clear and initially estimation of water depth is difficult. Also, as the surroundings are full of beauty and interest, it is easy to lose track of time. Remember that there is only one decompression chamber in Queensland (at the Australian Institute of Marine Science at Cape Cleveland, near Townsville), and in most cases there would be a long delay before you could be placed in such a facility.

Unfortunately, a major difficulty attends the use of scuba in Great Barrier Reef waters. This is the paucity of filling stations for scuba tanks in the area. A portable compressor can be used, but there is then the trouble of transporting the compressor along with tanks to reefs that are often remote from mainland centres. A few tourist resorts have facilities for filling scuba tanks, and scuba gear may be hired at some resorts. A certificate of competency in the use of scuba gear is required before tanks will be filled or scuba gear hired. The blue and white international diver's flag is required to be flown when diving in Queensland waters. Failure to do so could result in a heavy fine. Remember that a lot of boats move about in waters near tourist resorts.

When diving with face mask and snorkel in Great Barrier Reef waters, care is required to prevent over-exposure to the tropical sun. Old clothing provides protection against sunburn and also helps to prevent cuts from coral. Many scuba divers find wet-suits uncomfortably hot in the tropics as well as a nuisance to transport, and they, too, frequently enter the water clad in old clothing.

It is necessary to take some care with marine animals that are encountered while reef-walking or diving. Some are venomous and capable of inflicting painful stings. They should not be touched. A list of these is given in chapter 19. A few of the larger sharks are dangerous, and it would be wise to leave the water if large sharks, particularly tiger sharks or hammerheads, show any aggressive behaviour. However, most sharks encountered will show no obvious interest in humans intruding into their watery domain and in many cases will actually flee.

One face-to-face encounter with a large shark in shallow water on an outer reef east of Bowen is vividly remembered. The sea was flat calm, and the present author, snorkelling, had quietly rounded a coral pinnacle. A large object appeared directly ahead cruising slowly on a collision course. The unmistakable broad snout, large circular eyes, and crescent mouth-slit of a tiger shark materialized and approached inexorably. When it was within about two metres the water seemed to explode and vision was blotted out by a great cloud of material in the water, thought for an instant to be blood. Then it was realized that the material suspended in the water was whitish. The startled shark had defaecated before hurtling off towards blue water.

23

Natural Agencies Causing Destruction of Coral Reef Communities

The physical environment of most of the coral reef communities found in Great Barrier Reef waters is benign and free from any marked seasonal change. Mean sea water temperatures at different points along the length of the Great Barrier Reef approximate the ideal for the growth of the coral species present, and the annual temperature range is narrow. Salinity is normal for sea water, variation in salinity throughout the year being significant only in waters washing fringing reefs near the mainland following heavy rain. The sea water is saturated with oxygen. It is normally of great clarity, so that light penetrates to a maximum extent. Since the reefs are in the tropics, solar energy flow is essentially constant. In view of all this, it is not surprising that most of the coral reef communities, particularly those found on platform and ribbon reefs, are considered to be adapted to a low-stress environment. Indeed, it is a feature of coral physiology that most reef-forming coral species are able to live only within a narrow range of temperature and salinity; the extremes of the ranges of environmental temperatures and salinities normally encountered are near their lethal limits. In this connection it should be appreciated that corals play pivotal roles in the construction and maintenance of coral reef communities, and factors that affect corals must affect the intregity of the whole coral reef community. Thus the adaptation of corals to regimes virtually free from stress makes the coral reef community vulnerable to environmental changes outside the range normally encountered.

Significant fluctuations in physico-chemical conditions of their environment often leads to localized destruction of corals and their associates, which no doubt is responsible for the spatial heterogeneity — the variation in space occupancy discussed earlier — found on coral reefs. Total or very near total destruction of coral reef communities by natural events (e.g., the destruction of coral reef communities at Krakatoa in Indonesia as a result of the volcanic eruption of 1883) is extremely rare, but extensive destruction involving perhaps a significant sector of a coral reef owing to major fluctuations in physico-chemical conditions in this environment is more common. One or a few such episodes of extensive destruction of coral reef communities may be observed in human lifetime. Natural agencies that are capable of causing such destruction are listed below.

Cyclonic Storms

Almost every year one or more severe tropical storms — known as cyclones and given names such as "Dinah" or "Althea" — move into the Great Barrier Reef area. Heavy seas generated by these storms produce a pounding surf on coral reefs. The sheer mechanical force exerted by the surf is capable of tearing hemispherical coral colonies from their points of attachment and hurling these corals onto the reef crests. There they are subsequently bared to the atmosphere at low tide and their polyps die. The perimeters of many reefs of the Great Barrier Reef are delineated by these large coral boulders, often called "bommies" by the locals. Branching corals, too, are frequently torn loose and then smashed against other corals. Particularly is this so if the cyclone-driven seas strike what is normally the lee side of a reef, where fragile branching species of coral commonly occur. Although often extensive, coral destruction caused by cyclones is usually confined to shallow-water areas in the reef sector exposed to the full force of the cyclone-driven seas. Other sectors usually escape any significant damage.

Sedimentation

Because of the activities of cilia in ciliary tracts and the copious production of mucus, coral colonies are normally able to remove fine sediment in the form of silt that falls on them from above or encroaches on them from below. Their ability to cope with coarser sediments varies with the species of coral, the type of sediment, and the rate of sediment deposition or accumulation. Colonies belonging to species that have relatively large polyps are more successful than others at ridding themselves of sediment. However, corals cannot withstand burial under sediment for periods longer than one or two days, and excessive sedimentation may result in the deaths of corals. Such excessive sedimentation may occur in the vicinity of river mouths after major flooding on the Queensland mainland, or it may occur during cyclonic storms. For example, sections of the reef crest and adjacent regions of the reef flat on the northern side of Heron Island reef were blanketed with large amounts of coral sand and rubble during a cyclone in March 1972. Numerous corals that had been buried under the sediment for a few days were dead when exposed subsequently by water movements associated with normal tidal flow and wave action.

Temperature Changes

Although corals can live only within a narrow range of water temperature, the temperature of the sea water in the Great Barrier Reef area lies within this range. Hence corals growing on the edges of reefs are not normally subjected to fluctuations in sea-water temperature that would impose stresses. However, corals growing in shallow lagoons and reef-flat moats that are effectively isolated at low tide from the sea water surrounding the reef are in a different position. Shallow-water heating by solar radiation may be sufficient to impose stresses on corals living in these situations. Such heating is believed to be responsible for the paucity of corals near the shores of islands surmounting reef flats and may be responsible, in part, for differences in the distribution of the various species of coral found on reef flats.

It should be noted that the minimum temperature of the ambient sea water limits the geographical distribution of reef-forming corals. In general, corals cannot live in waters having a minimum annual temperature below 18°C. Even within the Great Barrier Reef system there is an attenuation of coral species with increasing latitude that is probably related to differences in temperature tolerance by the different species of coral.

Salinity Changes

Corals cannot withstand exposure to fresh water for periods longer than approximately thirty minutes, and even exposure to 50 per cent sea water for a few hours may cause the deaths of corals. Of course, violent fluctuations in the salinity of the surrounding sea water do not normally occur. However, corals in shallow water near the Queensland mainland may be killed as a result of the dilution of the ambient sea water following flooding on the mainland. Then too, corals growing on fringing reefs around continental islands are frequently subjected to lowerings of salinity, particularly during periods of rain associated with cyclones. The large-scale destruction of corals on fringing reefs in the Whitsunday area that occurred during the cyclone in 1918 was attributed to this cause. Dilution of the sea water in lagoons associated with platform reefs may occur during periods of heavy rain coinciding with low tide and may result in corals there being subjected to stress.

Emersion at Low Tide

Emersion at low tide can cause the deaths of polyps exposed to the atmosphere for periods longer than two to three hours. For this reason corals do not usually grow above mean lower water. Desiccation and excessively high or low air temperature are responsible for killing exposed coral polyps in many cases. Exposure of emersed corals to heavy rain has also been shown to be lethal to the exposed coral polyps.

On some reefs, waters on the reef flat are dammed back at low tide by the reef crest or by ramparts formed of coral rubble in drainage channels. At such times the level of the dammed water may be considerably higher than the actual sea level around the reef. Breaching of the ramparts by violent water movements associated with tropical storms will lower the water level in the dams, resulting in deaths of polyps in the portions of coral colonies thereby exposed to the atmosphere at low tide.

Changes in Current Flow Patterns

A well-marked drainage pattern is evident on most reef flats as the water level falls during the low-tide period. Also, during the ebb and flood, local tidal currents are quite strong over those reef flats where the tidal range is considerable. Water currents associated with tidal movements and with drainage patterns cause coral rubble and finer sediments such as coral sand to be deposited in some regions of reef flats, while such detritus may be removed from other regions. Accumulation of such material could result in the burial of whole coral colonies or portions of coral colonies and their consequent destruction. Any interference to drainage patterns such as might occur during cyclones could also cause similar effects.

Changes in Dissolved Oxygen Levels

Wave action and associated turbulence of water at the perimeters of reefs ensure that the water in these regions is fully saturated with oxygen. However, the oxygen content of the water in reef-flat pools and lagoons often falls significantly at low tide, and corals growing in these regions may be stressed at such times. Complicating factors would be created by the relative biomasses of animals and plants present and the extent of photosynthesis occurring in the plants (including symbiotic zooxanthellae) present. Of course, the extent of photosynthesis and hence oxygen production by plants would vary diurnally, being minimal at night.

Some coral species appear to be more tolerant of low oxygen concentrations in the surrounding sea water than others, and this may be reflected to some extent in the distribution patterns of different coral species on the reef flat.

Other Changes in Physico-Chemical Conditions

A critical factor controlling the depth at which corals are capable of growing is illumination. Any factor that reduces the depth to which light penetrates is inimical to the growth of corals in deep water. After prolonged periods of rain on Queensland coastal regions, the water near the coast becomes markedly turbid because of increases in the amount of suspended material present. The extent to which the growth of coral in shallow regions bathed by the turbid water is adversely affected is not known but may be significant at such times.

Corals growing in some parts of the tropics are often adversely affected by volcanic activity, earthquakes, and tectonic activity which causes rapid subsidence or uplifts. Such geologic activity is not marked in the Great Barrier Reef region at present.

Predation by Animals

Several species of fish have been observed to crush branches of living coral on the Great Barrier Reef. It is not clear in many cases whether they smash the coral in order to obtain algae or invertebrates that live on the interstices of branching corals or whether they feed primarily on living polyps. However, a few species of fish belonging to several different families do feed on coral polyps themselves. Several polychaete worms, several crustaceans, several gastropods, and the starfish, *Acanthaster planci* and *Culcita novaeguineae* also prey on coral polyps. In the waters of the Great Barrier Reef only these two species of starfish and one species of gastropod, *Drupella cornus*, have been observed to kill entire colonies of hermatypic corals. Even so, when present at normal population densities these coral predators cause negligible damage to the hard coral cover of reefs, the relatively small amount of destruction caused being compensated for by rapid recolonization.

As we have seen, a number of methods is used by coral reef organisms to acquire and hold space. Some species overgrow others. Some species of coral, for example, are sometimes overgrown by some of the larger algae, sponges, soft corals, and zoanthids, resulting in the deaths of the corals. The extent to which the release of antibiotic substances is involved in facilitating this overgrowth warrants investigation. On the other hand, some corals are able, by the use of mesenterial filaments or "sweeper tentacles", to kill other organisms, including other corals, that encroach on their living space. The extent to which these competitive interactions for space result in destruction of coral colonies awaits clarification.

Recovery

Recovery of coral reef communities that have been devastated by natural destructive agencies is basically dependent on the continued growth and reproduction of coral colonies that have survived and on the recolonization of devastated areas by coral larvae that settle from the plankton. Complete recovery will involve the return of those species typically associated with corals and the re-establishment of the complex relationships normally existing among these species. A distinct succession of species, with those settling first — the pioneer species — being supplanted by later colonists, can be expected. Ultimately the climax will be reached when a pattern of stable community relationships exists. The rate of change in early succession is rapid but slows as the climax is reached.

On the Great Barrier Reef, recovery of coral reef communities after varying degrees of destruction caused by cyclones and by *Acanthaster* has been studied. It was found that the rate at which recovery occurs is largely related to the extent of the damage inflicted on the hard coral cover by the destructive event. If destruction is localized or patchy and numerous mature colonies remain undamaged and able to produce larvae, the recolonization can be rapid. However, if few mature colonies have survived and recolonizing larvae have to be transported long distances from other reefs in currents, then recolonization may be delayed. Other factors such as the presence of large amounts of unconsolidated rubble, the availability of suitable substratum, the abundance of competing species such as algae and soft corals, and the degree of success attending larval settlement will influence recolonization rates. Recovery from small-scale localized destruction generally requires less than ten years, while periods of time ranging from ten to twenty years are required for full recovery of affected areas following heavy coral mortality. It is possible that if coral destruction has been exceptionally severe over a wide area, several decades might be required for complete recovery.

24

Damage to Coral Reef Communities Induced by Humans

As already noted, the adaptation of coral-reef communities to regimes free from stress renders the community very sensitive to environmental changes. Indeed, localized destruction of corals and their associates as a result of the operation of normal physical agencies occurs regularly. Sometimes the destruction that occurs as a result of a natural agency such as a severe tropical storm is extensive, but damage is soon repaired as a result of rapid growth of surviving corals and rapid recolonization by larvae. It would appear too that coral reef communities in the Indo–West Pacific region are well buffered against changes wrought by biological agencies. Despite the structural complexity of the mature coral reef community, population sizes of individual species are essentially stable, or at least vary only within narrow predictable limits. This stability or predictability appears to stem from the operation of a multiplicity of checks and balances that have been acquired during the evolutionary history of coral-reef communities.

Although coral-reef communities have evolved mechanisms that resist perturbations induced by normal agencies that have operated continuously or intermittently for millennia, they may not be buffered against perturbation induced by novel factors. Certain human activities may constitute such novel factors against which they have no defences, and as a result destruction of catastrophic proportions might ensue.

It would appear that in the past catastrophic destruction of coral reef communities was an extremely rare event. In many areas these communities have had a long history of continuous development, although the communities have moved laterally from time to time because of eustatic changes in sea level. Observed episodes of recent catastrophic destruction are limited to a few reefs and bear no comparison with the episodes of mass extinction of organisms documented in the fossil record. Some of these episodes simultaneously involved organisms living on land and in the sea. In some cases organisms inhabiting ancient coral reefs were involved in these mass extinctions, the rugose corals of the Palaeozoic era being one well-known example. However, the episodes of mass extinction were millions of years apart and infrequent if considered in relation to the age of the earth, which is estimated to be some four thousand million years old.

Nevertheless, the catastrophic destruction of coral-reef communities that has been witnessed in some regions in recent years may represent only the beginning of much more extensive destruction which will occur if human activities that produce adverse affects on such communities are allowed to continue unchecked. It should also be appreciated that although the reefs of the Great Barrier Reef are separate entities, they constitute an ecosystem, and what occurs on one reef may influence what occurs on another.

Many forms of human activity adversely affect coral-reef communities. Although for a variety of reasons the Great Barrier Reef has not as yet been affected to any great extent by most of these activities, it has been seriously affected by some. It is instructive to examine all these activities so that we can be made aware of what is likely to happen on the Great Barrier Reef if they operate there in the future and so that we may devise the means that could be adopted to counter their adverse effects.

Marked increases in the load of sediment carried to coastal waters by rivers and streams have occurred in some coralliferous areas in recent years because of unplanned agriculture and deforestation leading to accelerated erosion of land surfaces. High islands and continental land masses fringed by coral reefs are frequently areas of high rainfall and lush vegetation. They are particularly susceptible to erosion when the vegetation is removed. As well as an increase in the sediment load carried from eroded land by streams, larger volumes of fresh water than usual may pass down the streams draining much eroded land to the shoreline where coral reefs occur. On many parts of Okinawa, for example, deforestation associated with land development projects for agriculture, tourism, and housing construction have been carried out at an increasing rate over the past ten years; as a result, a heavy sedimentation of clay particles is occurring on coral reefs in many areas and coral mortality is extensive. It is likely that similar conditions prevail elsewhere, including the Great Barrier Reef region. It is possible, for example, that recently observed siltation at Low Isles, near Port Douglas, has stemmed from deforestation on the adjacent Queensland mainland.

Mining, dredging, and filling are activities that frequently lead to increased sedimentation rates that result in damage to reef communities. Where reef limestone is quarried, a great deal of mechanical damage can be inflicted on the animal and plant life of a reef as a result of the mining activities themselves, as has happened in Malaysia, India, and Mauritius. No limestone mining has occurred in the Great Barrier Reef as yet. Dredging operations have caused significant damage to coral reefs in various localities in the Pacific, in Singapore, and at the Seychelles. In Queensland, dredging has occurred at a few coral-reef localities, and the effects are known. Spoil from dredging activities in the vicinity of Townsville harbour released over several years into waters near Magnetic Island has caused destruction of many of the coral colonies that formed fringing reefs at the island; platform corals were particularly susceptible to the rain of fine sediment produced when the spoil was dumped. At Heron Island a channel and swing basin which served as a harbour were excavated from the reef flat in 1967. Bund walls were raised around the channel and the swing basin to prevent excessive drainage of water from the reef flat at low tide (water is normally dammed on the reef flat by the reef crest at low tide). However, a series of cyclones in the early 1970s made breaches in the bund walls, thereby causing an abnormal lowering of water level at low tide on the reef flat in the vicinity of the harbour. This led in turn to a large-scale mortality of the upper portions of colonies of branching coral near the harbour.

Explosives are often used to kill coral reef fish in the West Pacific ocean. Sometimes the capture of fish by this method is highly organized. In the Philippines, for example, blast fishermen surround sizeable coral formations with underwater lights to attract fish. They also lure them into the selected areas by using baits consisting of pieces of fish and molluscan flesh. Periodic checks on fish numbers in each area are made, and when numbers seem adequate, dynamite placed strategically throughout the area is exploded. Scuba divers are used to collect the fish killed or stunned by the explosion, but frequently only the larger fish are retrieved. At some localities the reefs have been virtually denuded of living coral. On the Great Barrier Reef, explosives are used to capture fish but only infrequently. However, the so-called "bang-sticks" or "power heads" — spears with .303 bullets or 12-gauge shotgun cartridges cradled at their tips in such a way that the charge is fired on impact — have been used extensively to kill reef sharks and large fishes such as groper.

Explosives are sometimes used to blast channels through reefs or to move coral pinnacles that constitute navigational hazards. Surplus United States Navy explosives used to clear a channel through the reef at Kayangel Atoll, Palau, in 1973 caused extensive damage to coral in the vicinity. Military bombardment of reefs around the tropical Pacific islands during World War II caused marked destruction of hard corals on these reefs. In the Great Barrier Reef region the reef at Fairfax Island in the Bunker Group was used for bombing practice during World War II, and craters in the reef were still visible in the late 1950s. However, most other reefs of the Great Barrier Reef do not appear to have been abused in this way.

Although the mechanical damage inflicted on coral-reef communities as a result of blast when nuclear weapons are exploded in coralliferous areas is obviously extensive, it is probable that the associated radioactive contamination of food chains has a much greater significance for survival of coral-reef organisms. A single nuclear blast may contaminate thousands of square kilometres of reef. Fortunately, no nuclear explosions have occurred in the Great Barrier Reef area.

Shallow-water tropical regions where coral reefs occur are known to be particularly susceptible to chemical pollution. However, the extent of chemical pollution in coral reef regions has not been studied. There is, for example, a dearth of information on the effects of heavy metal pollution in coral reef areas. In Queensland, mercurial compounds are used in the sugar cane industry as fungicides and nematocides. It would be of interest to examine the mercury content of organisms on reefs nearest the mouths of rivers draining from sugar-cane-growing areas.

It is well known that pollution of the world's oceans by man-made organic chemicals, particularly DDT, has occurred. Other chlorinated hydrocarbons such as dieldrin and endrin, which are more toxic for marine organisms than DDT, have been widely used in certain coral reef areas, including mainland regions adjacent to certain parts of the Great Barrier Reef in recent years. Chronic effects elicited in members of the coral reef community by chemical pollutants have not been studied. It is possible that some species may be especially susceptible to these pollutants while others are particularly resistant. Selective elimination of specialized predators, for example, could profoundly affect community structure.

Some of the detergents now being released in increasing quantities into waters bathing coral reefs may have adverse effects on corals. It has been found that a mild household detergent in common use, at concentrations as low as 0.5 per cent, is capable of killing corals.

In some parts of the world, deaths of corals have been attributed in part to the release of large volumes of sewage into the surrounding sea water. It is believed that in Kaneohe Bay, Hawaii, increased levels of phosphates and other plant nutrients associated with the sewage are responsible for the rapid growth of an alga, *Dictyosphaeria cavernosa*, which has invaded and in some cases obliterated corals growing in the southern portion of the bay. Although a similar phenomenon has not been witnessed in the Great Barrier Reef area, the possibility of its occurrence should be borne in mind when planning new housing or tourist developments on or near coral reefs.

Heated effluents from large power plants using sea water as coolant have caused coral destruction in Florida and Hawaii. Heated and highly saline effluents from desalination plants have been responsible for coral mortality in other areas. Again, the possibility of coral destruction stemming from such causes in the waters of the Great Barrier Reef should warrant consideration by planning authorities.

Because corals appear to flourish in some areas subject to chronic oil pollution, and because of a lack of reports of damage to coral reef communities stemming from oil spills, it has been generally believed that corals are resistant to oil pollution. This belief was heightened as a result of experiments involving the floating of oil over submerged corals carried out both in Queensland and in Hawaii. No visible signs of damage to the submerged corals was observed. However, it was found by American researchers that floating oil can kill coral tissue if it adheres to corals exposed to air. Under these circumstances, oil adheres strongly to branching corals such as species of *Acropora* and *Pocillopora* and may be retained for weeks. On the other hand, oil did not adhere strongly to corals such as *Fungia* and *Symphyllia*, which possess large fleshy polyps and secrete abundant mucus, and was soon removed when the corals were submerged. These results have significance for coral reef communities growing on reef flats of the Great Barrier Reef which are frequently exposed to the atmosphere at low water spring tides.

Of greater importance than any immediate mortality to corals caused by oil pollution is the effect of chronic oil pollution on subsequent recruitment of new coral colonies. In experiments carried out in the Red Sea near Eilat, on the Gulf of Aqaba, during 1969–73, community structure and species diversity of corals on the reef flats of two reefs were studied. One reef flat was chronically polluted with oil and minerals; the other was free from oil pollution and served as a control. In 1970, approximately 90 per cent mortality of corals occurred on both reefs as a result of an extremely low tide. Three years later there were few signs of recolonization on the chronically polluted reef, but extensive recolonization and regeneration had occurred on the control reef. It was suggested that chronic oil spills prevent normal settlement or development of coral larvae. This study and others indicate that the effect of oil pollution on coral recruitment is more important than any immediate coral mortality caused.

The human activity that has probably had the most devestating and widespread effect on coral reef communities, particularly in the Great Barrier Reef region, is the selective removal of elements of the fauna. Some species, particularly fishes, molluscs, crabs, turtles, and worms, have been collected for food for centuries by the indigenous peoples inhabiting islands in coralliferous seas. Other species, especially molluscs that produce materials that could be used as receptacles or as ornaments, have also been collected by these people. It would appear that, in the main, removal of these coral-reef species from any particular area was on a restricted scale and well within the replacement capability of the coral-reef community.

In recent years, however, the situation has changed. Commercial fisheries have been established in coralliferous areas. Most of the earlier fisheries involved the hand-collecting by divers of elements of the fauna. The trepang, or *bêche-de-mer*, fishery involved the collection of various species of holothurians which, after treatment, provided stock for stews, soups, and curries that were much favoured by some Asian peoples. The pearl-shell and pearling industry involved initially the hand-collecting of species of *Pinctada*, some of which were found on coral reefs. The trochus shell, *Trochus niloticus*, was much sought after on coral reefs before the large-scale introduction of plastic buttons caused a collapse in the market for trochus shell during the 1950s. Giant clams, particularly *Tridacna gigas* and *T. derasa*, have for long been collected from reefs. Some Taiwanese clam fishermen still make journeys from Taiwan to the reefs of the Great Barrier Reef. What effects, if any, the large-scale removal from reefs of holothurians, pearl shells, trochus, and giant clams, all of which feed on minute organisms, has had on the coral reef community is not known but warrants study.

In more recent times, species that occupy key positions in food webs have been collected intensively. Thus the introduction of self-contained underwater breathing apparatus and spear-guns (some with explosive heads) and the advent of high-powered outboard motors for small craft have led to a spectacular increase in the numbers and variety of coral-reef fishes captured for food in some areas. For example, on many accessible reefs of the Great Barrier Reef there is a dearth of sizeable specimens, particularly of site-attached fishes. Those still to be seen are timid and readily flee from divers, a behaviour pattern indicating that the fish have been subject to repeated spear-fishing. In some cases it is known that the reefs had been visited by spear-fishermen who move systematically over the reefs spearing as they move.

One of the largest fishes found on the Great Barrier Reef is the groper, *Promicrops lanceolatus*. In 1974, fourteen reefs in the central region of the Great Barrier Reef were searched for specimens of *P. lanceolatus*. A total of only five sizeable specimens, the largest estimated to weigh 150 kilograms, was observed. Although the normal population density of *P. lanceolatus* on reefs is not known, on protected reefs or reefs that are relatively inaccessible because of the distance from coastal towns, groper are commonly encountered.

The implications for the coral-reef community of the selective removal of large predatory fishes, particularly those occupying key positions in food webs, can only be guessed at. Groper will prey on juvenile specimens of the coral-eating starfish *Acanthaster planci*, and removal of groper by humans may have been a factor in triggering population explosions of the starfish. Perhaps other site-attached serranids whose numbers have been depleted on some reefs also prey on juvenile *Acanthaster planci*.

In recent years a flourishing trade in aquarium fishes from coral reefs has developed, and in some areas reefs are rapidly being depleted of aquarium fishes. Cleaner-fish, which remove parasites from other coral reef fishes, are among the aquarium fishes eagerly sought after by enthusiasts.

Since World War II, great interest has been shown in the collection of the shells of molluscs by dealers throughout the world. Because of the great variety of form and colour exhibited, the shells of coral reef molluscs generally have been eagerly sought after by collectors, and those of many species now command high prices. However, the shells of large coral reef gastropods such as balers (*Melo* species), giant helmets (*Cassis cornuta*), and giant tritons (*Charonia tritonis*) have been the prime targets of collectors. Unfortunately, precise quantitative data on the extent to which these species have been collected throughout their range are not available. In Barrier Reef waters there has been an obvious reduction in the number of giant helmets. During the 1950s, specimens of *Cassis cornuta* were commonly encountered on sandy areas of reefs. The large bumps they made in the sand were obvious even to inexperienced collectors. During the 1960s an apparent decline occurred in numbers of *C. cornuta* observed, and in the 1970s the species became a rarity in most sections of the Great Barrier Reef. Likewise, there appears to have been an obvious reduction in the numbers of the giant triton on many reefs since the 1950s. During the 1950s thousands of specimens were collected by the crews of trochus luggers operating in Great Barrier Reef waters.

Again, it is not known what effects selective removal of predatory gastropods such as balers, giant helmets, and giant tritons would have on the structure of reef communities. However, the results could be far-reaching. The giant helmets and giant tritons are specialist carnivores, the giant helmets preying on sea-urchins and the giant tritons preying on starfish and holothurians. It is known that the giant triton will prey on juvenile and adult crown-of-thorns starfish, and it has been proposed that removal of giant tritons by humans could have been a major factor in triggering population explosions of *A. planci*.

It is possible that the introduction of marine species to a coralliferous region such as the Great Barrier Reef from which the species has been previously excluded may have profound effects on the coral reef community. Certainly the devastating ecological disturbances caused by importing alien terrestrial species such as the rabbit and toad to Australia are well known. Introduction of alien species into coral reef communities has already occurred at Hawaii. Other introductions may have occurred on the Great Barrier Reef and elsewhere but have gone unnoticed to date. It has been shown that the crown-of-thorns starfish will eat Caribbean corals, and there has been speculation about the fate of Caribbean corals if the Pacific and Atlantic Oceans are linked with a sea-level canal across Panama.

The phenomenal increase in tourist establishments in coralliferous areas such as the Great Barrier Reef that has occurred in recent years is apparent to anyone who has travelled through these areas. The construction of new tourist resorts and the expansion of existing ones will obviously continue, and these will bring with them problems relating to pollution in various forms. They will provide access to coral reefs for increasing numbers of tourists. The damage tourists themselves inflict on reefs by walking across reef flats smashing coral, collecting molluscs and fish, overturning coral boulders, etc., can only be guessed at, but where narrow fringing reefs are involved the damage may be substantial. There is a need for baseline data on the normal structures of coral reef communities to be collected on those reefs of the Great Barrier Reef that have not as yet been affected by the human activities just discussed. Changes in the structures of the coral reef communities stemming from known activities could then be readily detected and appropriate counter measures instituted. The need underscores the desirability of creating adequate marine parks where the fauna and flora are totally protected and the desirability of having available a group of biologists specially trained to monitor reefs of the Great Barrier Reef with a view to detecting changes in coral-reef community structure caused by human activities.

There is a general belief that destruction of coral-reef communities stemming from human activities is likely to be more serious and to have more long-term consequences than destruction caused by natural agencies. Whereas destructive natural agencies tend to operate sporadically, some forms of human activity leading to destruction of coral communities operate almost continuously. Also, coral communities have not had time to evolve defence mechanisms against those human activities which produce changes of a novel kind.

25

Crown-of-Thorns Starfish Infestations — a Warning?

Acanthaster planci is a many-armed species of starfish which attains a size of up to 60 centimetres in diameter and is covered with prominent spines, a feature that has given rise to its common name — the crown-of-thorns starfish. The spines are venomous and have been responsible for numerous human injuries. The species is found on coral reefs throughout the Indian and Pacific oceans, where it preys chiefly on hard corals, digesting away the flesh and leaving only the calcareous skeleton of its prey.

Available data indicate that specimens of *A. planci* occur on every reef of the Great Barrier Reef. However, as elsewhere on the well-developed reefs of the Indian and West Pacific oceans, the crown-of-thorns starfish is normally sparsely represented. Normal population densities are about six specimens per square kilometre of reef. Each specimen eats about ten square metres (flat projection) of coral per year. Hence, when present at normal population densities, *A. planci* kills only about sixty square metres of coral per million square metres of reef per year. The coral destroyed is soon replaced. Thus, under normal circumstances, *A. planci* causes negligible damage to the hard-coral cover of a reef.

In recent years, however, very large numbers of starfish have appeared on certain reefs, particularly in the central region of the Great Barrier Reef, and the feeding activities of the starfish have resulted in the destruction of the bulk of the hard-coral cover of entire reefs. (About 37 per cent of the surface of a reef in the central region of the Great Barrier Reef is covered by hard corals.) It has been found that the bulk of the hard-coral cover of a reef of average size (approximately ten square kilometres in flat projection) may be killed within two to three years. Calculations reveal that a mean figure of about fourteen thousand adult starfish per square kilometre of reef would be required to cause such destruction of coral. Actual estimates of starfish numbers on infested reefs of the Great Barrier Reef range from tens of thousands to millions, but it should be noted that on infested reefs starfish aggregate and move in large groups over the reef.

As the bulk of the hard-coral cover of a reef is destroyed, the whole ecology of the reef changes from a coral-dominated reef to one dominated by algae. There is a concomitant change in the associated fauna, leading to an obvious reduction in species diversity, and for two to three years the reef assumes a drab, lifeless appearance. Having devastated the bulk of the hard coral cover of a reef, adult starfish leave the reef and apparently migrate to adjacent reefs.

Population outbreaks of *A. planci* were first observed on reefs in the Cairns region during 1961. By 1962, Green Island Reef, an inner platform reef and tourist centre near Cairns, was infested with crown-of-thorns starfish that were causing obvious damage to hard corals of the reef. No well-authenticated reports of the occurrence of population outbreaks of *A. planci* on these reefs before the 1960s have been forthcoming.

Although reefs near Cairns were certainly infested by 1962, it is not known precisely which reefs were among the first to be infested. However, it is known that by the mid-1960s population outbreaks of *A. planci* had occurred on most, if not all, of the inner platform reefs lying between Pickersgill Reef (lat. 15°51'S) and Beaver Reef (lat. 17°50'S). Subsequently the infestations spread to the south and to the north of this region. By the mid-1970s most of the approximately three hundred platform reefs lying between latitudes 14°40'S and 20°S had experienced population outbreaks of *A. planci*. A massive destruction of the hard-coral cover of infested reefs occurred. In most cases the bulk of the hard-coral cover of numerous reefs examined was destroyed within two to four years. After destruction of the hard-coral cover of a reef, crown-of-thorns starfish disappeared from the reef. No mass mortality of the starfish was observed, and it is assumed that they migrated from the reef, possibly to a neighbouring reef or reefs. It is now apparent that certain inner platform reefs in the region under consideration became infested first, and these acted as foci for the infestation of adjacent platform reefs in each area.

A few reefs lying outside the central region of the Great Barrier Reef became infested in the period 1961–75. The most southerly of these were reefs in the Bunker group. In 1973, reports were received that reefs in the northern part of the Swain Reefs complex near latitude 21°S were infested. A visit made in January 1975 confirmed that some reefs near Lavers Cay (lat. 21°10'S approximately) and Mystery Cay (lat. 21°20'S approximately) were infested. Although these reefs are remote from centres of human population, they are among the reefs most frequently visited by charter boat operators. Visitors to these reefs engage in activities such as spear-fishing, line fishing, and shell collecting.

In 1967 the most northerly reef known to be infested with *A. planci* was Eye Reef, near latitude 15°S. In 1975 Clack Reef, near latitude 14°S, which was not infested in 1966, carried numerous starfish and much dead coral. In 1979 it was reported that reefs near Portland Roads (lat. 12°30'S) were infested. Then, at the end of 1979 it was found that the hard-coral cover of Green Island was again under attack by *A. planci*. Estimates of starfish numbers found on the reef at the time ranged from 160,000 to 450,000. Subsequently the estimate was raised to 2,000,000 and other reefs in the area as far north as Pickersgill Reef and as far south as Peart Reef, off Innisfail, were found to be infested in 1981. It would appear that the invasions of the 1960s of reefs in the central area of the Great Barrier Reef are being repeated in the 1980s.

many factors, such as reef topography, degree of exposure of the reef to oceanic waves, the extent of coral cover, the mean size of starfish present, the number of starfish present, and the state of infestation of the reef reached. On infested reefs, specimens of *A. planci* are not uniformly distributed but tend to aggregate in large herds each containing hundreds of individuals. When present in such large herds, adult *A. planci* can kill the hard coral cover at a surprisingly rapid rate. When first exposed, the coral skeletons are white, but within a few days they acquire a coat of fouling algae.

A precise figure for the actual percentage of the hard-coral cover of any reef killed by *A. planci* during an infestation has not been obtained because the obtaining of such data would be a major undertaking. However, the extent of the damage inflicted on the whole hard-coral cover of affected reefs is unequivocal. In major areas of those affected reefs that were surveyed, most coral colonies were usually killed. Only corals growing in very shallow water usually survived the *A. planci* infestations. In a few cases starfish departed from reefs in Great Barrier Reef waters before killing the coral in major sections of the reef, but this was the exception rather than the rule.

Studies on the sequence of events that occurred on some reefs devastated by *A. planci* reveal that within two to three weeks the exposed skeletons of corals killed by the starfish began to acquire an algal coating that subsequently thickened and darkened. During this period, there was an obvious breakdown of typical reef community structure, coral-associated animals being particularly affected by the change from a coral-dominated to an algae-dominated community. Coralline algae did not become apparent among the algae or the skeletons until several months after the skeletons had been exposed.

Within a few months after a reef had been devastated by *A. planci*, an obvious increase in the soft coral cover occurred, particularly in lagoons and back-reef areas. Frequently these soft corals grew over the skeletons of corals killed by *Acanthaster*. In some regions stalked algae (e.g., *Turbinaria* species) proliferated and covered coral skeletons. In other cases the skeletons of branching corals fragmented and formed piles of rubble. The rubble accumulated in lagoons and back reef areas, especially around the bases of coral pinnacles.

Within three to four years after *A. planci* had devastated a reef, the first coral recolonizers were noted. However, few species were represented among the recolonizers. Well-known opportunistic species such as *Pocillopora damicornis*, *Seriatopora hystrix*, *Stylophora pistillata*, and *Acropora hyacinthus* were among the first corals to settle. There was an

Vindication. Peter James, author of *Requiem for the Reef* and the present author standing alongside one of the signs erected at Green Island by the Queensland government to warn visitors of the danger of treading on the spines of venomous crown-of-thorns starfish, tens of thousands of which were present on the reef during the period 1979–1982. Both authors had warned of the threat to the hard coral cover of The Great Barrier Reef posed by the starfish population outbreaks. The hard coral cover of the reef at Green Island and other reefs was devastated by *Acanthaster planci* during the 1960s and the present author had predicted that reinfestation would occur as soon as sufficient hard coral cover had been re-established.

294

295

296

297

298

299

apparent relationship between the rate of recovery of an area and the extent of coral destruction in the area caused by the starfish initially. The greater the initial destruction, the slower the recovery. There are strong indications that recolonization by hard corals was fastest in shallow water on seaward slopes in the vicinity of patches of hard corals that had survived the *A. planci* infestations. On the devastated reefs examined, these patches were found mainly near reef crests and upper seaward slopes in situations exposed to considerable wave action. Wave action was usually most marked at the south-eastern tips of the reefs studied, and usually shallow-water corals had survived in this region. Conversely, recolonization was slowest in deeper water on seaward slopes and in lagoons and back-reef areas where fewer hard corals had survived.

Coral regrowth over a period of six to ten years following devastation was impressive on a few reefs, particularly where fast-growing tabular (platform) colonies of *Acropora hyacinthus* were well represented among the recolonizers. On many other reefs, however, recolonization by hard corals over the same period of time was surprisingly slow; in some situations, particularly in back-reef areas, it was negligible. In some cases the presence of an extensive cover of soft corals and of mats of filamentous and stalked algae hampered recolonization by hard corals, as did the presence of huge amounts of loose rubble formed from the fragmented skeletons of corals killed by *A. planci*.

It was suggested by the present author some years ago in scientific papers that a period of more than twenty years, and possibly periods ranging from twenty to forty years, would be required for complete recovery of reefs of the Great Barrier Reef, provided that affected reefs were not reinvaded by *A. planci* during the course of recolonization by hard corals. Unfortunately, as evidenced by recent events at Green Island Reef and neighbouring reefs, large numbers of starfish are indeed likely to reinvade a reef when sufficient coral to provide adequate food supplies has recolonized the reef. The possibility must now be entertained that affected reefs in the central region of the Great Barrier Reef will be impoverished for long periods of time or until such time as effective control measures are instituted.

There has been considerable argument about the causes of the starfish infestations. Some scientists believe that they represent normal fluctuations in the population density of *A. planci*, and some even believe that these infestations occur in cycles. The discovery of *A. planci* spines and other debris in sediments from some areas of several reefs was claimed to be evidence of previous plagues of *A. planci* on these reefs. However, the normal resident *A. planci* populations on all reefs frequently lose arms and portions of their bodies to predators. Hard skeletal parts such as spines are not digested and would be voided onto the reefs. The mere presence of such material in reef sediments does not signify that plagues have occurred in the past. Of course, the material would be moved by physical and biological agencies, and there is no way of telling how many skeletal remains of *A. planci* per kilogram of sediment represent a past plague. Moreover, difficulties are encountered in accounting for the retention of *Acanthaster* debris on platform reefs which reached the sea surface hundreds of years ago and which cap knoll-like antecedent structures. Then too, there are no scientific or historical records of the occurrence of population outbreaks of *A. planci* on the Great Barrier Reef before the 1960s.

Most scientists who consider the *A. planci* population outbreaks to be normal phenomena base their beliefs on the fact that although *A. planci* breeds for only a short period each year, each female is capable of releasing millions of eggs which give rise to planktonic larval stages of long duration. It is argued that in some years environmental conditions (temperature, salinity, availability of food, etc.) are particularly favourable for production and survival of larvae. In those years many more larvae settle on reefs and metamorphose into juvenile *A. planci* than at other times, thereby giving rise to greatly increased *A. planci*

Facing page
Illustration 294
Part of a population explosion of the crown-of-thorns starfish, *Acanthaster planci*, on a reef in the Slasher reef complex.

Illustration 295
A boatload of *Acanthaster planci* collected on a reef near Cairns in 1969.

Illustration 296
The white skeletons of corals freshly exposed by the feeding activities of crown-of-thorns starfish, *Acanthaster planci*, on a reef in the Swain reef complex in 1974. The rapidity with which corals may be killed by large numbers of crown-of-thorns starfish is apparent since the skeletons acquire a coat of algae and become greyish within two weeks.

Illustration 297
The algae-covered skeletons of plate corals that had been killed by a population explosion of crown-of-thorns starfish at Broadhurst reef in 1970.

Illustration 298
The beginning of recovery. Recolonizing corals amidst algae at Feather reef, August, 1971.

Illustration 299
Part of a population explosion of *Acanthaster planci* on a reef near Cairns in 1981.

populations on reefs. However, *A. planci* infestations on the Great Barrier Reef have continued since the early 1960s, and several year classes (identified by size ranges) were represented on most infested reefs studied. This rules out the possibility that the outbreaks are the direct result of exceptional recruitment in one or two favourable years. At any one time, some reefs in an area may carry *A. planci* population outbreaks while others in the same area do not. This would seem to indicate that some reefs in an area are more prone to infestation than others in the same area.

As mentioned earlier, many biologists consider that coral reef communities have a stable or predictable organization because they possess many mechanisms for buffering any tendency for marked change in the population densities of constituent species. Numbers of *A. planci* on a reef must normally be regulated within narrow limits, as only a moderate increase in the population density of the species will result in destruction of the hard coral cover of the reef and loss of its normal food supply. In view of the massive increases in the population densities of *A. planci* that have been observed on infested reefs in recent years, it would appear that a new form of perturbation has been introduced into the system. At any one time this perturbation may affect some reefs but not others in a particular area. What is this perturbation?

In the present author's view it is significant that the Great Barrier Reef starfish infestations appeared to occur first on accessible reefs nearest centres of human population. This is in accord with the general picture that has emerged for the distribution of *A. planci* infestations in the Indo–West Pacific region. Normally reefs remote from centre of human population are free from *A. planci* infestation unless they are regularly visited by humans, as is the case for certain reefs in the Swain Reefs complex, which became infested in the 1970s. All this indicates that some recent form or forms of human activity could have triggered the starfish infestations.

One way in which humans could have been involved is the large-scale collecting of natural predators of juvenile and small adult *A. planci*. Of particular significance here could be the overcollecting of the giant triton, *Charonia tritonis*. There is evidence that large-scale collecting of the giant triton occurred during the 1950s and subsequently on the Great Barrier Reef and elsewhere in the Indo–West Pacific region. Another predator of juvenile and small adult *A. planci* is the groper, *Promicrops lanceolatus*. Again, there is evidence that on accessible reefs large-scale collecting of groper and other large resident predator fishes has occurred in recent years following the advent of scuba, spearguns, and high-powered outboard motors.

There are indications that the starfish infestations are having repercussions on reef fishing. The usual assemblage of coral-associated fish disappears after the bulk of the hard coral of a reef has been killed by the starfish. Catches of premium food fish such as coral trout have declined markedly in recent years in the central region of the Great Barrier Reef, and commercial fishing for reef-associated fish has now virtually ceased on reefs between Cairns and Innisfail. However, it is not known whether the current dearth of reef fish in the region is a direct consequence of reef fishing or of the destruction of the hard-coral cover of reefs by *A. planci* or whether both factors have contributed. In the long term the population outbreaks could also affect Great Barrier Reef tourism.

A more insidious effect of the starfish infestations could be the apparent increased incidence in Queensland of ciguatera — a type of poisoning that follows the ingestion of coral reef fish. The initiators of the toxin responsible for this poisoning are microscopic organisms that flourish on skeletons of recently killed corals. These organisms are eaten by small fish and their toxins are concentrated during passage along food chains leading to carnivorous fish and finally to humans.

The long-term ecological consequences of the destruction of the bulk of the hard-coral cover of the majority of reefs in the central region of the Great Barrier Reef — a huge amount of coral — can only be guessed at. Because population outbreaks of *A. planci* are now recurring on previously devastated reefs as their hard-coral cover is re-established, and because population outbreaks are now occurring on reefs that were not infested during the 1960s and early 1970s, it seems likely that many reefs in the central region of the Great Barrier Reef will be impoverished for long periods of time, and it is possible that the whole Great Barrier Reef ecosystem could be affected ultimately by the outbreaks.

To date, little has been done to control the starfish infestations on the Great Barrier Reef. Attempts were made at Green Island to control starfish numbers on a small area of the reef flat visited by glass-bottomed boats — an estimated twenty-seven thousand starfish were collected from the area in 1964 and an undisclosed number were collected during the period 1979–80. Elsewhere the infestations have been allowed to continue unchecked. This situation contrasts markedly with the strong measures adopted by many other countries in the Pacific region to control *A. planci* outbreaks in their territories. Following receipt of a report prepared by the present author in 1969, the Queensland government legislated to confer protection on the giant triton; and recently, following publicity about the adverse effects of commercial spear-fishing on the resident fish population of reefs, it legislated to ban the use of spear-guns in conjunction with scuba for the taking of reef fish. Unless these regulations are rigidly enforced, it is possible that the whole Great Barrier Reef ecosystem will be impoverished for decades. The crown-of-thorns starfish outbreaks have provided ample warning of the adverse effects of human activities on coral reefs generally and those of the Great Barrier Reef in particular. The time for action is now.

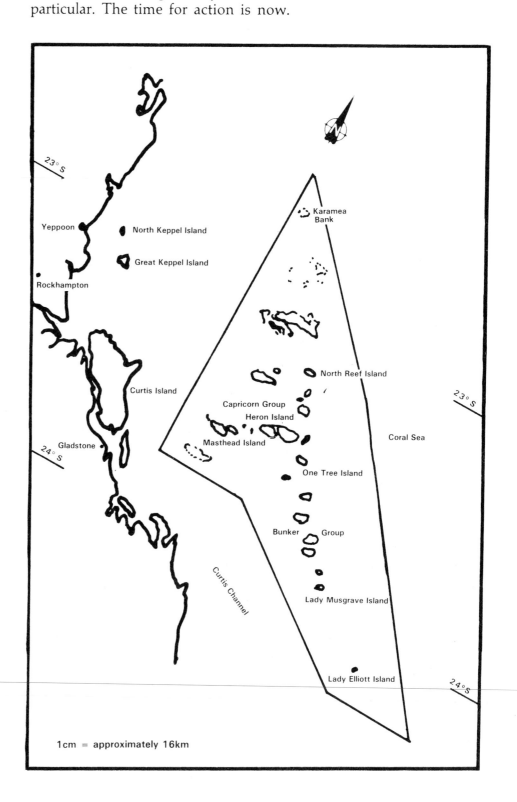

Map 5. Great Barrier Reef Marine Park, Capricornia area.

26

The Future of the Reef

In the past, Australians have been decidedly apathetic about conservation issues generally and about the fate of the unique fauna and flora of their country in particular. They have witnessed, with little protest, the destruction of the bulk of Australia's forests, the decimation of the Australian fauna, the widespread erosion of Australian soils, the pollution of waterways and the despoilation of onshore coastal regions. Yet attempts to mine limestone and drill for oil in the Great Barrier Reef region have met with opposition that has been intense, widespread and spontaneous. In most cases this opposition does not have its roots in a close association with the reefs of the Great Barrier Reef since it is estimated that fewer than 50,000 Australians per annum actually set foot on or swim over these reefs. Nor does it stem basically from a need to protect rare structures or a rare fauna and flora. There are hundreds of reefs in the Great Barrier Reef system and there are numerous coral reef systems in the tropical oceans of the world, some of these reef systems, such as the Louisiade Pallisade on the opposite side of the Coral Sea from the Great Barrier Reef, being very large. Despite the existence of a few differences in structural organization of the coral reef communities found on the Great Barrier Reef compared with that of other coral reef communities of the Indo-West Pacific region, the similarities are striking. Most of the numerous species found on the Great Barrier Reef are wide-ranging Indo-West Pacific species, and there are very few species that appear to be restricted to the Great Barrier Reef. Why then should conservation of the reefs of the Great Barrier Reef and of their fauna and flora have become such an emotive issue.

Possibly some Australians are impressed by the sheer size of the Great Barrier Reef. The fact that it is the largest system of coral reefs on this planet is, of course, a source of great national pride. Others have visited or seen films of the reefs and the reef communities, and these have appealed to their aesthetic senses. Indeed, the colour of the water around reefs, the variety of colour and shape exhibited by the fauna and flora of reefs and the extraordinary behaviour of many of the animals found on reefs cannot fail to impress the observer who would tend to resist any threat, real or imagined, to the integrity of the reefs and their fauna and flora. Some see the reef communities as storehouses of foodstuffs, new therapeutic drugs and new natural products. Others see the reefs as the future mainstay of the Australian economy because of their tremendous tourist potential. Still others see the reefs, particularly the complex reef communities, as repositories of new knowledge waiting to be tapped. Most of these people would also tend to resist any large scale interference with the reef communities.

Then, too, there appears to have been a marked change in the attitude of Australians to conservation issues in recent years. A surprisingly large number have embraced the conservation ethic with enthusiasm. Many of them believe that, because of their isolation and inaccessibility, the reefs of the Great Barrier Reef are still in their pristine state. Also, they believe that, unlike most situations on the Australian mainland, they still have the opportunity to prevent despoilation of the Great Barrier Reef. Its conservation has become something of a *cause célèbre*. However, the Great Barrier Reef has not emerged unscathed from its encounter with humans. As noted in preceding chapters, urgent action is required to prevent further damage to the reef communities and to prevent their long-term impoverishment.

Exploitation of Biological Resources

Exploitation of the biological resources of the Great Barrier Reef by Europeans has been occurring since the early 1800s when bêche-de-mer collecting for Asian markets began. Since then, corals, the shells of various species of mollusc — particularly green snail *(Turbo marmoratus)*, trochus, pearl shell and clams, crayfish, various reef fishes and turtles have been collected intensively. What effects, if any, this past collecting of Great Barrier Reef animals has had on the structure of coral reef communities are unknown but may be considerable. The probable effects of the large scale removal in recent years of giant tritons and large, site-attached reef fishes, such as groper, that are predators of crown-of-thorns starfish have already been commented on. To a large extent Australian nationals have been responsible for the extensive collecting of Great Barrier Reef organisms. Indeed, extensive collecting of coral reef shells, aquarium-fishes, large site-attached fishes and reef crayfish by Australian nationals is still occurring. In many cases the collectors are unlicensed and the activities are clandestine. The effects of their activities on reef communities require urgent study. In recent years their activities have been overshadowed in the news media by reports of the activities of foreign nationals in Great Barrier Reef waters.

Over-collecting of reef animals by foreign nationals has had its biggest impact on giant clams. The adductor muscles, which are responsible for closing the valves of clams, are highly prized both as a delicacy and as a health food in several Asian countries. For decades, Taiwanese fishermen have plundered reefs to the north of Australia of their giant clams. By the late 1950s these reefs were virtually fished out and the Taiwanese junks descended on the Great Barrier Reef. On the northern reefs of this system the giant clam, *Tridacna gigas*, was taken whilst on southern reefs, particularly in the Swain Reefs complex, the somewhat smaller *Tridacna derasa* was the object of attention. Almost the entire crew (numbering usually from twelve to twenty) of a junk, participates in the collection of clams. Two or three dinghies transfer the collectors from each junk to the shallow water of a reef. The collectors then move systematically back and forth across the reef seeking clams. When these are encountered the sharpened blades of spade-like implements are thrust between the valves of the clams and their adductor muscles severed. The fleshy mantle and viscera are then trimmed from the muscles which are subsequently refrigerated or dried.

In the late 1960s prosecutions of illegal clam poachers began, and during the next decade the crews of over thirty vessels were apprehended. Initially fines were light and had a negligible deterrent effect. Subsequently fines became heavier and vessels were confiscated and their skippers jailed. Even so, the trade continued for the financial rewards were great. Eventually the clam poaching problem was raised at government to government level and by the 1980s poaching by Taiwanese nationals had been greatly reduced. However, the price paid has been great. The giant clam population of the Great Barrier Reef has been greatly reduced, with many reefs now littered with white empty shells.

Estimates based on actual counts reveal that approximately 50,000 specimens of *T. derasa* per trip are collected by the crew of each junk operating in the Swain Reefs complex, and perhaps 10,000 specimens of *T. gigas* per trip are collected by the crew of each junk operating on northern reefs. Judging by the number of arrests that have been made in recent years, it would appear that at least twenty Taiwanese junks have visited the Great Barrier Reef annually. If visits have been made to the Swain Reefs complex and to northern reefs with equal frequency, it is probable that about 500,000 specimens of *T. derasa* and about 100,000 specimens of *T. gigas* have been collected annually for about twenty years.

It has been estimated that a reef of average size in the northern sector of the Great Barrier Reef carries about 15,000 specimens of *T. gigas* while a reef of average size in the Swain Reefs complex carries about 40,000 specimens of the smaller *T. derasa*. There are about 350 reefs in the Swain Reefs complex and about 1,100 offshore reefs north of this complex. A rough calculation will reveal that considerable in-roads have already been made into the giant clam populations of these areas. If recruitment to the populations is low then a serious situation already exists. Unfortunately, the rate of recruitment of giant clams to any reef of the Great Barrier Reef is not known, but normally it appears to be low. Indeed, juvenile giant clams are rarely encountered. Juvenile giant clams grow rapidly initially but growth rates slow as they age. Giant clams are believed to be long-lived and large specimens may well be over 100 years of age. Research into the life histories of giant clams is urgently required. In addition to clams the Taiwanese poachers take fish, turtles, dolphins, terns and shells — such as giant triton shells — which command a ready sale on overseas markets.

On northern reefs in the Torres Strait region, problems have arisen relating to the collection of reef crayfish. At certain times female crayfish *(Panulirus ornatus)* leave the reefs in order to release their young. In the past the female crayfish have, at such times, been fished by foreign nationals as well as by Australian nationals. Research into the effects of such fishing on breeding stock is required.

Exploitation of Minerals and Oil

To date there has been negligible exploitation of the geological resources of the Great Barrier Reef although moves to exploit these resources have been made. These attempts have met with widespread opposition. In 1967 an application was made to dredge "dead coral" on Ellison Reef, near Innisfail. The objective was to provide lime for use on sugarcane crops. The application was fiercely contested by local conservation groups, particularly the Wildlife Preservation Society of Queensland and the Queensland Littoral Society. The applicant maintained that the proposed operation would not harm the reef communities as only dead coral was involved. However, the conservationists showed that numerous living organisms frequented the areas of apparently dead coral rubble found on the reef. (At the time Ellison Reef was under attack by the crown-of-thorns starfish and had been almost stripped of living coral in the deeper water around its periphery, a situation that was not commented on by anybody at the enquiry.) In the event the conservationists won the day and the application to dredge coral was ultimately refused by the Queensland government.

In retrospect, it seems unlikely that the type of operation proposed would have resulted in any long-term damage to the reef. However, the conservationists were fearful that granting of the application would set a precedent that could lead to large scale mining operations on numerous reefs. Rejection of the limestone mining application was a turning point as far as the conservation of the Great Barrier Reef was concerned. The application hearings provided a rallying point for conservationists dedicated to the preservation of the Great Barrier Reef and the protection of its fauna and flora. Thereafter the voice of the conservationist was one to be reckoned with in Great Barrier Reef matters, and conservationists have since provided a major brake on the uncontrolled exploitation of the reefs. Soon after their 1967 victory their resolve to defend the Great Barrier Reef against mining was to be tested further.

In 1958 an exploratory bore was drilled through Wreck Island reef in the Capricorn Group at the southern end of the Great Barrier Reef on behalf of Humber Barrier Reef Oil Pty Ltd. In the 1960s two bores were drilled in the nearby Capricorn Channel and another was drilled at Anchor Cay at the northern tip of the Great Barrier Reef. By 1969 almost the whole extent of the Great Barrier Reef was under title to oil prospecting rights. However, concern for the Great Barrier Reef had been steadily mounting during the late 1960s, sparked by issues such as the crown-of-thorns starfish infestations, the Ellison Reef coral mining application and Taiwanese clam poaching activities, and fanned by various conservation organizations such as the Wildlife Preservation Society of Queensland, the Littoral Society of Queensland and the Save the Reef Committee. In 1969 the immense off-shore oil leakages at Santa Barbara in California occurred. Pictures and accounts of the plight of oil-soaked birds, dead fish and blackened beaches appeared in the news media. The Australian public began to wonder what would happen to the coral reefs of the Great Barrier Reef if oil leakages occurred there as a result of the establishment of an offshore oil industry. The Queensland Trades and Labour Council decided that a total ban would be applied by all affiliated unions on oil-drilling on the Great Barrier Reef, and the Commonwealth and Queensland State governments decided to hold an enquiry into the possible effects of oil driiling on the Great Barrier Reef. In March 1970 a 58,000 ton tanker, the *Oceanic Grandeur*, struck a rock in Torres Strait and five of her fifteen oil tanks were ruptured. The released oil moved eastwards and ultimately passed between the reefs of the Great Barrier Reef to the Coral Sea. As far as it is known no damage was done to the fauna and flora of the reefs, but attempts to disperse the oil spills with detergents appear to have been responsible for the destruction of three of the five pearl-culture farms that operated in the region at the time. The proposed enquiry into oil drilling was upgraded to the status of a Royal Commission. The hearings of the Royal Commissions on Petroleum Drilling in Great Barrier Reef waters extended over two years. The conclusions and recommendations stemming from the Commissions were released in late 1974. Two of the three Commissioners came out in favour of drilling for oil under stringent conditions in certain areas of the Great Barrier Reef, but the Chairman of the Commissions recommended that all drilling in the Great Barrier Reef region be postponed until results of research recommended by the Commissions had been carried out. In effect, oil drilling on the Great Barrier Reef has not occurred since the Royal Commission was set up. Although oil drilling is to be excluded from areas set aside as marine national parks under the Great Barrier Reef Marine Park Act of 1975, leases held by oil companies still covered most of the Great Barrier Reef in early 1982.

In the author's view the oil drilling controversy advanced the cause of conservation of the coral reef communities by preventing uncontrolled oil drilling in the Great Barrier Reef region. Whether oil drilling operations that are under strict control should ever be permitted is another matter. However, the oil drilling controversy distracted attention from a far more important issue — the crown-of-thorns starfish infestations of reefs of the Great Barrier Reef. Even if oil were discovered on the Great Barrier Reef, and even if oil spills did then occur and did cause extensive damage to coral reef communities, an oil spill equivalent to the greatest in recorded history could not have done damage to the communities of the Great Barrier Reef that would approach that caused by the starfish infestations.

The Crown-of-Thorns Starfish *(Acanthaster planci)* Infestations

Ironically, the worst fears of those opposed to oil drilling on the Great Barrier Reef during the 1960s and subsequently were being realized as early as 1962, but coral-eating starfish, not oil, were responsible for the coral damage inflicted. In 1962 coral colonies on Green Island were observed to be attacked and killed by large numbers of crown-of-thorns starfish. By 1967 the bulk of the hard coral cover at Green Island reef had been killed. Tens of thousands of starfish were involved. In the period 1962 to 1974 inclusive, the majority of the approximately 300 platform reefs lying between lat. 14° 14'S and lat. 20°S experienced similar population outbreaks of crown-of-thorns starfish and a similar destruction of their hard coral cover. The number of coral colonies killed in this central region of the Great Barrier Reef was obviously in the millions and must represent the greatest mass-destruction of recent corals ever recorded. As a result of this coral destruction the structure of the reef communities changed from coral-dominated communities to algae-dominated communities.

At the request of the Queensland government the present author carried out research into the crown-of-thorns starfish infestations during the period April 1966 to May 1968. A report was then submitted in June 1968 to the Queensland government. The threat posed by the crown-of-thorns starfish to the integrity of the hard coral cover of reefs of the Great Barrier Reef was clearly defined in this report and recommendations were made for control of the starfish population outbreaks. These recommendations were supported by the then Chief Inspector of Fisheries (Mr G. G. T. Harrison). However, the report was not acted upon by the government. Subsequent reports of starfish infestations of additional reefs and widespread public unease forced the holding of an official enquiry into the crown-of-thorns starfish problem, an enquiry first proposed by the Commonwealth government. Three of the six members of the Committee set up for this purpose were appointed by the Commonwealth and three by the Queensland government. None had had any experience of the crown-of-thorns infestations or had carried out any research on the problem. They produced a report in 1971 in which they expressed the view that the crown-of-thorns starfish infestations did not pose a threat to the Great Barrier Reef, that damage to the hard coral cover of reefs had occurred on only a few reefs and that corals would soon grow back on affected reefs. They also expressed the opinion that similar starfish infestations probably occurred naturally at intervals and that destruction of corals by the starfish probably constituted part of the natural forces of destruction which are a prerequisite for the building of reefs. More importantly, they stated that action to control the starfish infestations was unwarranted. This opinion was used by governments to justify lack of action to control the starfish infestations. However, subsequent events, as outlined in the preceding chapter, have emphasized the threat that the crown-of-thorns starfish poses to the integrity of the coral reef communities of the Great Barrier Reef and have fully supported the author's contention that long-term impoverishment of many of these communities will occur unless action to control the infestations is taken.

Conservation of the Great Barrier Reef

One of the principal organizations concerned with the conservation of the Great Barrier Reef is the Great Barrier Reef Committee. This organization consists primarily of scientists and among its main aims, as set out in its Memorandum of Association, are "to carry on marine, biological and other scientific research generally and to protect and conserve the said Reef and to report upon and advise on the proper utilization of the said Reef". One of the first conservation issues in which it was involved concerned turtles.

During the 1920s and early 1930s, turtle soup canneries operated at Heron Island and North West Island in the Capricorn Group. During this period thousands of green turtles *(Chelonia mydas)*, all breeding females, were captured as they ventured ashore to lay. By the 1929–30 season it was apparent that numbers of turtles captured were on the decline. A Queensland government biologist, F. W. Moorhouse, examined the turtle soup operations in the Capricorn Group and recommended that the taking of green turtles during the early part (October and November) of their breeding season, be banned south of Cairns (lat. 17°S). This would ensure that at least some turtles had the opportunity to lay before being captured. The recommendation was accepted by the Queensland government and the necessary legislation soon gazetted. However, despite the subsequent failure of island-based operations, the trade in turtles continued. Large meat works on the Queensland mainland began butchering the animals principally for the export trade. Turtles were captured by fishermen for the trade.

In 1950 the Great Barrier Reef Committee discussed the turtle trade and recommended that an investigation be made of the ecological and economic status of the green turtle in Great Barrier Reef waters, and that this species should be totally protected pending the outcome of the investigation. This recommendation was accepted by the Queensland government and protection conferred on the green turtle south of Cairns. However, many years elapsed before any investigation was made into ecological and economic aspects of the turtle populations of the Great Barrier Reef. In 1964 a team led by Dr R. Bustard of the Australian National University began work on turtle populations. By

1968 Dr Bustard was able to state that a turtle fishery, based on the capture of breeding females, was not a practical proposition. Instead, he advocated that turtle farms, each with their own breeding stock, be established and that prior to the establishment of such farms all species of turtle should be protected throughout the whole of Queensland. Dr Bustard was supported by G. T. T. Harrison, Chief Inspector of Fisheries in Queensland, and by the present author who was at that stage Secretary of the Great Barrier Reef Committee. The proposals were accepted by the Queensland government and the necessary legislation gazetted on 18 July 1968. Since then turtles have been completely protected in Queensland waters. Turtle farming was subsequently attempted in the Torres Strait region. For a variety of reasons it was not an economic success and was soon abandoned. However, the idea warrants further consideration. It could lead to the establishment of a new industry in North Queensland based upon the controlled exploitation of a renewable Great Barrier Reef resource.

In 1963 the Great Barrier Reef Committee, acting in association with Mr R. Poulson, then manager of the Heron Island tourist resort, successfully lobbied the Queensland government to confer protection on the marine fauna and flora of Heron Island reef and the adjacent Wistari Reef.

By 1967 it was apparent that over-collection of some reef animals was occurring, that the mining of reef limestone for industrial and agricultural purposes was imminent, and that the large scale search for oil in Great Barrier Reef waters was about to begin. On behalf of the Great Barrier Reef Committee, the present author then prepared a document entitled "Proposals relating to the conservation and controlled exploitation of the Great Barrier Reefs" which was sent to the Queensland government and other interested parties. As well as putting forward a plan for assessing the effects of projected mining operations on the fauna and flora of the Great Barrier Reef it proposed that "an overall plan be formulated which will permit the controlled exploitation of areas of the Reefs in a way which will ensure that damage to the fauna and flora of the Reefs is kept to a minimum, that tourists and the Queensland public will have access to areas of the Reefs, that certain large areas will be reserved as marine national parks for conservation purposes and that certain key areas are reserved for scientific study". The document also called for "the establishment of a planning, co-ordinating and advisory body consisting of people with specialized knowledge of the Reefs and their resources. This body would have the task of formulating an overall plan and would make recommendations based on this plan to relevant government departments". The report was not directly acted upon by the government and was subsequently criticized by some conservationists because it advocated the controlled exploitation of Great Barrier Reef resources. However, it should be appreciated that at the time there were no effective controls on the exploitation of any of the resources of the Great Barrier Reef region and no plan for the management and conservation of the fauna and flora of the reefs. The Committee's document represents the first major attempt to control exploitation and formulate a plan for the conservation and management of the Great Barrier Reef. Subsequently the Commonwealth government became increasingly involved in Great Barrier Reef matters and the Great Barrier Reef Committee decided to seek the setting up of a statutory authority by joint Commonwealth and Queensland government legislation in order to secure the effective conservation and management of the Great Barrier Reef. The Committee's efforts were finally rewarded by the establishment of a Great Barrier Reef Marine Park Authority under the Great Barrier Reef Marine Park Act of 1975.

Prior to 1968 the enactment of legislation relating to conservation of the fauna and flora of the Great Barrier Reef was effectively the preserve of the Queensland state government. Initially legislation was introduced under the Fish and Oyster Acts, 1914 to 1945. This legislation was aimed at regulating by licensing systems the commercial exploitation of oysters, pearl shell, trochus, green snail, bêche-de-mer and reef fishes. In 1937 an Order-in-Council prohibited the taking of coral in waters around Green Island, Low Isles, Michaelmas Cay, Arlington Reef and Oyster Cay. By 1945 it was an offence to take corals anywhere in Queensland waters unless a licence was held. In 1957 an Order-in-Council conferred protection on all the fauna of Green Island within one mile (1.6 km) of the low water mark. Similar protection was conferred on the marine fauna of Heron Island Reef and Wistari Reef in 1963. Special protection was given to the molluscs known as giant tritons and giant helmets in 1969 following a recommendation to the Queensland government made by the present author in 1969. In addition, protection was conferred on the flora and fauna of several coral islands and continental islands by declaring them national parks under the Forestry Acts. Despite the obvious good intentions of successive Queensland governments towards the protection of the fauna and flora of the Great Barrier Reef, much of the legislation involved was of doubtful validity and enforcement of the various regulations relating to this protection was minimal. Insufficient inspectors and rangers were available to police the various regulations over the vast distances involved. In particular, the offshore platform reefs were not regularly patrolled. Consequently the conservation measures adopted were not effective in preventing over-collecting of elements of the fauna by Australian and foreign nationals.

In 1968 the Commonwealth government passed the Continental Shelf (Living Natural Resources) Act which controlled the taking of sedentary organisms on the continental shelf. This paved the way for the use of the Royal Australian Navy and Royal Australian Air Force in surveillance work relating to the protection of the marine fauna of the Great Barrier Reef. By the Seas and Submerged Lands Act of 1973 the Commonwealth further asserted its jurisdiction over the natural resources of the continental shelf including the Great Barrier Reef. However, the passing of this Act caused conflict between Commonwealth and Queensland state governments about their respective rights in the Great Barrier Reef region. A 1975 High Court decision held that the Australian states had no rights in the territorial seas beyond low water mark. This decision resulted in further conflict. An agreement thrashed out in 1980 between the states and the Commonwealth will ultimately give the states jurisdiction over waters 5.5 km from the coast but the Commonwealth has retained the right to exercise its powers in areas encompassed by the Great Barrier Reef Marine Park Act which was passed in 1975.

The Great Barrier Reef Marine Park Act of 1975

Under this Act an Authority was set up by the Commonwealth government to recommend areas of the Great Barrier Reef to be included in a Great Barrier Reef Marine Park. Plans for the management of each area so included were to be drawn up by the Authority under the provisions of the Act. The Authority was then to have responsibility for the care and control of the resulting Great Barrier Reef Marine Park. The Act also created a Great Barrier Reef Consultative Committee to provide expert advice to the Authority.

The gazetting of the Act was welcomed by most members of the general public who generally believed that creation of the Authority would lead to Great Barrier Reef issues being removed from the political arena and placed in the hands of an independent body of experts devoted to the conservation and scientific management of the Great Barrier Reef and its fauna and flora. However, despite the laudable intentions of those responsible for framing the legislation relating to the Great Barrier Reef Marine Park Act of 1975, for shepherding its passage through parliament and for implementing the provisions of the Act, progress in securing the conservation and scientific management of the reefs of the Great Barrier Reef and of their fauna and flora has been lamentably slow. Indeed, by early 1982 it was apparent that the Act would not, in itself, secure the conservation and management of the reefs and their fauna and flora this century. Moreover, implementation of the provisions of the Act tended to exacerbate an already difficult situation by involving a third party, the Great Barrier Reef Marine Park Authority, in matters relating to Great Barrier Reef conservation. As they stood, many of these matters, particularly those connected with Commonwealth government versus Queensland state government jurisdiction over islands and emergent reefs were certainly complicated. Following creation of the Authority but obvious retention of control over all major reef matters by Commonwealth and Queensland state governments (with occasional disputation between these governments) many members of the public became confused as to who was actually responsible for these matters. Confusion and apprehension replaced the strong concern for the future of the Great Barrier Reef that was expressed so forcibly by the general public during the late 1960s and early 1970s. It is instructive to examine some of the reasons for this state of affairs. Many of the reasons are bound up with the structure of the Authority and its satellite body — the Great Barrier Reef Marine Park Consultative Committee, in the mode of operation of these bodies, in their powers or lack of them, in their dependence on governments and in what may be viewed, in hindsight, as shortcomings of the Great Barrier Reef Marine Park Act.

In effect, the Authority has some form of control only over those sections of the Great Barrier Reef that have been declared part of the Great Barrier Reef Marine Park. By 1982, some seven years after gazettal of the Act, only the Capricorn and Bunker groups of islands and reefs at the extreme southern end of the Great Barrier Reef, and a section of the Great Barrier Reef near Cairns had been so declared. Collectively these areas account for less than 20 per cent of the Great Barrier Reef region. If that rate of progress is any guide, decades will elapse before the whole system comes under the protective umbrella of the Act, if indeed it ever does. In the interim, the plunder of reef communities by Australian and foreign nationals will continue. It is the present author's considered opinion that further delay in conferring protection on reef communities will lead to their long-term impoverishment. The piecemeal approach to declaration of the Great Barrier Reef Marine Park adopted, effectively forces the Authority to adopt a piecemeal approach to the conservation of the Great Barrier Reef. The zoning plan prepared for the Capricornia section of the Great Barrier Reef Marine Park gives the impression that it is Authority policy to perpetuate traditional forms of usage of the reefs by humans. The plan created six zones, each with a different set of restrictions. It will not be surprising if visitors find this plan confusing. If it can be used as a guide then the zoning plan being prepared for the Cairns section of the Great Barrier Reef Marine Park which contains many more reefs and islands than the Capricornia section, and which extends to the low water mark along 30 per cent of the Queensland mainland in the section under consideration is likely to be even more complicated and to bristle with restrictions. Straightforward plans for management and conservation which enable visitors to understand readily what they can and cannot do in the Marine Park are required. Also the need for restrictions should be fully spelt out so the need can be readily appreciated by the general public.

There is no statutory requirement that any member of the three-man Authority should be a recognized coral reef biologist, yet the major problems relating to the Great Barrier Reef with which the Authority has to deal are all biological ones. Although the Authority is widely held to be an independent body, its members are nominated by governments and according to the Act the Authority is under the absolute control of a Commonwealth minister. However, in practice, control appears to rest in a ministerial council consisting of two ministers from each of the Commonwealth and Queensland governments that has been established to co-ordinate the marine park policies of both governments. Furthermore, the Authority has no jurisdiction over those islands of the Great Barrier Reef that are not owned by the Commonwealth, no jurisdiction over the Queensland mainland adjacent to the Great Barrier Reef, and no jurisdiction over reefs in the Torres Strait region which have been specifically excluded from the provisions of the Act.

As sections of the Great Barrier Reef Marine Park are declared the day-to-day management is to be undertaken by Queensland. A massive injection of funds will be required to ensure that sufficient inspectors and rangers and sufficient fast boats, adequately equipped, are available to patrol the widespread reefs and islands in the sections included in the Great Barrier Reef Marine Park. It is essential for its future that enforcement of regulations relating to the management of the Great Barrier Reef Marine Park be effective. At present the prospects for effective enforcement appear remote.

As well as setting up an Authority, the Great Barrier Reef Marine Park Act required the formation of a Consultative Committee to advise the Authority on matters relating to the Great Barrier Reef. However, the majority of members of the Consultative Committee are drawn from and represent government departments. This could be viewed as a case of governments advising themselves. Most other members were appointed to the Consultative Committee as representatives of sectional interests. The constitution of the Consultative Committee (all members of which are nominated by Queensland and Commonwealth governments) appears inappropriate for a role as an independent and impartial advisor on Great Barrier Reef matters.

Despite all this, an organization of experts is required to advise governments on matters relating to the management of the Great Barrier Reef Marine Park and on scientific and technical matters related to the conservation of the fauna and flora of the reefs. The experts should be associated with and be assisted by clerical and research staff who are responsible for the routine administration of the marine park. A different organization is required to enforce regulations relating to the conservation and management of the marine park.

The following plan is proposed by the present author to overcome the difficulties and deficiencies that have become evident in the Great Barrier Reef Marine Park Act. The plan requires extensive modification of this Act but it should appeal to most people interested in Great Barrier Reef matters irrespective of their political affiliations and irrespective of whether they are ardent conservationists or potential exploiters of reef resources. It leaves the decision making on Great Barrier Reef matters to the elected representatives in Commonwealth and Queensland state parliaments but it provides these representatives with expert advice on scientific and technical matters relating to the reefs and their fauna and flora from independent experts. Specifically it provides these representatives with rational plans for the conservation of the reefs and their fauna and flora and for the controlled exploitation of reef resources where exploitation is indeed considered advisable. The plan is outlined below:—

1. The Great Barrier Reef should be officially proclaimed and regarded as a major wilderness area requiring urgent protection from adverse human activities and one that should be preserved in as natural a condition as is reasonably possible. It should also be proclaimed and regarded as a scientific and tourist asset of international as well as national importance. At this stage the benefits that are likely to accrue from scientific research in the area are incalculable but can be expected to be of major importance. As far as tourism is concerned, it is already apparent that if the tourist potential of the area were properly developed the Great Barrier Reef would become one of the world's principal tourist attractions and, in time, Australia's major earner of foreign exchange. Tourism, scientific research and preservation of wilderness areas are compatible if intelligent planning and adequate supervision are provided.

2. Each of the reefs of the Great Barrier Reef, including those at the northern end, should be included in a Great Barrier Reef Marine Park immediately and immediate protection conferred on the reefs and the reef communities so that these may be kept as free as possible from major perturbations induced by human activity.

This will require modification of the Great Barrier Reef Marine Park Act. It is essential that living resources be managed as ecological rather than political units.

3. The Great Barrier Reef Marine Park Act should also be modified so that the Authority and Consultative Committee set up under the Act can be merged to form a Great Barrier Reef Advisory Council. This should be an impartial planning and advisory body, independent of government control but reporting to both Commonwealth and Queensland governments on matters relating to the Great Barrier Reef. It should be comprised principally of scientists (particularly biologists and geologists with recognized expertise in coral reef biology and geology respectively), but have representation from relevant industrial and commercial organizations such as tourist and commercial fishing organizations and relevant recreational and sporting bodies. The Council of the Great Barrier Reef Committee (which is an association of coral reef scientists independent of government control), would appear to be an ideal body to form the nucleus of the proposed Advisory Council. Adequate funds should be provided to enable the Advisory Council to function efficiently.

4. The proposed Advisory Council should concentrate attention on the conservation and management of the fauna and flora of reefs and islands of the Great Barrier Reef. It should advise on the degree of exploitation of the renewable resources (e.g. fishing, mining for coral sand, shell collecting, etc.) and of its non-renewable resources (e.g. oil and minerals) that should be permitted. Special attention should be given to resolution of problems relating to oil drilling and transport of oil in Great Barrier Reef waters.

5. A major task of the Council should be to arrange for an investigation of the general condition of the fauna and flora of each reef of the Great Barrier Reef beginning with the most accessible reefs. The impact of past and present human activities on reefs, particularly the over-collection of giant clams, giant tritons and other molluscs and site-attached fishes should be assessed. At the same time the reefs of the Great Barrier Reef could be properly charted.

6. Particular attention should be given to a determination of the extent of recent destruction of the hard coral cover of reefs by the crown-of-thorns starfish *(Acanthaster planci)* and the extent of current infestations of reefs by the starfish. Urgent consideration should be given to devising the best method of controlling the starfish infestations. Measures already adopted by other countries (e.g. Okinawa and other islands in the Ryukyus, Western Samoa, American Samoa, Fiji, Tahiti, Hawaii, Guam, Palau and the islands

and atolls of the U.S. Central Pacific Trust Territory) to control crown-of-thorns starfish infestations should be examined.

7. As a matter of urgency, the Council should make recommendations for the drafting of legislation to curb the activities of Australian and foreign nations that are harmful to the fauna and flora of the Great Barrier Reef. Particular attention should be given to the institution of practical measures for prevention of excessive collection of site-attached reef organisms such as territory-holding fishes and of molluscs such as giant clams and giant tritons and to the prevention of the introduction of alien species to reefs.

8. The Council should make recommendations for the siting of new tourist resorts and facilities, including moored surface vessels, moored submersibles and semi-submersibles, marinas and helicopter platforms. Assessments should be made of the number of tourist establishments that should be permitted in each section of the Great Barrier Reef and of the optimal sizes reef-based tourist establishments should attain. While there is ample scope for increased tourism, tourism should be so regulated in each region that it is compatible with the conservation of the fauna and flora of the Great Barrier Reef. An overall plan for the controlled development of tourism and tourist resorts in the Great Barrier Reef region should be drawn up and implemented as soon as possible.

9. The extent to which professional and amateur fishing on reefs of the Great Barrier Reef should be permitted should be determined. Also, the species of fish that can be taken from the reefs and the method of capture should be considered. It will obviously be necessary to close some reefs completely to fishing so that adequate baseline data for the devising of fishery conservation measures can be obtained. The names and positions of those reefs should be determined as soon as possible so that their fauna and flora remain in as near a natural state as possible.

10. The Council should make recommendations to governments for the carrying out of any scientific research necessary to provide baseline data for its deliberations.

11. Interested members of the general public should have reasonable access to the data the Council obtains and to the advice that the Council gives governments. Also, the Council should make public the reasoning (and any assumptions) upon which its major recommendations are based and its activities should be open to public and scientific scrutiny.

12. The Commonwealth and Queensland governments should, as a matter of urgency, devise a mechanism whereby complementary legislation incorporating and implementing those of the Council's recommendations that are found to be acceptable and practicable by the respective governments can be quickly drafted.

13. The general staff of the present Great Barrier Reef Marine Park Authority should be retained and expanded. In addition to dealing with the general public, industry and commerce on matters relating to the Great Barrier Reef and other clerical and administrative duties, the staff should be involved with the gathering of data and the carrying out of routine conservation-oriented research including the obtaining of baseline data and the monitoring of reefs for population explosions of crown-of-thorns starfish and other adverse effects of human activities. These activities should be directed towards facilitating the task of the proposed Great Barrier Reef Advisory Council by providing data necessary for the Council's deliberations.

14. Adequate funds should be provided by Commonwealth and Queensland governments for the operation of reef-based research stations such as the Heron Island Research Station. The status of this station could readily be raised to a position where it would be universally recognized as one of the world's leading centres for coral reef research.

15. The policing of regulations relating to the conservation of the fauna and flora of reefs should be placed under the control of a type of coastguard service especially established by the Commonwealth government to protect Australia's marine resources and to prevent illegal entry of people and goods. In any case, a service of this type is now required with the advent of the 320 km offshore resources zone.

16. The policing of regulations relating to islands (above high water mark) should be left to rangers associated with the Queensland National Parks and Wildlife Service who might be expected to liaise with the proposed Coastguard Service. Special attention should be given to the protection of birds and turtles breeding on these islands as well as their flora. It should be appreciated that many activities on islands and the Queensland mainland adjacent to reefs will have an impact on coral reef communities.

Implementation of a plan for the future of the Great Barrier Reef similar to that outlined above is urgent. Already, as evidenced by the continued massive destruction of the hard coral cover of reefs belonging to a major sector of the Great Barrier Reef caused by crown-of-thorns starfish infestations, time could well be running out for the fauna and flora of these reefs as it obviously is for the fauna and flora of their terrestrial counterparts, the world's tropical rainforests. The time for action is now. If effective action is not taken now the reefs of the Great Barrier Reef could be impoverished for decades and their future could be bleak. However, if such action is taken one might expect the future of the Great Barrier Reef to be particularly rosy.

The Future of the Great Barrier Reef

The future of the Great Barrier Reef region would appear to be inextricably bound with conservation, tourism, scientific research and controlled exploitation. One might expect to see dozens of new tourist resorts established in the region. In order to minimize the impact of human activities on reef communities and in order to share out among coastal communities the economic benefits arising from tourism, the new tourist resorts will probably be spaced at strategic intervals along the length of the Great Barrier Reef. A few of these new resorts will be of the conventional island-based pattern. However, large islands are rare on offshore reefs and, on present indications, many resorts will be based on ships, submersibles and semi-submersibles moored in the vicinity of reefs. Some of the semi-submersibles will probably be designed to resemble coral islands. Most of these moored resorts will possess helicopter landing facilities or be associated with helicopter landing platforms built on reefs or with landing areas in reef lagoons for amphibious planes. Some of the reef resorts will be in the nature of boatels catering primarily for the boating fraternity. A variety of boats, hovercraft and free submersibles will be used for short distance travel among the reefs. No doubt many of the new resorts will feature underwater walkways with transparent walls, underwater cableways, conference and entertainment areas and, perhaps, underwater accommodation designed expressly for divers. Low cost accommodation will probably be provided on some reefs by educational bodies interested in exposing youngsters to a novel and challenging educational experience.

Probably some coral reef associated industries such as coral jewellery and some forms of souvenir production involving the use of coral, shells and forams will continue to flourish. However, because of the obvious dangers posed to the integrity of coral reef communities the collecting of reef organisms for such industries will be carefully regulated. Although commercial fishing involving reef associated fish will continue it will probably be confined to specific reef areas and to certain species. Probably some collection of other edible reef organisms such as bêche-de-mer, crayfish, turtles and some molluscs will be permitted in some areas, but also will be carefully regulated. In the long term, some or all of these animals will probably be farmed for human consumption. There will probably be a marked increase in dredging and trawling the seafloor among reefs and between reefs and the Queensland mainland for demersal fishes, crustaceans such as prawns, and molluscs such as scallop and squid. Possibly some removal of coral sand in the vicinity of reefs using dredges with modified suction heads will be permitted. The establishment of an oil industry anywhere in the Great Barrier Reef region will depend, of course, on whether oil is indeed present in commercial quantities in the region. If so, it can be expected that production wells will be drilled. Obviously, however, the drilling operations will be carefully controlled and drilling rigs will not be permitted to be set up on top of coral reefs. The minimum distance at which they should be set back from the reefs will have been determined by research into water movements near reefs likely to be affected should any major spill occur.

Overall there will be a long-term need for the intelligent planning and enlightened application of controls on the type and extent of human perturbation of coral reef communities that will be permitted. Surveillance of the reefs and enforcement of regulations relating to the activities of foreign and Australian nationals on reefs will be a major task of some agency such as the proposed coastguard service whose members, no doubt wearing distinctive uniforms, should be a common sight in Great Barrier Reef waters in the future. Unless such a coastguard service is instituted the Great Barrier Reef area could develop into a haven for drug runners and pirates as parts of the Caribbean are fast becoming. As well as dealing with poaching on the reefs by Australian nationals the coastguard could liaise with the Australian Armed Forces in dealing with poaching by foreign nationals.

A great deal of conservation-oriented research will be carried out at reef-based research stations in the future. Also, management of the Great Barrier Reef Marine Park will rely heavily on baseline data obtained from reefs where fauna and flora are totally protected. Research into the structure of the coral reef communities of the Great Barrier Reef should lead to a marked increase in our understanding of the structure of what is generally regarded as the most complex of the world's ecosystems.

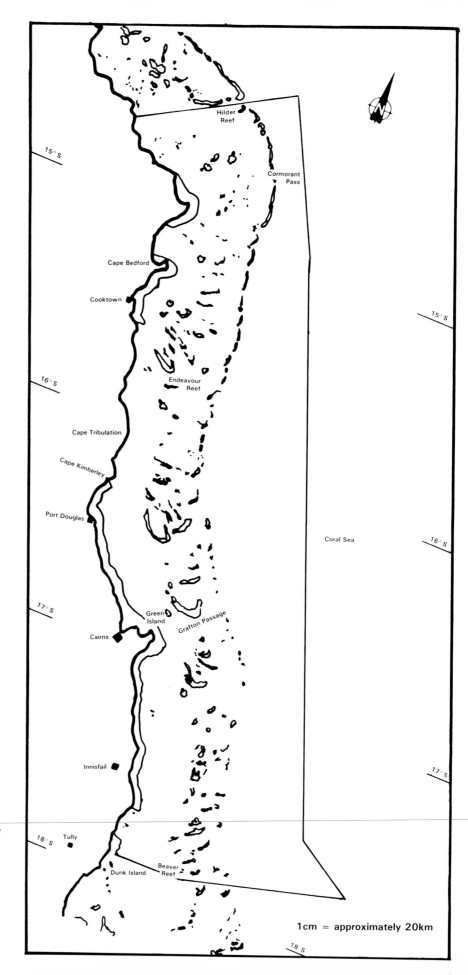

Map 6. Great Barrier Reef Marine Park, Cormorant Pass area.

1cm = approximately 20km

Index